-- PENGUIN BOOKS

# THE NATIONAL SOCIETY OF
# FILM CRITICS ON MOVIE COMEDY

Stuart Byron is the film critic for Boston's *Nightfall* and has written for *The New York Times, The Village Voice, Rolling Stone, Creem, Movie, Film Quarterly,* and *Gay.* He was for two years on the staff of *Variety* and for another two the film editor of the *Real Paper.* He is a contributing editor of *Film Comment.*

Elisabeth Weis serves the National Society of Film Critics in the position of secretary. She teaches film at Brooklyn College of the City University of New York and has written for *The Village Voice, Film International,* and *American Film.*

# THE NATIONAL SOCIETY OF FILM CRITICS ON

# MOVIE COMEDY

## EDITED BY STUART BYRON
## AND ELISABETH WEIS

**PENGUIN BOOKS**

Penguin Books Ltd, Harmondsworth, Middlesex, England
Penguin Books, 625 Madison Avenue, New York, New York 10022, U.S.A.
Penguin Books Australia Ltd, Ringwood, Victoria, Australia
Penguin Books Canada Limited, 2801 John Street, Markham, Ontario, Canada L3R 1F
Penguin Books (N.Z.) Ltd, 182–190 Wairau Road, Auckland 10, New Zealand

First published in the United States of America by Grossman Publishers 1977
Published in Penguin Books 1977

LIBRARY OF CONGRESS CATALOGING IN PUBLICATION DATA
Main entry under title:
The National Society of Film Critics on movie comedy.
Includes index.
1. Comedy films—History and criticism.
2. Moving—pictures—Reviews.
I. Byron, Stuart. II. Weis, Elisabeth.
III. National Society of Film Critics. IV. Title.
V. Title: Movie comedy.
PN1995.9.C55N35 1977b     791.43′09′0917     77–10106
ISBN 0 14 00.4578 3

Printed in the United States of America, by
Offset Paperback Mfrs., Inc., Dallas, Pennsylvania
Set in Videocomp Times Roman

Acknowledgment is made to the authors and to the following for permission to use the material listed:

American Guild of Variety Artists (AGVA): "A Tribute to Jerry Lewis" by Stuart Byron, in 1964 Jerry Lewis Program book; reprinted by permission of AGVA, with thanks to Mr. Lewis.

Basic Books, Inc., Publishers: from *The Movies: A History of an Art and an Institution* by Richard Schickel, Copyright © 1964 by Richard Schickel; reprinted by permission of the publisher.

Boston Phoenix: reviews of *Shampoo* and *Swept Away . . .* by Janet Maslin; reprinted by permission of the publisher.

Chicago Sun-Times: "Of Comedians, Clowns and the Cinema" and reviews of *The Great Dictator, City Lights, The Firemen's Ball,* and *Love Affair* by Roger Ebert; reprinted by permission of the publisher.

Citadel Press: from Arthur Knight's Introduction to *The Films of W.C. Fields* by Donald Deschner; reprinted by permission of Citadel Press, Inc., a Division of Lyle Stuart, Inc., Secaucus, New Jersey.

*(Page 307 constitutes an extension of this copyright page.)*

# PREFACE

When we began this book, we assumed that the result would be a random collection of articles on film comedy by members of the National Society of Film Critics. We soon found, however, to our delight, that almost all of the high points in the history of screen comedy had been covered at one time or another by the members of a Society that, according to its by-laws, is limited to critics who are the regular reviewers for general-interest periodicals.

And even though anything written by an active member anywhere (including outlets as diverse as testimonial-dinner program booklets and scholarly journals) was eligible for inclusion, *Movie Comedy* is still, and deliberately, a journalists' book—a group of *immediate* responses. Fully three-quarters of the pieces included were originally written as part of the regular work of a reviewer or columnist for a daily, weekly, or monthly publication. Even many of the articles on older films were written in response to reissues and revivals. Thus, this is also a concrete book; few of the Society's members see it as a reviewer's function to discourse in print on the nature of comedy, or of screen comedy as distinct from other forms. Occasionally such theorizings have crept into reviews, and we have included a selection of them as an Afterword. But most reviewers probably understand the response of Tennessee Williams (as reported by Pauline Kael) to some sympathetic but unexpected laughter at the premiere of *The Rose Tattoo:* "If they laugh, it's a comedy."

The eclectic nature of the volume means that some pretty varied, even contradictory approaches are used, and they show how many points of view can be brought to bear on the subject. Directorial, aesthetic, sociological, reflective, and immediate approaches follow one another. We tried to include as many different kinds of criticism as possible, and in some instances we have included two or more considerations of the same film as examples of critical methods.

The only other general survey of screen comedy currently in print, Gerald Mast's *The Comic Mind* (1973), is written at least in part as a textbook and, as befits that perspective, is conservative about which comedy films will live on: more than half of its pages are devoted to the silent period, and only one film of the sixties *(Dr. Strangelove)* is considered to have achieved the classic status deserving extended treatment. If in *Movie Comedy* we have included a good deal of material on comedy that is recent and American, this is not to say that time has yet sorted out the ephemeral from the lasting. Rather, it seemed to us a subject most sorely needing attention in a form of print more lasting and accessible than last week's newspaper.

Some regrets: In trying to delimit such a broad subject as movie comedy, we had to leave out extensive discussion of comic actors and screenwriters of the sound era. In some cases the omission of certain directors (Vigo, McCarey, La Cava, the Ozu of such pure comedies as *Ohayo*) or some individual films *(Divorce—Italian Style, The Apartment)* was due simply to the fact that nothing appropriate by any of our current members was available.

Other comic films have been excluded by choice. Opinions as to what films are funny vary not only from critic to critic but from year to year. Certainly distinctions are becoming progressively less clear. As long ago as 1937, Alfred Hitchcock noted the decline of the film comedian per se and predicted that the distinction between drama and comedy would blur as actors replaced comedians. Some writers would place this development at a later date, but it's probably true that there was less an abrupt break from the strict generic divisions of the silent days than a gradual change. At any rate, it's certainly true that a few directors have developed unique comic styles but that they utilize them *within* films that are almost always dramas. Hitchcock himself is among these as are John Ford, Claude Chabrol, and Bernardo Bertolucci. Space considerations ultimately ruled these directors out here.

Some personal notes: Thank you to Ellen Posner, our editor, for her advice and patience, and to Penelope Gilliatt, who, as the Society's chairman during a period of financial crisis, devised the idea of this volume and went through the tedious process of steering it to a receptive publisher. We have tried to put forth a view of film comedy that represents a consensus of the members of the Society. Undoubtedly we have allowed, in our introductions and selection of material, some of our own prejudices to slip through. These should not be attributed to anyone but ourselves.

—Stuart Byron
Elisabeth Weis

# CONTENTS

# CONTENTS

# II. CONTEMPORARY TRENDS

## 3  SPOOFING    *102*

## 4  SEX AND MARRIAGE    *138*

# CONTENTS

# CLASSICAL TRADITIONS

# THE SILENT ERA

Ever since James Agee's seminal article of 1949, "Comedy's Greatest Era," the twenties have experienced both the glory and the burden of being called by that name. For years the decade had been neglected, but when the pendulum swung it did so in a manner which swept everything else away. Silent comedies were inherently best *because* they didn't talk, the argument went; sound comedies were by definition merely canned theater. Critical efforts of more recent years have tended to redress the balance, with emphasis on the social and behavioral realism of thirties comedy—a relief, some feel, from the relentless "poetry" of the great silent comedians.

In retrospect, the whole question would seem to derive from a polemical insistence on ranking what are essentially two different kinds of comedy, not a better and a worse kind. The style of comedy we associate with the big silent names—Charles Chaplin, Buster Keaton, Harold Lloyd, Harry Langdon—is unique, and we shall not see its like again. As is mentioned often in the following selections, it derived from vaudeville, the music hall, and pantomime, and then passed through a crucial stage: Mack Sennett, whose short chase comedies, celebrated here by Richard Schickel, have seemed to other critics most important for the training they gave to others.

Chaplin, Keaton, Lloyd, and Langdon all spent some time with Sennett, but by the mid-twenties all of them were on their own, and they are seen as the artists most responsible for the character of their films. These four silent "clowns," even more than such early sound successes as W. C. Fields and the Marx Brothers, are given the extraordinary credit of being the *auteurs* of their movies even when they didn't direct them. They were personae, with screen characters so developed that situations were devised to fit them; most comedy, including screen comedy, works the other way around, with the situation devised first and then an actor chosen to add his contribution.

Of late, critics have begun to esteem Keaton as a greater artist than Chaplin. For one thing, his absurdist view seems more modern than the sentimentality attributed to Chaplin. But even so, Chaplin remains the most fascinating—and most written about—of the great silent comedians. In part this is because almost all of his feature films were unavailable for years and thus occasioned reviews as if for new pictures when they were rereleased with great fanfare in 1972. But aside from timing, Chaplin's greater range and complexity are more provocative of debate than Keaton's depth, grace, and unity.

Indeed, the length and evolution of Chaplin's career have sparked the Chaplin debate. Of the four great silent clowns, Chaplin alone continued to make films throughout the sound era. And the later films all proposed philosophical attitudes that could not be ignored. His moralizing grew more and more central while his technique remained the same. The question: Did Chaplin's famous lack of technical sophistication help or hinder his meaning, did it lend a forceful directness or an embarrassing awkwardness? And was Chaplin's moralizing an interruption or an integral part of his later films? The selections here can be seen as a debate on these issues, with Schickel on one side and Ebert and Williamson on the other.

It shouldn't be supposed that the "balletic" comedies of Chaplin, Keaton, Lloyd, and Langdon constituted all of silent comedy; but they so eclipsed in reputation even the praised efforts of De Mille, Stroheim, Vidor, Lubitsch, and others that the social comedy of the silent era remains a relatively unknown field. As more of these films are brought back into circulation, re-evaluations will surely become more common.

## MACK SENNETT
### Richard Schickel

"You know," said the late Snub Pollard, one of the original Keystone Kops, "I guess I've been bathed in no less than ten tons of very wet cement. I figured up once I'd caught about fourteen thousand pies in my puss and had been hit by six hundred automobiles and two trains. Once I was even kicked by a giraffe."

These hardships occurred in the pursuit of a most peculiar art, an art which flourished only briefly, then disappeared, done in by technology, pseudo sophistication, and, perhaps, a decline in the creative energy of the group which forged the unique, the incomparable style of silent screen comedy in the manic atelier of Mack Sennett.

The Keystone Kops in particular, Sennett's entire group in general, achieved stardom en masse. From time to time a particularly strong personality, like Chaplin, would emerge from the gang and strike off on his own, having developed his trade in this school of hard knocks. But by and large the Kops and their quarries stand as anomalies in the history of stardom. A good many strange people have achieved stardom, but no group of this size—and nature —made it, either before or since. This is in character, for the Keystone group always stood a little outside the mainstream of film history. There was really only one thing they could do—make Keystone comedies—and very few of them survived the coming of sound. Even at the height of their powers the kind of film they were making had about the same relationship to the rest of moviemaking as the work of S. J. Perelman has to the art of the novel. The same basic tools (camera and film, pen and paper) are used, but after that the similarity ends.

The Kops were the sole creation of Mack Sennett, an indifferent actor who worked for Griffith at Biograph, graduated to scenario writing, then to the supervision of rube comedies. He paid generous tribute to Griffith as the man who "was my day school, my adult education program, my university," and indeed his emphasis on movement in the comedies is certainly related to the theories of Griffith, as is his editing technique. But the source of Sennett's work lies inexplicably deeper. It seems that all his life he regarded the policeman as one of God's more absurd creations. Probably it was the silly majesty the law attempts to maintain in the pursuit of minor offenders, its pitiful attempts at dignity in the face of man's obvious irrationality, which attracted Sennett to his great theme. In any case, he tapped a basic American feeling about policemen and allowed the nation to vent its dislike of regulations in gales of laughter. Law is such a sad thing, trying as it does to capture the basic absurdity of human behavior and pen it behind walls of rationally conceived rules. Our instinctive knowledge of the hopelessness of the task is what triggers our laughter at the Sennett comedy.

In this we are aided by the Kops themselves. We think of Sisyphus, toiling to push his rock up the hill, fully aware that, at the moment of triumph, the gods will send it tumbling back to the ground below. The Kops seemed to sense the futility of their activities, but the game itself was the fun, and their hope-lessly befuddled chase after the miscreant—typically in a decrepit flivver from which their blue-clad arms and legs protruded in wild tangles, their faces meanwhile maintaining a stolid dignity that defied us to comment upon the mess they were making—was something into which you could read a dozen meanings. A wild swerve around a trolley car, a near miss of a wandering mongrel, a brush of the bumper with a speeding train, the sudden disembarka-tion as the car crashes against tree or hydrant (how was it that the Kops always missed the moving hazards and hit the stationary ones?). Then the chase on foot, through the alleys and backyards, in which all the sprinklers were unac-countably turned on, finally the quarry coming to ground, naturally, in a pastry shop or restaurant, offering its tempting array of missiles to be hurled by one and all.

What did it all mean? The chase offered a dozen possibilities of interpretation: it was a comment on all who pursue goals with too much zeal and not enough sense, it was a dramatization of the individual's struggle against society or organization, it was a grand thumb in the eye of authority. But, beyond all this, there was the beautifully simple cinematic style in which these splendid fellows went through their paces. Sennett believed speed and grotesquerie were the basis of comedy. Few Sennett gags took more than ten seconds of screen time from initial statement, through elaboration, to culmination. Ideally, the next gag was built off the first and sight gag followed sight gag in dizzying succession. Even when he was supervising the entire product of his busy studio and directing very little, he reviewed every scene shot, the creakings of his projection-room rocker an index to his responses. He always called for more speed. As to his liking for the grotesque, one need only look at the faces and figures of the actors he employed. They were parodies of the human form, and that made their parodies of poor man's attempts to cope with the essentially unmanageable modern world even more delicious. The backgrounds against which they moved, the wasteland of southern California when it was a sub-divider's paradise, with only the skeleton of the megalopolis to come sketched in, enhanced the mood of dreamlike realism in Sennett's films. Finally, the girls, really quite lovely, and the first direct screen statement of the pleasures inherent in the female form were a perfect touch. The bathing beauties represented a healthy kidding of our sexual preoccupations. They were neither simpering nor blatant in manner. They simply existed, delightful, not quite bright, ideal foils for the cavorting grotesques around them.

The Sennett star faded quickly after the coming of sound. His most talented mimes had already left him, and then tastes changed, and the verbal gag replaced the visual one in films. Sennett ended his days broke and—like so many movie pioneers—almost forgotten by the industry he helped create. Most of the artists who followed his traditions and work were also ruined by sound. It is only now—too late—that we see in the artless art of Mack Sennett more real worth than in all but a handful of the more grandiose productions of his contemporaries. He is one of the few who made genuine folk art while working in the mass media.

[1962, 1964]

# HARRY LANGDON
## *Penelope Gilliatt*

Keaton, Chaplin, Lloyd, Langdon—and the unsung of these is Langdon. If Harold Lloyd looks like a schoolboy who is hitting the awkward age and who is also a bit of a swot, Harry Langdon looks like a small girl with high hopes of one day being eight. The exquisite Bessie Love face is hung with panniers of puppy fat. The make-up, which weirdly manages not to seem androgynous, gives him the likeness of a child who has been mooning for hours in front of a looking glass with its mother's lipstick and mascara. The mouth looks babyish and jammy, and the eye black has been put on in a state of trance; the whole face has then been dreamily smothered in talcum powder. When Langdon gazes into the distance in a film—when he is playing a soldier looking for his regiment in country too hard for him—his lineless, unpanicked face is the mask not of a mind hard at work, like Keaton's, but of a mind gently lolling at anchor, like a punt. He seems to be contemplating not a problem but his own reflection, with an interest too infant to be called vanity. Any intrusions of thought would be perilous, like noises that could make a sleepwalker break an ankle. The face exudes great sweetness and placidity. When cunning takes over, it is the response of someone premoral. Langdon is very much an only child, and it has made him a duffer at games. As a 1914–1918 private in *The Strong Man*—the only private in the whole army who might easily fail someday to absorb the fact that the war is over—he takes abstracted aim at a tin can and then at a German officer's helmet, using army biscuits slung from a catapult. Only a girl would find such a rotten form of bullet, and only a girl would be so thrilled and surprised to get a hit—a girl with aspirations not to be a butterfingers, but doomed in the hope, and solitary. Langdon automatically goes his own way, without troubling himself to get in touch with the rest of the world. The position seems to be shared by all the great cinema comedians; the movies' double acts, the fables about alliance, derive from the stage, and never seem to be as glorious on screen as they can be in music hall.

When Langdon is in mufti—when he isn't being a soldier, or isn't dressed up in a morning coat to marry some scheming, avaricious bride—he generally wears a hat with the brim turned up all the way around, an outgrown jacket of which only the top buttons will fasten, baggy trousers, and large, amoebic boots. He stands with his feet in the first position of ballet, toes out—again like a girl without much of a clue. There can never have been such a spry comedian who gave such an impression of unathleticism. He looks as if he couldn't run for toffee. The best of his films—including some that he directed himself—reflect his schoolgirl torpor and move along with a beautiful dumbbell liquidity. He has a child's blitheness in egoism, a child's greed and hope and otherworld criminality, and if the characterization ever slips into a moment of adult, this-world proneness to wounds, the film falters. Keaton is entirely grown up, stoic, decisive, ancient; Langdon seems most himself when he is unformed and seraphically naïve. He is a virtuoso of infant twitches that signal some tiny, fleeting worry, and a master of the beguilingly fatuous motions of beings who are still at the stage of experimenting to find their muscles. He can be especially splendid when he is working at a slant, trudging around the precipitous floor of a shack in a cyclone as if he had only just learned to walk.

The girls in his films are filthy grownups, treacherous and not very pretty. There is a terrible harridan in *The Strong Man* who cons him into thinking that she was the flower-faced girl who was his pen pal at the front; back home in America, she slips a stolen wad of bills into his pocket to off-load detection by a dick behind her, and then faints massively outside her choice of mansion.

Langdon is told severely by a servant that one can't leave one's women lying around like that. He lugs her inside as if she were a very large roll of carpet, keeling under her weight and avoiding several nasty blows from her *diamanté* jewelry. Her neck looks like a boxer's. Langdon staggers, sees the immense curving staircase that she wants to be carried up, and staggers some more. Starting the long haul, he gets his foot stuck in a flowerpot. There is a joyful moment when the overdressed burden, who is still pretending to be in a swoon, has to be propped on the marble banisters for an instant and then slides all the way down on her stomach. Langdon anxiously begins over again, sitting down on the stairs and carting the woman up step by step on his lap. He has indoctrinated himself so sternly into making the taxed movement that he plugs on with it, still backward, up a stepladder at the head of the stairs, right to the top of the ladder, and then beyond and over. It is a marvelous passage of mime. Maybe inflexibility, automatism, abstractedness, and unsociability are great staples of funniness; Langdon's films sometimes have them all.

Unlike Chaplin and Harold Lloyd, he doesn't wheedle. We might as well not be there. He is subject to attacks of entirely private petulance, and doesn't give a damn that they're dopey. He will kick a cannon, or throw things irritably, and with a girl's aim, at a cyclone. In one celebrated set piece in, again, *The Strong Man,* he has a cold and attends devotedly to curing himself with stinking remedies in a crowded vehicle. The other passengers object, especially when he rubs his chest with Limburger cheese instead of liniment. A fusspot on his left is incensed. Langdon, hampered by feeling lousy, gives him an effete punch and also manages to spatter cough syrup over the dandyish enemy. His revenges are always serene and his movements oddly meditative. As with the business of lugging the hefty woman thief upstairs, his physical gags often come out of the old vaudeville-comedy discipline of repeating a movement mechanically after the need for it has gone. In *Tramp, Tramp, Tramp,* he somehow gets himself into and out of a prisoners' work camp in the middle of a cross-America walking race; he has grown entirely accustomed to walking with a ball and chain when he rejoins the race, and when a train happens (never mind how) to run over the chain and cut it loose he picks up the ball gamely and carries it as if it were a given of life. Sometimes he will stoop to pull up the iron links around his legs because they have drooped like sock garters. You can see that the things have given him pins and needles. He rubs the circulation back. Comedy is to swallow a camel and strain at a gnat.

Comedy is also to be tenacious in pursuit of hermetically peculiar tasks. In *Long Pants,* Langdon tries desperately to train a ventriloquist's dummy to run, doing demonstration sprints again and again, and coming back each time to see if the lesson has taken. He is fine with props, and a great punster with objects. Planning radiantly to murder his prospective bride in a wood, he drops his pistol into the undergrowth and retrieves in its stead a pistol-shaped branch, which he carries on with for a while. In England, the Goons used to do this sort of thing in their great early days at the BBC. Spike Milligan would suddenly pick up a passing banana in the recording studio and plant it in his ear as a telephone receiver for an improvised call to Peter Sellers, blandly ignoring the fact that they were doing radio, not television.

Harry Langdon was born in 1884, child of two Salvation Army officers—which was a start. He worked as a cartoonist, a prop boy, a barber, and a performer in a patent-medicine show and then in vaudeville for twenty years before he went to Mack Sennett. It was Frank Capra, a Sennett gag writer at the time, who invented *Tramp, Tramp, Tramp* for him. Capra apparently understood Langdon's comic personality perfectly and begged to be allowed to work with him. (Later on, it was Capra who directed the two films that are probably Langdon's best—*The Strong Man* and *Long Pants*.) In *Tramp, Tramp, Tramp,* Capra correctly shows him coming out on top, as infants do, and winning the cross-continental marathon in spite of the ball and chain and in spite of infatuation with a girl played by Joan Crawford. The spiritual load for Langdon of loving Joan Crawford is inspired.

In Langdon's most characteristic films, the girls tend to be armor-plated. While he slips them love notes, they are likely to be immersed in some manly correspondence with other criminals about loot and dope. His attitude toward them is distant and spiked with decorum. He may sleep with a framed poster of the beloved's face in his bed, but this is as far as he will go. The strapping lady thief in *The Strong Man* tries to seduce him; though he is prefectly polite, the occasion is beyond his experience, and all he knows is that it tickles. There are some Langdon pictures in which the misogyny becomes delicately surreal. In *Three's a Crowd,* which he directed, he has a nightmare about having to fight in a brightly lit boxing ring, with his girl rooting against him, eyes hard as quartz; in the end, loopy with blood lust, she bites her straw hat to pieces. Girls are never much help to Langdon. His best friend is providence—some fall of a stone in the nick of time, some Old Testament collapse of a saloon filled with stronger enemies. There is one cast list in which the characters include "His Bride," "His Downfall," "His Finish"; all three, predictably, are girls. Nonetheless, he is chivalrous. There are standards to be kept up. Sometimes he will explain these standards in a subtitle. They have a charming impatience and oddness: "Can't you see, Pa, when your sweetheart's in distress you can't go around marrying other women?" His love letters have the same straightforward idiosyncrasy: "I love you, I love you, I love you, I love you, and hope you are the same. Harry."

The America of his films is grounded in the twenties. It is a world of marathons and patent medicines and bootlegging, of religion that has a thunderous edge to it, of wedding rings in hock, of keeping one's end up. There is an out-of-work strong man who wears a brocade waistcoat for bravado; he boasts, to maintain his spirits, "I lift the heaviest weights in the world, and when I shoot myself from a cannon to a trapeze it's a sensation." Sometimes Langdon's films movingly catch the desperate, squalid courage of the epoch. His father in *Tramp, Tramp, Tramp* is a smalltime cobbler on his way out because of the coming of mass production. "I can't battle those big shoe manufacturers," Pop says tremulously from, of course, a wheelchair. The sentimentality about crafts and private enterprise also belongs to the times; it seems half mock, but meant, too. The great silent comedians demonstrate a philosophy of me-against-the-world, of small-town decency against metropolitan mayhem, of the loner against the propertied. Greed whirls over the landscape in a dark cone, drawing with it everyone except the tramp comedian and his kin. But though the tramp doesn't have a bean, he has a benedictive luck. In one of Langdon's famous stunt sequences, he has leaped over the fence of a yard enticingly labeled PRIVATE. KEEP OUT, to be saved on the other side only by a nail from falling down a cliff face. Whoever wrote that notice had a satanic passion for property and no great feeling for the lives of natural daredevils. Langdon's belt catches on the nail, and so does his sweater. He removes the sweater from the nail carefully and starts to unbuckle the belt. Then he sees the drop below him, absorbs it gravely, and does up the buckle, going on to cover up the sight of it with his sweater, in one of my favorite hopeless moments in silent comedy. Langdon did the stunt himself. "There was no one else to do it," he told a friend later, after the talkies had come in and his career had hit bankruptcy, "so I had no alternative." He was apparently deeply worried at the time because there wasn't a titter from the crew as he hung there. He didn't allow for their being fond of him; he thought it meant the sequence wouldn't be funny.

[1971]

# HAROLD LLOYD
## Richard Schickel

By the time he died, on March 8, 1971, at the age of seventy-seven, Harold Lloyd had become an obligatory name on the short, nostalgic—sometimes falsely nostalgic—list of the great comedians of the silent screen: Chaplin, Keaton, Harry Langdon, sometimes Laurel and Hardy—and Lloyd. No one dared omit his name. He had been so greatly popular in his time and he was obviously such a nice man, living in prosperous retirement in his legendary home in Beverly Hills, that it would have seemed both antihistorical and unnecessarily cruel not to at least mention him in passing. Besides, no illustrated history of the movies—indeed, of the social history of twentieth-century America—seemed complete without that famous still from *Safety Last* of Lloyd hanging from the hands of a clock, its face itself dangling from the huge timepiece's mainspring, some twelve stories above a busy downtown street. Somehow, better than any other, that picture seemed to summarize the inordinate lengths to which Lloyd and his peers in the great, lost art of silent comedy would go for a laugh. And if few knew exactly how and why Lloyd came to this unlikely and obviously temporary predicament, fewer still cared to investigate the matter. It was difficult to see his films, since they had long since gone out of general release and two compilations of their best sequences, put together by Lloyd himself in the early sixties, had aroused only mild, and certainly not critically acute, interest. There were no calls for a general revival of his work, as there were for that of Chaplin and Keaton. It would have been fair to say that when he died Harold Lloyd was recalled fondly, and even warmly by those who had grown up on his films in the 1920s. But he was not remembered, not in the fullest sense of the word.

There were two reasons for this. In 1971, when Richard Griffith, former curator of the Museum of Modern Art film library, came to write an introduction to the reprint of Lloyd's reticent, primitive venture into the as-told-to autobiography, *An American Comedy,* he noted the lack of interest in Lloyd, a lack of interest so profound that not a single substantial book had been written about him. This reflected, Griffith commented, "the disesteem in which he has traditionally been held by the movie high-brows. They do not like his optimism. His calculated comedy methods have been labeled 'mechanical' and let go at that. His wealth and success have been held against him. . . ." So far as these remarks go—and Griffith did not live to finish the introductory essay —they are entirely accurate. For example, in *The Comic Mind,* a study devoted entirely to screen comedy, and largely to silent comedy at that, Gerald Mast spared but sixteen pages for Lloyd, and though he gives grudging acknowledgments to Lloyd's skill as a creator of incredibly long and intricate gag sequences, he calls him "deliberate, cold-blooded, and detached . . . superficial." Ultimately, Mast tells us, "Lloyd comedies say nothing about life." The problem, as he sees it, is that Lloyd (and Langdon) lacked "that perfect unity between soul and surface, internal feeling and external gag, comic business and serious implication, subjective reaction to human life and objective depiction of it in the film medium." This bias was even shared by James Agee, whose 1949 piece, "Comedy's Greatest Era," remains one of the few essays in film criticism that combines grace of expression, thoughtfulness of analysis, and judiciousness—and which did more than any single work of criticism to revive interest in the silent comedians. Agee felt it necessary to balance his generally affectionate remarks about Lloyd by remarking, "If great comedy must involve something beyond laughter, Lloyd was not a great comedian."

If the critics found a lack of what we would now call "soul" in Lloyd's films, they found a similar lack of emotional resonance in his life off screen. It seems to have contained only one serious crisis, which (typically) Lloyd himself went to some lengths to disguise, and so far as anyone outside his immediate circle knew, no tragedies, though again, there was more unhappiness in Lloyd's life than met the uninformed eye. Essentially, his road to success—an enormous success in his time, quite comparable to Chaplin's, economically—had been a smooth one. His childhood was apparently emotionally stable, if rather less geographically rooted than most—though, interestingly, all the great silent comics had rather foot-loose beginnings. Lloyd's struggle to establish himself professionally was both brief and without major frustration. He made the transition to the sound era more easily and more profitably than most of his peers, though without the glorious results that Chaplin, after much creative anguish, achieved in *City Lights* and *Modern Times*—if, indeed, it is fair to call these sound films in the full sense of the term. In any event, he was not ruined as Keaton and Langdon were, not forced into the sometimes humiliating low-budget pictures that Laurel and Hardy had to make in order to keep going. Then, when public taste gently, without rancor or shocking haste, veered away from him, he was able to quietly withdraw, never officially announcing a retirement, and indeed, keeping himself before the public in a variety of dignified ways during the last three decades of his life—as a producer, as the host of a radio show for a brief time, and, most important to him, as Imperial Potentate—the national president—of the Shrine. He was even the star of a Preston Sturges movie, though it didn't come out as successfully as it might have. Later, of course, there were his compilation films to attend to, and the inevitable old man's round of retrospectives, film festivals, seminars, and lectures, as well as extensive real-estate holdings to oversee, and a succession of obsessive hobbies to fill the hours between his public and business engagements.

Of such things legendary status as a cultural hero is not made. What is required is some sort of tragedy. An artist who dies before his time—F. Scott Fitzgerald is the classic example in our era—is in a sense fortunate; if he had any ability at all we mourn not only for the indifference visited upon him by a world which underestimated his mortality but also for the work that might have been. But death is not necessary to achieve tragic status. For example, Buster Keaton was effectively silenced as an artist by drink and by the insensitivity to his gifts of his last employer, Metro-Goldwyn-Mayer, who gave up on him too quickly, too brutally, when his first sound films proved unprofitable. Charles Chaplin, in a sense, produced and directed his own fall from grace. His marital difficulties and his earnest, if innocent, left-wing political views did not jibe with the benign image of the Little Fellow (indeed, his compulsion to lecture the world about how it ought to think and behave politically fatally marred his last movies). Unable or unwilling to sue for a renewal of the affection he had once found in his adopted country, he withdrew in bitter exile and did not return until he could return to the prodigal's welcome that was arranged for him on the occasion of his receipt of a special Academy Award in 1972—an event that, not accidentally, coincided with the carefully managed reissue of his old films by shrewd promoters. Even poor Harry Langdon, the least conscious of silent comedians, and the one with the briefest period of stardom, came to be seen as a tragic figure. As Frank Capra, who was part of the team at Mack Sennett's studio that concocted a screen character for him —something close to *The Good Soldier Schweik*—and who directed his first independent feature, tells it, Langdon was afflicted with a sudden swelling of the head. He dismissed most of the group, Capra included, who had helped create his success, floundered for a bit, and then after the coming of sound sank entirely—into short subjects, then bit parts, then silence. Agee's article did not merely rescue his reputation, it made it, for he had never really established himself in his time, as Chaplin, Keaton, and Lloyd had; without Agee, Langdon would have been almost completely forgotten. Now, if anything, his ranking exceeds Lloyd's in the estimate of many scholars.

Thus the congeries of factors that have condemned Harold Lloyd to the fringe of historical consciousness. And thus the need to re-examine his achievement. In this essay I am not going to argue that received opinion about him is completely wrong. Nor am I going to attempt to prove that there was some hidden psychological wound or some previously unsuspected depth of vision or feeling that only now, at some distance in time, we can perceive, and thereby find new values in his films. Yet it seems to me self-evident that any performer who achieved and sustained over a period of years the enormous popularity that Lloyd enjoyed must have had virtues that his more recent critics have ignored. It also seems to me, having had the opportunity lately to study the body of his work, that it has, for the most part, an overriding virtue which is so obvious that it is easy to overlook—namely that it is simply and consistently more hilarious than the work of any contemporary other than Keaton. Or, as Agee immediately added after acknowledging that Lloyd, for lack of heart, might not be a "great" comedian, "If plain laughter is any criterion—and it is a healthy counterbalance to the other—few people have equalled him, and nobody has ever beaten him."

It is a point to be borne firmly in mind. And there are others that come to mind as his work unfolds before one, some three or four decades after it was done. For one thing, the world through which Lloyd moved was the "realest" of all the comic worlds of the silent screen, the freest of exaggeration and stylization, both physically and in terms of the other characters encountered by Lloyd's character, often identified in the credits only as "The Boy." There are few freaks or grotesques here, and the streets, shops, and homes he moved through were more often than not locations rented for a few days' shooting, and so far as one can tell, scarcely changed or decorated by the moviemakers. And, because Lloyd himself is usually such a normal, everyday sort of chap, fitting so easily into these ordinary surroundings, one gains from the films now a quite extraordinary sense of the physical reality of a period fast receding from living memory.

One point seems particularly worth emphasizing, if only because Lloyd and his coworkers (probably unconsciously) emphasized it. That is that the decade or so between the end of World War I and the stock-market crash in 1929 was a period of contrast between the older, essentially rural America—nineteenth-century America that had, in fact, continued to flourish at least as a repository of values for the first two decades of this country—and the new urban America that was developing. This new nation inside the old seemed nothing less than a miracle to a goodly portion of the citizenry, especially to those who, like Lloyd himself, had been born into rural small-town America but had been irresistibly drawn to the glamour and the economic opportunities of the growing cities. This all seems odd to us today, oppressed as so many of us are by the ugliness and decay of city life. But to Lloyd's generation everything about the city seemed fresh and enthralling. The automobile, for instance, represented a wondrous convenience, an object of almost indescribable longing, not a source of pollution and, indeed, death. No wonder one of his greatest comic sequences—Harold taking his wife and his in-laws for a first spin in a new car in *Hot Water*—is so beautifully orchestrated and so strangely touching. One understands what the car means to its new owner as a first symbolization of rising status and as a demonstration to his thoroughly awful relatives that he is a more substantial figure than they had reckoned him to be. Thus, its gradual demolition as he attempts to master both the mechanical intricacies of the vehicle and the confusions of the city's traffic regulations is not only suspenseful and funny, but oddly moving. One gains the sense from this sequence that Lloyd's befuddlement and his increasingly desperate attempts to maintain his *savoir-faire,* to project mastery in a situation for which he had no training, emotional or otherwise, was instantly and entirely recognizable to his audience —and that it was one for which they had instant empathy. Indeed, one does not have to work very hard to rekindle, some forty years later, a similar emotional response, for there are still complicated objects we long for but which can undo our dignity, our *amour-propre,* when we attempt to bring them under our control. Simply replace the *Hot Water* car with something like a camper and place in it an urban American attempting to embrace the outdoor life, from which we are now as alienated by birth and training as Lloyd and his generation were from the city and its tools for living, and the comic point becomes self-evident. Similarly, it seems to me, Lloyd's obsession with high places, his literally nightmarish discovery of himself clinging to the ledges, decorations, flagpoles, clocks of skyscrapers, makes perfect sense for his time—and has a resonance for us as well. *Safety Last* may contain the most famous of these sequences, but he had begun experimenting with similar work in his two- and three-reelers of 1920 and 1921, *High and Dizzy* and *Never Weaken,* and he may have topped all these "thrill" sequences with the great one contained in an otherwise indifferent sound film, 1930's *Feet First.* At any rate, they were all products of a period in which the whole nation was mightily impressed by our relatively new-found ability to build upward, ever upward. The skyscraper was perhaps the greatest symbol of the age's technological achievements—a thrilling, yet in some sense a scary, thing. (It still is, only now anxiety outruns pride—witness the interest in the 1974 superproduction, *The Towering Inferno,* an adaptation of two best-selling books about the currently lively fear that the great buildings downtown may be firetraps in which hundreds could be killed by accident.) In any event, there is no need to emphasize that skyscrapers almost immediately became a feature of our dream world, as any psychoanalyst can testify. Nor is there much need to stress the dreamy quality of Lloyd's high-rise thrill sequences, the (again unconscious) surrealistic air about them. They afford us, now, the opportunity to reflect on how recently our attitudes toward our environment were diametrically opposed to what they have become, how quickly we have reversed ourselves, and—perhaps more to the point—how Lloyd's always disastrous entanglements with the contraptions of modernism seem to predict the exasperation with them that more and more of us would feel in the years to come. Again, it is impossible to believe that this rather simple soul, always in rather narrow-minded pursuit of the strongest possible gag line, had anything like social criticism in mind. He was not writing on film an early version of *Future Shock.* But it is all there to see if one has the eyes to see it.

Along this line, it is interesting to note how accurately his pictures reflect the exquisite confusions of a time of vast environmental transition. For example, in that same sequence in *Hot Water,* one of the things Lloyd, his family, and his car get entangled with is a fire engine answering an alarm. The engine is horse-drawn. Yet this encounter with a remnant of nineteenth-century technology follows almost immediately their eluding a traffic cop who is mounted on what appears to be the latest model motorcycle. Similarly, there is a great sequence in the film immediately preceding, *Girl Shy,* in which

Harold must stop a wedding before the girl he loves marries a sly bigamist. He must get from city to country, and in the process he uses—or attempts to use—every mode of land transportation then available (including, most spectacularly, a runaway trolley car). The point is not merely that this is as beautifully orchestrated a sequence as anything in Keaton, but that horses and horse-drawn vehicles come as readily to his desperate hand as motor-driven conveyances. The confusion of the old-fashioned and the modern, doubtless accepted without thought by audiences of the day, since it is accepted unblinkingly by Lloyd, adds a note of peculiar interest to the movie today—a strange displacing note—that often occurs in other Lloyd movies as well, and gives them a special value on rediscovery. Indeed, there is something of this quality —the familiar made casually unfamiliar by quirks of costume, décor, or what have you—lurking in the corner of nearly every frame of every silent film. It is one of the things that make them so endlessly fascinating to study today.

In reviewing Lloyd's work today, one is also struck by how purely it seems to be the product of the movies and of nothing else. This is often held against him by critics like Mast, who point out that Chaplin and Keaton were "international" stars of vaudeville and music hall before coming to film, that even Langdon served a long—if not particularly distinguished—apprenticeship in the same environs. It is perfectly true that, aside from the most modest kind of work in amateur theatricals and in some professional stock companies, Lloyd had only a small amount of stage training, and no vaudeville background whatever. It is also undoubtedly accurate to say that he knew next to nothing of the comedic traditions, established in the dim reaches of theatrical history, that informed Chaplin's work in particular. Lloyd's schools were the movie-comedy factories, mainly Hal Roach's, but also, for a short interval, Mack Sennett's. And as Agee said, "The early silent comedians never strove for or consciously thought of anything which could be called artistic 'form,' " although, as he also says, "they achieved it."

The basic Sennett and Roach films, especially in the early days when Lloyd was apprenticing, consisted of setting up an excuse for a chase or "rally" (as the device was known around Sennett's) and then getting it going—at undercranked speeds, of course, so movement would be (Agee's phrase again) "just a shade faster and fizzier than life." Sennett, in particular, was uninterested in the comedy of character (though perhaps he achieved a comedy of humors from time to time), and while film scholar William K. Everson finds more character development in the Roach films, it remains difficult to advance very elaborate claims for them either in this respect. At any rate, Chaplin left Sennett precisely because the opportunities for his delicate pantomimic characterizations were few and he feared being lost in the general uproar. Keaton also had only brief Sennett experience, taking a cut from his two-hundred-fifty-dollar-a-week vaudeville salary to learn the craft of film comedy for a starting fee of forty dollars a week, at first working mainly in the Fatty Arbuckle series. In fact, of the legendary top bananas of the silent screen, only Lloyd worked for any length of time at either of the premier comedy studios. And that may very well account for the fact that it was he who developed to its highest point the comedy of thrills and movement—the "rally" raised to its highest levels

—though there is nothing in any of Lloyd's work that would suggest the balletic parallels a number of critics, especially the French, have found in Sennett's rallies.

But that's all right, too. Sennett himself used to reserve his bluntest derision for critics of that school, noting happily that he had never seen a ballet in his life. What's more important is that Sennett in the beginning, then Keaton and Lloyd with greater sophistication, were able to use the first machine capable of capturing and reproducing motion in order to satirize an age of machines that had set the whole society into accelerated motion. It scarcely detracts from Chaplin to say that except for *Modern Times* his films seem scarcely aware of the mechanization of life. The Little Fellow had other fish to fry. Similarly, it seems unfair to criticize Lloyd for his failure to develop a tragic sense of life. He, too, had his eye on other matters. And besides, there do not seem to have been any incidents in his early life that might have set him to brooding about injustice, about the pathetic and the absurd qualities of existence. In his films he did suffer, as Andrew Sarris has acutely pointed out, "terrible humiliation . . . on the social ladder," and these moments can generate more potent shocks of recognition than most critics care to admit (*The Freshman,* for example, is full of them). Still, it is fair to say that Harold Lloyd had every reason to suppose that the most banal of American philosophies—the pluck-and-luck dream by which a poor but eager youth is elevated above the crowd because he is willing to work hard to develop his God-given talents—actually worked. It had for him, and he had the good fortune to place before the public his best and most carefully developed work at precisely the historical moment when that public as a whole had every reason to share his belief in this most common form of the American dream. He was comedian to the Age of Prosperity, and no more than his audience did he have any reason to suppose that the age would not last, that a moment ought to be spared for the thought that trouble and tragedy are timeless, and, for the individual, quite resistant to the movements of the business cycle. But if, indeed, Chaplin and to a degree Keaton had the depth and sensitivity to comprehend this and to encompass it in their art, one may also note that Lloyd's sublime unawareness of it can be refreshing in its innocence, its naïveté.

Indeed, it might even be correct to suggest that Lloyd is rather unfairly lumped with Chaplin, Keaton, and Langdon. They are considered together largely, it would seem, because they were the leading producer-stars of feature-length comedies in the 1920s. But it has always seemed to me that Lloyd's eager youth, slender and well-groomed, with nothing but his lensless glasses —themselves a completely natural, everyday sort of appurtenance—to set him apart, to establish his "character," owed more to the early Douglas Fairbanks screen character than it did to stage convention, which insisted on grotesque make-up and costume for "low" comics, and which Lloyd's competitors, each in his own way, adapted to the screen. Fairbanks, like Lloyd, though on a grander scale, had come from legit, where he had been mostly a juvenile, and the character he played in his early movies, before he turned to historical spectacles, was a variation on the kind of youths he had been playing on stage. Like Lloyd's character later, this character was usually introduced either as an inept and wealthy idler who discovers within himself untapped depths of courage and physical inventiveness when he stumbles into some sort of danger, or as a rather dreamy lower-class youth entertaining fantasies of heroism behind his clerkly counter who is given the opportunity to act out those dreams in reality—usually because the girl he loves requires rescuing from some peril or other. These, precisely, are the situations Lloyd found himself coping with in his features, and it seems interesting that Fairbanks made the last picture of this kind *(The Nut)* in 1921, a year after he had made the first of his swashbucklers, *The Mark of Zorro,* whose success determined his new direction. For in that same year Lloyd, who had begun in 1918 to experiment with his "glasses character," as he liked to call his only enduring screen persona, made his first feature, *A Sailor-Made Man,* which is astonishingly close to the early Fairbanks formula. In other words, consciously or not, Lloyd saw a niche in the process of being vacated and nimbly hopped into it.

It did not take him long to make it his own. Fairbanks had never been averse to getting a laugh, but he also fancied himself, quite correctly, as a considerable romantic figure, and his stunts, thrilling as they were, were primarily designed to show off his graceful and dashing athleticism. Lloyd, however, depended on looking as comically awkward as possible when he was confronted by difficult circumstances, and, of course, he was required to draw out his chases to the point where an audience's fears for him were converted first into nervous laughter, then into the pure boffo thing. This, obviously, left but small space in which to build up the romantic side of his screen character, which also had its ridiculous side—this shy, pale four-eyes, the kind of kid who plays clarinet in the high-school band, has trouble getting a date for the prom, and hopefully takes the business course (though it is hard to imagine him mastering the courage to sell anything except from behind a modest notions counter). Still, Lloyd's relationship to the Fairbanks character, who was also an all-American optimist, a four-square believer in what amounted to Rotarian values, is clearer and closer than his relationship to the creations of the screen figures we more generally regard as his closest competitors and to whom we most frequently compare him, mostly invidiously.

To summarize the matter briefly, then, Harold Lloyd's relatively undramatic personal life, its lack of obvious tragic overtones, has led to a regrettable lack of popular interest in his creative output; also, his work is more bound to his times than the work of most silent comedians, although that begins to seem something of an advantage now, as his films, because of their naturalistic air, help us to gain a historical purchase on his age; his films also owe less to literary and theatrical tradition than those of the other great silent comedians, but that may mean that they have a pure "movieness," a significance in the establishment of a film aesthetic that owes less to the other arts than some critics would like; his work is less "universal," more "American," in its underlying values than that of other actors, Chaplin in particular, though this lack of pretension can be refreshing and something of a value in itself; and in any event, it is unfair to overstress his relationship with the other masters of screen comedy, because his work seems to have grown out of a tradition quite different from the one which informed them. Finally, and this may be the most significant point of all, Lloyd's personal history led him inescapably to the kind of art he created, and was thus responsible for its virtues and its defects. Indeed, one could say that the linkage between Lloyd the man and Lloyd the primitive screen artist was closer, more direct, than that of any other comedian, any other screen personality one can think of. One could say, in fact, that Harold Lloyd's early life—his later life was far darker than most people know —reads very much like the script for a Harold Lloyd movie.

[1974]

# BUSTER KEATON
## Penelope Gilliatt

"You don't go out of your way *not* to talk in a film," Buster Keaton says to me, "but you only talk if it's necessary." Two-minute pause. He is now sixty-eight, two years from his death in 1966. He is sitting in his rather poor ranch house in the San Fernando Valley, quite a drive from the stars' hangout in Beverly Hills. (Keaton—whose work is running now, in 1970—always talked about making films in the present tense, and you don't easily use any other yourself about him.) He is trying to explain to me, on the basis of what he started learning in vaudeville from his parents' act when he was rising three, the machinery of silent jokes. The pause goes on, and the beautiful profile looks out of the back window onto the plot of land where he has built his hens a henhouse that has the space of an aviary and the architecture of a New England schoolhouse. The great master of film comedy, who is one of the true masters of cinema, suddenly gets up and climbs onto a dresser and does a very neat fall, turning over onto his hands and pretending that he has a sore right thumb. He keeps it raised, and then stands stock still and looks at it, acting. "Suppose I'm a carpenter's apprentice," he says after a while. Chest out, manly look, like a Victorian boy with his hands in his pockets having his photograph taken. "Suppose the carpenter hits my thumb with his hammer. Suppose I think, God damn, and leap out the window. Well, I'm not going to *say* my thumb hurts, am I?" He sits down in his chair again and thinks. He is wearing a jersey with piratical insignia on the front, and the sort of jaunty trousers that people wore on smart yachts in the thirties. "The thing is not to be ridiculous. The one mistake the Marx Brothers ever make is that they're sometimes ridiculous. Sometimes *we're* in the middle of building a gag that turns out to be ridiculous. So, well, we have to think of something else. Sit it out. The cameras are our own, aren't they? We never hire our cameras. And we've got a start, and we've got a finish, because we don't begin on a film if we haven't, so all we've got to get now is the middle."

He lays out a game of solitaire. The room has a pool table in it, and a lot of old photographs. On the table between us there is a card that a studio magnate left stuck in his dressing-table mirror one day soon after the talkies had come in, giving him the sack in three lines. "In the thirties, if there's a silence," says Buster, "they say there's a dead spot." Stills from his films come to mind: images of that noble gaze, austere and distinctive even when the head is up to the ears in water after a shipwreck, or when Buster is in mid-flight of some sort. Partly because of his vaudeville experience and partly because of his temperament, he obviously reserves great respect for those who retain a stoic attitude toward calamity and imminent death in the middle of being flung from one side of life to the other. He admires the character of a performing animal—a gorilla, as I remember, called Peter the Great—who expressed a Senecan-sounding serenity as he was being thrown around the stage of Buster's childhood.

Keaton's first film entrance was in *The Butcher Boy*. His character is clear at once. We are in a world of slapstick chaos, but he emits a sense of wary order. The scene is a village store. Everyone else moves around a lot, to put it mildly. When Keaton enters, the unmistakable calm asserts itself. He is wearing shabby overalls, big shoes with a hole in one sole (which later turns out to be usefully open to some spilled molasses), and already the famous flat hat. He then goes quietly through a scene of almost aeronautic catastrophe and subsidence, the whole parabola photographed in one take. Only a child brought up in music-hall mayhem from toddling age could have done it. The shop—hung with posters promising FRESH SAUSAGES MADE EVERY MONTH, run by a Roscoe Arbuckle who puts on a fur coat to go into the freezer locker (Keaton never calls him Fatty; it is always Roscoe), and inhabited by a club of aloof card players with Abe Lincoln faces clustered around a stove—turns into a whirlwind. Molasses sticks, and bodies fly, and flour powders the air. We are in a world of agile apprentices and flung custard pies and badly made brooms that Buster scathingly plucks by the individual bristle, like suspect poultry. And through it all there is the Keaton presence: the beautiful eyes, the nose running straight down from the forehead, the raised, speculative eyebrows, the profile that seems simplified into a line as classical as the line of a Picasso figure drawing. After a bit, Roscoe Arbuckle throws a sack of flour at him. Throughout his life, to many people, Buster has repeated his admiration of the force and address of that throw.

In spite of the peculiarly heroic austerity of his comic temperament, Keaton maintains firmly that he is a low comedian. This is a simple piece of old vaudeville nomenclature. "The moment you get into character clothes, you're a low comedian," he says. There are also, among others, tramp comedians and blackface comedians—a category that was stylized for purely technical reasons but that drew some of Keaton's shorts into looking Uncle Tom-ish. "What you have to do is create a character. Then the character just does his best, and there's your comedy. No begging." This is the difference between him and Chaplin, though he doesn't invite comparisons and talks more eagerly about technical things. The system of vaudeville comedy that he works by is methodical, physically taxing, and professionally interpreted. "Once you've got your realistic character, you've classed yourself. Any time you put a man into a woman's outfit, you're out of the realism class and you're in *Charley's Aunt.*"

There are one or two films of Keaton's, early in his career, in which someone wears drag; leaving aside modern unease about transvestism, the device goes against what Keaton can do.

Keaton's logical and vitally realist nature gradually got rid of the farfetched, or what he amiably calls just "the ridiculous." His whole comic character is too sobering for that, though infinitely and consolingly funny. Nothing much changes, it says. Things don't get easier. He will be courting a girl, for instance, and have to make way for a puppy, which the etiquette of the girl's demonstrativeness demands that she hug; the proposal that he meant to make to her goes dry in his mouth. He leaves with an air. Seasons pass, the puppy grows to frightful size, and he is still outwitted by her intervening love of pets. Finally, against every sort of odds, and only by great deftness, he manages to marry her, but the chance of kissing her is still obligatorily yielded to others—to the minister, to the in-laws, to the rival suitor, and to the now-monstrous slobberer, which ends the picture by sitting between the wedding couple on a garden seat and licking the bride's face. All the same, whatever the mortification, Keaton is never a pathetic figure. He stares out any plight. Perhaps because he has an instinctive dislike of crawling to an audience by exploiting any affliction in a character, including any capacity for being victimized, his figures never seem beaten men, and after a few experiments in his early work he never played a simpleton. He has perfected, uniquely, a sort of comedy that is about heroes of native high-brow intelligence, just as he is almost the only man who has ever managed to establish qualities of delicate dignity in characters with money. Comedians don't generally play the highborn. The fortunate, debonair, tongue-tied central character of *The Navigator* is one of the rarer creations of comedy: rich, decorous, possessed of a chauffeur and of a fine car that makes a U turn across the street to his fiancée's house, infinitely capable of dealing with the exchange and mart of high-flown social marriage, jerking no heartstrings. Keaton's world is a world of swells and toffs as well as butcher boys, and mixed up in it are memories of his hardy past in vaudeville that give some of his films a mood of the surreal. In *The Playhouse,* which he made after breaking his ankle on another picture, he plays not only nine musicians and seven orchestra members but also a music-hall aquatic star, an entire minstrel show, a dowager and her bedeviled husband, a pair of soft-shoe dancers, a stagehand, an Irish char, her awful child. We see the Keaton brat dropping a lollipop onto the Keaton *grande dame* in the box below; the dowager then abstractedly uses the lollipop as a lorgnette. He also plays a monkey who shins up the pros arch—something that must have been rough on the broken ankle. The film has a peculiar aura, not quite like anything else he made. It is dreamlike and touching, with roots in a singular infancy that he takes for granted. Vaudeville is what he comes from as powerfully as Shakespeare's Hal comes from boon nights spent with Falstaff. In *Go West,* there is a music-hall set piece about a slightly ramshackle top hat that is kept brilliantly in the air with repeated gunshots. "It has to be an old hat," says Buster. "You couldn't use a new hat. Otherwise, you don't get your laugh. Audiences don't like to see things getting spoiled."

Keaton has a passion for props. Especially for stylish things like top hats, for sailing boats and paddle steamers, and for all brainy machinery. He finds ships irresistible. A short called *The Boat* forecasts *The Navigator;* there is also *Steamboat Bill, Jr.* Facing many calamities, Buster as a sailor works with a sad, composed gaze and a resourcefulness that never wilts. In *Steamboat Bill, Jr.*, he leans on a life preserver that first jars his elbow by falling off the boat and then immediately sinks; Keaton's alert face, looking at it, is beautiful and without reproach. In *The Boat,* where he is shipbuilding, though deflected a good many times by one or another of a set of unsmiling small sons, his wife dents the stern of his creation with an unbreakable bottle of Coke while she is launching it; Keaton helps by leaning over the side to smash the thing with a hammer, and then stands erect while the boat sinks under him in water that comes quickly up to his neck, leaving us to watch the august head turning round in contained and unresentful bafflement. In *Steamboat Bill, Jr.,* his last independently produced film, he turns up, looking chipper, to join a long-lost father who runs a steamboat. The son will be recognizable by a white carnation, Buster has bravely said in a telegram, delivered four days late. He keeps authoritatively turning the carnation in his lapel toward people as if it were a police badge. No one is interested. His father eventually proves to be a big, benign bruiser, and not the man his son would have expected; nor is Buster the sort of man his father instantly warms to. He is much put off by the beautiful uniform of an admiral that Buster wears to help on the steamboat. It is not, maybe, fit for running a paddle steamer, but it is profoundly hopeful. It represents an apparently mistaken dapperness and an admission of instinctive class that turn out to be as correct in the end as the same out-of-place aristocratism in *The Navigator,* that poetic masterpiece of world cinema. There is nothing anywhere quite to equal the comic, desperate beauty of the long shots in *The Navigator* when Buster, the rich sap, is looking for his girl on the otherwise deserted liner that has gone adrift. The rows of cabin doors swing open and closed in turn, port and starboard in rhythm, on deck after deck; the debonair, tiny figure with the strict face and the passionate character runs round and round to find his dizzy girl, who is looking for him in her own quite sweet but less heartfelt way. The flower-faced fiancée played by Kathryn McGuire in *The Navigator* is a typical Keaton heroine. She is rather nice to him when he has got into his diving suit to free the rudder and has forgotten, with the helmet closed, that there is a lighted cigarette in his mouth. (This is a mistake that apparently happened while Keaton was shooting. "They've closed the suit on me," he says, coughing, the memory bringing on his present bronchitis, "and everyone just thinks I'm working up a gag.")

Keaton's characters are outsiders in the sense of spectators, not of nihilists or anarchists. He isn't at his best when he hates people (unlike W. C. Fields, for instance—whom he talks about with regard, doing a brotherly imitation of the voice of men who are martyrs to drinkers' catarrh). A short called *My Wife's Relations* has some of the Fields ingredients, but Keaton muffs the loathing. The picture has its moments, though. The wife is a virago with Irish relations who are devout but greedy; the only way to get a steak, Buster discovers, is to turn the calendar to a Friday. The blows that he manages to give her in bed when she thinks he is only thrashing in his sleep are pretty funny. So are the hordes of rapacious brides in *Seven Chances,* rushing after him on roller skates and wearing improvised bridal veils to make a grab for him because he will inherit a mint if he marries by seven o'clock. But Keaton is really at his best when he is being rather courtly. He has great charm in a feature called *The Three Ages*—about love in the Stone Age, the Roman Age, and the Modern Age—when he stands around among primordial rocks in a fur singlet and huge fur bedroom slippers chivalrously helping enormous girls up boulders. In that Age prospective in-laws assess the suitors by strenuous blows with clubs, and people ride around on mastodons that are clearly elephants decked out with rococo tusks by Keaton's happy prop men. In the Roman Age episodes, Wallace Beery as the Adventurer has a fine chariot, and Keaton has a sort of orange crate drawn by a hopeless collection of four indescribable animals. The Romans throw him into a lions' den, but he remembers only the pleasantest thing to remember about lions, which is that they behave well if you do something or other nice to their paws. He takes a paw, washes it, manicures it, and dries it. The interested beast responds affably. We switch back to the Stone Age. Keaton, looking more than usually small in the surroundings, is dealing courageously with the colossal opposite sex and hoping privately for more lyric times. He gets them for a moment in the Roman sequences: there is a wonderful shot of a girl's worshiping face as she thinks of Buster when she is in the middle of being pulled by the hair in some impossible Roman torment. But nothing vile in antiquity, Keaton implies by the sudden, pinching end of this revue film, can equal the meager-spiritedness of Los Angeles; the Stone Age and the Roman Age episodes both finish with shots of Buster and his bride surrounded by hordes of kids in baby fur tunics and baby togas, but the Modern Age episode finishes with the happy couple walking out of a Beverly Hills house followed by a very small, spoiled dog. Such minutes of tart melancholy are often there in Keaton. They go by fleetingly and without bitterness, like the sad flash in *The Scarecrow* when a girl takes it that his kneeling to do up a shoelace means that he is proposing. His beloveds sometimes have overwhelming mothers; one battle-ax, in *The Three Ages,* causes a pang when she makes him produce his bank balance, which is in a passbook labeled LAST NATIONAL BANK and obviously not up to scratch. One thinks, inevitably, of the hard time that Keaton was to have with his ambitious actress wife, Natalie Talmadge, which left him flat broke when the talkies came in. The Keaton hero, with the scale he is built on, and with his fastidious sense of humor, is obviously the born physical enemy of all awesome women. The girls he loves are shy and funny, with faces that they raise to him like wineglasses. But his idyllic scenes are very unsentimental. There is a nice moment when his loved one in *The Navigator* says to him, in reply to a proposal of marriage, "Certainly not!" Chaplin was once said to have given comedy its soul; if so, it was Keaton who gave it its spine and spirit.

"They have too many people working on pictures now, you know," says the aging, unsoured man whom the talkies threw on the dust heap although he could probably have gone on making great films in any new circumstance, and on a minute budget, and editing in a cupboard. "We had a head electrician, a head carpenter, and a head blacksmith." The blacksmith seems to have been crucial. There was a lot of welding to do. Keaton himself did his stunt work, magically and beautifully. Who else? He could loop through the air like a lasso. When he is playing the cox in *College* and the rudder falls off the boat, it is entirely in character that he should dip himself into the water and use his own body as the rudder. The end of *Seven Chances* is an amazing piece of stunt invention, inspired by cascades of falling boulders, that would have killed Keaton if he hadn't been an acrobat. Most of his stunt stuff isn't the sort of thing that can be retaken, and Keaton doesn't care much for inserts. "I like long takes, in long shot," he says. "Close-ups hurt comedy. CinemaScope hurts comedy. I like to work full figure. All comedians want their feet in."

He has just been asked to the premiere of *It's a Mad, Mad, Mad, Mad World,* which he has a part in after spending decades doing nothing much but commercials. *Mad World* is in the mode of wide screens with a vengeance. Buster has seen the picture. It can't be much to his taste, but he doesn't say so. He likes working; even making commercials doesn't strike him as such a cruel outcome to a life. He wants to go to the premiere. He looks vigilant and spry.

The wife of his last years thinks he shouldn't go to the premiere, because he might get a coughing fit and have to leave.

"We have aisle seats," he says.

"You're not well," she says.

"I can take my cough mixture," he says. "I can take a small container. I can get ready to move in a hurry."

[1970]

# CHARLES CHAPLIN

## A CHAPLIN OVERVIEW
### *Richard Schickel*

Praise, at this point, seems superfluous. Chaplin has received it, in fullest measure from his peers ("the greatest artist that was ever on the screen"—Stan Laurel, "the greatest comedian who ever lived"—Buster Keaton, "the greatest artist that ever lived"—Mack Sennett, "the best ballet dancer that ever lived, and if I get a chance I'll kill him with my bare hands"—W. C. Fields); from the critics ("It seems unlikely that any dancer or actor can ever have excelled him in eloquence, variety and poignancy of motion"—James Agee, "one of the few great comic geniuses who have appeared so far in history"—Robert Warshow, "Chaplin's career is a cinematic biography on the highest level of artistic expression"—Andrew Sarris); and from the highest levels of the literary world ("the only genius developed in motion pictures"—George Bernard Shaw, "among his age's first artists"—Edmund Wilson).

One could fill an essay with such quotations and still have plenty left over.

Moreover, one would, in the end, have a sentence or two from nearly every critic and every artist one respects. So it is disturbing not to join, full-voiced, in a chorus where only Fields, that lovely man, manages to sound an unawed, human note. It is especially difficult to maintain a degree of critical reserve after Chaplin, following a quarter century of self-imposed exile, came among us again—two weeks short of his eighty-third birthday, so obviously on a sentimental, farewell journey to a land that is to him, as Sarris wisely put it, "a fantasy and a delusion, marvelous world that he may . . . revisit, but will never reconquer," at least in the way he once did when he graciously accepted our unconditional surrender to his art. One is so anxious not to appear insensitive before a creator whose chief stock in trade was a preternatural sensitivity, so anxious not to be mistaken for the kind of right-wing crazy who hounded him about his really quite innocent politics and morals, coloring his essential loneliness with the terrible bitterness that seems only now to be fading to bearable levels.

It is, I think, a measure not merely of Chaplin's art, but of his really incredible ego, that one simply cannot find an article that presumes to criticize him—or even to view his life and work with decent objectivity—which does not begin as this one has: apologetically. He has made us feel that any flaws we detect in his work must be flaws in ourselves. He has involved us, as no performing artist ever has, in the drama of his life, the longest-running soap opera on record, and he has forced us for the most part, to discuss it in the terms he has dictated. To put the matter simply, no entertainer in history has so imposed himself on the consciousness of his times for so long a time— almost a half century now.

Nearly everyone who has cared about Chaplin's art has been convinced that in the Tramp or the Little Fellow, to use the terms invariably employed in discussing Chaplin's great creation, we had a very direct expression of the artist's personality—"so simple and unaffected," despite the onslaught of previously unimagined celebrity. Certainly Chaplin has wanted us to believe that. And up to a point, one does. Surely what is best and wisest in him can be found in the Tramp.

But are we really to think that's all that is significant about the man? If we were talking about the great primitives in his line—Buster Keaton, for example, or Stan Laurel—the matter could rest there. Between what we knew of them as men and what we saw of them on screen there was no important discontinuity. That is simply not true of Chaplin. The feeling of anyone born after, say, 1930 for the Little Fellow is bound to be rather abstract; we simply did not experience the excitement of discovery, that sense of possessing (and being possessed by) the Little Fellow that earlier generations felt. We knew who he was, of course, and our elders endlessly guaranteed his greatness to us. But he remained something of an abstraction: a figure to be appreciated, but impossible to love in the way he was loved by those who had been present at the creation.

What we were involved in was the larger drama of Chaplin's life—a drama, as it turned out, in one of the classic twentieth-century molds, that of the artist-visionary in conflict with his age. It was, and is, infinitely more fascinating than any of the Little Fellow's adventures—with its author even now engaged in creating for us an aesthetically satisfying conclusion.

This drama is divided, as all classic, epic works should be, into five acts, which might be subtitled "Self-Discovery," "Success," "Struggle," "Tragedy," and—when the audience at the Academy Award presentations rose to give him an ovation, and everybody forgave everybody—the last act, "Triumph."

Like his greatest routines, the Chaplin drama has a simplicity, an inevitability (and a self-consciousness) that is awesome. Of course fate helped him out a little bit, especially with his opening scenes, for he was born into poverty, the son of a drunken father and a mother who went mad. It was a Dickensian childhood, but one which turned out to have its uses as the source of his art, which he began to perfect at an early age, becoming the leading comedian in one of the Fred Karno comedy troupes where he learned the classic English music-hall style. As everyone knows, it was with a Karno company that Chaplin came to the United States—a leading comedian at age twenty-one—and it was while working with it that he was discovered by Mack Sennett in 1914.

The English comic style was not Sennett's; Chaplin's relationship with his new, roughneck colleagues was edgy. A lot of his best bits were cut out of his early Keystones, Chaplin claims. As the world would soon know, however, Chaplin has always had what any unique artist must have to survive: utter confidence in the correctness of his own judgment. He fought out the stylistic issue with the Keystone crowd, finally finding a way to demonstrate what he had been trying to tell them. It happened one day when Sennett was observed glumly studying a hotel-lobby set, chewing on his cigar. "We need some gags here," he muttered, then turned to Chaplin and told him, "Put on a comedy make-up. Anything will do."

At which point, if life were as well-managed as a movie, the clouds should have broken and beams of sunlight should have lit Chaplin's way to the wardrobe. For his time had come. "I thought I would dress in baggy pants, big shoes, a cane, and a derby hat. I wanted everything a contradiction: the pants baggy, the coat tight, the hat small, and the shoes large." The mustache was added, he says, because Sennett had expected him to be much older and Chaplin thought it would age him without hiding his expression.

He continues: "I had no idea of the character. But the moment I was dressed, the clothes and make-up made me feel the person he was. I began to know him, and by the time I walked onto the stage he was fully born." He claims—and one is a trifle dubious about this—that he was able instantly to describe his creation to Sennett in rather poetic terms *before* a foot of film had been shot: "You know this fellow is many-sided, a tramp, a gentleman, a poet, a dreamer, a lonely fellow, always hopeful of romance and adventure. He would have you believe he is a scientist, a musician, a duke, a polo player. However, he is not above picking up cigarette butts or robbing a baby of its candy. And, of course, if the occasion warrants it, he will kick a lady in the rear—but only in extreme anger."

Perhaps he really was that articulate that quickly. Perhaps not. No doubt, however, he was inspired, sensed there was something more here than just another role, something through which he could express more of his feelings and visions than he ever had before. Most critics, however, believe it required most of the rest of his year with Sennett, plus a good bit of the following year (with the Essanay production company), before the Tramp began to demonstrate all the dimensions Chaplin ascribes to him on, as it were, their first meeting. In particular, the undercurrent of pathos, which in time was to become a veritable torrent, was not visible for another year.

Still, the public almost immediately observed that something wonderful had been wrought. The demand for films featuring the Little Fellow was immediate and huge. The 1915 Essanay contract called for $1200 a week and a $10,000 bonus on signing. A year later he was to receive $675,000 for a year's work with Mutual, and a little more than a year after that, in 1917, Chaplin signed his famous million-dollar contract with First National. Close with his money, and determined never to suffer again the kind of poverty he had so recently escaped, Chaplin began accumulating one of the great show-business fortunes.

He was entitled to it. For in an age when forty or fifty prints of a movie comedy could satisfy the demand for other actors' work, distributors had to make up close to two hundred prints of Chaplin's films—for which they could charge well above the going rates. It was a golden time. It required only a simple poster of the Tramp bearing the legend I AM HERE TODAY to bring the people in. And the two-reel length of these early comedies was perfectly suited to his gifts. Agee wrote: "Before Chaplin came to pictures people were content with a couple of gags per comedy; he got some kind of laugh every second," mainly "through his genius for what might be called *inflection*—the perfect, changeful shading of his physical and emotional attitudes toward the gag." Every writer has his favorite moments in these two-reelers. Agee, for example, loved Chaplin's drunken bout with a malevolent Murphy bed in *One A.M.;* Gilbert Seldes cites *The Pawnshop,* where Chaplin includes business with a feather duster, then a sequence in which he tries to dry dishes by passing them through a clothes wringer, and then some nonsense with a clock where a simple inspection leads to disaster, as all the clockworks litter the screen. Both men mention, as the quintessential Chaplin moment, a sequence in *A Night Out* where Ben Turpin, himself far gone in booze, is dragging a stiffened Chaplin through the streets after the bars have closed. Chaplin awakens, sees how splendidly his friend is serving him, and reaches out to pluck and delicately sniff a flower.

There are lots of ways to put it: he found poetry in the ordinary, he transcended reality, he extended the range of pantomime to previously unimagined dimensions. Yet none of them quite explain his phenomenal appeal. Chaplin has never been generous in acknowledging influences, but some critics have noticed a correlation between his work and that of Max Linder, who had earlier brought something of the European comic tradition to the screen through his Pathé shorts. Edmund Wilson has emphasized how much Chaplin owed to the classic turns of the English music halls. And despite his protests, it is clear that Chaplin learned a great deal from Sennett, especially about pacing and the use of the chase as a climax.

In short, he summarized much that had gone before, linking the art of screen comedy to a much older tradition. This was very significant to those intellectuals who began to take the movies seriously in the teens and twenties of this century. For, if nothing else, it gave them a classy frame of reference in which to place Chaplin. In turn, their writing has been extremely valuable to Chaplin, ensuring his reputation as an artist against both direct assault and the more insidious danger of neglect during the long periods when he was absent from the screen. In effect, they committed us to him irrevocably. Through all the long years when most of them were exercising their contempt for movies in general, Chaplin was always cited as the medium's one unquestioned, unquestionable artist, the individualist amid the corporate herd, a man clinging to his peculiar vision while everyone else went hooting off in pursuit of momentary fads. Or submitted to degrading manipulation by the studios. Or simply faded away as his great contemporaries (and sometime United Artists partners) did —Griffith, Fairbanks, Pickford.

Yet this fact remains: Chaplin never again achieved the perfection of those first years. The little films of the Little Fellow were, in effect, solo ballets. As such, they had no more need of plot, of subsidiary characterizations, of great themes than one of Nijinsky's variations did. Despite the reams of appreciative analysis written about the early films, the pleasure we derived from them was essentially kinesthetic and therefore non- (and even perhaps anti-) intellectual. One could go on watching them for a lifetime. Indeed, one has.

But popular arts like the movies are cruel in their demand for novelty. And so are the intellectuals who have taken such arts for their province. No matter what they *thought* they thought, there was in their endless nattering over Chaplin an implicit demand for "development," for big ideas and statements. No doubt Chaplin made the same demands on himself. Beginning with *The Kid* in 1920 he began to inject larger and larger doses of pure sentiment into his work. No less than Griffith's, his was essentially a Victorian sensibility and he turned naturally to a rather cloying sweetness when he was forced, by the public demand for feature-length films, to extend his works.

There were other problems as well. As Edmund Wilson accurately noticed in 1925, "His gift is primarily the actor's, not the director's or the artist's. All the photographic, the plastic development of the movies, which is at present making such remarkable advances, seems not to interest Chaplin. His pictures are still in this respect nearly as raw as *Tillie's Punctured Romance* or any other primitive comedy." He added, presciently, that Chaplin "is jealous of his independence . . . he is very unlikely to allow himself to be written for, directed, or even advised."

The issues were more complex than Wilson could possibly have known at the time. In retrospect it seems significant that Chaplin did not appear in an important role in *A Woman of Paris*—a 1923 picture which was, after all, his first production for United Artists, the company he had helped establish. It betokened, perhaps, a certain restiveness with the Tramp character. Or was it the beginning of a lack of confidence in the Little Fellow as a means of expressing all that Chaplin was beginning to feel about modern life? At any rate—despite the notable exception of *The Gold Rush*—Chaplin's art and his production pace grew hesitant. From the time *A Woman of Paris* was completed to 1940, when *The Great Dictator* appeared, Chaplin made just five films, the last of which, of course, contained his final appearance as the Tramp —and in a role that was quite overwhelmed by Chaplin's impersonation of Hynkel, the dictator.

The coming of sound, naturally, was a threatening problem, solved in *City Lights* and *Modern Times* by the simple expedient of ignoring the microphone and filling the track with music, sound effects, and an occasional burst of gibberish. But dramatic as Chaplin's confrontation was with a technological advance he disliked, and exciting as his triumph over it was (no other screen artist dared so radical a strategy), I do not think it was fear of movies that talked which stayed Chaplin's hand.

Andrew Sarris has pointed out that "for Chaplin, his other self on the screen has always been the supreme object of contemplation," adding that his much-disapproved late work, *Limelight,* about a clown who lost his hold on the audience, was "an imagining [of] his own death, a conception of sublime egoism unparalleled in the world cinema," since "to imagine one's own death, one must imagine the death of the world."

Here, I think, we approach the center of the Chaplin enigma, the reason why he has discomfited so many observers for so many years. It is that every stylistic and technical change which has come to the movies since the end of World War I has implicitly interfered with his (and our) contemplation of his screen self. Length, of course, implies the necessity for subplots and the presence of other actors in significant roles. Very distracting. The growth in movie "plasticity" that Wilson spoke of was similarly likely to disrupt our concentration on the nuances of his art. And talk was perceived to be fatally interruptive.

He was in a double bind. He was an artist universally beloved because he had created a universal symbol of the common man's virtues, flaws, and aspirations, a man whose presence had helped to create a great audience for a new medium at the same time that he had given the medium respectability as an art form. Yet as the century wore on, the common man increasingly showed himself to be capable of the most terrible crimes and indifferences; to be the dupe of such evil mass movements as fascism.

At the same time, the movies, Chaplin's medium, underwent radical change, became more and more resistant to his particular gifts. Otis Ferguson, the first great populist critic of movies since Vachel Lindsay, said of *Modern Times* that it was "about the last thing they should have called the Chaplin picture. . . . Its times were modern when the movies were younger and screen motion was a little faster and more jerky than life, and sequences came in forty-foot spurts." Ferguson called it "a feature picture made up of several one- or two-reel shorts" and proposed titles like *The Shop, The Jailbird, The Watchman, The Singing Waiter.* Like everyone else, he could see the momentary beauties of these sequences, but they did not, he thought, make Chaplin "a first-class picturemaker. He may personally surmount his period, but as director-producer he can't carry his whole show with him, and I'll take bets that if he keeps on refusing to learn any more than he learned when the movies themselves were just learning, each successive picture he makes will seem, on release, to fall short of what went before."

This is a sadly accurate prediction. There is not a subsequent Chaplin film that does not contain its sublime moments: the dance with the balloon globe and the scenes with Jack Oakie in *The Great Dictator,* the sequence where he tries to bump off Martha Raye in *Monsieur Verdoux,* the wonderful concert with Buster Keaton in *Limelight.* Still, the Tramp was dead, done in, as Robert Warshow observed, because the essentially innocent relationship between him and his society could no longer be sustained. "The satiric point of the relationship lay precisely in [the] element of fortuitousness . . . it *happened* that the Tramp and the society were in constant collision, but neither side was impelled to draw any conclusions from this. The absurdity in the Tramp's behavior consisted in its irrelevance to the preoccupations of the society; the viciousness of the society consisted in its failure to make any provision for the Tramp, its complete indifference to his fate."

In truly modern times, this kind of relationship was impossible. "Now the two were compelled to become conscious of each other, openly and continuously, and the quality of innocence . . . could no longer be preserved between them." As Warshow observes, the factory in *Modern Times* is "a living, malevolent organism," as is the state in *The Great Dictator.* There is no longer even a thin margin where the Tramp could survive. And so he was put to rest.

Now Chaplin began to act out in life the drama that Warshow saw going on close to the surface of his art. There was the desperate preachment of love-as-panacea at the end of *Dictator,* embarrassing because the speech is not truly felt, remains merely an empty oration—though one imagines Chaplin thought he meant it at the time. In *Verdoux* the climactic speech is bitter: How is Verdoux, the murderer of a handful of lonely women—and for the justifiable end of supporting his dear family—worse than all the munitions manufacturers, etc., etc.?

In these pictures the stale ideologies of the age fill the gap between the world's reality and an artistic vision now inadequate to that reality. Finally there is the self-pity of *Limelight,* the reported savagery of *A King in New York,* the sheer emptiness and lack of energy of *A Countess from Hong Kong.* Yes, age had taken its toll and our expectations about great men are excessive, unsatisfiable. But there is something more disturbing than that in the late films. For what we see surfacing in them is something that we may well have been aware of right from the start, yet dismissed as unworthy of us.

That, of course, is the increasingly shrill egoism of the artist, a quality transcending mere self-consciousness, and preventing those of us who were not part of the first, uncomplicated love affair between Chaplin and the public from surrendering to his insistent demand for a continuance of that affair in the old simple terms.

Of course, one despised Chaplin's enemies and their inquiries into his politics and his morals; and yet one responded automatically, not with the warmth and spirit with which one might try to defend a public figure with whom our relationship was less complex. There was a sense, which we could not articulate at the time, that Chaplin had, no doubt unconsciously, conspired in the creation of that comfortable exile which he wanted us to understand as tragedy. One could see that he was increasingly bewildered by the world, increasingly unable to encompass his feelings about it (and prescriptions for it) in the metaphors he employed in lieu of the Little Fellow in his films. One was aware, too, of his loss of touch with his roots—and ours.

He was seen abroad only occasionally and then largely in the company of those few world-class celebrities who were his peers. When he addressed the rest of us he was distant, abstract, patronizing. He preached love of mankind in general, but appeared incapable of affectionate gestures toward anyone outside his family circle, that ever-expanding extension of himself. And the art was not what it had been—not even so brilliant a rationale as Warshow's could save *Verdoux* for us. Or *Limelight*. The world had changed and he had changed.

Awed by accomplishments we had to rediscover, trying to re-create the innocent times in which they had seemed so astonishing, one found one's direct suspicions confirmed by *My Autobiography* in 1964. The first third of it is wonderful, one of the great portraits of turn-of-the-century life, rich in color, anecdote, feeling. But the last two-thirds? They are cold, simplistic, a dreary listing of the great man's encounters with other great men, none of whom are as interesting as he is. And he is too interesting, too complex to be discussed. Now all the doubts, all the hesitations that the good critics had noted in their appreciations rose hauntingly before us. And one sensed that the most important reservations one had harbored were not based on the accidents of age, of political nonsense, of the tragedy of history. One saw that his art was based not on holding a mirror up to life, but up to himself, that our presence, necessary as it was to satisfy his drive for power (which Samuel Goldwyn, who knew something about the subject, called the most developed he had ever encountered) was essentially an intrusion on what was, really, a perfect love, that of the artist for his creation—which was, alas, himself.

The guilt that wells up as one writes those words is palpable. Even now one imagines the failure to be one's own, not his. And anyway, one does not wish to spoil, even in a small way, the conclusion of the Chaplin drama, the necessary, inevitable reconciliation between him and his public. The art *was* there. Every man who loves the movies is in his debt. And as long as that love persists we will take our children to see his first works, that they may know the beauty and innocence of film's beginnings, before the corruption began, before the distortions of power, of celebrity, of the alienation of men from their idols and from their very selves, were incorporated, enhanced by this terrible, wonderful machinery.

The ironies of this life, this career are endless. Let us stop. Let us, at last, honor him as simply as we can. As he seems to want us to, the King—and not only in New York.

[1972]

## CITY LIGHTS
### Roger Ebert

Charlie Chaplin's *City Lights* (1931) came near the beginning of two eras, the Depression and the talkies, and had fun with both. But it didn't depend upon topical realities for its humor. Chaplin's films age so well, I think, because his situations grow out of basic human hungers such as lust, greed, avarice. Those are the hungers on the other side, of course—the side inhabited by policemen, millionaires, mayors, and boxing promoters. All Charlie sends against them is his Little Tramp, eternally hopeful, concerned only with escaping from the dilemma of the moment.

*City Lights* was Chaplin's first production after talking movies were introduced. He avoided sound, wisely as it turns out, since the awkward sound equipment of the early days would have trapped his films in sound stages and sets. Chaplin said at the time (and has been endlessly quoted as saying ever since) that comedy is in long shot, tragedy in close-up. He was right, as a moment's thought will reveal, and synchronized sound would have made it necessary for the Tramp to spend too much of his time too close to the camera.

The few sounds he does use in *City Lights* underline the silent comedy without distracting us. In the famous opening scene, when the mayor unveils a civic statue to find Charlie sleeping in its arms, the mayor's speech is represented as a series of unintelligible squawks and squeaks. It sounds more speechlike, somehow, than real words would. There's also the sequence after Charlie swallows the whistle and inadvertently stops a concert, hails a cab and surrounds himself with dogs.

Apart from these two scenes (the first no doubt intended to make his feelings about sound unmistakable), the film is silent, except for the original Chaplin musical score. There is a bare minimum of subtitles, too; everything is made perfectly clear by the genius of Chaplin's pantomime.

The story involves some of the Tramp's most familiar adventures. He falls in love with a blind flower girl, is taken in tow by a drunken millionaire, does a shift as a municipal manure-sweeper (gazing in despair at a parade of horses followed by an elephant), and finally wins the blind girl's gratitude after a term in jail.

*City Lights* includes one of the funniest sporting events ever filmed, the immortal boxing scene in which Charlie's footwork bedazzles both the referee and his opponent. It also includes a great deal of sentiment, which some of the 1931 critics found excessive. I don't think so. Chaplin goes only so far with sentiment, then makes his getaway with a gag.

Sometimes the sentiment and the gag grow so organically out of the situation that you don't know whether to laugh or not. That's the case in the opening sequence with the blind flower girl. Charlie buys a flower, leaves, tiptoes around the corner, positions himself beside a water tap, and gazes at her adoringly. She makes her way to the tap, fills her water can, sloshes it around, and throws the water into Charlie's face. His reaction to this misadventure is so complex that comedy hardly seems the word for it.

[1972]

# THE GREAT DICTATOR
## Roger Ebert

Charlie Chaplin's *The Great Dictator* (1940) came some twelve years after the introduction of sound, but it was Chaplin's first all-talking picture, and the first in which we heard the Little Tramp speak. The dialogue turned out to be his last words; Chaplin never used the Tramp character again after this film.

In a way, the Tramp's heartfelt closing plea for peace and human brotherhood is spoken by Chaplin himself, stepping out of character to make a personal statement on the eve of the war with Hitler. The speech does not fit into the fabric of the rest of the film (as many critics noted at the time), but the passage of years has made it seem uncannily appropriate.

Chaplin conceived and filmed *The Great Dictator* during a period when an accommodation with Hitler was still thought possible in some quarters; indeed, he must have been filming when Neville Chamberlain went to Munich. But Chaplin himself had no such optimism, and his portrait of Adenoid Hynkel, dictator of Tomania, was among the first declarations of war on Hitler. The film also prophesied the persecution of the Jews, and the scenes of storm troopers terrorizing the ghetto were thought at the time to go too far. What a sad joke that seems today.

The film itself is filled with sad, pathetic little jokes; this is Chaplin's most serious, most tragic, most human work. He did not find Hitler at all funny, needless to say, and so although he uses his own comic genius to inspire the movie, the comedy is never neutral. It is jugular, as he creates a Hynkel who is a vain, strutting buffoon, given to egomaniacal rages and ridiculous posturing. Charlie never for a moment allows us to laugh with Hynkel, but only at him, and Hynkel thus becomes the only totally unsympathetic character Chaplin has ever played. To balance him, Chaplin also plays the part of a Jewish barber who happens to be Hynkel's exact double (and who also happens to look exactly like the Little Tramp).

There are some good belly laughs in the movie, most of them involving a state visit by Benzini Napaloni, dictator of the neighboring nation of Bacteria. As played by Jack Oakie, Napaloni is a loud, cheerful, idiotic clown whose natural zest for a good time cuts right through Hynkel's phony dignity.

It's during the Oakie scenes that we get many of the film's most famous comedy moments: the futile attempt to seat Napaloni on a very low chair, so Hynkel can tower over him; the negotiations during the banquet, when Hynkel says he will destroy his enemies just like this (and attempts to rip apart a handful of spaghetti, but can't), and of course the classic barber-chair scene, in which each dictator tries to pump himself higher than the other.

There are also immortal moments of Chaplin pantomime. He shaves a customer in time to classic music. As the Jewish barber, dressed in the stolen uniform of the dictator, he nonchalantly reviews "his" troops and then sits in a folding chair that collapses, causing complete confusion. And, as the dictator, he does the famous ballet with the world globe painted on a balloon.

[1972]

# THE LATE CHAPLIN FILMS
## Bruce Williamson

With the United States release of his next-to-last film, *A King in New York*—made in 1956 and long delayed as a consequence of Charlie Chaplin's love-hate relationship with America—evidence is now at hand for a full study of the lovable Little Tramp. A provisional happy ending to the Chaplin story was written in the spring of 1972, when the prodigal movie master returned to the United States for the first time in twenty years. (He was banished during the McCarthy hysteria for his leftist political views and scandalous private life, which included several marriages to child brides and a conviction on a paternity suit.) All was forgiven, however, amid a blitzkrieg of publicity and bonhomie at last year's Lincoln Center "Salute to Chaplin" and at the Oscar ceremonies in Hollywood. Even then, the good will was tinged with a profit motive, since Chaplin's United States invitation was engineered to benefit the Lincoln Center film society and to ballyhoo a multimillion-dollar private deal for redistribution of nine major Chaplin films.

Nevertheless, the Chaplin renaissance that has followed demonstrates again the generosity of genius, which repays a fickle public with enduring works of art. Currently dubbed by some "the Picasso of cinema," his Tramp called "the greatest comic creation of the twentieth century," Chaplin now plays to almost unanimously exuberant reviews. Which is justifiable, except that such critical reappraisal doesn't show us how the Little Tramp became the mature, reflective, self-indulgent, masterful, and frequently misunderstood clown of later years.

Though it is fashionable to call Chaplin's film style primitive because he seemed to ignore technological innovations, he was actually a purist, who used the camera with straightforward efficiency to emphasize what was essential to his art—a method comparable to Picasso's rendering a dove with a few definitive brush strokes. In *The Gold Rush, The Circus,* and the miraculous, rueful *City Lights,* Chaplin's portrayals delicately balanced indomitable aspiration, bad luck, and naïve fallibility to capture the imagination of millions. The Tramp's slapstick not only made poetry of the pratfall but achieved the heights of human comedy. And though traces of sentimentalism and social comment were always evident, Chaplin's comedy was invariably saved by his ability to kick an adversary in the pants or run himself up a flagpole just when things were about to drown in pathos.

The classic Tramp began giving away to the social critic as early as 1936, in *Modern Times,* Chaplin's view of Everyman going nobly berserk in an assembly-line society. Today a new generation of doubting consumers and dropouts sees *Modern Times* for the masterpiece it is and overlooks the flaws stemming from what one critic of the period called Chaplin's "restless longing for profundity." That need to preach was even more pronounced in the closing moments of *The Great Dictator,* when an impassioned hymn to brotherhood suddenly played havoc with a comedy based on the striking resemblance between Chaplin's Tramp and Adolf Hitler. Chaplin talking, in his most political of movies, up to that time, was not universally applauded. In fact, a Congressional committee was preparing to investigate him when the United States entered World War II. Yet *The Great Dictator* is strewn with comic gems, such as the unforgettable ballet sequence in which dictator Adenoid Hynkel dreams of world domination in a dance with an inflatable globe.

Seven years and several scandals later, Chaplin brought forth *Monsieur Verdoux,* a biting black comedy about a modern Bluebeard. This was in 1947. The war was over, the Tramp was dead, and audiences were aghast that Chaplin—a certified lady-killer, according to hostile press accounts—would have the chutzpah to cast himself as a mild-mannered bank clerk who supports his invalid wife and child through a world war and a depression by marrying and murdering a series of stupid, wealthy women. Furthermore, he even dared moralize about murder and sent his unrepentant hero off to the guillotine declaring that "numbers sanctify" and that the small businessman in homicide is condemned, whereas "munitions manufacturers and the professional soldiers who contribute to murder on a mass scale are given great honors and monetary rewards." *Verdoux,* based on a brainstorm by Orson Welles, was years ahead of its time. Today, Chaplin's sardonic fable of good and evil is both devastating and hilarious—particularly when Verdoux meets Martha Raye, a raucous girl who was born lucky and cannot be done in. This so-called comedy of murder hasn't a moment of explicit violence—a lesson to us all in an era of surgical cinema—and may well be the best and boldest of all Chaplin talkies.

Chaplin had already begun his bitter involuntary exile when *Limelight* opened in 1952, in the face of a boycott. Such opposition was scarcely necessary to discourage movie-goers from watching Chaplin as a washed-up, once-great comedian in love with a paralyzed ballerina (Claire Bloom, making her film debut). *Limelight* may not have been a masterpiece, but it was surely the work of a master—corn of rare vintage, laced with wit and wisdom and featuring some superlative bits of comedy by Buster Keaton. Chaplin seemed to be playing himself. "What a sad business being funny," he says in character. "I'm through clowning . . . truth is all I have left."

The truth as Chaplin perceived it during his years of near-total eclipse was touched upon only fleetingly in his 1964 autobiography. Words were never his chosen weapons, but time puts all artists to the cruelest test, and time has been kind to Chaplin. Without him, the history of screen comedy would be an impoverished saga. As performer, director, and writer, Chaplin put aside the endearing image that had earned him fame and fortune, to explore new dimensions of comedy. Often reported missing, he was seldom truly lost, for his intuitive grasp of human frailty governed every turn. It seems fitting that the final important work in the Chaplin canon should be so full of great and small surprises.

The least funny of Chaplin's movies, *A King in New York* is nonetheless fascinating. There's wry humor of a high order in an early sequence when Chaplin—as an exiled European king seeking refuge in the United States—is quietly fingerprinted while he talks to reporters of America's "native warmth and noble generosity," his inky finger tips emphasizing every phrase. Later, before the visiting monarch becomes a marketable commodity—plugging Royal Crown whisky in TV commercials—he is introduced to the hard-sell American way at a dinner party, where his seductive companion (Dawn Addams) interrupts their conversational intimacies to talk about an underarm deodorant for a hidden camera. Dropping in at a Broadway movie house, the king catches fragments of a feature called *Sex Changes,* plus another epic concerning "A killer with a soul . . . you'll love him . . . bring the family." Such satirical broadsides are less subtle than accurate, projected in a spirit of amused indulgence that makes *King in New York* seem positively benevolent compared with advance press reports that called it a savage and vindictive "labor of hate," intended as Chaplin's revenge on an ungrateful America. As a matter of fact, Chaplin's king, fairly brimming with good will, carries blueprints for a plan to create an atomic utopia. No one in the government has time to see him, being too busy confronting the Red Menace. In fact, the film's sharpest barbs are directed at an Un-American Activities Committee that persuades a young boy (played by Chaplin's son Michael) to inform on his parents. Even this does not deter Chaplin from a final wistful hope that such aberrations are not reflective of the real America. America's bumptious fast-buck commercialism is pinned down in less time than it takes to endorse a check ("I know it's beneath your dignity," coos the promoter of whisky, "but there's fifty thousand bucks in it"). The gorgeous creature who finally persuades the king to sell himself becomes the film's chief symbol for all-American energy and innocence combined with plenty of forward drive. An instinct for survival in the face of disaster was the hallmark of Chaplin's Little Tramp, whose genius and sweetness are still visible through *A King in New York*'s cynicism and disillusionment. Fundamentally, Chaplin performing anything at all is an event, even if this strident calliope of a comedy turns out to be his swan song.

[1973]

# THE SEXES

## WOMEN AND THE SILENT COMEDIANS
### *Molly Haskell*

Women comedians, even at their most rambunctious, are more accommodating to society, while their male counterparts, even at their most docile, are more heretical. The woman's need for a man (even Min had her Bill) takes precedence over unbridled self-expression or transgression of the rules that were thought to be created for her protection. To the extent that it flies in the face of these rules, most comedy is masculine (or to the extent that most comedy is masculine, it flies against these rules . . . and is antifeminine). It instinctively sets out to destroy, through ridicule or physical assault, the props of an orderly society over which woman presides. Comedy is a gust of fresh air, anarchic and disruptive; it spills the tea, shatters glass and conversation; it is a mad dog that shreds the napkins and the tablecloth, and along with them the last vestiges of romantic illusion.

Understandably, women audiences have never responded with great warmth to physical comedy, with its misogynous overtones. As film buffs, women may appreciate the comedians intellectually, but women in general, responding at a more instinctive level, reject low comedy and knockabout farce. M-G-M forced the Marx Brothers to feature a romantic love story in *A Night at the Opera* to attract women audiences. To this day, many older women remember the film for the thrush-throated courting of Allan Jones and Kitty Carlisle rather than for the Marx Brothers' antics, which they found an irritating intrusion. Even among modern, liberated audiences, women seem to prefer Woody Allen's more conventionally romantic *Play It Again, Sam* to its nuttier predecessors, in which the romantic interest was only comical and incidental.

Of all the silent comedians, Laurel and Hardy are perhaps the most threatening to women, as they combine physical ruination with misogyny. One epicene and gross, the other emaciated, they are an aesthetic offense. With their disaster-prone bodies and their exclusive relationship that not only shuts out women but questions their very necessity, they constitute a two-man wrecking team of female—that is, civilized and bourgeois—society. The male duo, from Laurel and Hardy to Abbott and Costello, is almost by definition, or by metaphor, latently homosexual: a union of opposites (tall/short, thin/fat, straight/comic) who, like husband and wife, combine to make a whole. Practicing heterosexual (machismo twice over) partners like Martin and Lewis are likely, in real life, to clash at some point and "divorce."

By their absurd but compatible physiques, Laurel and Hardy are at one and the same time disqualified from the world of normal heterosexual activity and united against it, the misfits against the fits. Constantly expressing affection for each other, they form a parody male-female couple. In *Their First Mistake*, they "elope," adopt a baby, feign breast-feeding it, sleep together (as they did often in their movies), and try out various male-female roles. But the sexual implications are not so much hidden beneath, as arrested at, the innocently anal idiocy of child's play. In contrast, the Marx Brothers, who are heterosexually aggressive and, being natural brothers, don't need surrogate ones, show genuine, if not particularly genteel, warmth and love in their relations with women. However brutally they may treat poor Margaret Dumont in *A Day at the Races* and *A Night at the Opera,* they secretly adore her—the poise and unruffled splendor with which she graces their films is ample testimony to her place in their hearts and in film history. Laurel and Hardy—and to an even greater and unpleasanter extent, Abbott and Costello—ridicule older women and, by implication, all women. Laurel and Hardy's best films—like the exhilarating *Big Business,* in which they start out selling Christmas trees and end by dismembering a car, destroying, piece by symbolic piece, this pride of the capitalist economy—escape the sexual bias in a splurge of irresistible anarchy. But most of their routines are unequivocally antifemale and make one appreciate the self-contained misogyny of a blackguard like W. C. Fields. Though no less a woman-hater, he expresses his antipathy in a language—verbal rather than physical—women can respond to, and his isolationist elegance is less threatening to the borders of female hegemony than the bull-in-a-china-shop antics of Laurel and Hardy.

The real surprise is that women have always seemed to react more adversely to physical aggression than to misogyny, have seemed to find the desecration of property and the home more threatening than the violation of their spiritual and sexual value. Actually, it is probably because women identify in spirit with certain male comedians and respond to the "feminine" side of their nature. Women project themselves into the place of the comic rather than into that of the women he ignores or rejects.

Ambivalence toward women, if not misogyny, was practically the stock in trade of silent comedy, whose activating force was a kind of compensation—physical or *spirituelle*—for the comic's social maladjustment. The social maladjustment in turn became the trophy, the hoop of fire, the chip on the shoulder of his comic act. The comedian had a vested interest in his social ineptitude, but as he became professionally more successful, the illusion of helplessness was more difficult to maintain.

The contradictions in all men—between arrogance and insecurity, between innocence and calculation, between idealism and misogyny—are more apparent in the comedian whose self-image is the substance of his art, but, with geniuses like Chaplin and Keaton, they achieve a brief reconciliation and illumination in comic relief.

Again, size was all-important. Sharing with many comedians the small frame of the "weakling," the little man, Chaplin and Keaton developed wit and ingenuity the way other men develop muscles. In creating their comic personae, they used size as a metaphor for the outsider (Chaplin always more self-pityingly than Keaton). By placing themselves in competition with champion boxers or towering Confederate soldiers, they accentuated the incongruity and multiplied their disadvantages. And they felt their size most keenly when they competed with their rivals for the hand of a girl. She, in turn, was never a "realistic" partner, with defects like their own, but the most beautiful and exquisite of creatures, a paragon suited not to the ants of the earth but to it giants, not to its poets but to its athletes. Thus, they created a situation which could only lead to disappointment, and a woman who, in her blindness to th comedian's true values, could only reflect the shallowness and vanity of al women. Like the sadomasochist, the comic—or the idealist/misogynist—cre ates a woman who will quicken the pulse of his own self-hatred, who will, in her unapproachable perfection, justify his misogyny and, if he is an artist simultaneously shape and fuel his art. But then, much of the animating spiri of misogyny (indeed, the male *anima*) is a self-fulfilling prophecy derivin, from the particular image of the mother (or any other key female in early life that predates, and in a sense predetermines, the women who will come to elici it.

Beside such legendary misogynists as Strindberg and Swift, the more gentl Chaplin and Keaton look mild indeed. Yet an excess of reverence for women which leads, upon disappointment (and it must be disappointed), to profoun( misogyny, unites them all. Still, to dismiss them as misogynists would be to( simple, for their attitude toward women is characterized by anything bu undifferentiated hatred. The biographies of Swift, Strindberg, and Chapli reveal that all were continuously attracted to, obsessed with, and even adore( by, women. In the abuse he took from women in life, Chaplin seems mor justified in his misogyny than Swift and Strindberg do in theirs, but Chaplin like the others, and in a peculiar mixture of arrogance and obsequiousness, wa driven to seek out the very woman, the "ideal," who would end by disappoint ing him and destroying his illusions.

In their films, built around a romantic female image, Chaplin and Keaton both illuminate the love-hate feelings that lie dormant in most men and show the progression from one to the other. For the idealist to turn misogynist, the princess must turn shrew, a metamorphosis that, for both Chaplin and Keaton was conveniently represented by the transformation of a woman from sweet heart to wife. Misogyny was cloaked in the acceptably American and automat ically comic form of misogamy, the hatred of marriage and, by extension, th wife. In Keaton's *College,* the happily-ever-after ending was ironically under cut by successive shots of the couple with children, the couple grown old, an( the headstones of two graves—a startlingly corrosive ending for a romanti comedy. In *The Three Ages,* his spoof of Griffith's *Intolerance,* Keaton intro duced the figure of the Amazon; she would crop up, in different forms, in several of his later films. One of the bitterest and funniest comedies on sexua relations ever made is Keaton's uxorious *Seven Chances.* In the first half, th hero endures the supreme social torture of having a marriage proposal whis pered from one to another in a roomful of women, and then, when everyon has gotten the word, he is mocked in a chorus of laughter. The same kind o nightmare proliferation turns the second half from fun-house ingenuity int( horror, with the beleaguered hero racing down Main Street pursued by a trib of termagants, a thousand prospective dowager-brides who have responded t( an ad for a wife he has placed in the paper. In that one master stroke of a visua gag, Keaton runs the gamut of male fears—fears of female supremacy, o entrapment by marriage, and of woman as "wife," of the little man pitte(

against the big woman and dwarfed by her overriding competence, and, most of all, of castration.

There is a similar, if more gallant, awe of women in *Balloonatics,* a short film in which Keaton plays a Lothario on a back-to-nature trip, living in the wilds and struggling unsuccessfully with fish, bears, the rapids; into his midst, a young woman materializes and overcomes all these difficulties with humiliating ease. The Amazon heroine is offset by the sweetheart, a hardy if foolhardy specimen, who can be counted on to do something enchantingly imbecilic at the crucial moment. In *The General* there is the scene (Andrew Sarris has rightly called it "one of the most glorious celebrations of heterosexual love in the history of cinema") in which Keaton turns to his girl friend, who is busily stoking the engine of the train with pieces of wood the size of pencils, makes as if to strangle her, and suddenly changes his mind and kisses her. Keaton is not upset by woman's incompetence; on the contrary, he is alarmed by her competence. In this he perhaps reflects not only his personal fears but also those of a period in which women were taking the initiative and threatening the bastions of male supremacy. And yet Keaton was one of the few directors, or artists of any kind, to envision (and envision himself with) both kinds of women—the soft, feminine dodo, the towering Amazon, and even (in *Balloonatics*) a soft, feminine Amazon and (in *Seven Chances*) a towering dodo. Keaton's women (we can almost hear them, like the secret amplified into a roar) rise up in a glorious cacophony of mixed moods and emotions, a testimonial to the tolerance of their creator.

If Chaplin never achieved the sublime equanimity with women that Keaton did, it is perhaps because women were more traumatically crucial to his life and to the ego at the center of his art. Keaton was detached, almost complacent; for him, women, like the elements and the machines with which he achieved rapport, were part of the scheme of things, a technological-sociological-meteorological harmony of parts with which his own motions wondrously synchronized. We hardly know the names of Keaton's actresses, whereas Chaplin's, though not stars in their own right, enjoyed a one-to-one relationship with him and were psychologically central to his stories.

There is a discernible progression in Chaplin's heroines. He begins with Edna Purviance, the frailest, the most idealized and otherworldly of his women, in the two-reelers and in the features, *The Kid* and *A Woman of Paris.* She is the model for what the great French critic André Bazin, in his definitive essay on Chaplin, called the Edna Purviance myth, the feminine ideal, the inspiration for Chaplin's spasmodic attempts at moral rehabilitation. She is succeeded by Georgia Hale, the dance-hall demimondaine in *The Gold Rush* (and, incidentally, a Sternberg discovery), who is a tougher version of the ideal woman. Initially, she responds only to power; in the end, she is reconciled with Chaplin, but in a union that seems inspired less by her own feelings than by the obligatory need for a happy ending. The two films made with Paulette Goddard, *Modern Times* and *The Great Dictator,* reflect a relationship of something like sexual equality with a normal woman, although, as gamine and waif, soul mate to the Tramp and streetfighter like him, she is normal only in the solipsistic terms of Chaplin's world. Still, the last image of the two trotting hand-in-hand down the road of life suggests a collaboration of equals, in contrast to the last shot of *City Lights*—a close-up of Chaplin as the self-deprecating suppliant at the altar of love. In the relationship between Chaplin and Claire Bloom, the fading vaudevillian and the rising ballerina of *Limelight,* it is the relationship rather than the woman herself that is idealized, a fusion of personal love and love of art that remains a perfect mystery.

But Chaplin's idealism is not softened, like Keaton's, by tolerance, and when he reaches out to strangle, he does not change his mind at the last minute. The virus, so long suppressed, has grown into a monster, the way Keaton's demons multiplied. In *Monsieur Verdoux,* Chaplin cowers in the back of a rowboat, a would-be murderer, drawing his legs under him and his expression into that familiar wormy, fastidious grin. In this, Chaplin's most scathing film, he uses the Bluebeard tale not just to expose the absurdities of capitalism but to express the final rage of his disillusionment with women, all poured into the quintessential shrew figure played by Martha Raye. She is the virago, the overblown slob, the distorted mirror image of all the women who took advantage of him and deceived him, the Lita Greys and the Mildred Harrises; but now the tables are turned and he is the philanderer, the thief, the murderer.

There are, as Bazin has indicated, two kinds of Chaplin women: the fragile, helpless wife, the Edna Purviance myth extended into matrimony, who is dependent on Chaplin and whom he kills because he can no longer protect her and no longer hopes to be reconciled to society through his love for her; and the shrew who, by the very abrasiveness Martha Raye imparts to her, vindicates Verdoux's crimes and turns him into a sympathetic victim. But these two types are closer to each other than is at first apparent. They share an alliance born of Chaplin's schizophrenia, prefigured in the split, in *The Great Dictator,* between Chaplin the Jewish barber and Chaplin the mad dictator. United by the word "wife," both women have to be killed. "Wife" is the loaded word which, like the blade of the guillotine that kills Verdoux, spells death to the ideal of woman. She dies so that the myth of the sweetheart can live. Chaplin/Verdoux kills her rather than revise his opinion of woman to include a more proportionate balance of good and evil. But, as if in retaliation, Verdoux is defeated by her ghost, her avenging spirit—Martha Raye as the negative, the evil he refused to recognize, refused to integrate into a total picture of an individual woman. She is Edna Purviance's opposite and twin, just as Verdoux is the Tramp's, the one a direct outgrowth of the other. The man who splits women in two splits himself in two, or vice versa. The wife must take the blame for the illusion of the sweetheart, must pay for the whore-birth of the son; woman must be raped, or murdered, because the lover was foolish enough to believe in a perfection she never promised.

[1974]

# 2

# THE SOUND ERA

The talkies killed vaudeville, but many graduates of vaudeville training remained—some with well-defined personalities around whom films were built, as they had been for Chaplin and Keaton. Like Chaplin, the team of Stan Laurel and Oliver Hardy simply continued their career into the sound era. On the other hand, the raspy, insulting one-liners of W. C. Fields required sound; only the talkies brought about the complete expression of a personality that could not have been fully developed on the silent screen. Such irreverence, indeed, was the hallmark of most of the "talkie clowns"—Mae West's irreverence toward sexual mores, the Marx Brothers' toward social mores, Fields's toward family life—in that free-for-all period before New Deal paternalism and Production Code neo-Victorianism re-established and reinstitutionalized more conventional respect and morality.

In fact, it was Mae West's combination of *décolletage* and *double-entendre* which most specifically prompted the Catholic Church in 1934 to form its Legion of Decency and the industry to enforce more strictly a Production Code explicitly forbidding the portrayal of everything from extra- or even postmarital sex to miscegenation and white slavery.

Actually, by the time they were tapped by Hollywood, both West and the Marxes had long escaped their vaudeville backgrounds for the more sophisticated ambience of Broadway. To be sure, Hollywood had raided Broadway from the beginning, and the brittle high-society tone of the typical Broadway comedy was often reproduced on the silent screen. But the coming of sound turned Coast eyes eastward as never before, and the Broadway influence, marginal in the twenties, became dominant in the following decade.

If Broadway did provide much of the initial inspiration and talent, however, the new screen comedy of the thirties soon took on a life of its own, developing two main (and sometimes overlapping) formats: High comedy, which stressed the cosmopolitan life of the wealthy at home and abroad, is described here by Bernard Drew. Screwball comedy, the label attached to such films as *My Man Godfrey, The Awful Truth,* and *Nothing Sacred,* is remembered for its madcap heroines involved in zany actions which nevertheless were gestures of reconciliation. As Andrew Bergman has said, "Their 'wackiness' cemented social classes and broken marriages; personal relations were smoothed and discontent quieted."

Both Howard Hawks's *Twentieth Century* and Frank Capra's *It Happened One Night* could lay claim to be the "first" screwball comedy, but both directors created so personal a body of work that it seems reductive to discuss them mainly in terms of genre history. In their comedies, Capra and Hawks aimed, if from different directions, at the same issues and values that concerned them in their other films, and sometimes were even more serious and explicit. In Hawks's comic films, for example, his protagonists lose the very same professional "pride" and "dignity" that they value so highly in such melodramas as *Only Angels Have Wings, Red River,* and *Rio Bravo.* As for Capra, while his comedies in the thirties have their share of screwball acts and plot turns, his characters are best seen as mouthpieces for his particular brand of optimistic populism.

However much they differ, Capra and Hawks share a certain benign attitude toward America and its institutions. They deliver their critiques with a remarkable absence of negativism or cynicism. Their films fall within a romantic tradition deriving from D. W. Griffith, a tradition which in Hollywood seems to have been practiced by directors who were native-born or, like Capra, came to this country as infants.

Almost from the beginning of Hollywood history this romantic tendency was countered by the worldliness provided by the European immigrant. Before turning to the naturalistic melodrama, Erich von Stroheim created a sensation with two comedies, *Blind Husbands* (1919) and *Foolish Wives* (1922), which were startlingly frank and cynical in their approach to sexual relations. In the thirties, Ernst Lubitsch's name became synonymous with this middle-European tradition. *Trouble in Paradise, Design for Living,* even the Chevalier–MacDonald operettas displayed a sophisticated approach to sexuality, though Lubitsch took care to place them in European settings.

An astute businessman as well as an artist (at one point he was production chief at Paramount), Lubitsch was in a position to exert influence not only through his own work but also through that of his followers. His influence is seen in the work of native-born George Cukor, who brought to the cinematization of such Broadway comedies as *Holiday, The Women,* and *The Philadelphia Story* a sarcastic wit that seemed as distant from the relative cheeriness of Capra or Ford as was that of the "official" Europeans. It was not until the late forties, however, that Cukor turned his major attention to questions of marriage and society. His series of comedies with Katharine Hepburn and Spencer Tracy, which featured troubled relations between the sexes, were, as Molly Haskell points out, very much against the American norm of the time.

It was even after that, in the late fifties, that Lubitsch's most direct disciple, Berlin-born Billy Wilder, turned his talents totally to comedy. Having brought the illusionless vision of the outsider to American institutions in such melodramas as *Sunset Boulevard* and *Ace in the Hole,* Wilder now took advantage of the screen's new boldness to turn American sexual hypocrisy into a personal comic target. He was particularly fascinated with the ways in which sex connected with the American myth of success. His suspicion was that every American will prostitute himself or herself to get ahead, and he presented that thought with such visible delight that there have been frequent charges of vulgarity, never more than with 1964's *Kiss Me, Stupid,* in which a wife sleeps with a famous singer in order to help her song-writing husband. In contrast, four years earlier, Wilder's *The Apartment* had been greeted with unanimous praise. In that film the director expressed the immigrant's cool view of American social institutions by setting his story of sexual favors in the kind of gigantic service organization that epitomized the postwar transfer of power in America from "high society" to a bourgeois managerial elite. In retrospect, *The Apartment* is a seminal film in the history of American comedy, the prototype of all of the sixties films that have been so concerned with the deteriorating American marriage.

Until Wilder shifted from melodramas to comedies, American comedy had been relatively moribund. As opposed to the golden age of the thirties, the forties and fifties were not very interesting periods for comedy. Many comedies were still made—including vehicles for popular talents such as Bob Hope, Lucille Ball, Danny Kaye, and Red Skelton—but few are memorable. In some ways, this decline seems a by-product of the much-noted change in the status of women in American films after World War II. Whether or not they were working girls, thirties film women had had much more vital and equal roles. As Richard Schickel has pointed out, "Comediennes were the new wave of the thirties. What was funny about them was that they always turned out to be more realistic than the men in their pictures. They had a sharper sense of right and wrong, were better students of tactics and were masters of the mannish wisecrack. In a movie world where women had, prior to the Depression, been either innocents or exotics, they were refreshingly down-to-earth. In comedy, previously dominated by males —with women used only as foils or decoration—they actually set the style of the period." In contrast, postwar films emphasized the family and, as part of that, the woman's "traditional" role. The characteristic postwar comedy was a hymn to marital togetherness such as *The Egg and I, Mr. Blandings Builds His Dream House,* or *Father of the Bride.* And when "sophistication" returned in the fifties, it was in the dubious form of the acquisitive and buxom dumb blondes often played by Jayne Mansfield and Marilyn Monroe. By the end of the fifties, such man-vs.-woman farces as *Pillow Talk* and *That Touch of Mink* revived the screwball kind of story, but the years of middle-class family comedy had taken their toll: characters had to be bourgeois to achieve any sort of audience identity, and the screwball plots seemed empty outside of a high-society context in which people were rich enough to act silly without looking silly.

Of course there were some exceptions to the general decline in comic talent in the forties and fifties. At Paramount Preston Sturges, in an extraordinarily concentrated period from 1940 to 1944, made eight films which finished off the screwball tradition while starting several of his own. In fact, his Brueghelesque use of crowds of minor characters is so distinctive that no one ever really tried to duplicate it. Frank Tashlin earned a Parisian cult with a group of films that curiously combined the breast-fixation of the mid-fifties with an anticipation of Wilder's critique of the American cult of success. And Blake Edwards struggled to revive slapstick in an era more attuned to the relatively sober situation comedy. But these were clearly anomalies during a barren period.

# THE THIRTIES

## LAUREL AND HARDY
### *Vincent Canby*

Oliver Hardy, who was fat, superior, and short-tempered (but always the first to ask: "Can't you take a joke?"), died in 1957. Stan Laurel, the thin one with the George Price face and a gift for Zen ("You can lead a horse to water, but a pencil must be lead"), died in 1965. By that time, to the horror of such clear-eyed movie historians as William K. Everson, the author of *The Films of Laurel and Hardy* (Citadel Press), the comedy team, which had been most active in the 1930s, was well on its way to becoming the object of the kind of cult worship that is as patronizing as it is faddish.

During the last ten years or so, movie producers have been ravaging Laurel and Hardy features and shorts for scenes that they have then compiled into anthology features, some more lovingly and intelligently put together (Robert Youngson's *The Golden Age of Comedy* and *The Further Perils of Laurel and Hardy*) than others, especially Jay Ward's *The Crazy World of Laurel and Hardy*. Because (in my adult life, anyway) I've always liked Laurel and Hardy, without ever being a fanatic, I was disappointed but not really surprised when I saw the Ward compilation for the first time recently. *The Crazy World of Laurel and Hardy* (1966) is all peaks and no valleys, bits and pieces from too many comedies, climaxes presented without lead-ins, a kind of surreal symphony of immersions, skull fractures, shattered windows, punctured posteriors, and zonk-pow-splat sound effects. Laurel and Hardy seemed as grotesque and brutal now as they seemed when I was a child.

The Hal Roach Studios, under whose auspices all of the team's best films were made, has corrected that impression with the reissue of what must be one of the most consistently funny Laurel and Hardy features, *Way Out West* (1937), along with five fine short subjects, *The Hoose-Gow* (1929), *Brats* (1930), *Hog Wild* (1930), *Helpmates* (1931), and *Busy Bodies* (1933). The program is so special, so exuberant, that it must be shown for as long as there are people who like to test their nostalgia against the reality of an actual movie experience—and for as long as there are people who simply like to laugh without recourse to analysis. The most obvious virtue of the program is that it presents Laurel and Hardy unedited, complete in their own time and space, rather than excised and juxtaposed in ways that destroy the very conscious, internal rhythms of their gags. (For anyone who wants to pursue that matter more deeply, I'd recommend the University of California Press's *Laurel and Hardy* by Charles Barr, who, among other things, discusses the typical Laurel and Hardy "triple gag," in which gags are set, one within another, like Chinese boxes.)

*Way Out West* was produced by Laurel, directed by James Horne, who did a number of the team's short films, and written in part by James Parrott, who directed four of the five shorts in the current reissue program. It's one of their most economical features, both in running time (65 minutes) and in time elapsed within the film (a day and a night). Its story is atypically a triumph-through-failure (most of their shorts end in either loss or collapse): Stan and Ollie come to Brushwood Gulch to deliver a gold-mine deed to Mary Roberts (Rosina Lawrence), the daughter of a dead prospector-friend. Mickey Finn (James Finlayson), the owner of the bar where Mary works, gulls them into giving the deed to his wife. In their efforts to retrieve the deed, and to free poor Mary from her servitude as barmaid, Stan and Ollie are subjected to all sorts of indignities, most of their own making.

The film includes at least two classic Laurel and Hardy routines. In one, Stan is literally tickled into helplessness by the bar owner's wife, played by Sharon Lynn, who is billed within the film as "Lola Marcel, the Serio-Comic Entertainer." In another, Stan and Ollie, trying to sneak onto the second floor of the bar at night, employ a block and tackle and wind up by somehow putting their mule into the bar owner's apartment. (The tickling routine, which comes off as a kind of cheerful rape, was excised for use in *The Crazy World of Laurel and Hardy*, where it's only dimly amusing.) *Way Out West* also features three of the most charming musical numbers that the comedy team ever did, including a soft shoe, and some harmony ("In the Blue Ridge Mountains of Virginia") in which Stan lip-syncs everything from bass to contralto, to Ollie's slow irritation.

All five of the shorts are hilarious, but several are noteworthy for very specific reasons. *The Hoose-Gow*, in which Stan and Ollie find themselves on a prison farm (having been arrested in a speakeasy raid), closes with a classic custard-pie confrontation. Instead of custard pies, however, the combat medium is rice, freshly boiled in the radiator of the car that has brought the Governor to the farm on an inspection trip. *Helpmates* details the total destruction of Ollie's house when Stan attempts to help his friend clean it up before Ollie's wife returns from Chicago. Although Ollie (as he does in all the films) is constantly looking at the audience with knowing resignation each time Stan makes a new blunder, neither Hardy nor Laurel ever makes any real bid for our sympathy. They get it, but they never ask for it—which, I think, is one of the reasons they wear so well. As he was in *Helpmates*, Ollie is rather unhappily married in *Hog Wild*, in which Mrs. Hardy forces Ollie to put an aerial on the roof so that she can get Japan on the radio. With Stan's help, a fifteen- or twenty-minute chore is transformed into complete disaster—for the house (the chimney collapses), for Mrs. Hardy (who gets crowned—or is it "beaned"?—with great chunks of plaster), for Ollie (who falls off the roof repeatedly). The final sequence is an extraordinary ride through Los Angeles streets, with Ollie hanging from a ladder, standing upright in the back of the car, and Stan trying to cope with the driving.

This film, as do most of the others, provides subsidiary joys in its views of Los Angeles, especially Culver City (where the Roach Studios were situated), circa 1930. I doubt that there was much thought given to landscapes when the films were made, but landscapes are very much a part of what we see in the films today. I'm not referring to the trolley cars and flivvers in the backgrounds, but rather to the vistas of the flat, partly developed, semiurban landscapes that you can see from Ollie's roof in *Hog Wild*. It's Los Angeles, all right, but it also looks like the sort of setting in which Fellini's Guido could afford to build his great, skeletal space-toy in *8½*. It's not a place where land values are exactly soaring.

The kind of physical mayhem featured in Laurel and Hardy films (cars sliced in two by buzz saws, cars turned into accordions in head-on accidents, people falling through picture frames, windows, roofs) is not really funny when it is removed from the context of the original films, which provide mad logic for everything that happens. Youngson, by using longer excerpts from individual films, made some quite delightful anthologies, but nothing is as satisfactory as seeing the best of the original films, unaltered and unedited, as is this reissued program from Roach.

[1969]

# THE MARX BROTHERS
## *Richard Schickel*

The root of Marxism lay in the conflict of the Brothers with their setting. They appeared always as interlopers in a place of power or, at least, high fashion (at a house party; in the cabinet of a mythical kingdom of which Groucho was inexplicably the prime minister; at the opera; at a Saratoga-like spa). Once established, they immediately started to destroy their milieu. Theirs was the maniac humor of nihilism.

They were natural men, unhindered by those notions of good taste and proper behavior which so inhibit the world of the bourgeoisie. Immediately upon arrival, Groucho would establish (a) that he wished to steal a great deal of money by means of a complex confidence scheme, and (b) his love-hate relationship with Grande Dame Margaret Dumont. His technique for interpersonal relations was always the same—insult upon insult. The upshot was a characterization in which hatred for the conventional was so immense that he could not forbear his insults even if they placed his economic goals in jeopardy.

Groucho stood at the center of the Marxian plot; it was he who set all the wheels to spinning madly. His brothers worked a series of inventive variations on the basic melodic line he established. Periodically a comely blonde, in a state of dishabille, would scamper through, Harpo, horn tooting madly, tiny eyes aglitter, in hot pursuit. His silence disguised the fact that he was completely amoral. Outside, his relationship to the great scheme of things unclear, was Chico in his pointy hat, his Italian accent a bar to the world of fashion, busily pursuing a more modest form of crookedness than Groucho's. Unlike Groucho, he hid his aggressions and, in the end, displayed more shrewdness than the self-proclaimed mastermind. Usually, in desperation, Groucho would have to enlist Chico's aid to make things come out all right. The end always came suddenly in a Marx Brothers movie—as if they suddenly tired of it and decided to end the nonsense as quickly as possible.

As a team, they were the perfect bridge between silent comedy and sound. Harpo, of course, was the last of the great pantomimists, his special forte being direct action. In a moment of peril he could be relied upon to bring forth from his capacious coat pockets some tool or gadget with which to save the day— a pair of scissors, say, for cutting the phone line over which his enemies were relaying their plans. Groucho was, conversely, among the first of the fast-talking masters of insult, setting a style that was to be the accepted standard among the radio comics of the thirties and forties. Chico, of course, was a dialect comedian familiar to the vaudeville of a slightly earlier time.

Among them, the Marx Brothers represented all the great American comedy styles. Together they transcended all style to answer a felt national need —the utter denigration of upper-class values, values which were widely believed to have caused all the troubles of the decade in which the Marx Brothers achieved their great popularity.

[1962]

# THE MARX BROTHERS
## Andrew Sarris

The Marx Brothers so completely dominated the slapstick scene in the early sound era that few movie-goers mourned the demise of pantomime. Except for Leo McCarey's relatively integrated *Duck Soup*, the Marx Brothers burrowed from within an invariably mediocre *mise en scène* to burst upon the audience with their distinctively anarchic personalities. They were a welcome relief not only from the badness of their own movies but also from the badness of most of the movies around them. Except for Groucho's bad habit of doing double and triple takes after every bon mot to give his audience a chance to laugh, the Marx Brothers have worn reasonably well in the three decades since they burned themselves out somewhere between *A Night at the Opera* and *A Day at the Races*. Their more intellectual admirers have compared them with everyone from the Brothers Karamazov to the Beatles. A case can be made for Groucho as Ivan, Harpo as Aloysha, and Chico as Dmitri. Groucho, the skeptic of the sound track, was often pitted against Harpo's Fool of silence. The high-brows laughed louder at Groucho, but they smiled more sweetly at Harpo. The Fool fell in more easily with the lingering aesthetic guilt over the demise of the silent film. There were really only three Marx Brothers; Zeppo and Gummo never counted, and Allan Jones was never anything more than one of Irving J. Thalberg's stray tenors. However, Groucho was aided in no small measure by the exquisite dignity and self-abasement of Margaret Dumont, one of the greatest character comediennes in the history of the screen. Groucho's confrontations with Miss Dumont seem much more the heart of the

Marxian matter today than the rather loose rapport among the three Brothers themselves.

The limiting factor of the Marx Brothers is their failure to achieve the degree of production control held by Chaplin throughout his career, and Keaton and Lloyd in the silent era. The Marx Brothers often had to sit by in compliant neutrality while the most inane plot conventions were being developed. *Monkey Business,* particularly, suffers from a studio-grafted gangster intrigue in mock imitation of the gangster films of the time. It may seem trivial that Chaplin, Keaton, and Lloyd were always trying to get the girl, whereas the Marx Brothers were trying to get the girl for whatever straight man happened to be around at the time, but that is what made Chaplin, Keaton, and Lloyd major and the Marx Brothers minor.

Nonetheless, the best bits of the Marx Brothers were as funny as anything the sound film has produced. For starters, there is Groucho's land auction in *The Cocoanuts,* Harpo and Chico's bridge game in *Animal Crackers,* Harpo's madness with the passports and the puppets in *Monkey Business,* Harpo and Groucho's bunny-nightcap confrontation in the magical mirror of *Duck Soup,* and the stateroom scene in *A Night at the Opera.* On the other side of the ledger were a profusion of piano and harp solos, bad puns from Groucho and Chico, and, toward the end, the desecrations of B-picture budgets and shooting schedules. As for the comparison between the Marx Brothers and the Beatles, the Marx Brothers, to borrow Priestley's phrase, tried to be mad in a sane world, whereas the Beatles try to be sane in a mad world.

[1969]

# W. C. FIELDS
## Judith Crist

[. . .] True appreciation of Fields comes to some of us instinctively and to others with experience and with maturity; he was that rare comedian who is not superficially "accessible" to all comers in the guise of lovable tramp, cross-eyed buffoon, or spastic clown. The complexity of his character and of the comedy that sprang therefrom bear minute analysis.

Fields in essence was an American Falstaff at war with the twentieth century and its total Establishment, an aged-in-the-cask Gargantua trapped in middle-class morality, an alter ego for all of us in our daily frustrations, our petty rages, our dishonesties, and our dreams of glory, superhuman in his survivals and human enough to touch the heart—just a little—after pounding the funny bone. He was anti-Establishment before the phrase became facile, but he opposed it right from the middle, the white-collar man at war with all the social machinery that entraps the middle class, from foul family life to professional persecutions from doctors and lawyers and bankers to the abominations of just-folks folks, particularly the children among them. His comedy was black before the fashion came, and he was the ultimate antihero before the armpit-scratching slouchers took over the role, the totally unregenerate fraud who mouthed the pomposities and mumbled the insults and conned his way in and out of disaster with a carney's assurance that a fraud can triumph in a fraudulent world. He was Mr. Middle America, the poseur, the pitchman, the Falstaffian fake full of asides and alibis at home—but at home and in command everywhere *but* at home. As who among us is not?

With the born-yesterday perspective that each generation claims, we find Fields curiously avant-garde in retrospect, but then, what genius is not? After all, he bestrode a half century of American entertainment like a Colossus, from the music halls and vaudeville stages of the nineties to the turn-of-the-century tour circuits to the Broadway stages of the teens and twenties, to Hollywood of the thirties and forties, to radio—and had he not died at sixty-seven in 1946, he would have gone on without doubt to become one of the early greats of television. He was a vaudeville headliner at nineteen, his master juggling turn a "dumb" act (without commentary or patter and therefore eligible for international tours without language difficulty) that led to Royal Command performances and world-wide acclaim.

He made his first movie at thirty-six, immortalizing his pool-game routine in *Pool Sharks* in 1915, and continued to make silent films (among them *Sally of the Sawdust* and *That Royle Girl* for D. W. Griffith) while wowing Broadwayites in the Ziegfeld Follies for six years, George White's Scandals, and Dorothy Donnelly's smash hit, *Poppy,* the source of *Sally of the Sawdust* and of a far more successful remake in 1936, as *Poppy,* with Fields's root character, the conniving Professor Eustace McGargle (supersalesman of talking dogs and doer-in of country bumpkins) in full voice. The "dumb act" and the silent Fields (usually adorned with a fake mustache) had departed en route (Fields settled in Hollywood in the mid-twenties) and the double-dealing double voice —bombastic and booming for the fraud, a mumbling adenoidal drawl for the inner man aware that there are no honest men to be cheated and that only suckers get even breaks—had been established as part of the new whole humorist.

For Fields without voice, as his silent films attest, is an entirely different cup of comedy, a master pantomimist indeed—but largely appreciated by the talkie generations, I suspect, because we "hear" that gravelly swoosh-and-slide of vocal-nasal chords, the rhythm of the circumlocutions that convert a hit on the head to "a crack on the noggin," accompany a gallant hand-kiss with "What symmetrical digits!" and do in an enemy with a "Michael Finn." He was, after all, the one comic star of silent films who came to talkies and conquered new worlds by talking.

At his best, he talked pure Fields—on screen and off. Like the true humorists—Chaplin, the Marx Brothers, Mae West, Jimmy Durante—he was a total personality on screen as well as off, capturing a facet of the American personality and holding it up against the structure of "normal" society in all its hypocritical moralities. Fields, however, drew blood because (like Miss West and Chaplin and Fred Allen and virtually no latter-day comedians with the exception of the brilliant Woody Allen) he did not "assume" his character but kept it to himself; he did not put it in the hands of others but provided his own materials. He took over other screenwriters' creations by sheer force of personality (and mastery of the ad lib *in excelsis*), but he was in his finest flower as his own writer (a euphemism, really, since Fields's "screenplays" and "stories" were jots and scribbles on the backs of envelopes and whatever came to mind on the set). His best early work, four shorts for Mack Sennett (*The Dentist, The Fatal Glass of Beer, The Pharmacist,* and *The Barber Shop),* in 1932, were "original screenplays" by W. C. Fields, a name he used again in collaboration with Mae West for *My Little Chickadee* in 1940. It was as Charles Bogle (a long "o," he insisted) that he supplied the original story for *The Old-Fashioned Way* and *It's a Gift* (with J. P. McEvoy) in 1934, *The Man on the Flying Trapeze* in 1935, and *You Can't Cheat an Honest Man* in 1939. As Mahatma Kane Jeeves, he provided both story and screenplay for what indeed stands as a classic of pure Fields as well as a classic American screen comedy, *The Bank Dick,* in 1940, and in 1941 he provided the original story for *Never Give a Sucker an Even Break* as Otis Cublecoblis (pronunciation unspecified).

Consider the quintessentials of Fields's comedy in *The Bank Dick,* wherein his Egbert Souse (*accent aigu* on the "e," of course) is an improvident citizen of Lompoc saddled with a houseful of repulsive women (mother-in-law, wife, and two daughters whose mouths are filled with food and/or venom); his major worry is that he might have lost twenty dollars the night before instead of spending it in the Black Pussy Café. As he's loafing, an escaping bank robber stumbles over him and is knocked cold; Souse claims credit for the capture and is rewarded with a job as bank dick. This enables him to proceed with a scheme to get his prospective son-in-law, a bank teller, to embezzle five hundred dollars to invest in a phony beefsteak mine, a scheme that involves zonking out a bank examiner; disaster looms but Souse, again inadvertently, gets involved in a second robber's getaway and wins not only a reward but is handsomely paid for a screenplay he managed to peddle to a visiting movie company (while taking over briefly for its drunken director); the beefsteak mine proves a gold mine as well. And Souse, at fade-out time, is a hero abroad and in his lavish new home where his fawning wife urges upon him "a second noggin of café baba au rhum." And in the course of this 74-minute virtually one-man show (although such fine comics as Franklin Pangborn, Cora Witherspoon, Una Merkel, and Shemp Howard are on hand) Fields has managed to vent his spleen on women, children, directors, producers, actors, doctors, bankers, and even little old ladies while proving himself a fraud, a phony, a cowardly nebbish, a pompous lecher, and a fool—all with the grace and style of the mahatmas of the world! And he's managed to touch base with all of us because we know what it's like in the Lompocs of this land and he's touched upon all our frustrations (whether it's the bank teller's window closing in our face or finding the grapes we munch on are made of plastic) and given us a taste of fraudulence paying off in the way of this fraudulent world.

Fields is not likable. Children with half a wit to see (whether it's the boot in Baby Leroy's behind or the urn about to be cracked on his daughter's noggin or his deft theft of the bologna from the sandwich he's to share with his son) can see nothing lovable there. And misogyny is rampant, along with the long underwear, bulgy belly, and bulbous nose: Eddie Sutherland, who directed nine Fields films, said the comedian missed superstardom because women did not like him. Pauline Kael agrees, declaring, "For women, he is an acquired taste—like sour-mash bourbon. But then," she advises her sisters, "you can't go on sipping daiquiris forever." But from a purely humanistic point of view, as one examines the structures and details of the work of this angry artist— a man made paranoid by the early hardships of his struggle for success and by success itself, a Horatio Alger hero who refused to turn mealymouthed and forget and forgive just because he made it to the top—then indeed we find in Fields's art what Otis Ferguson rightly termed something "more real, more touching than the froth and fizzle of wit."

For Fields's is not the easy path of the pantomimist, or good "actor," equipped with glittering one-liners. His every move is choreographed, his total concept orchestrated. The seeming rambling plotlessness (and consider, in the context of Hollywood slickeries of production and Mom-and-apple-pie-isms of the era, the courage of his producers in permitting him his free-form structures, let alone his iconoclasms) puts an aura of carelessness on his work. But Fields knew—from those first vaudeville moments and the disciplines of his primary art as a juggler—that there is structure and expansion at the base of comedic entertainment. There is the situation and the joke—but one laugh is not enough, just as a one-liner is inadequate. His genius was that each of his classic moments builds from funny to funnier to funniest.

In this *Bullitt*-imitating era, there is still not a car chase to build in thrill or comedic effect quite the way the car chase in *The Bank Dick* did three decades earlier. Not since has anyone prepared with more hilarious sloth to respond to his wife's plea to rout singing burglars from the cellar as Fields does in *The Man on the Flying Trapeze* or suffered more relentless an assault from an insurance salesman than our sleep-starved hero in *It's a Gift.* The building of the ballad of his son's tragic fate in *The Fatal Glass of Beer* on Fields's apology to his listener for "playing my zither with my mittens on"; the debacle of the poker game wherein our man has dealt himself five aces and draws nothing but aces thereafter; the glorious prelude to blowing the head off an ice-cream soda . . .

These are but a few of my favorite flowers of the Fields creativity. There are others for you to savor and to study. "The funniest thing about comedy," Fields once wrote, "is that you never know why people laugh. I know *what* makes them laugh but trying to get your hands on the *why* of it is like trying to pick an eel out of a tub of water."

[1972]

# FIELDS VS. CHAPLIN
## Roger Ebert

Walking away from the camera, down a dirt road, his cane bobbing behind him, Charlie Chaplin is not a comedian but a clown. Emmett Kelly was the same kind of clown, smiling through a painted-on frown.

In Chaplin's films, the frown is painted on with a camera, and the audiences have to supply the smile themselves. Chaplin's deadly seriousness makes it clear that he does not understand why the joke should be on him.

When his hat lands on his cane rather than his head, when he is insulted by rude customers in a restaurant, when he must defend his honor and pulls a broken-off blade from an enormous scabbard, these are not bits of comic business but the genuine misfortunes of a little man against the world.

Such thoughts are called to mind by the first new film in ten years to bear the Chaplin name, *A Countess from Hong Kong.* It has been a long time since we last saw a new Chaplin film; nearly fourteen years since *Limelight.* When it opened, Charlie was still a controversial figure not yet allotted his footstool among the immortals. Indeed, the film was picketed because of his politics (medium rare) and his exile from the United States.

But all crimes are forgiven those who die young or live to an old age, and this year we can read Bertrand Russell's memoirs, erect Picasso's statue, and look again at Chaplin's work without signing a loyalty oath.

The difference between Chaplin and the other great screen comics was that Chaplin played a clown. The others, by and large, played comedians, with a few exceptions such as Lahr, Keaton, and possibly Jerry Lewis.

Comedians and clowns aim in opposite directions. Comedians live in imaginary worlds that look just like our own. In *The Apartment,* for example, Jack Lemmon inhabited a flat as realistic as it was unlikely.

Clowns, on the other hand, live in real worlds which consist of a few props. No worlds are more real than the clown-worlds of *Waiting for Godot* or Chaplin's early shorts.

Comedians use fantasy to make the real world seem funny. Clowns use reality to make our fantasies seem ridiculous. (End of metaphysics.)

If Chaplin was the greatest film clown, W. C. Fields was probably the greatest comedian. The sets in a Fields film are likely to seem pretty realistic, looking something like barbershops and Yukon cottages. But the strangest things happen on them. Bass fiddles have babies, Mae West is replaced by a goat on a wedding night, and golf carts become airplanes. If we thought we could count on everyday life, we were wrong.

Fields, by sneering at conventions, appealed to what we thought was our cynicism. Sure, we agreed, we really hate old ladies and fat men. Honeymoons are ridiculous. All parents hope their ex-convict sons will cut them in on the loot.

But we didn't really believe in Fields's negative world. Secretly, every last one of us trusted in romance, nobility, and heroism. Fields could destroy our faith in the real world, but he couldn't even touch our idealism.

That was Chaplin's target.

The world of his films usually consisted of only the necessary props (and, more often than not, looked more convincing than the phony naturalism of Hollywood sound stages). Into this world, where everyone else dressed conventionally, Chaplin went dressed as a clown.

Chaplin was also the only one in his world who believed in its conventional morality. He believed honor should be defended. He believed customers in restaurants should be polite. He believed little flower girls, especially if they are beautiful and virtuous, will be treated kindly by the world. In short, he was naïve.

It's almost as if everyone in Chaplin's world was a W. C. Fields, and everyone in Fields's world was a Chaplin. Fields took great relish in beating down the naïve idealists ("Out of my way, you fools," he once snarled at a flock of chickens). But Chaplin never did quite learn how to handle the cynics. And that was the point of his art.

One of Fields's favorite gestures was a brisk dusting of his hands after he had satisfactorily dispatched the caddies, old ladies, young children, and animals who made demands on his sentimentality.

Chaplin hardly ever used this gesture. When he did, it came right before a pratfall. Most of his films ended with a despairing look, a sentimental good-by, or a walk alone down the road.

[1967]

# HIGH COMEDY IN THE THIRTIES
## Bernard Drew

Whatever happened to high comedy in the movies and theater? I asked Peter Ustinov not too long ago.

"Whatever happened to it in life?" he smiled.

A few months later, I was having dinner with Ina Claire, happily retired for the past twenty-five years in San Francisco, and she told me she'd never planned to end her career when she did. "It was just that my kind of comedy went out," she explained. "You know, where there was a maid for practically every major character and a footman for every other one. Phil Barry died, George Kelly retired, and Sam Behrman went on to other things. So finally, after waiting around for several years with nothing in sight but one play by T. S. Eliot, did I."

In 1929 and 1930, when sound had irrevocably come to Hollywood and even Garbo had to Talk, there was, after the first consternation and panic over ethereal love goddesses who were revealed by the new sound equipment to have Pitkin Avenue souls and speech, a wholesale importation of the finest talent from the Broadway and London theater.

Ivor Novello came to Paramount to costar with Ruth Chatterton, who had herself only arrived from Broadway two years earlier, and Claudette Colbert,

Fredric March, Sylvia Sidney, Miriam Hopkins, and Kay Francis were virtually packed into the same Broadway-to-Paramount boxcar. Within a year, Mae West, Cary Grant, and Tallulah Bankhead would follow.

Ina Claire, Alfred Lunt and Lynn Fontanne, Katharine Hepburn, Helen Hayes, Paul Muni, James Cagney, Spencer Tracy, Humphrey Bogart, Ann Harding, Edward G. Robinson, Irene Dunne, Elissa Landi, Jeanette MacDonald, Clark Gable, Melvyn Douglas, Bette Davis, Maurice Chevalier, Herbert Marshall, Alice Brady, Lee Tracy, and Joan Blondell checked into Warners, Metro, RKO, and Fox to replace the now-obsolete and unvocal Norma Talmadge, John Gilbert, Vilma Banky, Mae Murray, Leatrice Joy, and dozens of others.

And now that the cumbersome sound equipment hampered the movement the great silent directors had finally achieved by the late twenties—cameras were virtually bound to remain in a fixed position in one room—the studios had no recourse but to purchase the hit Broadway plays of the teens, twenties, and early thirties.

The Lunts transmogrified their Broadway smash *The Guardsman* by Molnár to the screen, Ina Claire made *The Awful Truth, The Royal Family, Rebound,* and *The Greeks Had a Word for Them,* and Ann Harding essayed a fine *Holiday* at the beginning of the decade, which Katharine Hepburn would repeat, with equal success, at its close.

Mittel-europa soufflés and pouffes were purchased en masse from Molnár, Vayda, Fodor, Biro, Bus Fekete, and less-talented Hungarians, while Noël Coward, Ivor Novello, John van Druten, Benn Levy, Frederick Lonsdale, and later in the thirties, Terence Rattigan, sent on their wares from London. Donald Ogden Stewart, Philip Barry, S. N. Behrman, George Kelly, and Robert E. Sherwood kept the home fires burning.

Creaky old melodramas like *Madame X, The Green Hat, The Yellow Ticket, Smilin' Through,* and *The Sin of Madelon Claudet* were exhumed to provide tear-jerking vehicles for La Shearer, La Bennett, La Chatterton, La Landi, La Hayes, and La Dunne, and to no one's great surprise, it was discovered that they could still jerk a tear in 1932. One was even treated, that year, to a Puccini-less *Madame Butterfly,* with La Sidney bowing and singsonging to Cary Grant, "Honorable Rieutenant, most best nicest man in all the world."

Fannie Hurst's studies of mother love and tenement life—*Back Street, Symphony of Six Million, Humoresque,* and *Imitation of Life*—were virtually an industry in themselves and nearly every great female star at least once walked the streets in order to pay for milk for her illegitimate child, who would be taken from her in the second reel and grow up to defend her in a murder trial without knowing who she was by the ninth.

It is hardly surprising that these rampant melodramas do not hold up today, but most of the comedies of the same period do. Deriving from the theater, they were frankly artificial comedies of manners—and who else had manners but the rich?

The Crash had occurred a couple of years before, the Depression was setting in, and everyone was feeling the pinch, so that the comparative handful of rich people became not only a remote species but a mythic one. Few of the movie audiences who paid a dime a ticket could identify with the highborn ladies Ina Claire, Ann Harding, and Diana Wynyard were playing, ladies who had all the time in the world for sacred and profane love, who could change their Adrian gowns every five minutes, who could dally with one lover in the boudoir, another in the drawing room, while the husband was off on Wall Street, paying for her caviar. It was a world as fantastic and improbable as the white-on-white one Astaire and Rogers were dancing in, as Ruritanian as Lubitsch's, inhabited, in the main, by Chevalier and MacDonald.

The rich could do anything, because how many in the audience, who were getting their free dishes and playing bingo in the theaters, knew what the rich were doing?

So movie heiresses were *always* dizzy, madcap, charming, and irresponsible. Carole Lombard would discover hobo William Powell on a scavenger hunt in *My Man Godfrey,* runaway Claudette Colbert would meet plebeian Clark Gable on a transcontinental bus in *It Happened One Night,* Katharine Hepburn's pet leopard would run off with Cary Grant's brontosaurus's clavicle in *Bringing Up Baby.*

A decade which had begun in so genteel a fashion, with the civilized pleasantries of *Holiday, Rebound,* and *Topaze,* was becoming more and more screwball. Such dignified ladies as Irene Dunne went Wild as Theodora and in the remake of *The Awful Truth,* and idle-rich William Powell and Myrna Loy had nothing to do in their married life as Mr. and Mrs. Nick Charles but to track down murderers and utter wisecracks.

There were, of course, some comedies a little lower on the social scale, and Jean Arthur had the proletarian heroine almost all to herself, thanks to Frank Capra and *Mr. Deeds Goes to Town, You Can't Take It with You,* and *Mr. Smith Goes to Washington.* In them, she and Gary Cooper or Jimmy Stewart would battle the villainous rich or teach them a simple lesson in humanity. She did the same duty for Edward Arnold in Mitchell Leisen's *Easy Living,* which boasted a screenplay by Preston Sturges.

Sturges would begin to direct his own screenplays by the early forties (as would Billy Wilder). Meanwhile, he and Charles Brackett had to content themselves writing for other directors—Lubitsch in *Bluebeard's Eighth Wife* and *Ninotchka,* Howard Hawks in *Ball of Fire,* and Leisen's *Midnight,* which starred Claudette Colbert, who continued her gallery of madcap heiresses well into the forties.

The most notable of these was in Sturges's *The Palm Beach Story,* about which Mary Astor wrote in *A Life on Film:* "It was all about mad, mad people in Palm Beach or the South of France or something, the forerunners of our jet set. . . . I wore a blond wig and waved a lorgnette around and I could never please Sturges. It was just not my thing. I couldn't talk in a high, fluty voice and run my words together as he thought high-society women did, or at least mad high-society women who had six husbands and six million dollars."

Delightful as that film is even today, by 1942, when it was released, it was already something of an anachronism. The Japanese had bombed Pearl Harbor and the climate of the country had abruptly changed. Those not off to war were working in defense plants and making more money than they ever had. Thus the rich were not as remote as they once were, now that so many of the Depression audiences were comfortable themselves. In any case, to be rich no longer meant that one was automatically funny.

Katharine Hepburn would team with Spencer Tracy in far more realistically comic situations than she had with Cary Grant; Irene Dunne had to discover the war in *A Guy Named Joe* and *The White Cliffs of Dover;* Claudette Colbert would be a wartime nurse and wartime mother in *So Proudly We Hail* and *Since You Went Away;* Carole Lombard would switch to drama in *In Name Only, Vigil in the Night,* and *They Knew What They Wanted* before ending her career so gloriously in Lubitsch's wartime *To Be or Not to Be;* and Jean Arthur, after enduring the Washington housing shortage so memorably in *The More the Merrier,* would retire for a few years.

Robert Montgomery put away his tennis racket and went away to the real war, as did such other boulevardiers as Douglas Fairbanks, Jr., and Melvyn Douglas, while Cary Grant fought it on the screen in *Destination Tokyo* and *Once Upon a Honeymoon.*

And when the war was over, so was the insouciant comedy of the thirties, the elegance and the style. Brackett and Wilder would grow mordant in *A Foreign Affair,* Frank Capra would content himself remaking inferior versions of his thirties hits, George Stevens would rediscover *An American Tragedy* in *A Place in the Sun,* the Old West in *Shane,* and would even Remember Mama, and George Cukor would devote most of his energies to such melodramas as *A Double Life, Edward, My Son,* and *A Life of Her Own,* while stubbornly attempting to keep the comedic aspidistra flying in the Tracy-Hepburn *Adam's Rib* and *Pat and Mike.*

But Lubitsch was dead, Sturges in a serious decline, and high comedy was as moribund in the theater as it was in films. On Broadway, Arthur Miller had discovered the Common Man and Tennessee Williams the Uncommon Woman, and the Actors Studio had been founded to provide actors with a Method of performing Willy Loman and Blanche du Bois and other introverts, psychotics, and disoriented souls who were beginning to take over the theatrical stages.

Soon, that tragic but exciting world of red and green lights, created almost singlehandedly by Elia Kazan, would ascend over Hollywood and a new gallery of heroes and heroines would be born—Marlon Brando, Montgomery Clift, later James Dean—and they would bring the truth and power of Kazan's theater to the movies, and sound the death knell for the Beautiful People of the thirties, truth and power being the enemies of style and grace.

The Park Avenue boudoir of Lubitsch was finished. Hepburn and Bogart would have to go to the Congo to find comedy in *The African Queen,* Cary Grant clamber across Riviera roofs and Mount Rushmore in Hitchcock's *To Catch a Thief* and *North by Northwest,* and though here and there, there might be a passing rueful glance back to a vanished world, as in Wilder's *Sabrina,* Wyler's *Roman Holiday,* and Mankiewicz's *All About Eve* and *Five Fingers,* the perpetual house party on the huge North Shore estate was as dead and gone as Adrian's gowns and Ina Claire's maids and footmen and Robert Montgomery and Franchot Tone's "Tennis, anyone?"

Life would henceforth be real and earnest, and in the sixties and seventies a new generation of audiences would come along which would have as little truck with humor as its stars. To be amusing would be as heinous a crime as to be beautiful. The beautiful and light of heart had been the ones responsible for the rotten world they'd inherited, so the hell with them.

And so the Age of Aquarius became the Age of the Apocalypse and The Graduate graduated into Godfathers and Exorcists and Stings and comedies like *A Touch of Class* and *Blazing Saddles,* which might be black, zany, low, or middle-brow, but never high, never, never, never again, high.

[1976]

# AMERICAN MADNESS

## HAWKSIAN COMEDY
### *Andrew Sarris*

*Twentieth Century* is one of Hawks's three favorite films, the other two being *The Dawn Patrol* and *Scarface*. The first of the screwball comedies of the thirties, it is performed at the frenetic pace which has distinguished all of his later comedies. Released in 1934 with a sophisticated Hecht-MacArthur script, *Twentieth Century* was a few years ahead of its time, and, as might be expected of a Hawks masterpiece, did not receive the popular and critical acclaim it deserved. Hawks can take the credit not only for John Barrymore's best bravura comedy performance but also for the film which first established Carole Lombard as the finest comedienne of the thirties. Although this is a play adaptation, it enables Hawks to exploit two of his favorite devices for cinematic narrative: the odyssey and the enclosure, in this instance combined by the inner and outer aspects of a train—the Twentieth Century—speeding across the continent.

Hawksian comedy is even more bitter than Hawksian adventure as it confronts the disordered world of the twentieth century, and the title here is quite inspired as a key to Hawks's attitudes toward modern life. Exhausted by her frenzied theatrical experiences, the heroine tries to escape into a normal existence, but is thwarted by a series of farcical intrigues which would never have succeeded if she had not been unconsciously drawn to the very insanity she sought to escape. However, unlike other comedy directors of the period such as Cukor, McCarey, and La Cava, Hawks never pauses long enough to exploit the inherent pathos and emotional involvement of the situation. Without invoking the sentimentality of the theater except as a last resort, the director in *Twentieth Century* is simultaneously involved in the lunacy of the stage and yet determined to master it on his own terms. *Twentieth Century* is notable as the first comedy in which sexually attractive, sophisticated stars indulged in their own slapstick instead of delegating it to their inferiors. [. . .]

*Bringing Up Baby* (1938) is undeniably the screwiest of the screwball comedies. Even Hawks has never equaled the rocketing pace of this demented farce in which Cary Grant and Katharine Hepburn made Barrymore and Lombard in *Twentieth Century* seem as feverish as Victoria and Albert. This film passes beyond the customary lunacy of the period into a bestial *Walpurgisnacht* during which man, dog, and leopard pursue each other over the Connecticut countryside until the behavior patterns of men and animals become indistinguishable. Grant is a distinguished scientist who has labored for years to reconstruct a dinosaur. While seeking a donation for his museum, he collides literally and figuratively with a madcap heiress played by Miss Hepburn with a frantic style unlike that of any of her other performances.

Some critics have mistakenly defined Hepburn in terms of this isolated performance, but it is the Cukor-and-Stevens blend of brashness and emotional vulnerability which is most typical of her career in the thirties. Here she demolishes in minutes what it took the scientist she loves years to develop, and the film ends with Grant and Hepburn embracing over the ruins of the dinosaur. The film is so fast that it is impossible for the audience to stop even to enjoy it, much less to speculate on its interior meaning. The "Baby" of the title refers to a tame leopard which Hepburn forces Grant to share as a problem. The very quest to which Grant is dedicated involves the reconstruction of man's bestial origins which, Hawks suggests, are not too far from man's present state, particularly in the disorder of the modern world where the possibilities of regression seem infinite. The regression of man to a lower order will henceforth be one of the dominant motifs of Hawksian comedy. [. . .]

*His Girl Friday* (1940) is a loose remake of *The Front Page,* with Hildy Parks transformed into Hildy Johnson, girl reporter, played by Rosalind Russell in her bright comedy period. The antagonistic male relationship of the original is thereby converted into sexual conflict. The film begins with the classic scene of Cary Grant ridiculing an unsuspecting Ralph Bellamy. Aside from permanently destroying Bellamy as a serious screen personality, this bit of hilarious sadism is consistent with Hawks's conception of Bellamy as the "square" outsider who attempts to rescue the heroine from the insane world of journalism, an attempt doomed to failure by the very structure of Hawksian comedy as the defeat of intelligence and dignity by the gratuitous elements of modern life. The dialogue and slapstick hurtle across the screen at such a fast tempo that a comparison is suggested with Milestone's *The Front Page* to determine whether Milestone's montage is actually faster and more cinematic than Hawks's pacing within a frame. [. . .]

*Ball of Fire* (1941) marks Hawks's only collaboration with the writing team of Brackett and Wilder and is remarkably consistent with previously developed Hawksian conceptions. Once more a learned man concerned with the quest for knowledge is subjected to the inhuman excesses of the modern world. Gary Cooper is working with a group of professors on an encyclopedia. When he reaches "Slang" he enlists the services of a burlesque dancer (Barbara Stanwyck) who is fleeing the police. He is then forced out of his academic sanctuary in order to win the dancer from the gangster. The regression of intellectual man to the level of the caveman is accomplished here in the fast raucous style which is invariably the Hawksian trademark. [. . .]

*I Was a Male War Bride* (1949) bitterly records the emasculation of sexes in the modern world to the point of transvestism, Ann Sheridan in trousers and Cary Grant in a skirt; the corruption of European culture by Americanistic energy; and the dehumanization of man by modern bureaucracy to the extent that Grant is driven to the frenzy of an animal by his inability to find a place to sleep in accordance with the perforations of IBM mentalities. *Monkey Business* (1952) demolishes the poignant myths of childhood in its depiction of savagery and brutish self-indulgence, qualities amplified in the unforgettable image of George Winslow, the cigar-smoking toddler who is on the make for Marilyn Monroe in *Gentlemen Prefer Blondes* (1953). [. . .]

On the whole, Hawksian comedy is faster and funnier than anything Hollywood has done since the silent days of slapstick. Hawks lacks the comic density of Preston Sturges, the lightness of Lubitsch, the psychological intensity of Cukor, the sharp bite of Mankiewicz and Wilder, and the warmth of Capra, McCarey, and Stevens. What then does Hawks not lack in his comedies? For one thing, he does not lack a personal attitude toward his work. One can always see the director disentangling himself from the most grotesque situations with that distinctive intelligence which is shared by both the Hawksian hero and the Hawksian buffoon. Another indispensable ingredient in Hawksian comedy is Cary Grant, the most gifted light comedian in the history of the cinema. (Chaplin and Raimu are essentially tragedians with a comic flair while Olivier and Jouvet are the screen's great dark comedians.)

[1961]

## *THE FRONT PAGE* AND *HIS GIRL FRIDAY*
### Richard Corliss

Welcome to Chicago, the city of *The Front Page*, with an outstanding tradition of competitive journalism. Another tradition has been the excellent rapport between the Chicago police and working newsmen. You can be assured of our continued cooperation as you report to the nation about the 1968 Democratic Convention.

—Press handout, Chicago, August 1968

Ben Hecht had died four years before the Democratic National Convention of 1968, and he and Charles MacArthur had written *The Front Page* forty years earlier—but Hecht's big, tolerant heart might have warmed, even as his liberal blood would have curdled, at this press release from the Chicago Police Department, with its unconscious irony worthy of *The Front Page*'s own Sheriff "Pinky" Hartwell. It proved that four decades of twentieth-century progress had been powerless in altering Chicago's image from its traditional one as the breezily medieval Gun City of Al Capone. An Irishman might now be sitting on that estimable Sicilian's throne, but business went on as usual. Even the Chamber of Commerce still seemed to be controlled by Murder, Inc.

Hecht and MacArthur rose, or escaped, from the very milieu they half-canonized and half-cauterized. Their cynicism, toward both City Hall and those who would fight it, might be confused with misanthropy if they weren't so cheerful, so energetic—and so compromising, for they were too much a part of Chicago not to love it a little without hating themselves a lot. After all, the only game in town was prostitution of one kind or another, so you might as well lean back and enjoy it.

The reporters in *The Front Page,* play and movie, and in *His Girl Friday* (the adaptation Charles Lederer and Howard Hawks made a decade later), take it for granted that every aspect of life, themselves included, is completely and gloriously corrupt. *His Girl Friday*'s pair of idealists—Earl Williams (the convicted killer) and Bruce Baldwin (reporter Hildy Johnson's fiancé)—are treated as amiable fools. Earl Williams is considered a sympathetic, if psychotic, character because the man he'd killed was only a Negro policeman, whose death the unscrupulous city government is using to whip up the "race vote," and because anyone who preached radicalism in the twenties *must* be crazy. As for Bruce, he's so palpably out of place, a kitten in the lion cage, that *he* seems to be the aberration; and he's such an obvious mismatch for the resourceful, peripatetic Hildy that for once we don't want the nice guy to get the girl. Hildy winds up with the man she deserves: her domineering managing editor, Walter Burns.

As pungent and invigorating as it is, *The Front Page* is neither foolproof nor actorproof. The breakneck speed at which the play is usually staged cleverly conceals the fact that it rather sits back on its haunches for more than an act, cranking up the plot and character machinery that will explode once Walter Burns enters in Act III. And, while the fast pacing demands a certain technical facility of the actors who play those sarcastic denizens of the Criminal Courts pressroom, it's even more important that the actors be able to balance the antagonistic feelings of capriciousness and maliciousness that they are alternatingly to convey. The press gang must act both as a chorus and as conspirators, and it takes real finesse to juggle both functions without jumbling them.

(Cynicism and despair hung over the whole *Front Page* enterprise. Actor Louis Wolheim, who had worked for *The Front Page*'s director, Lewis Milestone, in *Two Arabian Nights* and *All Quiet on the Western Front,* was anxious to play the Walter Burns role for Milestone, and, according to a contemporary source, "dieted to bring himself down to a suitable weight, losing twenty-five pounds in a few days. At this time he underwent an operation for cancer, and his weakened condition caused his death"! One can easily imagine this appalling story being told during the *Front Page* poker game, and eliciting a cantata of wisecracks.)

The Milestone version, on which Charles Lederer worked as an itinerant dialogue-polisher, introduces Walter Burns earlier—even taking Burns and Hildy out for a drink—and boasts a competent group of scene-stealers as the poker-playing press corps. But it remained for Lederer and Howard Hawks, with an uncredited assist from Hecht himself, to get to the root of the problem and bring on Walter Burns in the first scene. If Burns had kept out of sight, an *éminence grise, noire, et bleue* pervading and shaping the smoky atmosphere of the Court pressroom, Hawks's other grand maneuver—switching Hildy Johnson, Walter's ace reporter, from a man to Walter's ex-wife—would have fallen flat.

A general rule of romantic comedy is that, in a triangle situation, the boy and girl who are to end up together must be seen together first, thus establishing the couple's iconographic unity before the intruding third party enters. If we had seen Bruce and Hildy together for half the film, without Walter's overbearing presence, it might have taken even more than Cary Grant's incomparable charms to alter our sympathies from poor schmuck Bruce to manipulative dervish Walter.

I'm considering *The Front Page* and *His Girl Friday* as part of Charles Lederer's career, rather than Ben Hecht's, because it was the Lederer screenplay for *His Girl Friday* that crystallized the themes and moods Hecht and MacArthur were really only fooling with. The first third of *His Girl Friday*—in which Walter begins to undermine Hildy's professed preference for Bruce and his plodding, domestic, Albany life style—is primarily Lederer's achievement. Though Walter bullies, lies to, and spills things on Bruce, the film convinces us that Walter and Hildy were made for each other, if only because angelic boredom is a greater movie sin than stylish corruption.

*His Girl Friday* is Hawks's best comedy, and quite possibly his best film. Robin Wood has perceptively analyzed the benefits Hawks accrued when he changed Hildy's sex. But the inspiration can be exaggerated, since literally dozens of thirties comedies featured man-woman reporting-romancing teams. Nor should Hawks's influence on what even Wood cites as "the film's chief virtue—its brilliant dialogue" be overemphasized. Even the overlapping dialogue perversely attributed to Hawks can be found in the Hecht–MacArthur playscript, as well as many of the film's delightful behavioral gestures—like the moment when Walter lifts the lid of the desk hiding Earl Williams, fans a little air Earl's way, and promptly shuts it again. Still, Hawks's realization of the Hecht–MacArthur–Lederer script does it the fullest possible justice, as can be seen by comparing his direction with that of Lewis Milestone in the 1931 version.

In nearly every scene, Hawks proves his superiority to Milestone as a director of both actors and camera. *His Girl Friday*'s famous, frenetic dialogue delivery is actually slower than *The Front Page*'s. But, whereas Milestone's performers tend to speak very loud and fast, with stagy pauses after each punchline, Hawks has his actors speak at a lower level and slightly slower, but with no pauses. On the most immediate level, Hawks makes it easier for the audience to catch what is being said, while *The Front Page* audience has to strain to make sense of the dialogue. (Milestone may have been trying to beat the record set by George S. Kaufman, whose direction of the stage version was notoriously fast-paced.) Moreover, Hawks's attitude suggests a respect for the dialogue *and* provokes a more benign state of exhaustion; in *His Girl Friday*, the dialogue is not faster-paced but the film is. What these newspapermen are saying, after all, often lurches past journalistic sarcasm into genuine misanthropy, and Walter Burns's ploys have a touch of the clever psychotic about them. Hawks's steady pace never gives us time to question the characters' motives. Molly Malloy jumps out the window and is promptly forgotten; Walter kidnaps Bruce's mother and is promptly forgiven. Only in retrospect does this delightful comedy reveal itself as possibly the most subtly cynical film Hollywood has produced.

Hawks's camera observes these inanities and insanities with the detachment of a visitor to the Marat-Sade play-within-a-play, again letting us concentrate on the dialogue and situations. But Milestone is so busy trying to make *The Front Page* "cinematic" that we often don't know who's speaking, let alone what he's saying. Great pains are taken to establish that the pressroom does indeed have four walls; there are meaningless shock cuts to the gallows outside; the camera is on the move far more than any of the characters. It's a case of too many tracks spoiling the froth. Milestone's greatest indulgence is a follow-the-bouncing-camera effect that accompanies the reporters in song, and which nobody I've asked can justify or even understand. Hawks hardly bothers with the pressroom's "fourth wall"; but by then the film has moved from Walter's office to his city room to a restaurant, so there's no need for a hyperthyroid *mise en scène* later on. Further, since almost everything in the pressroom is played against one wall, the desk in which Earl Williams hides, fearing for his life, is almost always in sight, and thus his predicament is kept in mind even as Walter courts Hildy in his own peculiar fashion.

Maybe it's unfair to compare *The Front Page* with *His Girl Friday,* since the only available print of the earlier film is cursed with a sound track that is, on occasion, maddeningly indistinct. According to Dwight Macdonald, *The Front Page* "was widely considered the best movie of 1931," and critics must have been grateful for a film that *moved,* though in the wrong direction and for the wrong reasons. But a Hawks picture of the same year, *The Criminal Code,* can be seriously preferred to *The Front Page* for its natural use of the moving camera and its sophistication of dialogue delivery. By 1939, Hawks had sharpened his sense of pacing and direction of actors and Lederer had refined his own considerable talent for movie adaptation to the point where they were ready to transform the liveliest stage play of the twenties into the finest, most anarchic newspaper comedy of all time.

[1974]

# FRANK CAPRA
## *William S. Pechter*

I suppose that merely to bring oneself to see a film with a name like *Pocketful of Miracles,* no less like it, it is necessary simply to like the movies, and, at least in part, in a strictly noncerebral way. I saw it, and I liked it, and I can't say that the experience of it much involved the faculty of mind. Nor, even on the level of mindless diversion, can Frank Capra's new movie, his second following a retirement of eight years, be said to be impeccable. It is an expensive job and gives occasionally onto those big, dull, vacant spaces which money seems infallibly to buy; it suffers from the Hollywood disease—elephantiasis ("A ninety-minute picture, Jules? You must be talking about the coming attractions!"). At its best—a bravura performance by Bette Davis as "Apple Annie," some wonderfully funny bits and pieces, a knockdown brawl which assails and exhilarates by its sheer kinetic energy—the insubstantiality of the whole is almost justified. At its bad moments—particularly those featuring an incredible ingénue and her Valentino-like Latin fiancé, in whom even Capra does not seem to believe—one has the sense not so much of talent lacking as of talent not engaged. Yet Capra is his own producer, wholly independent; he hops to no mogul's barked command. Among important Hollywood directors, only George Stevens has recently had this kind of independence, and, with the financial collapse of his last film, he now has probably lost it. Indeed, with the exceptions of John Ford and De Mille,[1] Capra is perhaps the most conventionally successful director Hollywood has ever known: consistent maker of profit; winner of several Academy Awards.

And, despite these credentials, Capra *is* a director of considerable importance. Among Hollywood directors, perhaps only Preston Sturges has so consistently concerned himself with a comedy of the contemporary scene; yet, for all Sturges's cosmopolitan wit, he was essentially a *farceur,* and Capra, for all his occasional air of being merely topical and his apparent sentimentality, works in a much more Aristophanic tradition. Billy Wilder also comes to mind. But his films seem to me almost the inverse of Capra's; hard cynicism on the surface, soft sentimentality underneath; and, in a film like *The Apartment,* the surface becomes scarcely distinguishable from the core. What is sentimentality if not a deficiency of feeling expressed as an excess of response; and what is cynicism if not the reciprocal of this?

Capra has called his latest film a fairy tale, and this it is, a fable of innocence out of Damon Runyon. There are a number of things wrong with it, but never does it become sentimental; if anything, one is rather conscious of a sharp edge of cruelty running through the work, an edge which cuts. Capra has populated his film—and this is one of its pleasures—with the greatest array of character actors assembled since the thirties, but the familiarity of their faces serves a purpose beyond nostalgia. The faces, like the rest of the movie's artifice, seem there constantly to remind us we are in a theater, and, indeed, Capra seems always to be saying of his fairy tale, "You'd better enjoy it while you can because it only happens in the movies."

But the faces—epitomized by the marvelous mask of cosmic incompetence which is the face of Edward Everett Horton—serve still another function: inescapably, they date the work. One of the film's shrewdest strokes was in Capra's decision not to modernize his material, as, for instance, Billy Wilder refurbishes Molnár. *Pocketful of Miracles* is a fable of the twenties set in the twenties; its innocence remains inviolate. In the pervasive ambience of the fairy tale, even a joke on implied homosexuality is redeemed for innocence. The audience with whom I saw it laughed at the comedy and cried at the pathos as at no other film of my recent experience; in fact, my impression was of

1. In this, as with the question of independence, I exclude Hitchcock as a special case.

seeing, in the audience as well, faces that had not been inside a movie theater since the thirties. How one aches for the simple innocence of the world on the screen; I found myself nostalgic for a time in which I had not yet been born: clue, perhaps, that it was a time which never existed. Never, that is, but in our movies; and who would deny the reality of our experience of them? It is the movies themselves for which the film evokes nostalgia. But the pastness of *Pocketful of Miracles* exceeds mere nostalgia, being both more profound and more complex; the film, in its totality, has the aura of some earlier experience. And, in fact, the film is a remake of one of Capra's earliest successes, a remake in the sixties of a film made in the thirties and set in the twenties. The final effect left by Frank Capra's latest film is that of having seen a revival.

In an enterprise as vast and impersonal as the making of a film, it is rare enough that a director creates his own style; if, then, he also creates his own genre, it is indeed a signal accomplishment. That Frank Capra did both, and then abruptly climaxed his spectacularly successful career by a self-imposed premature retirement, would serve to make him an absolute conundrum. For Hollywood directors are notoriously like old soldiers in the way in which they just fade out and away.

The unique Capra genre has been defined by Richard Griffith, the film historian, as the "fantasy of good will," and he has also described its archetypical pattern. "In each film, a messianic innocent, not unlike the classic simpletons of literature . . . pits himself against the forces of entrenched greed. His inexperience defeats him strategically, but his gallant integrity in the face of temptation calls forth the good will of the 'little people,' and through their combined protest, he triumphs." This ritual of innocence triumphant did little to ingratiate Capra to an intellectual audience to whom he represented only the triumph of the *Saturday Evening Post*. But though the apparent vein of cheery optimism which informs this ritual's re-enactment *is,* of course, precisely that quality which both endears Capra to his popular audience and alienates an intellectual one, yet, in seeing the films again, this quality seems strangely elusive, forever asserting itself on set occasions, but always dissipating itself finally in a kind of shrill excitement. There are even intimations of something like melancholy constantly lurking beneath the surface glare of happy affirmation.

The sense of this becomes particularly emphatic if one views the films—and I restrict myself to his most famous and characteristic comedies—in chronological sequence. From this perspective, although the pattern is already set in such early work as *The Strong Man,* a 1926 Harry Langdon seven-reeler, *Mr. Deeds Goes to Town* is its first major exposition, at once the prototype and the exception. Compared to Capra's subsequent films, it is the most unreservedly "positive" in tone. Longfellow Deeds does, indeed, win out, and innocence triumphs. The rustic poet-*cum*-tuba confronts the powerful presence of metropolitan venality, and not only effects a personal victory but manages to impress the cynical—a reminder of their own lost innocence—with his exemplary goodness as well. The memory of innocence lost is a crucially disturbing one in Capra's films, and central to any understanding of them. While the progress from small-town purity to big-city corruption may not, in fact, be part of the audience's personal history, it remains a fact of its acquired cultural legacy. That is, it is part of the inherited myth of an American past—of quiet, shady, tree-lined streets of white wood homes—which is so concretely a part of an American childhood that it persists into adulthood as a psychological fact, with the force of memory. And while the audience is asked to, and indeed must, identify with the innocent hero, it cannot fail to recognize itself, if not quite consciously, more nearly depicted in the images of his antagonists—the cynics, smart guys, hustlers, chiselers, opportunists, exploiters, hypocrites: all the corrupt; all our failed selves; what we have become. We respond finally to the classic Capra hero, whether Mr. Smith or John Doe, the uniquely American Everyman, with a kind of reluctant longing. He is our conscience *manqué*, the image of our childhood selves, reminding us, as we do not wish to be reminded, of the ways and degrees to which we have failed this image; all reaching some comic apotheosis in the figure of Jimmy Stewart, as Mr. Smith, in Washington, quite literally, a big Boy Scout.

What moderates the merely Sunday-school piety of the Capra hero, what keeps his meaning just short of the moralizing "essay" on the page before the murder case in our Sunday supplements, is always some specifically foolish, specifically human trait which becomes the comic correlative of virtue: Mr. Deeds plays his tuba, John Doe plays his baseball, and Mr. Smith is not simply a patriot but an absurdly fanatical one, who cannot pass the Washington Monument, however casually, without adopting some posture of ridiculously extravagant reverence. The virtue of the characters seems inseparable from their absurdity, and, bound up as it is with this absurdity, passes from the ideality of the Sunday moral to the reality of a concrete human embodiment. It becomes a human possibility; that is to say, the peculiar impact of the Capra hero is as an assertion that it is possible to be that good . . . and human, too.

It is the formularized happy ending which has always seemed the fatal weakness of Capra's films; the apparent belief that everything will turn out all right in the end serves, finally, only to nullify any serious moral concern. Yet this convention of the happy ending seems, on closer look, to be curiously quarantined in Capra's films, and the observance of it has often been strangely perfunctory. Only *Mr. Deeds Goes to Town* appears comfortably to adopt a happy ending, and, while this film remains the prototype of the others, much of their interest derives from the variations they work on the original pattern. In *Mr. Smith Goes to Washington,* the dramatic climax is brought off with such astonishing abruptness as to be over before we can consciously comprehend it. The filibuster has dragged on interminably. Mr. Smith seems defeated, and with the arrival of the hostile letters he suddenly becomes aware of his defeat. More suddenly still, the corrupt Senator leaps to the railing—admits the truth of Smith's accusation—Smith collapses in exhaustion and disbelief—wild commotion—Jean Arthur smiles—The End. The entire dramatic reversal takes place in less than a minute. The finale of *Meet John Doe* is almost the reverse in quality. With John Doe's suicide an apparent inevitability, the film closes on an episode of almost dreamlike tranquillity. It is Christmas Eve; there is an all but unendurably slow elevator ride to the top of a deserted skyscraper; the snow is falling, thick and silent; John Doe appears and moves to the edge of the roof; Edward Arnold appears with his henchmen; the Girl appears with specimen types of little folk who have regained faith in the idea of John Doe, and Doe allows himself to be persuaded to return to life. Distant church bells. In both cases, the tone and tenor of the final sequence are seriously at odds with the rest of the work: in *Meet John Doe,* it seems to take place in a vacuum; in *Mr. Smith Goes to Washington,* on a roller coaster. I am not at all sure that Capra rejects the validity of the happy ending, but what one detects, in the abrupt changes of style, is some knowledge, if less than conscious, of the discrepancy between the complex nature of his film's recurring antitheses and the evasive facility of their reconciliation.

To understand this is to come to a film such as *It's a Wonderful Life* with a fresh eye. For it is in this film that Capra effects the perfect equipoise between the antitheses he poses and the apparatus by which he reconciles them; there being, in fact, no recourse in "real life," the end is served by the intervention of a literal *deus ex machina.* And, as George Bailey, the film's hero, jumps into the river to commit suicide as the culmination of his progress of disastrous failures, he is saved . . . by an angel! This is, of course, the perfect, and, in fact, only, alternative for Capra; and the *deus ex machina* serves its classic purpose, from *Iphigenia in Tauris* to *The Threepenny Opera*—namely, to satisfy an understanding of the work on every level. It creates, for those who wish it, the happy ending par excellence, since it had already become apparent, in the previous Capra movies, that the climaxes, by the very extremity of the situations which gave rise to them, were derived *de force majeure.* Yet, for those who can accept the realities of George Bailey's situation—the continual frustration of his ambitions, his envy of those who have done what he has only wanted to do, the collapse of his business, a sense of utter isolation, final despair—and do not believe in angels (and Capra no more says *we* must believe in slightly absurd angels, although *he* possibly does, than Euripides says we may not believe in slightly absurd gods, although he surely doesn't), the film ends, in effect, with the hero's suicide.[2]

*It's a Wonderful Life* is the kind of work that defies criticism; almost, one might say, defies art. It is one of the funniest and one of the bleakest, as well as being one of the most technically adroit, films ever made; it is a masterpiece, yet rather of that kind peculiar to the film: unconscious masterpieces. Consciously, except in the matter of his certainly conscious concern with the mastery of his medium's technique, I don't imagine Capra conceives of himself as much different from Clarence Budington Kelland, from whose story *Mr. Deeds Goes to Town* was adapted. *It's a Wonderful Life* is a truly subversive work, the *Huckleberry Finn* which gives the lie to the *Tom Sawyer*s; yet I am certain Capra would not think of it in this way, nor boast of pacts made with the devil. I mention Twain and allude to Melville not haphazardly; Capra's films seem to me related in a direct way to the mainstream of our literature;

---

2. I don't mean to give the impression here that Capra employs his *deus ex machina* with any Euripidean irony (all the film's irony is contained in its title). The agonizing pathos of the film's climax derives precisely from the tension one senses between Capra's deeply felt desire to save his protagonist and his terrible knowledge that he cannot.

and the kind of case Leslie Fiedler makes with regard to the American novel, leaving aside questions of its truth or falsity, might equally have been derived from the American film. Just as *Pull My Daisy* is clearly out of *Huckleberry Finn,* so *A Place in the Sun* (once one forgets Dreiser, as the film itself was quite ready to do) is pure *Gatsby;* and Capra seems to me, in many ways, the analogue of Twain, always but once flawing his genius. I would not wish to press this analogy, for, as artists, Twain and Capra are vastly dissimilar; yet they seem to me comparable in their situation with respect to art and consciousness. And, like Twain also, Capra is a "natural," a folk artist in the sense of drawing imaginatively for his substance on some of the most characteristic matter of our national folklore.

Capra (whose life, in actuality, was in imitation of that most classic American cliché: poor Italian immigrant makes good) has made our clichés the stuff of his art; compounding his most significant films of the ritual elements of the peculiarly American mythos of innocence. The image of metropolitan corruption, the hatred of the city slicker, the suspicion of sophistication, the distrust of politics and the fear of government, the virtue of the rural: what is this if not a compendium of the beliefs of populism and of progressivism, which, in turn, are Jeffersonianism, grown ossified and anachronistic. Even the agrarian quality of Jeffersonianism has been curiously preserved; Mr. Deeds wants to use his twenty-million-dollar inheritance to aid homeless farmers with free land and seed, and Mr. Smith wants the disputed tract of land to be used as an outdoor camp for boys. And there is, in addition, in Capra's work, a preoccupation with still another aspect of our national subconscious. All of his heroes are made to undergo some extraordinarily harrowing ordeal before their final triumph: Mr. Deeds is placed on trial; Mr. Smith is forced to filibuster; John Doe is hissed, jeered, and ridiculed before an assemblage of his followers; George Bailey is humiliatingly bankrupt. There is, as Dwight Macdonald has observed, something very American in the idea of an uncrucified Christ.

But Capra's genius is a comic one, and there remains that quality of irreducible foolishness in the Capra heroes, a foolishness that is the emblem of their humanity: Mr. Deeds's tuba and awful poetry, Mr. Smith's patriotic mania, John Doe's hobo language and legends, George Bailey's consummate awkwardness. And their innocence, their virtue, their beauty is inextricable from this. In a world of cleverness and corruption, they have allowed themselves to be "fools for Christ's sake"; and it hardly seems a flaw in this scheme that George Bailey's antagonist in *It's a Wonderful Life* is made a Dickensian caricature of villainy, embodying his single trait; rather, he becomes an abstracted converse of the George Baileys, the incarnation of pure, natural malignity. He exists not so much as a human being as as an operative force in this world; and, by the suicide of George Bailey, the triumphant one; in the end, the cross will not be cheated of its suffering.

I have mentioned the breaches of Capra's style, but it remains to mention the style as such. It is a style—although one might never guess it from the most part of his recent work—of almost classic purity; and it seems somehow appropriate to the American ethos of casual abundance that the director of quite probably the greatest technical genius in the Hollywood film, post-Griffith, pre-Hitchcock—a genius, as Richard Griffith has suggested, on the order of those of the silent Russian cinema at its zenith—should have placed his great gifts at the service of an apparently frivolous kind of comedy. It is a style, one is tempted to say, based solely on editing, since it depends for its effect on a sustained sequence of rhythmic motion. There is very little about Capra's style which may be ascertained from a still, as, say, each still from Eisenstein has the carefully composed quality of an Old Master. A Capra still is unbeautiful; if anything, a characteristic still from Capra will strike one as a little too busy, even chaotic. But whereas Eisenstein's complex and intricate editing seems, finally, the attempt to impose movement on material which is essentially static, Capra's has the effect of imposing order on images constantly in motion, imposing order on chaos. The end of all this is indeed a kind of beauty, a beauty of controlled motion, more like dancing than like painting, but more like the movies than like anything else.

A comic genius is fundamentally a realistic one, and, in his films, his various conclusions notwithstanding, Capra has created for us an anthology of indelible images of predatory greed, political corruption, the cynical manipulation of public opinion, the murderous nature of private enterprise, and the frustration and aridity of small-town American life. There is always a gulf between what Capra wishes to say and what he actually succeeds in saying. He seems obsessed with certain American social myths, but he observes that society itself as a realist. The most succinct statement of this discrepancy between intention and accomplishment is put by Richard Griffith, in his monograph on Capra, simply by juxtaposing a commonplace phrase of Capra criticism—"engrossing affection for small American types"—against a still of the witnesses at the trial of Mr. Deeds. Their faces remain more expressive than any comment one could make upon them: mean, stupid, vain, petty, ridiculous; they form an imposing catalogue of human viciousness.

And Capra seems always to realize this. His films move at a breath-taking clip: dynamic, driving, taut, at their extreme even hysterical; the unrelenting, frantic acceleration of pace seems to spring from the release of some tremendous accumulation of pressure. The sheer speed and energy seem, finally, less calculated than desperate, as though Capra were aware, on some level, of the tension established between his material and what he attempts to make of it. Desperation—in this quality of Capra's films one sees again the fundamental nature of style as moral action: Capra's desperation is his final honesty. It ruthlessly exposes his own affirmation as pretense, and reveals, recklessly and without defense, dilemma.

Perhaps mention should be made, in passing, of what was, in effect—the rest being only a few remakes, a few frank time killers, and eight years of silence—Capra's last film, *State of the Union;* despite its prodigal talent and virtuoso style, an acknowledgment of defeat. With *It's a Wonderful Life,* the ideal form for the Capra comedy had been established, but it was a form which could be employed only once. Despite the fact that, in *State of the Union,* such actual names as Vandenberg and Stassen *(O tempora! O mores!)* are mentioned with considerable irreverence, these ostensible signs of daring only serve to emphasize a more fundamental lack of it. Unlike any of Capra's other films, *State of the Union* seems anxious to retreat into its subplot, one of romantic misalliance. And all the hoopla of its finale, as frenetic and noisy as anything Capra has put on the screen, cannot disguise the fact that the hero resigns from politics with the implication being that he is, in fact, *too good* to be involved. In one sense, this is Capra at his most realistic, but also at his least engaged. For the artist, withdrawal from the world—the world as he perceives it—is never achieved without some radical diminution of his art.

Perhaps, having made *It's a Wonderful Life,* there was nothing more Capra had to say. His only fruitful alternative, having achieved a kind of perfection within his own terms, had to be to question the very nature of those terms themselves. Without a realization that the dilemma existed inherently in the terms in which he articulated it, he could, in effect, go no further. It remains only to note that he went no further.

[1962]

# LUBITSCH AND HIS DISCIPLES

## ERNST LUBITSCH
### *Richard Schickel*

Of the many [Hollywood directors] who were called from abroad, only a few remained chosen for very long. Among them, the greatest success was scored by Ernst Lubitsch, who somehow managed to capture the wit and style of a drawing-room comedy without benefit of sound track. Alone of the directors in America he managed to create, in a medium still purely visual, the screen equivalent of the written or spoken epigram. A shrewd, cigar-shredding showman, he was the De Mille of the sophisticates, turning out a cycle of films full of witty images and deft camera comments on the manners and morals of the well-bred. He was a laconic director, economical in the use of a camera that was both sly and seemingly self-effacing as it moved about settings that had both spaciousness and uncommon "rightness" of detail. Withal, Lubitsch had a refreshing cynicism about what he was doing: "The American public—with the mind of a twelve-year-old child, you know—it must have life as it ain't." Of all the great silent directors, Lubitsch would most easily survive the transition to sound, when "the Lubitsch touch" was to become a byword for high style in a medium where comedy tended to be at its best when it was at its broadest.

[1964]

# ERNST LUBITSCH
## Arthur Knight

Ernst Lubitsch, by 1929 the top director at Paramount, made the important discovery that a talking picture did not have to be *all* talking, nor did the sound track have to reproduce faithfully each sound on the set. In his first talkies, *The Love Parade* (1929) and *Monte Carlo* (1930), he included many passages that were shot without dialogue or any other synchronized sound. For these, he was able to bring the camera out of its soundproof box and proceed in the old silent techniques, moving his camera freely, changing its position frequently. Music or effects were put in later. One of the high points of *The Love Parade* was a running gag with Maurice Chevalier telling a risqué joke to members of the court. Each time he approaches the tag line, his voice sinks to a confidential whisper, a door closes, or the camera leaps outside to view the effect of his story through a window. Audiences of 1929 were delighted to find a new element in the talkies—silence!

Working mainly on the Maurice Chevalier–Jeanette MacDonald musicals, Lubitsch quickly established himself as one of the most inventive directors of the period. With his strong feeling for the relationship between music and visuals, he brought back some of the rhythm that had been present in the silent films. In *Monte Carlo*, for example, Lubitsch cuts together the sounds of a train getting under way. As it picks up speed, the characteristic tempo of the wheels is translated into the music of the theme song, "Beyond the Blue Horizon." The impressive wedding ceremony in *The Smiling Lieutenant* (1931) was staged without the confining microphone, but each opening door, every step down the great flight of marble stairs, every gesture of the players was timed to the beat of a score that was dubbed in later. He was the first to be concerned with the "natural" introduction of songs into the development of a musical-comedy plot, the first to find a cinematic way to handle verbal humor in the new medium.

[1957]

# ERNST LUBITSCH
## Andrew Sarris

In the well-mannered, good-natured world of Ernst Lubitsch, grace transcends purpose. *To Be or Not to Be,* widely criticized as an inappropriately farcical treatment of Nazi terror, bridges the abyss between laughter and horror. For Lubitsch, it was sufficient to say that Hitler had bad manners, and no evil was then inconceivable. What are manners, after all, but the limits to man's presumption, a recognition that we all eventually lose the game of life but that we should still play the game according to the rules. A poignant sadness infiltrates the director's gayest moments, and it is this counterpoint between sadness and gaiety that represents the Lubitsch touch, and not the leering humor of closed doors. Describing Lubitsch as the Continental sophisticate is as inadequate as describing Hitchcock as the master of suspense. Garbo's pixilated speech in *Ninotchka* is pitched delicately between the comic and the cosmic, and in one breath-taking moment, Garbo and Lubitsch sway on the tightrope between grace and purpose. [. . .]

Lubitsch has had the last laugh in that the magical qualities of his films have survived the topical distractions of his detractors. If *Angel* evokes Pirandello as *The Shop Around the Corner* evokes Molnár, it is because Lubitsch taught the American cinema the importance of appearances for appearance's sake (Pirandello) and the indispensability of good manners (Molnár). Lubitsch was the last of the genuine Continentals let loose on the American continent, and we shall never see his like again because the world he celebrated had died—even before he did—everywhere except in his own memory.

[1969]

## TROUBLE IN PARADISE
### Richard Corliss

*Trouble in Paradise* (1932) inhabits a world of bogus nobility and disloyal family retainers, in which charm is acquired not for its own sake but to give the swindler an acceptable upper-class façade, and in which *noblesse oblige* is worth about as much as the failed stocks kept sentimentally in the vaults of the still rich and the *nouveau* poor. This milieu, uncharacteristic for Lubitsch, has led some critics to argue that the director abandoned Ruritanian romance for elegant muckraking à la Stroheim, allowing milady's mudpack to harden into an appropriately grotesque mask, and m'sieur's Vichy water to go flatter than his current bank account. Well, the milieu may have changed, but Lubitsch's tone did not. The Depression did not affect him nearly so deeply as Hitler's territorial imperatives would a decade later. *Trouble in Paradise* remains the most perfect expression of Lubitsch's—and [screenwriter Samuel] Raphaelson's—urbanity, whereas *To Be or Not to Be* possesses a tone determined to an off-putting extent by the boorish personality of Nazism.

There is even some question as to whether Lubitsch and Raphaelson are exposing the dishonesty of romance in Depression-ridden Europe or extolling the romance of dishonesty. The opening sequence is often taken as an image of disillusion and dissolution: "a romantic tenor . . . turns out to be the captain of a garbage gondola," as Richard Koszarski describes it. What the scene actually shows is a man with a garbage can who turns out to be a romantic tenor. Although the filmmakers may be robbing the upper class of its expensive pretenses (just as Gaston, the hero, and Lily, the heroine, are doing), they are also investing the working class—garbage men and con men alike—with romance and respect.

We know, almost from the start, that "Baron" Gaston and "Countess" Lily are opportunistic phonies. Later on, we learn that they are more gracious and graceful, more honest and honorable—in a word, more *noble*—than the nobility they are working so hard to impoverish. In this twilight of the aristocracy, manners are rules that can be played by the rich, the servants of the rich, and the would-be rich; so it's often difficult to know whether that distinguished man in the drawing room is the very model of a modern major general, majority stockholder, major-domo, or master criminal (like Gaston). The first dialogue sequence finds "Baron" Gaston on his Venetian veranda, being met by a waiter.

> WAITER *(offering menu):* Yes, Baron. *(No answer.)* What shall we start with, Baron?
> GASTON *(absent-mindedly):* Hmm? Oh, yes. *(He scans the menu.)* That's not so easy. Beginnings are always difficult.
> WAITER: Yes, Baron.
> GASTON: If Casanova suddenly turned out to be Romeo, having supper with Juliet, who might become . . . Cleopatra . . . how would *you* start?
> WAITER *(momentarily nonplussed—then, brightly):* I would start with cocktails.
> GASTON: Mm-hmm. Very good. Excellent. *(He sees Lily—his assignation for the evening—in a gondola, and waves to her.)* It must be the most marvelous supper. We may not eat it—but it must be marvelous.
> WAITER: Yes, Baron.
> GASTON: And, waiter . . .
> WAITER: Yes, Baron?
> GASTON: You see that moon?
> WAITER: Yes, Baron.
> GASTON: I want to see that moon in the champagne.
> WAITER: Yes, Baron. *(He writes.)* Moon . . . in champagne.
> GASTON: I want to see . . . *(His mind wanders back down to the canal.)* Umm . . .
> WAITER *(understands):* Yes, Baron.
> GASTON: And as for you, waiter . . .
> WAITER *(expectantly):* Yes, Baron?
> GASTON: I don't want to see you at all.
> WAITER *(the slightest bit disappointed that the Baron has thought it necessary to mention this):* No, Baron.

The waiter's professional chagrin at this last remark is so beautifully understated that I can't be sure whether I'm inferring it or inventing it. What is certain is that Herbert Marshall's false *sang-froid* is far more assured here than the real thing would be a few years later in *Angel*. But of course Marshall—like nearly every other actor who ever played an aristocrat or a plutocrat—is a swindler himself, convincing his audience that he is to the manner born when he has really only snuck into it through the servants' entrance. Indeed, Gaston and Lily can be seen not as thieves but as thespians who are fooling viewers used to "defining essences in terms of surfaces" (Andrew Sarris's description of "the highest art of the cinema"), just as they trick their wealthy suckers into accepting them as equals so they can steal from them and *become* their equals.

Gaston and Lily may be able to fool their "marks," and us, but they can't fool each other. Gaston is the perfect gentleman-on-the-make, removing Lily's wrap with a panache that implies the most sensual seduction. But Lily is on to him. We know that Gaston has just robbed foppish Edward Everett Horton of 20,000 francs, because the waiter has removed a leaf, which had clung to Gaston's coat during the getaway, from his dinner jacket. Now Lily says, "Baron, I have a confession to make. You are a crook. You robbed the gentlemen in two-fifty-three, -five, -seven, and -nine. Would you please pass the salt?" The rest of a delightful dinner is spent filching things and returning them. Gaston steals Lily's pin, and appraises it for her. Lily pinches Gaston's watch, and regulates it for him. It is love—or, at the very least, mutual admiration and collaboration—at first sight, the perfect liaison of business and pleasure.

The Depression began in the banks, then put the poor out of work, and finally kept the rich from buying any new jewelry—which threatens to deprive Gaston and Lily of a livelihood. Stocks and lovers tend to depreciate without warning; only cash is trustworthy. So our plucky thieves switch to a "cash business," which Gaston doesn't mind but Lily does. Lily is an *amateuse,* and it takes the heart out of her work to steal something she can't wear. She is also slightly less secure in her role of noblewoman than Gaston is as a bankrupt baron (in fact, she *dunks,* a habit later Lubitsch-Raphaelson films will condemn as the nadir of gaucherie), so she needs jewelry as an emblem of the status that Gaston carries in his diction and his discretion. Whereas Gaston radiates the understated arrogance of the wealthy even when he works as private secretary to a woman he plans to swindle, Lily finds it easy to assume the working-class attitudes appropriate to Gaston's assistant, when he later hires *her.*

Mme. Colet, Gaston's employer and Lily's ultimate rival, is a woman with money enough to finance her exquisite taste. She finds a 3,000-franc purse too expensive, but buys a 125,000-franc purse because it's "beautiful." It is this handbag that Gaston steals, only to return it to its owner when the reward comes to twice its black-market value. Mme. Colet appraises Gaston—rather as Gaston and Lily had appraised each other—and, deciding he is worth more than a handbag, takes him on, first as a secretary, then as a lover. This arrangement infuriates Lily ("I wouldn't fall for another man if he were the biggest crook on earth!") and she plots her revenge on both of them.

The romantic and financial complications that ensue are too complicated to synopsize here. Suffice it to say that Mme. Colet discovers that her French lover is a Rumanian thief, but that he has saved her loss of both face and fortune by getting out of her life, after leaving her with a choice bit of information (namely, that the family retainer—C. Aubrey Smith, no less—has been embezzling her husband's company for more than forty years). "Do you know what you're missing?" he asks, bidding an amorous adieu. "Yes," she says, expressing the ecstasy of things lost. "No," he replies. *"This* is what you're missing"—and pulls out a rope of priceless pearls—"a gift to Lily. . . ." She smiles and says, regally, ". . . with the compliments of Colet . . . and Company."

As in *The Lady Eve,* the leads fall in love again as they had at first. In a taxi, Gaston reaches into his pocket for Mme. Colet's gift—but Lily has it. She pulls out Mme. Colet's 125,000-franc handbag—but something is missing. Gaston pulls out 100,000 francs (which Lily had threatened to rob, then thrown back at Mme. Colet)—and hands the notes to Lily. "Gaston!" They embrace. Fade-out on the first film in which Lubitsch's visual subtlety and Raphaelson's verbal sophistication combine to produce a triumphant immorality play.

[1974]

# MARRIAGE CUKOR STYLE
## *Molly Haskell*

[. . .] The delicate equilibrium between a man and a woman and between a woman's need to distinguish herself and the social demands on her become the explicit theme of George Cukor's great films of the late forties and early fifties, specifically the Judy Holliday films and Hepburn–Tracy vehicles written by the husband-and-wife team of Ruth Gordon and Garson Kanin. Gordon and Kanin wrote a series of seven screenplays for Cukor, three of which dealt, comically and sublimely, with the problems and the chemistry of the couple.

Almost as a parody of the extraordinary individuals represented by Hepburn and Tracy in *Adam's Rib* and *Pat and Mike,* Aldo Ray and Judy Holliday were a typical, dumb, middle-class, well-meaning, ordinary married couple in Cukor's *The Marrying Kind.* Almost a parody, but not quite. For it is one of the glories of the film that the two characters, without ever being patronized and at the same time without ever being lifted above the class and the cliché in which they are rooted, are intensely moving. Ray and Holliday, on the brink of divorce, have come to a woman judge (who, in her relationship with her male assistant, shows both authority and warmth). Through a series of flashbacks reconstructing their marriage we, and they, come to realize that together they are something they never were apart: a unit, a whole. Two ordinary, less-than-complete individuals who have grown into each other to the point where they can be defined only by the word "couple" have no right to divorce. Separately, they are two more swallowers of the American myth, two more victims of its fraudulence: but together, with their children, they add up to something full and affirmative. In losing their child, they are at first destroyed —their "meaning" evaporates. But in that nothingness, old roles dissolve and they must rediscover themselves. Cukor, Gordon, and Kanin are very much aware of the sexual insecurities that arise from too rigid a concept of male-female roles, and suggest, in the visual and verbal motifs of these "companion" films, that through some kind of "merger" of identities, through a free exchange of traits (as when Holliday, in defiance of the law whereby it is the man who "storms out" of the house in a fight, throws herself into the night), a truer sense of the self may emerge.

In the growing isolation of the New York cultural elite from the rest of

America in the sixties, this is the side of marriage and the middle class that has been lost to us. We seem to be able to approach middle-America only through giggles of derision (*The Graduate, Sticks and Bones,* "All in the Family"); and, in dismissing the housewife as a lower form of life, women's lib confirms that the real gap is cultural and economic rather than sexual. In the difference between the couple in *The Marrying Kind* and *Adam's Rib,* Cukor and company acknowledge the most fundamental intellectual, spiritual, and economic inequality between the educated elite and the less privileged and less imaginative members of lower-middle-class America; but they never deprive them of their dignity, or deny them joys and sorrows and a capacity to feel as great as the poets of the earth. The true emotional oppression—the oppression of blacks by whites, of housewives by working women—is pity. For in such lessons in life as we get from suffering, degrees are granted without reference to class or sex. Finally, most honestly, Holliday's Florence and Ray's Chet are the sheep of the world rather than its shepherds: they are the victims of emotions they haven't the words to express, the tools of a mechanical-industrial society they haven't the knowledge to resist. Their greatest defense against its monolithic oppressiveness, against being overwhelmed by routine, inhumanity, and their "proletarian" identity, is each other, is their identity as a couple. In the final, quite noble strength we feel in them as a couple, they confirm the theory Cukor, Gordon, and Kanin seem to be endorsing: that marriage is an institution ideally suited to the people at both the bottom and the top—the truly ordinary and the truly extraordinary, those who are preserved and protected by it, and those who can bend it to their will.

Hepburn and Tracy were nothing if not extraordinary. While preserving their individuality, they united to form a whole greater than the sum of its parts. As Tracy says to Hepburn in *Pat and Mike,* in a line that could have been written by Kanin-Gordon, Cukor, or Tracy himself and that finally tapers off into infinity, "What's good for you is good for me is good for you. . . ."

This was true of them professionally. They came together at a time when their careers were foundering: misfits in the Hollywood mold, they were not in any way typical romantic leads. Hepburn had grown older, the face that once blushed in gracious concession to femininity now betrayed in no uncertain terms the recalcitrant New England spirit. And Tracy, too short and dumpy for conventional leading roles, hadn't found the woman who could lure him from the rugged, masculine world he inhabited. Out of their complementary incongruities, they created one of the most romantic couples the cinema has ever known. His virility acts as a buffer to her intelligence; she is tempered by him just as he is sharpened by her, and their self-confidence is increased, rather than eroded, by their need for each other.

*Adam's Rib,* that *rara avis,* a commercial "feminist" film, was many years ahead of its time when it appeared in 1949, and, alas, still is. Even the slightly coy happy ending testifies to the fact that the film strikes deeper into the question of sexual roles than its comic surface would indicate and raises more questions than it can possibly answer.

Tracy and Hepburn play a couple of married lawyers who find themselves on opposite sides of a case; he is the prosecuting attorney, and she, seizing upon the crime and its implications, takes it upon herself to defend the accused. A dopey young wife—Judy Holliday, in her first major movie role—has shot, but not killed, her husband (Tom Ewell) over another woman. Hepburn, reading an account in the newspaper, is outraged by the certainty that the woman will be dealt with harshly while a man in that position would be acquitted by the courts and vindicated by society. Hepburn goes to visit Holliday at the woman's prison, and, in a long, lovely single-take scene, Holliday spills out her story, revealing, comically and pathetically, her exceptionally low consciousness. One of the constant and most relevant sources of comedy in the film is the lack of rapport between Hepburn's militant lawyer, constructing her case on feminist principles, and Holliday's housewife, contrite and idiotically eager to accept guilt. The film raises the means-and-end dilemma which has long been the philosophical thorn in the side of our thinking about the rights and reparations of minority groups. Hepburn marshals evidence of women's accomplishments to prove their equality with men, even to the point of having a lady wrestler lift Tracy onto her shoulders and make a laughingstock of him. She goes *too* far and humiliates him, while he remains a gentleman. She stoops to unscrupulous methods while he maintains strict honor and decorum. But, then, he can afford to, since the law was created by and for him.

Even down to his animal magnetism, Tracy wears the spoiled complacency of the man, but Hepburn, ambitious and intelligent, scrapes the nerves of male authority. An acute sense of the way male supremacy is institutionalized in the "games people play" occurs in two contrasting situations of one-upmanship: Hepburn, fiery about the case she is about to take, is describing it to Tracy on the telephone; Tracy, in a familiar male (or marital) riposte, effectively cuts her off by teasing, "I love you when you get caus-y." This is greeted with delight by audiences, who usually disapprove of Hepburn's "emasculation" of Tracy in court, a more obvious but perhaps a less damaging tactic of bad faith. Cukor gives Hepburn an ally in the Cole Porter–type composer played by David Wayne, a character who seems to stand, at least partially, for Cukor himself. He identifies with Hepburn and, in marital feuds, takes her side against the virile, meat-and-potatoes "straight" played by Tracy. Thus the neutral or homosexual character, when he is sympathetic, can help to restore some of the balance in the woman's favor. But as soon as the Hepburn-Wayne collusion becomes devious or bitchy, the balance shifts, and our sympathy goes, as it should, to Tracy.

The film brilliantly counterpoints and reconciles two basic assumptions: (1) that there are certain "male" qualities—stability, stoicism, fairness, dullness—possessed by Tracy, and that there are certain "female" qualities—volatility, brilliance, intuition, duplicity—possessed by Hepburn; and (2) that each can, and must, exchange these qualities like trading cards. It is important for Hepburn to be ethical, just as it is important for Tracy to be able to concede defeat gracefully, and if she can be a bastard, he can fake tears. If each can do everything the other can do, just where, we begin to wonder, are the boundaries between male and female? The question mark is established most pointedly and uncomfortably when, during the courtroom session, the faces of Holliday and Ewell are transposed, each becoming the other.

But Hepburn and Tracy are not quite so interchangeable, and the success of their union derives from the preservation of their individuality, not rigidly but through a fluctuating balance of concession and assertion. Tracy can be humiliated and still rebound without (too much) loss of ego. Hepburn occasionally can defer to him and still not lose her identity. A purely political-feminist logic would demand that she be given Tracy's head, in unqualified triumph (an ending that some small part of us would like to see), rather than make an equivocal, "feminine" concession to his masculinity. But marriage and love do not flourish according to such logic. Their love is the admission of their incompleteness, of their need and willingness to listen to each other, and their marriage is the certification—indeed, the celebration—of that compromise.

This finally is the greatness of Hepburn's superwoman, and [Bette] Davis's and [Rosalind] Russell's too—that she is able to achieve her ends in a man's world, to insist on her intelligence, to insist on using it, and yet be able to "dwindle," like Millamant in *The Way of the World,* "into marriage," but only after an equal bargain has been struck of conditions mutually agreed on. It is with just such a bargain, and a contract, that Cukor's great Tracy–Hepburn film of the fifties, *Pat and Mike,* is concerned.[. . .]

In *Pat and Mike,* Katharine Hepburn is a gym teacher caught between her enthusiasm for sports and a growing sense of pressure to marry and become a "woman." Indecision increases her guilt and lack of self-esteem. The situation crystallizes when, during a golf tournament (and again, later, at a tennis match) her fiancé (William Ching) appears. And what a brilliant conception he is—a bland, comic-horror figure, the "eternal male" as woman's nemesis, society's emissary on a mission to deflate woman before she can find out and gain confidence in her true powers. Alternately whispering to his companions or beaming at Hepburn with a fatuous grin, he is overconfident, insensitive, hearty, and, through it all, apparently harmless, mystified by her self-doubts, wanting "only the best" for the little lady. The moment he arrives on the scene, her confidence evaporates and her game falls apart. But from another shadow of the male spectrum comes Spencer Tracy, a Brooklynese sports promoter with dubious connections and a vocabulary studded wid dems and dose. He first tries to make her throw a golf match (and even at that his dishonesty is cleaner and more open than Ching's "honor"), but then, realizing she is incorruptible, signs her up as one of his three most valuable properties, along with a race horse and Aldo Ray. Tracy puts her through her paces (and we are treated to displays of Hepburn's real-life skill at golf and tennis), and enters her in professional competition. It is by gaining Tracy's respect and—in the film's most delightful irony—by becoming a commercial "property," that Hepburn is free to become herself. The support Tracy gives her is not the flattery or adoration of the lover—they don't kiss once in the whole movie—but the admiration of the pro, directed at her skill rather than her sex. Love follows, of course, but without compromising their professional relationship, and in that sense, because of the terms (professional *preceding* marital) and fit (manager-performer) of their "contract," theirs is a less competitive, more congenial relationship than in *Adam's Rib.* In *Pat and Mike,* Hepburn demonstrates with strength and reflex what in *Adam's Rib* she proved with her brains: that women can easily get along without men. Thus, we see her vanquishing, with little more than a flick of a wrist, three crooks who have assailed Tracy. But then, she seems to say as she defers to him in some other way, "Who wants to get along without men?"—especially if the relationship is and always will be, as Tracy says, "Five-oh, five-oh."[. . .]

[1974]

## THE PHILADELPHIA STORY
### Penelope Gilliatt

George Cukor's film of Philip Barry's *The Philadelphia Story* was made in 1940, with Katharine Hepburn, Cary Grant, and James Stewart. All three give performances of such calm comic judgment that one wonders whether Cukor's legendary reputation as an actress's director does him honor enough. It is true that Katharine Hepburn, cast as a rich girl who thrives on fights and who seems to be marrying her deadneck second husband as some sort of penance for flamboyance, has never seemed more invincible; her faultless technical sense makes one feel that she could play a scene with a speak-your-weight machine and still turn it into an encounter charged with irony and challenge.

But Cary Grant, as her first husband, flourishes under Cukor's direction almost as much. For once, his style of unwounding mockery seems to come out of the character; and though it is partly due to the editing that his glances at his recalcitrant ex-wife are as shrewdly fond as they are, they would never have been thrown at all if it had not been for the atmosphere of trust and intimacy that Cukor palpably creates for his cast. One could not imagine them in a Billy Wilder picture.

James Stewart, playing a dryly self-loathing gossip-journalist, head perpetually inclined as though he were going through a doorway in some quixotic Tudor cottage, seems to have bloomed in the same way. For some reason, mutters on the screen are always comic and beguiling: Stewart here is an incorrigible mutterer, tending to wander off into corners by himself and throw low insults like grapeshot at the palatial Philadelphia homestead he has invaded. In the circumstances his abrupt declaration of love for Katharine Hepburn in a public library, spoken away from camera in an undertone that infects her own bronze caw, demonstrates the most precise control of mood. Beneath the stinging repartee he implies a romanticism that makes it perfectly believable that he should work for an equivalent of *Confidential* and at the same time gently detest himself for it. "We'd love to see those pictures one day," says the engaged couple, having been compromisingly photographed by journalists whom they take to be guests. "You will," says the photographer grimly.

A good deal of the credit for *The Philadelphia Story* must be laid squarely at the feet of the writer. In most sophisticated comedies about sex among the rich the question of money is ignored, as though the author did not really like to remark on how well-heeled his characters are, and the sexual situations are acted out as though they were a mime by uncomprehending children. Neither of these generalities is true of Donald Ogden Stewart's owlishly witty screen version of the Philip Barry stage play, which embodies a view of life as critical and formed as one would expect of any serious dramatic writer. I am not sure why, in a century widely versed in Marx and Freud, we should somehow have agreed to accept snobbery about money and infantilism about sex with little resistance as long as they occur in a comedy; for one reason and another, *The Philadelphia Story* is to be saluted as a rare film as well as a good one.

[1961]

# BILLY WILDER
## *Richard Corliss*

Some appraisals of Billy Wilder's career are too critical to be taken seriously as criticism. John Simon's and Andrew Sarris's dismissals of Wilder sound like the filmmaker himself on one of his bilious binges. The virulent reaction to Wilder's work at least indicates the unavoidable presence of an *auteur*—if the word is to have any meaning at all—who has investigated the theme of role-playing for over four decades. It's no coincidence that Wilder's best films involve various forms of deception *(Ace in the Hole, Witness for the Prosecution, Some Like It Hot)*, detection *(Emil and the Detective, Double Indemnity, The Private Life of Sherlock Holmes)*, dementia *(The Lost Weekend, Sunset Boulevard, The Apartment)*, and, finally, transformation *(Hold Back the Dawn, Ball of Fire, Love in the Afternoon)*. His women often begin as victims of directorial misogyny and end as vessels of Christian regeneration, while his attitude toward those polar opposites of fifties child-women, Audrey Hepburn and Marilyn Monroe, vacillated from the cruel to the caressing.

Wilder is one of the few strong-willed screenwriters who function best with a genuine collaborator (as opposed to the rewrite men and studio hacks who often received shared credit on screen). But the films Charles Brackett and I. A. L. Diamond, Wilder's most frequent partners, have written on their own enforces the belief that their role has been that of the resourceful private secretary to an immigrant never completely confident in his grasp of English. Thus, though he may have used other men as mediums, Wilder's message comes through loud and clear—from the avant-garde *People on Sunday* in pre-Hitler Germany to the backward-glancing *Avanti!* of forty-three years later.

[1974]

## SOME LIKE IT HOT
### Richard Corliss

It begins with a mad car chase—gangsters, cops, bootleg whisky and a funeral. After all this, a superfluous title card flashes on: CHICAGO 1929. The scene of *Some Like It Hot* is America's largest small town in a year whose memory evokes both the pinnacle of Prohibition and the depths of the Depression. Its theme song is a jazzy, jarring antiphony of the roar of the Roaring Twenties and the pratfalling crash of the stock market. And its film style straddles two eras: "movies," with a frenetic pace and strategically placed chases, and "talkies," with a pair of male stars who manage to apotheosize, in different ways, the early-talkie actor—brash, flamboyant, show-tough; in a word: effeminate. Just as Marilyn Monroe combines the raunchiness of the silent-movie vamp with the resilience of a Colleen Moore flapper, so do Tony Curtis and Jack Lemmon combine to produce a set of variations on the acting style of the talkies' most durable and archetypal romantic-comedy actor, Cary Grant—and to put his brutal good looks and flossy gestural extravagance into a sensible critical perspective.

Wilder had played off voluptuous female against ineffectual male before (notably in *The Seven Year Itch*), and would do so again (ignobly in *Kiss Me, Stupid*). Time and again Wilder heroes set out to transform an earthy heroine, only to be transformed themselves in the process, from the traditional *Ball of Fire* to the transcendent *Sherlock Holmes* thirty years later. When Wilder worked with Monroe *(Itch* and *Hot),* he reaffirmed her guileless sexuality even while kidding it, and both times by casting her against harmless satyrs who were as childish in pursuing her gifts as she was in dispensing them. Wilder could tap Monroe's sex as no director of her dramatic films would dare, because the censors would say, "It's only comedy," and shrug it off. But, like Garbo in *Ninotchka,* Monroe played comedy with a bizarre intensity—neither actress seemed to make any distinction between what was to be played for laughs and what was not—so that her "seduction" of Tony Curtis on "his" yacht reveals Monroe (looking pendulous, diaphanous, and great) at her most erotic as an exuberant missionary for sexual rebirth.

Tony Curtis was young and pretty when he came to Hollywood, so his studio, Universal, cast him "visually," in Fairbanks–Flynn swashbuckling epics. But what he had, lurking beneath those cartoon looks, was a spine-wide streak of Bronx moxie; he was always more a Bernie Schwartz than a Tony Curtis. The essence of moxie is hustling and, in marled twilight of Broadway, hustling is best expressed by a show-bizzy amalgam of tough talk and sweet talk ("You want a perforated stomach?" and "I love ya, sweetie baby"). Curtis finally got a chance to play himself—Bernie Schwartz—in the sublimely titled *Sweet Smell of Success:* peripatetic, rodentoid, ulcerous, and almost Jewish. The film was a financial flop. But meanwhile Curtis had been honing a desire even keener than playing himself: namely, playing—being—Cary Grant. Blake Edwards, who had turned a Grant film, *Mr. Lucky,* into a successful TV show, and built another series, "Peter Gunn," around the resemblance of star Craig

Stevens to Grant, helped Curtis achieve his ambition by starring him in a string of lightweight comedies—the last one *(Operation Petticoat)* costarring Cary Grant. But by this time *Some Like It Hot* had intervened, and Curtis had gotten his chance to *pretend* to do what he had been *trying* to do for years: play a nearsighted, impotent Cary Grant.

Even when Curtis is not playing his Grant-like millionaire intentionally, there's enough of Grant's manic, hand-on-hip, moi-good-mayin bantering (from *His Girl Friday*) in his performance to establish spiritual kinship. In his early scenes with Jack Lemmon—who in turn is busy mimicking Joe E. Brown, with a touch of Jimmy Durante's head-shaking pant—the two flirt with each other and everyone else. Curtis, the Lothario, is romantic-effeminate, Lemmon, the kvetch, is whiny-effeminate. As Curtis seduces a girl out of her car keys, Lemmon looks into the camera and effuses, "Isn't he a bit of terrific!" In a way, *Some Like It Hot* tells how Monroe helped Curtis shrug off the accouterments of an early-talkie acting style—to become the more subdued, sophisticated Grant of *An Affair to Remember* and other late films —and how Joe E. Brown trapped Lemmon into the awful transsexual consequences of an effeminate movie presence.

To escape from some Chicago mobsters, Curtis and Lemmon don matted wigs and padded bras and join an all-girl jazz band. "Being" a girl—and falling in love with a real girl whose love life has been pocked with fast-talking heels like himself—teaches Curtis generosity; his role as the Grant millionaire is a distorted mirror image of his own character, since both avoid contact with the girls who chase after them. At any rate, Curtis is far more comfortable as Grant than as a girl. Lemmon "lives" his part too well: he becomes the role he plays, a flapper in search of a millionaire. When Lemmon takes off his wig, he looks ridiculous and incomplete, like the girlish second bananas in many early-talkies (Glenn Tryon). At first Lemmon had to convince himself that he was a girl; after becoming engaged to Brown, he keeps repeating: "I'm a guy, I'm a guy. I wish I was dead."

Curtis's masculinity is asserted for good when, again dressed as a girl and in the middle of the final chase sequence, he stops to hear Monroe singing "I'm Thru With Love." Music was hardly the making of Monroe's career, and yet that sad and remarkable decade of stardom can be summarized by two songs she performed. "Diamonds Are a Girl's Best Friend" (in *Gentlemen Prefer Blondes*) expresses a delicious comedy timing that was too often exploited and distended by Hawks, Wilder, and her other directors. And "I'm Thru With Love" is worth all the Method performances she never gave; it encapsulates a tawdry childhood, three disappointing marriages, the adulation-mockery of curious fans, even a final, abortive phone call. Astoundingly enough, Monroe's singing builds audacious swirls of tremolos and breathiness on the solid foundation of a confident vocal technique.

It's this combination of audacity and assurance that marks a great performance—one thinks of Garbo in *Camille,* Vivien Leigh in *A Streetcar Named Desire,* Anna Magnani in *The Miracle.* Because these actresses excelled in other roles, while Monroe played simple parts well and difficult ones insecurely, the tendency is to shrug off her few epiphanies as happy accidents. Say rather that Monroe's more obvious attributes, at least as they were apprehended by moviemakers and movie-goers alike, deprived her of the chance to exalt instead of merely to excite. Twenty years later, when Hollywood had died and been replaced by Nashville, she might have been a greater singer than she was an actress—and as great a star.

Wilder caps this brilliant sequence with Curtis's entrance. He steps onto the stage, holds her face in his hands, kisses her, and, seeing her tears, says, "None of that, Sugar. No man is worth it." It is a moment as bizarre and powerful as anything in *Sunset Boulevard,* and yet as tender and tragic as the Garbo–Douglas apartment scene in *Ninotchka.* For the gabby, grabby little men whose portraits Wilder so often drew, it marks a coming of age, almost a redemption. And those who think of Wilder as a smalltime cynic, peddling imitation Berliner *Weltschmerz,* will find their definitive refutation in the conviction, technique, assurance, and audacity of a simple kiss between an aging sex queen and a Bronx boy in drag.

[1974]

# THE FORTIES AND FIFTIES

## PRESTON STURGES
### Andrew Sarris

There has been a flurry of Preston Sturges revivals around town in recent months, and they promise to continue. But who is this Preston Sturges, and why is he so frequently revived? I have written on the subject of Sturges's films for the past twenty-five years, and this is where I stand at the moment.

Sturges enjoyed his greatest success between 1940 and 1944 as the acknowledged successor to Ernst Lubitsch on the Paramount lot. *The Great McGinty* and *Christmas in July* (1940), *The Lady Eve* (1941), *Sullivan's Travels* and *The Palm Beach Story* (1942), and *The Miracle of Morgan's Creek, Hail the Conquering Hero,* and *The Great Moment* (1944) expressed a satiric, often savage vision of American life at a time when movies tended to be smothered in sanctimoniousness. Hence, even at the time of his greatest success, he was overshadowed by the emotions aroused by the war and the stylistic revolution ushered in by *Citizen Kane.* He received an Academy Award for the script of *The Great McGinty* in 1940, and was nominated for *The Miracle of Morgan's Creek* and *Hail the Conquering Hero,* though again as a writer rather than as a director. If anything, he was considered too much of a one-man circus for the good of the studio system. The romantic agony of *auteur*ism was not appreciated in Hollywood then if indeed it has been to this day. At that, Sturges was regarded as infinitely less subversive than Welles, and considerably more adaptable to the public's needs. By the same token, Welles's greater solemnity was taken as greater seriousness. And the young, particularly, prefer solemnity to hilarity in their cult heroes, which is why Stroheim and Welles have tended to fare better than Lubitsch and Sturges in the film histories.

What distinguished Sturges from his contemporaries was the frantic congestion of his comedies. The Brueghel of American comedy directors, Sturges created a world of peripheral professionals—politicians, gangsters, executives, bartenders, cab drivers, secretaries, bookies, cardsharps, movie producers, doctors, dentists, bodyguards, butlers, inventors, dilettantes, and derelicts. These were not the usual flotsam and jetsam of Hollywood cinema but self-expressive cameos of aggressive individualism. With his sensitive ear for dialect humor Sturges managed to preserve all the lumpiness in the melting pot. In this context, Akim Tamiroff's quintessentially crooked political boss in *The Great McGinty* spoke for all of Sturges's genial rascals when he declared with ringing, heavily accented conviction: "America is a land of great opportunity." Unlike Capra and Riskin with their Christian populist melodramas, Sturges never sentimentalized the "little people" of the earth. Hence, his bit players never coalesced into a monolithic mob but, rather, dispersed into a brawling aggregation of aggrieved babblers. Indeed, Sturges was severely criticized in 1944 for toying with the emotional expectations of his audience by transforming an apparent lynch mob in *Hail the Conquering Hero* into a crowd of well-wishers. In a way, both *Hail the Conquering Hero* and *The Miracle of Morgan's Creek* can be considered as sophisticated parodies of *Mr. Smith Goes to Washington* and *Meet John Doe*. Even in the casting of jug-eared Eddie Bracken as the persecuted innocent, Sturges seemed to caricature the Capra-esque Christ-like agony of such icons of folksy idealism as James Stewart and Gary Cooper.

Sturges was criticized at his peak by James Agee and Manny Farber for an ambivalence in his work derived from a childhood conflict between a culturally demanding mother and an admired businessman stepfather. This unusually Freudian analysis of the director's work—unusual, that is, for its time—sought to explain the incongruity of Continental sophistication being challenged by American pragmatism. Sturges himself was seen as an uneasy mixture of savant and wise guy. On the one hand, his extreme literacy, rare among Hollywood screenwriters, enabled him to drop words like "ribaldry" and "vestal" into their proper contexts without a pretentious thud. On the other, he seemed to retreat into playful evasion whenever his deepest feelings were engaged. His movies therefore reflect a civilized skepticism about old conventions without the radical sensibility to create new ones. He could thus make jokes about the binary inevitability of boy-meets-girl scenarios, and then turn around and write the most lyrical love scenes of his era. Consequently, an appreciation of Hollywood movies for their own sake is necessary if one is to perceive the nuances of Sturges's talent. He made good movies, but not anti-movies, which is to say that he needed the system as much as the system needed him.

After 1944 when he left Paramount to form a short-lived partnership with Howard Hughes, Sturges's career suffered a precipitous decline. His three subsequent Hollywood films—*Mad Wednesday, Unfaithfully Yours,* and *The Beautiful Blonde from Bashful Bend*—were remote from the tastes of their time, and during his long exile in the fifties, his one realized European project, the bilingual *Les Carnets de Major Thompson (The French They Are a Funny Race),* was a singularly lethargic letdown. He died of a heart attack at the Algonquin in 1959, and he was never mourned or memorialized in the movie colony as he should have been.

Fortunately, the place of Preston Sturges in film history will remain secure as long as his movies continue to circulate widely. Seen in a block, the Sturges *œuvre* reveals a consistent stylistic pattern. Like most effective comedy directors, he depended more on the pacing of action and dialogue than on visual texture and composition. His canvas was flat, his sense of space shallow. Sturges employed long, uncut, "single-take" scenes to establish the premises of his elaborate scripts. In this he resembled the other directors who came to cinema after sound (Ophüls, Cukor, Mamoulian, Preminger). But when Sturges shifted to slapstick, he often cut to reactions before the action had been terminated. Indeed, his instinct for timing comedy montage made his films the funniest of their era in terms of audience laughter. He was capable of cinematic license with a talking horse or a portrait that changed expression. When he wanted to speed up the plot, he dispensed with dialogue altogether as he filled the screen with the hurtling bodies of silent farce. In *Mad Wednesday,* he went so far as to begin with the last reel of Harold Lloyd's 1925 classic, *The Freshman,* after which he embellished Lloyd's vertiginous comedy effects with even wilder Sturges variations. Curiously, the very critics who lamented the Lost Golden Age of Silent Comedy failed to appreciate Sturges's rousing efforts of resurrection. Admittedly, some of the Sturges slapstick was clumsy and forced. There are a few too many slugging matches between Brian Donlevy and Akim Tamiroff in *The Great McGinty,* and a bit too much fruit-throwing in *Christmas in July.* Eugene Pallette throws too much of a tantrum at the breakfast table in *The Lady Eve,* and Joel McCrea and Veronica Lake splash down once too often in the swimming pool in *Sullivan's Travels.*

On the credit side of the comic ledger are the tumultuous tell-all honeymoon night of Barbara Stanwyck and Henry Fonda in *The Lady Eve* (complete with train steaming into tunnel), the Mack Sennett chase of a midget race car by a studio land yacht fully equipped with slapstick and cheesecake elements in the Swiftian (in more senses than one) *Sullivan's Travels,* the convulsions of the contest jury in *Christmas in July,* the morning-after confrontation of Eddie Bracken and William Demarest over a daughter's (Betty Hutton's) honor in *The Miracle of Morgan's Creek,* the election night frolic in *The Great McGinty,* and the instant masochism of Rudy Vallee's courtship of Claudette Colbert in *The Palm Beach Story.* In each instance, a piece of physical action is either set up or capped by a clever line of dialogue.

Still, the delicate mechanism of a Sturges scenario cannot be considered simply as a laugh machine. The dramatic structure is too intricate and convoluted, the mood invariably mixed. In the very midst of a loud guffaw one is surprised to find a lump in one's throat and tears in one's eyes. Unlike most contemporary filmmakers Sturges could generally balance buddy-buddy camaraderie with man-woman comradeship. An exception is *The Great McGinty,* which is actually diluted by the school-marm reformism of Muriel Angelus when all Brian Donlevy and Akim Tamiroff really want to do is to wallow in the trough of civic corruption. But from *The Great McGinty* on, Sturges developed a gallery of tough, intelligent, and yet vulnerable females with Ellen Drew in *Christmas in July,* Barbara Stanwyck in *The Lady Eve,* Claudette Colbert and Mary Astor in *The Palm Beach Story,* Veronica Lake in *Sullivan's Travels,* Betty Hutton and Diana Lynn in *The Miracle of Morgan's Creek,* and Ella Raines in *Hail the Conquering Hero.* The distinctive sweetness of Sturges's films can be attributed to his deep emotional involvement with the roller-coaster rides to success and sexual fulfillment which he seemed to be satirizing. As a walking success story in his own right, Sturges never sneered complacently at the people coming up after him in his movie fables. There was in his restless and unruly characters none of the radical-chic litany of knowing one's place in the class struggle. People were always barging in where they weren't wanted in a Sturges movie, and if they were booted out, well, they just brushed themselves off and went about their business, their pugnacity and self-esteem miraculously undiminished. Indeed, the sheer likability of his American characters marks Sturges as a throwback to the long-ago-and-faraway forties, when Americans still liked themselves a lot.

Ultimately, Sturges can never be fully appreciated by non-English-speaking critics any more than Sacha Guitry can be fully appreciated by non-French-speaking critics. He was by far the wittiest scriptwriter the English-speaking cinema has known, even though he tended to lapse into garrulousness. He loved to play with words and names for their own sake (e.g., Diddlebock, Kockenlocker, Woodrow Truesmith) with the result that his asides were usually more devastating than other writers' punch lines. In a Sturgean context it did not seem unusual for a gravel-voiced bus driver to use the word "paraphrase" nor for a hoodlum to invoke the ruinous symmetry of "Samson and Delilah, Sodom and Gomorrah." A stereotyped performer like Eric Blore was virtually rediscovered savoring the line: "I positively swill in his ale." Similarly, Edgar Kennedy was resurrected from two-reelers to play an inspired bartender reacting to a customer's asking for his first drink ever: "Sir, you rouse the artist in me." The Sturges stock company was particularly noted for the contrasting personalities of William Demarest, the rowdy roughneck, and Franklin Pangborn, the prissy prune.

Yet Sturges was capable also of great eloquence, as is evident in his passionate prologue to *The Great Moment,* a piece of writing that is particularly admirable for having been turned out in the midst of all the propaganda of World War II: "One of the most charming characteristics of Homo Sapiens —the wise guy on your left—is the consistency with which he has stoned, crucified, burned at the stake, and otherwise rid himself of those who consecrated their lives to his further comfort and well-being so that all his strength and cunning might be preserved for the creation of ever larger monuments, memorial shafts, triumphal arches, pyramids, and obelisks to the eternal glory of generals on horseback, tyrants, usurpers, dictators, politicians, and other heroes who led him, usually from the rear, to dismemberment and death."

[1975]

# THE MIRACLE OF MORGAN'S CREEK
## Gary Arnold

Part of the delight in watching a Preston Sturges comedy like *The Miracle of Morgan's Creek* derives from sheer, admiring wonder. How, you ask yourself, did he get a name like Trudy Kockenlocker (which sounds no more innocent when it's spoken) past the censors?

Next you ask yourself how he got the whole sneaky plot past the censors. Sturges probably went even further in his subsequent picture, *Hail the Conquering Hero,* another audacious and peculiarly ambivalent comic balancing act that somehow, in the middle of wartime, managed to flatter America's sentimental self-images one moment and satirize the pants off them the next.

Reviewing *Miracle* in *The Nation* in February 1944, James Agee wrote:

> Sturges tells this story according to a sound principle which has been ne-
> glected in Hollywood—except by him—for a long time in proportion to the
> inanity and repressiveness of the age you live in, play the age as comedy if
> you want to get away with murder. The girl's name . . . of itself relegates
> her to a comic-strip world in which nothing need be regarded as real . . .
> and the wildly factitious story makes comic virtues of every censor-dodging
> necessity. Thanks to these devices the Hays office has been either hypnotized
> into a liberality for which it should be thanked, or has been raped in its sleep.

It's also possible that Hays-office chief Joseph Breen, not exactly a prude in private, was amused enough to play favorites or look the other way. At least it would be satisfying to believe that one great kidder recognized another— and acknowledged a superior attempt to beat the hypocritical game everyone in the business was compelled to play.

Among other underhanded tricks, Sturges includes an implicit parody of the Christmas story, as it might be retold by a shamelessly imaginative press agent, making it the kind of only-in-America success story that is destined to sell a million papers, as well as a million items of whatever products the lucky couple elects to endorse. Trudy Kockenlocker is the name of the heroine, a dumb fun-loving small-town girl played by Betty Hutton. She has a smart kid sister played by Diana Lynn and both of them are a torment to their irritable widower father, the local constable, played with a wonderful, scowling, slow burn by William Demarest, perhaps the greatest "type" in the Sturges stock company.

Officer Kockenlocker, disturbed by newspaper articles about war marriages, refuses to let Trudy attend the big social affair of the season, a farewell Saturday night dance for the boys at a nearby army base. Trudy, moved by patriotic fervor and self-interest, resorts to a ruse. She hoodwinks the poor schnook who adores her, a stammering, masochistic little bank teller named Norval Jones (who else but Eddie Bracken?), into covering for her.

While Papa thinks she's with Norval at a triple bill (Sturges gives us a glimpse of a poster advertising one of the films, *Wings Over Taos,* attributed to Paramount and starring those great favorites "Armando Torrez" and "Maria Robles"), Trudy is actually dancing the night away with our brave boys. Norval, a 4-F, accepts the facts of life stoically. His impassioned self-defense gets sidetracked—"They also serve who only stand and . . . well, whatever it is they stand and do; I forget what it is." Later he muses, "I guess you can't blame a girl for preferring soldiers to civilians. Maybe it would be different if we had uniforms."

As it happens, Trudy has been doing more than dancing the night away. She has no clear memory of anything that transpired after one of the boys lofted her during a jitterbug and cracked her head on a chandelier. However, she retains a vague, portentous memory of someone saying, "Let's all get married," and then of everyone doing it, only under assumed names. Probing deep into her memory, she believes the name of her mate might have been something "with a 'z' in it, like Ratskiwatski."

The cream of the jest, particularly in terms of censor-dodging, is that Sturges uses Trudy's loss of memory on this point to camouflage a rather more basic and unaccountable oversight: in the fullness of time Trudy discovers that she's pregnant. The obvious solution is to hoodwink poor Norval again. At first Trudy resists, saying, "I can't do that to him; we'll have to find someone else." Her sister asks, decisively, "Where do you think you'll find another clunk like Norval?"

Sturges constructed the finest talking comedy machines in movie history. It's a giddy pleasure to watch them operate and particularly to listen to the sounds they emit, that rapid, almost nonstop stream of dialogue, with virtually every character talking a surreal blue streak. In *Miracle,* the colloquies between Betty Hutton and Eddie Bracken leave you feeling slightly delirious, especially exchanges like the following, which occurs after Trudy has learned the embarrassing obstetric news:

> BRACKEN: I thought you enjoyed yourself at the dance, Trudy.
> MISS HUTTON: I did, Norval, but some kinds of fun last longer than others, if you get what I mean.

In recent years only the Italian comedy *The Pizza Triangle* has tried to operate on all the levels that Sturges once manipulated, mixing high- and low-comedy techniques, simultaneously satirizing and appealing to popular instincts and sentiments. While some of our best recent films have been comedies—*Bob & Carol & Ted & Alice, M\*A\*S\*H, Bananas*—none of them has reproduced the multiple pleasures of a Sturges show. Their styles are more leisurely or episodic or hit-and-miss, and there hasn't been a really funny plot since *The Producers.* Good as they are, these pictures don't have the comprehensive attack of a good Sturges effort, which kept dialogue, characterization, plot, social satire, slapstick, and topicality humming away in comic unison or counterpoint. We can click on certain cylinders, but Sturges seemed to click on all of them, while handicapped by the censor peering over his shoulder.

[1971]

# FRANK TASHLIN
## *Stuart Byron*

"In fifteen years' time," wrote a Parisian critic named Jean-Luc Godard in 1957, "people will realize that *The Girl Can't Help It* served then—today, that is—as a fountain of youth from which the cinema now—in the future, that is —has drawn inspiration." Well, it's now two years after Godard's deadline, and sure enough the movie—only a moderate success in its day—is being given an official reissue, just like *Gone with the Wind* or *The Sound of Music*, with a major advertising campaign. Is Godard's prediction justified?

Yes and no. *The Girl Can't Help It* was made by the late Frank Tashlin— a Hollywood director whose films of the fifties and early sixties were considered vulgar by American critics but who was lionized by the *Cahiers du Cinéma* writers in Paris who were later to make up the New Wave. Ironically, the reason for reissuing it has nothing to do with any perception on the part of 20th Century-Fox that it had in its vaults a movie that was seventeen years ahead of its time. Rather, it is the film's wealth of numbers by pop and rock groups of the era—The Platters, Fats Domino, Little Richard—which has caused the company to hook onto the nostalgia wave. The story is a satire on the music biz: A gangster's moll with no voice (Jayne Mansfield) is made into a pop star by an agent (Tom Ewell) at the behest of the mobster in love with her (Edmond O'Brien).

What makes the film a New Wave precursor? Its anarchic mixture of comedy and drama, with no attempt at smoothness—the very thing which made Tashlin seem awful to American critics. A scene will start ultraseriously —Ewell rehearsing with Mansfield, for example—and without warning a cartoon incident will take place: her voice will *literally* shatter glass. In one scene a group of gangsters will be as threatening as in any melodrama, and in the next they will be seen as buffoons. Although the whole point about the Mansfield character is that she wants to be nothing but a housewife and mother, psychology is thrown to the winds as she acts throughout like a caricature of a "sex pot"—even in scenes taking place in private.

Thus, Tashlin was an unconscious "Brechtian"—realism was shunted aside; he *wanted* you to be aware that you were watching a film, not a re-enactment of life, a position emphasized by having Ewell address the audience directly at the beginning and end of the movie. Is there a better definition of the New Wave sensibility? When Truffaut, in *Shoot the Piano Player,* does that famous insert shot of a mother dying immediately after her son has wished her death —there is Tashlin's influence. When Godard, in *Breathless,* presents the police inspector as a graceful pro in one scene and then as an awkward fool the next —there is the influence of Tashlin. There's no mistaking it: the New Wave— which is, after all, the most influential cinematic movement of the last twenty years—would have been impossible without Frank Tashlin.

And yet the funny thing is that as a piece of entertainment *The Girl Can't Help It* doesn't hold up—except, of course, for its rock numbers. Tashlin might have alternated his moods in a daring and unprecedented manner—but *what* he alternated was banal. Though his characters sometimes exhibit surprising depth, they never escape cliché—Ewell is little more than the standard show-business sellout rediscovering his integrity. And the jokes, original as they may be in their cartoon conception (Tashlin started out as a Disney animator), just aren't funny. Strangely enough, this instinctual director commands only intellectual interest now; film buffs can gasp at his influence, but like the general public they won't really be enjoying themselves in the process.

[1974]

# JERRY LEWIS
## *Stuart Byron*

"There is a certain something I have with young people. I think they feel that I am one of them. They see in me a noisy, raucous, jerky guy doing things for money that they would be doing anyway," says Jerry Lewis. "All kids need attention, consideration, love, and affection," he insists. "You can't tell a kid, every time he wants to ask you a question, 'Go away; don't bother me. I'm talking to Aunt Sarah now.' And then when he walks in one day with a switchblade knife in his hands, say to him, 'Oh, my darling, where did you learn such bad things? Certainly not from me.' "

Born Joseph Levitch in Newark, New Jersey, on March 16, 1926, to Danny and Rae Lewis (a stage name), Jerry was, in his own words, "an unwanted child right from the beginning, because I came from show people. My parents had a big problem as soon as they had me. They were on tour most of the time and it wasn't easy for them to look after me."

As a result, he was often placed in the care of friends or relatives. Sometimes he traveled with his parents. He attended thirty schools in two years during one stretch. Of course, he didn't put down roots or make friends. These years filled him with loneliness and a sense of rejection he has not altogether shaken off. So his heart goes out to a kid in trouble.

And it is this "Kid"—as he himself often refers to it—that has become his screen character, especially since the breakup with Dean Martin. In all the films since then—all but one directed and written by himself or by his friend and acknowledged "teacher" Frank Tashlin—Jerry has portrayed the adult whose emotions have been frozen at the mental age of about fourteen and who retains the desperate loneliness, the desperate sense of rejection, the desperate desire to please of the awkward and alone boy of that age. In his last two films especially, there have been long—and quite "serious"—flashbacks to traumatic adolescent incidents of this type. In *The Patsy,* for example, there is the beautiful sequence—done in a pantomime that without question equals the great silent comedians—in which Jerry, as a wrongly dressed and rejected outsider at a high-school dance, is turned down by all of the quite all-American-looking girls and finds a brief happiness dancing on an empty floor with another ugly duckling, Ina Balin. In *The Disorderly Orderly,* the emotional backwardness of the character is directly traced to his having been hopelessly in love with the standardly beautiful high-school cheerleader played by Susan Oliver.

Of late, certain critics—especially French and Latin-American ones—have come to realize that Lewis has really made this view of life into a true comic vision that can be discussed on a par with Chaplin's, Keaton's, and Laurel and Hardy's. But it is different from theirs in that it embodies a world based more on *nonsense* (à la Lewis Carroll) than on *slapstick* (Chaplin and Keaton).

It is a world, for example, where the physical properties of objects often are eliminated in a reflection of a child's unmechanical view of the universe. In *The Errand Boy,* for example, every object takes on its own independent life: transistor radios blare with no way of stopping them, bottles of champagne have absolutely inexhaustible supplies of liquid, puppets take on real and unmaneuvered life, the entire contents of a water cooler pour into a four-ounce cup. In *It's Only Money,* Jerry at one point, while shaving, notices his resemblance to the bearded personage in a painting; so he proceeds to shave the beard off the painting with his electric razor!

But this childlike attitude is reflected also in his uncontrollable happiness every time a small project is successfully accomplished. A moment of fantastic comic beauty is achieved in *The Disorderly Orderly* when Lewis plays a record on a juke box. In close-up, we see him grimace with satisfaction as the button is pushed, the selector correctly chooses the record he has picked, and the needle falls on the disc. There is also his childlike feeling that if he can't see something, he's lost it: his face in the shaving foam on a mirror, or a baby in a pile of talcum powder.

In every other version of Robert Louis Stevenson's book, Dr. Jekyll has been the handsome one and Mr. Hyde the ugly monster. But in *The Nutty Professor* it was the bucktoothed and clumsy professor who stood for heart-warming goodness and the smooth, handsome, and conceited Buddy Love who personified evil. This, one could say, is Jerry's vision: that the ugly and the awkward and the spastic are the beautiful. Jerry Lewis's well-known devotion to children's causes is no mere appendage to his art—not the normal feelings of an entertainer that he should be known publicly as a supporter of charitable enterprises. Rather, it is an integral part of his life, his art, his screen character, his comic and aesthetic vision.

[1964]

# BLAKE EDWARDS
### Stuart Byron

Peter Sellers's first two films for Blake Edwards, the Inspector Clouseau duo of 1964—*The Pink Panther* and *A Shot in the Dark*—are just as funny now as when first released, two of the best comedies an American has ever made. But the audience that sees them in 1974 doesn't do so in the same context as when I saw them a decade ago.

Nowadays the director is often a star, but in the early sixties there were very few directors whose names had any box-office power—Hitchcock and Wilder were in that company, but for all their Oscars, Ford and Zinnemann and Wyler and Stevens meant nothing to ordinary film-goers. But after the spectacular success of the Clouseau films, polls actually showed that the name "Blake Edwards" on a film was a marketable commodity. Commercially, his reputation had begun with his sixth film, the military comedy *Operation Petticoat* (1959), Universal's biggest grosser to that date, and critically it had started with *Breakfast at Tiffany's* (1961), Andrew Sarris's "directorial surprise" of the year and subject of Edwards's first full-length review (by Eric Rohmer) in *Cahiers du Cinéma.* After that, every one had at least one fave. If Pauline Kael raved about *The Pink Panther,* Bosley Crowther of the *Times* loved *A Shot in the Dark.* British critics were enraptured by 1963's melodrama of alcoholism, *Days of Wine and Roses.* And all of these were outstanding commercial successes.

But Edwards's emergence was significant because he was the first of the made-in-Hollywood directors to achieve such recognition. Unlike the early pioneers, he did not come to an embryonic Hollywood from a rural background. Nor did he serve the apprenticeship in the New York theater characteristic of the postwar generation of directors (Kazan, Ray, Losey). Nor did he emerge from the "Studio One"–"Playhouse 90" New York television group of around 1955 (Lumet, Frankenheimer, Penn). His father had been in the industry, he had spent most of his life in Los Angeles, he had pushed his way from the bottom of the Hollywood heap to the top by writing scripts for second features and writing and directing television series. He proved that Hollywood did not have to look to prestigious outside sources to find new directorial talent but could grow its own. Without the Edwards example, such people as Jewison, Schaffner, Altman, and Coppola might never have been given a chance.

But after *A Shot in the Dark,* the bubble burst. Edwards grew cocky—with his financial success and with his audience recognition. His next movie *The Great Race,* started out as a medium-budget six-million dollar comedy and ended up a big-budget twelve-million-dollar spectacular which never earned back its costs. And after that, nothing seemed to work, no matter how small or large the budget. Only the *auteur*ists supported him critically, and the public stayed away from *Gunn, What Did You Do in the War, Daddy?, The Party,* and *Darling Lili.* His going five million dollars over budget on *Lili* was "leaked" by Paramount to every columnist, and suddenly the man who once represented the New Hollywood became stigmatized as the symbol of the Old.

Only the settlement of an old deal at M-G-M kept him working—working at the studio with the most antidirectorial production policy, working at a studio whose president liked to rip apart directors' versions of films with a lawn mower. If the western *The Wild Rovers* was doomed from the beginning (I happened to read it in script form and didn't like it then), only Metro can be blamed for the failure of *The Carey Treatment*—a thriller that might have been Edwards's best and most popular film had M-G-M not whimsically cut it so that it didn't even make narrative sense. By the time Metro went under last year, the fifty-one-year-old man whose career it had definitively ruined had already moved, bitterly, to England with his wife Julie Andrews. The man whose feel for Los Angeles was second to none—the surreal collision between L.A. and Boston which Edwards tried to produce in *Carey* might have been clearer to Bostonians had Edwards's cut been released—now lives in London and is, for all practical purposes, a director in exile, having just made, for a British producer, *The Tamarind Seed,* an espionage thriller with Andrews and Omar Sharif.

Maybe I'm being unduly pessimistic; many of his best movies, after all, were made in Europe, including the Clouseau films. Yet Edwards seems so very American: he's the most urban, hard-boiled, glossy of directors, and his films deal so largely with the worlds of money and theater, of advertising and promotion, of the jet set, of gangsters and call girls. The one time that Edwards, who had never ventured further back into time than 1900, had attempted a true period piece, *Wild Rovers,* he had gotten lost in the Arizona wilderness. For all its personal touches, a few remarkably moving scenes, it was one of his few artistic failures.

With the singular exception of *Darling Lili,* I've never felt able to write about an Edwards movie as a single entity, a problem I don't have with other *auteurs*. His films meet Auden's test for the important artist: "his various works, taken together, make one consistent *œuvre.* " So what I have to say about the Clouseau films isn't so much about them as about how they reflect some common Edwards themes:

*Winners and losers.* As befits anyone who grew up in a Hollywood atmosphere, this was Edwards's earliest theme. His "Universal period" of the late fifties is characterized by three films with Tony Curtis: *Mister Cory, The Perfect Furlough,* and *Operation Petticoat,* in all of which Curtis played variations on the William Holden character in Wilder's *Stalag 17.* Rebuffed in his attempts to cash into high society, Curtis leaves the plush lake resort where he works in *Cory* and becomes a "winner" on his own terms: he wins over a deb after making a bundle in casino operations. *Furlough* and *Petticoat* have Curtis as the military "winner" who is past master at securing hordes of mattresses, blankets, chocolate bars, nylons, and women.

Clouseau was an original comic creation because, unlike Chaplin or Jerry Lewis—though perhaps a bit like Keaton—he's a loser who always *thinks* he's a winner. Everything always goes wrong for the French detective, but he constantly imagines it is going right—that he can secure anything instantly, including women. But unlike previous characters, he doesn't ultimately "really win"; in *Panther* it is he, and not the real thieves, who goes to jail for stealing the jewels. *The Pink Panther* is sometimes accused of cruelty and cynicism, but it's more a cold, dispassionate, "absurd" updating of traditional comedy themes. Edwards was the first "modern" director in his acceptance of comic pessimism.

*Gallantry.* But he's also the last classicist, which means the last *traditional* sexist. His nostalgia for an age when men were chivalrous toward women is too sincere to be denied its artistry. *Operation Petticoat* centers on the reaction of a World War II submarine crew to the presence of a group of women during a battle voyage, and the comedy derives from the necessity of the men to act gallantly in an age when such behavior had become a dimly remembered part of the past. If once a warrior carried his lady's standard, in *Petticoat* a necessity to paint the ship pink is misinterpreted; the U.S. ship is fired upon by American forces!

Clouseau plays out a gallant role. Maintaining his dignity—his self-image —is his overriding and absurd concern. He never ceases to believe in himself even as his maladroitness is denying it. In *A Shot in the Dark* especially, he sees himself as a Knight Gallant protecting a damsel in distress, though the age should deny him such a function.

*Fathers and sons.* Not the least curious and moving part of *Panther* does not concern Sellers's Clouseau at all, but involves son Robert Wagner's attempt to win the love of his father David Niven—whom he hasn't seen in years —by following him into the cat-burglar trade. Said Edwards, in an interview with me, when he was in New York for the opening of *Wild Rovers:* "Sure, *Rovers* is a 'love story' between two men, an older, William Holden, and a younger, Ryan O'Neal. There have been relationships like that since at least *Cory* in 1957, when Charles Bickford took Curtis under his wing and taught him the gambling trade. Something like that happens in *This Happy Feeling, Operation Petticoat, High Time, Panther,* and also in *Soldier in the Rain,* which I produced but didn't direct. Is it a search for a father? I won't dispute that. I always felt alienated, estranged from my own father, Jack McEdward, a veteran production manager in the industry. I wanted to be closer to him, and we're closer now—but it took a long time."

*Cartoon.* The man who decided upon those animated credit sequences for *Panther* and *Shot*— they caused a sensation at the time—has a financial but not a creative interest in their dreadful offshoots, the "Pink Panther" and "Inspector" cartoon series. Nonetheless, if any director has turned live-action characters into cartoonlike creations, it is Edwards. As Richard McGuinness has pointed out, James Coburn in *The Carey Treatment* is best understood as deriving from Bugs Bunny or Tom (of Tom and Jerry). Beaten to a pulp, the way Bugs or Tom are distorted into squares or stretched across miles, like them he immediately returns to normal and to his mission as if nothing's happened.

Clouseau has that same indestructibility, though he's almost never physically beaten. He's simply mindless, with no consciousness of the outside world's view of him, no sense of being hurt psychologically. You can't say or do anything to freak him out; he always returns to his bumbling detective work as if nothing had occurred. If Clouseau is screwed at the end of *Pink Panther,* he gets his revenge in *A Shot in the Dark.* Here the absurd cruelty saves him. There has rarely been a sequence quite so daring in an American comedy as the one when a gunman tries to kill Clouseau four different times and ends up killing four innocent bystanders. And the ending, when a bomb planted for Clouseau ends up by blowing all of the villains sky-high, is funny—*really* funny—because Edwards instills it with the nonhuman ethos of the animated cartoon.

[1974]

# CONTEMPORARY TRENDS

It wasn't the production of comedy that seemed dead by the late fifties, but the art. Hollywood kept churning them out. Every Broadway comedy hit from *Harvey* (1950) to *The Reluctant Debutante* (1958) was a sure Hollywood sale. As was already noted, domestic and family comedies were produced aplenty. And, toward the end of the decade, Doris Day was continually defending her virginity in a series of films which were simultaneously the delight of the mass audience and the despair of serious film critics, for whom they symbolized the dire state of film comedy. Meanwhile, Blake Edwards had not yet hit his stride. Only Billy Wilder seemed committed to fashioning funny films which paid attention to the great traditions of the past *(Some Like It Hot)* or extended them to new areas *(The Apartment)*.

The Hollywood situation was, in some ways, strange. In night club and coffeehouse, comedy went through its most profoundly original transformation since vaudeville. Improvisatory humorists (the Second City troupe, for example) probed love and marriage in ways that were freshly adult and modern, while the so-called sick humorists (notably Mort Sahl, Lenny Bruce) probed society and politics in ways that reflected the extreme skepticism of the nuclear age. But all that was, at the time, the entertainment of an educated elite, and if it didn't make it to a mass medium like the movies until the sixties, that perhaps provides additional evidence that Hollywood always "lags" behind high culture by a decade or so.

For film creators, the result of this anticomedy climate in Hollywood was often a deep frustration. Even such a conventional craftsman as writer-director Melville Shavelson found it impossible to escape from the routine Bob Hope vehicles he was making and still remain a comedy director. In 1964, he complained to Arthur Knight that because "a few years back, the studios were even afraid to do comedy, much less satire," he had been forced to turn a script originally written as a satire into a humorless drama.

The social factors that caused Hollywood to enter a "new era" at around 1963 have been much discussed. There seems little doubt that the most important was the coming of age of the huge generation produced by the postwar "baby boom." These children of prosperity— who benefited from a then-current belief in universal higher education, and were young enough to have a great deal of disposable income and leisure time—were hardly an elite. All of a sudden there was a large enough audience to make it profitable for Hollywood to cater to what had been only a few years before coffeehouse taste.

To more traditional observers, the first sign of the new sensibility was sexual, and here Hollywood had prepared the way. True, the constraining Production Code was not to be revised until 1966 (and then, in 1968, made essentially irrelevant by the ratings system). But by the time the new comedy era got under way with the sleeper success of the bawdy *Tom Jones* in 1963, the old Code was more honored in the breach than in the practice. Neither the transvestism in *Some Like It Hot* nor the explicit acknowledgment of extramarital relations in *The Apartment* would have been allowed, except under restrictively heavy camouflage, at the time when the Code was being strictly enforced. Major studios felt no compunction about releasing even franker comedies under the aegis of wholly owned subsidiaries created solely to avoid the Code—most notably Jules Dassin's big-grossing whore-with-a-heart-of-gold story *Never on Sunday* (1960). This relaxation about sex was the aspect of the new sensibility that the industry was most prepared for.

Other changes in the audience were more subtle, and more surprising. The generation proved a hardheaded, perhaps even cynical, one, at least insofar as it refused to accept unapologetic expressions of love or sentiment. No longer could comedy, as in its screwball phase, lead up to the kind of climax that could be characterized as a "mushy love scene." No more, as in Capra, Sturges, or Tashlin, could it be structured toward ringing declarations of faith in the common man, patriotism, or honesty. For the first time, comedy in the sixties was often to be accused of inhumanity. Directors, perhaps afraid that they would lose their audiences by any retreat into sentimentality, were sometimes criticized for sacrificing people to gags, for denigrating all emotion except derisive laughter. The very connotation of the word "comedy" took a 180-degree turn; once associated with warmth and softness, it came to suggest something cold and hard.

This development, however, brought comedy closer in tone to other traditional movie genres. If comedy couldn't mix any longer with romantic falderal, it now was accepted as an element in gangster, espionage, and melodramatic stories. The mixed genre was born. Or, rather, the unmixed genre—for the organic amalgam of diffuse elements, including comedy, in Capra's films or Renoir's was altogether of another nature, compared to the startling juxtaposition of burlesque and murderousness in New Wave films like Godard's *Breathless* and Truffaut's *Shoot the Piano Player*. With the James Bond films, mass popularity came to the kind of movie which simultaneously accepted and denigrated not only a genre but the values of heroism, loyalty, and social order which were its reasons for being. Many observers saw in this double vision the confusion about values which characterized the sixties. But it wasn't for long just a matter of spoofs, black comedies, and other traditional categories. By the mid-seventies, the mixed genre was so accepted and was created so casually that a movie like *One Flew Over the Cuckoo's Nest,* which ends with a strangling, a lobotomy, and a mercy killing, could be reviewed widely as a comedy—and not a black one, at that.

Although the great comedy revival of the sixties was begun by directors, like Stanley Kubrick and Tony Richardson, who were not totally committed to the field, still one of its major results was the emergence of the largest group of comedy specialists since the thirties. In large measure, their comedy careers preceded their film careers as they developed a craft in night clubs (Woody Allen, Mike Nichols, Elaine May) or on television (Mel Brooks, Carl Reiner, Paul Mazursky). But what is striking is that they are all Jewish. Jewish domination of comedy has existed at least since the days of vaudeville, and almost all the purveyors of Continental sophistication in Hollywood, from Stroheim to Wilder, were also Jewish. But the present instance probably reflects some contemporary realities as well. If the Jew is quintessentially urban, he is then the most prepared for the rapid urbanization of America. The Jewish sensibility, rooted to physical reality, to life in this world, is particularly suited to express the cosmopolitan, practical, and skeptical vision of the present film audience.

# 3

## SPOOFING

Only in the sixties did critics and sophisticated film-goers come to feel at ease with the fact that the American cinema is a cinema of genres. But by that time our film directors were too self-conscious about their work to present it straight any longer. The old pros in Hollywood were learning from French critiques and American dissertations that they were creating art—which was enough to stifle anybody. And the younger directors were too aware and in awe of their mentors to imitate them without putting tongue in cheek. So as soon as the genre traditions became mature enough to be seen with some perspective, they became immediately decadent. This is especially true of the spy-thriller genre. At the same time that they thrilled, they also smiled knowingly with their audience; the more they exaggerated, the more the audience was sure that Agent 007 or that man from Rio was spoofing his own existence.

But then few of the so-called spoofs of the sixties and seventies were "pure." If they weren't half-serious like *That Man From Rio,* or that harbinger *Beat the Devil* (reissued in 1964 as "the picture that was ten years ahead of its time"), they were audacious mixtures of spoof elements with other forms of comedy, such as satire, gags, slapstick, and camp. Purists who insisted on fine distinctions were bound to be disappointed, as the new films seemed to take as their models such anarchic flops of the thirties as *Duck Soup* and *Zero for Conduct.* Of course, a spoof that is nothing more than spoof can seem a hollow exercise. Delightful as were such "send-ups" of the western as *Cat Ballou* and *Support Your Local Sheriff,* they seemed to lack reference to anything outside of their own filmic worlds. And this opened them to the kind of attack suggested by Pauline Kael in a prescient warning issued just as the current wave of spoofs was beginning. Many have also found an insular outlook in a strain of underground films which burlesqued old

Hollywood styles by such directors as Jack Smith, the Kuchar Brothers, and Andy Warhol; Warhol's western spoof, *Lonesome Cowboys,* prompts this reaction here from Richard Schickel. But just as Warhol's pop-art paintings had interpreters who defended them against the charge of meaninglessness, so the films of Warhol and of his protégé, Paul Morrissey, received "readings" by more sympathetic critics who found content where most saw only form.

Like Warhol/Morrissey, Robert Downey is an underground director (though he disputes the appellation) who has achieved an aboveground success. His *Putney Swope* was basically a satire—that is, a comic work which attacked society rather than art. Yet it had the feel of a spoof because it was about a branch of show business, and there was no abrupt change of tone between the "satire" of the people who create television commercials and the "spoofs" of the commercials themselves.

Mel Brooks, too, adopted this formula for his first movie, *The Producers,* in which a spoof of a musical comedy was part of a larger satire of the Broadway theatrical world. But with his second movie, *The Twelve Chairs,* he made a classical satire. And it was only with the hugely successful *Blazing Saddles* that he followed the lead of Woody Allen and built his comedy around the outlines of a popular genre, a practice he followed with the even bigger hit *Young Frankenstein.*

Yet it's interesting that Brooks's concerns have not really changed. All four films are built around the relationship between two men; he's the buddy-buddy man among comedy directors. And the same questions of taste have dogged him from *The Producers* (Hitler) to *Saddles* (scatology), as has an anarchic style which shuffles satire, parody, even lyricism at will.

Indeed, it's conceivable that *Saddles,* with its emphasis on race relations, is more genuinely satiric than *The Twelve Chairs.* But Brooks learned that George S. Kaufman is still right: satire is what closes on Saturday night. By placing satire in a "spoof" format, directors can apparently give the audience a handle, and a subgenre which once seemed empty at its center is ironically now serving as a sly vehicle for meaning.

This artistic strategy was one that Woody Allen, unlike Brooks, always understood; from the beginning he accepted the fact that he could best structure his comic talents around existing genres. The remarkable thing, however, is how personal he has remained despite his use of generic formats. He is, after all, the closest equivalent we have

seventies to the silent comedians who created personae around
their movies were built—and who not only starred in their films
but also wrote and directed them. Yet even as Allen adapts established
genres to his purpose—whether gangster, spy-thriller, or science-fiction
stories—he creates an inimitable style. And he can be discussed in terms
of the major backgrounds which he shares with many contemporary
comic film makers. The following articles discuss him as night-club
monologuist, ex–TV writer, Borscht Belt comedian, maker of slapstick
chase comedies, intellectual and political satirist.

But the crux of the argument about Woody Allen boils down to this:
Is he a stand-up comedian, using films merely as a medium for his
strings of one-liners, however brilliant? Or is he making real movies?
In a review of Allen's first film as a director, *What's Up Tiger Lily?*,
Andrew Sarris wrote: "High-brow theories of dramatic and cinematic
structure aside, I can't see why a comic writer should be penalized for
being too funny." And yet Sarris himself was among the critics to
downgrade Allen on just those grounds less than a decade later. It is
not really a matter of changing one's mind, but rather the difference
between promise and achievement. What seemed a trivial put-down of
a first-time director looms as legitimate criticism of one being hailed as
a proven genius from many quarters. No further proof would seem to
be needed that Woody Allen is a success.

## AGAINST SPOOFING
### Pauline Kael

"I trust ya', Honey—but cut the cards."

Advertising experts look to the future and find—a new breed of sophisticates
that will not be so easy to convince.

They're coming. The new generation of young adults. Wise, hip, skeptical
—unlike any audience businesses and advertisers have ever known before.
A new breed of sophisticates who have been deluged by advertising since
they were three. Bred to new wisdom at television's knee. Able to "tune out"
automatically at the first sign of advertising puffery. Promising advertisers
no problem so great as that of sophisticated disbelief.

Purveyors of the advertising scene see this coming. The simplest social
analysis of the highly educated, worldly American society now emerging
indicates it.

This is an almost-full-page ad in *The New York Times,* May 11 and June
16, 1965.

And what is the ad for? *Good Housekeeping* and its Consumers' Guaranty Seal. The ad closes with "Seeing it in *Good Housekeeping* is believing."

The basic flattery of the customer is familiar, but the *kind* of flattery is new. Advertising, TV commercials, movies are trying to outwit disbelief by including it in the sell.

Are those who no longer "believe" the advertising they hear and see really "a new breed of sophisticates," part of "the highly educated, worldly American society now emerging"? If disbelief were the result of knowledge, every New York cab driver would be an educated man. What this generation was bred to at television's knee was not wisdom but cynicism: it is an indication of how self-important and self-congratulatory advertising men have become that they equate the cynical indifference of those wised up to *their* methods with wisdom.

Our society is disastrously utilitarian. We can no longer distinguish the ad from the entertainment, the front cover of the national magazine, in which an actor poses to plug his film, from the back cover, in which an actor sells cigarettes and indirectly also plugs a film. Television shows with groups of celebrities are a series of plugs (for books, records, night-club appearances, movies) interrupted by commercials. Movies are constructed with product tie-ins worked into their structure: mattresses, stoves, toothpaste, airlines, whisky, all with their brand names shining. The companies so advertised in turn feature the movie in *their* ads. Even without product tie-ins, modern-dress movies look just like ads and sell the advertising way of life. This is one of the reasons why our movies seem so slickly unreal: they look like the TV commercials that nobody "believes."

The acceleration in the standardization of mass culture since the end of World War II means that we are all hit by the same commodities, personalities, ideas, forces, fashions at the same time, and hit increasingly hard. If you drive across the country you'll find the same movies playing in every town and city, *Fanny Hill* and *Candy* on sale in every drugstore, pop and op in the bank and shop. At roadside restaurants you'll hear the same semiparodistic songs coming out of juke boxes; at a motel in the middle of nowhere you'll see the same TV shows, the same commercials you saw at home. The motel itself may be an exact reproduction of other motels, and you'll drive past supermarkets and housing developments that you could swear you'd already passed. The people in the small towns smell, look, read, react like the people in the big cities; there are no sticks any more.

Only "schtik"—the fraudulent uniqueness that sells when real individuality or difference is risky. Schtik is the special bit, the magic gimmick that makes the old look new, the stale seem fresh; it is what will "grab" the public. It is the desperate hope of an easy solution when the sellers cannot predict what the public, satiated increasingly fast, will buy.

What stories will seem believable, what themes will involve modern audiences, what will interest people? The problem that the "purveyors of the advertising scene" analyze is also being double-faced by the slick magazines and by Hollywood. Like the *Mademoiselle* editor explaining why a piece of Jean Harlow fiction was being printed ("We thought it would be sort of campy and fun"), they clutch at any little schtik.

They're afraid they can't do the same old stuff any more—not straight, anyway—so they do it "tongue in cheek." They pretend they're superior to it. There is a story told about Tennessee Williams at the opening of *The Rose Tattoo*. When a stagehand said in consternation, "Why, Mr. Williams, they're laughing," Williams is supposed to have replied, "If they laugh, it's a comedy." People all over the country were bored with or laughing at advertising, commercials, magazines, movies, so the purveyors found a face-saving device. Now advertising kids advertising, TV commercials kid TV commercials, movies kid movies. They go "way-out," become "send-ups"; they nudge us that what they're doing is just a "put-on." It's as embarrassed and halfhearted a strategy as that of the fat man who makes himself a buffoon so you can't make more fun of him than he has already.

Spoofing has become the safety net for those who are unsure of their footing. Unlike satire, spoofing has no serious objectives: it doesn't attack anything that anyone could take seriously; it has no cleansing power. It's just a technique of ingratiation: the spoof apologizes for its existence, assures us that it's harmless, that it isn't aiming for beauty or expressiveness or meaning or even relevance. To many in the advertising business and to those young artists who often seem to be in the same business, it's a way of life—or, rather, a time killer on the way to the grave.

Still, the purveyors are full of anxieties. In screening rooms, the publicity men and critics can be heard asking nervously, "Will audiences outside the big cities get the joke?" Is it perhaps that they're uncertain whether *they* get it either? What *is* the point? Who is being put-on? Way-out where? Send-up what?

We're sending ourselves up. We are reaching the point at which the purveyors don't care about anything but how to sell and the buyers buy because they don't give a damn. When there is no respect on either side, commerce is a dirty word.

But not all the new generation is buying. Many of them don't just " 'tune out' automatically at the first sign of advertising puffery" because they know there's no place to tune in again. They're surrounded by selling, and they tune out, period. They want some meaning, some honesty, some deeper experience, and they try to find them in romantic ideas of rejection and revolution based on their moral revulsion from the situation in the South, or in folk music, in underground movies, in narcotics.

Even the worst underground movies—the most chaotic, confused, and boring, the most amateurish—may still look more "real," more "sincere" than industrial products like *The Sandpiper* or *Harlow,* which you can't believe, or gigantic spoofs like *The Great Race,* which you're not supposed to believe. But though the desire, the need, the clamor, among college students particularly, for underground movies grows out of important kinds of rejection, the underground movement is infected by what the students are trying to escape.

The underground cinema is largely a fabrication of publicity: the students are put-on by *Film Culture* and the *Village Voice,* and then they're fobbed off with parodies of Maria Montez movies, Andy Warhol spoofs of experimentation, and underground variants of exploitation films. And if these films often spoof old movies, new big movies are already an imitation of the underground. *What's New Pussycat?* has the kind of jokes associated with underground movies; *The Knack* is already a fashionable, professionally "youthful" treatment of underground attitudes.

A movie that looks amateurish is not necessarily an answer to commercialism—it may be an innocent or a very shrewd form of commercialism; and commercial movies can all too easily imitate the amateurish look. Thus far, underground movies are too easy an answer: they're an illusory solution to a real problem—a commercialized society that nobody believes in.

[1965]

## BEAT THE DEVIL
### Charles Champlin

In early 1954 I was worrying about politics and other disasters for *Life* magazine out of Denver, and may well have been trailing a bizarre murder case through the Southwest when John Huston's *Beat the Devil* had its first release. I missed it, but then again so did almost everybody else.

Although it has since acquired a lively cult following, of which I am a member, it has never, so far as Huston knows, returned a dime of profit. Since *Beat the Devil* apparently cost not much more than a million dollars, this is another commentary on Hollywood's unique and zany bookkeeping. But it is also a commentary on a film which seems to have been years ahead not so much of its own time as of its exhibitors' time.

It was quite cordially reviewed. My predecessor at the *Los Angeles Times,* Phil Scheuer, found it "exhilaratingly funny." *The New Yorker* called it "hugely entertaining" and full of "bright lunacy." *Time* pronounced it the most elaborate shaggy-dog story ever told. But London's *Films and Filming,* of all voices, spoke what was apparently the industry's conventional wisdom on *Beat the Devil.* "An act of self-indulgence," said its critic. "It is a private joke, amusing only to the initiated." The review, quoted in William P. Nolan's *John Huston: King Rebel,* added that it was "a film for connoisseurs, who will treasure it highly—most highly perhaps, because it is valueless for the layman. . . . Divorcement from one's audience in a medium as commercially oriented as the cinema must be considered a dangerous trend." (A remarkable scolding, that.)

Whether layman agreed then is not clear, but exhibitors did. Talking about the film a couple of years ago, Huston recalled that one theater man, forced to show *Beat the Devil* under his contract with United Artists, used his display ads in the newspapers to apologize to his faithful clientele for having to offer them so inferior a work. He promised a return to normalcy the following week, and there probably was.

The movie had begun with Humphrey Bogart, who bought the James Helvick novel for his Santana Company in hopes it might make a hard-edged, suspenseful, colorful melodrama in the tradition of *The Maltese Falcon.* But the screenplay, worked on by Anthony Veiller, Huston, and Peter Viertel, turned Bogart off completely and he wanted out.

But Huston had found the ideal location—the steep, stunning mountain town of Ravello on the Castellammare coast of Italy near Naples—and he talked Bogart into coming over and going ahead. He was bringing Truman Capote in to work on a whole new draft of the script, he told Bogart.

Things began badly. Huston and Bogart and their adventurous driver had a near-fatal accident on the way to Ravello. Thereafter the location became a legend of icy martinis assuaging the exasperations and anxieties attendant upon getting the script in day-to-day pieces, after late-night collaborations by Huston and Capote. Gina Lollabrigida, learning her lines phonetically, complained that she had no idea what the hell was going on (a complaint shared by many viewers down the years). Yet alongside the convolutions of *Three Days of the Condor,* the plot of *Beat the Devil* is almost austerely simple.

And what emerged was neither the extension in kind of *The Maltese Falcon,* straight and tough, which Bogart had first envisioned, nor anything as grotesque as a parody or spoof of the *Falcon,* which *Beat the Devil* has imprecisely been called. (Later, numbed Hollywood hands would come up with something called *The Maltese Bippy,* a reminder even now of what a blessing forgetfulness can be.)

However antic and loopy the circumstances of its making may be, *Beat the Devil* holds up as a fast and disciplined comedy, with a richness of invention which even now, after fifteen or twenty viewings, I find astonishing. It is criminal intrigue executed as far-out farce, and the last thing in the world *Beat the Devil* is is self-indulgent. None of the boys'-night-out excesses or the look-Ma-no-restraints histrionics which have left a trail of gummed-up enterprises from Abbott and Costello to *California Split.*

From its tasty opening sequence of the four petulant villains—Robert Morley, Peter Lorre, Ivor Bernard, and Marco Tulli—being led handcuffed through the village, while the local bandsmen play a rousing, off-key march, *Beat the Devil* seems to know precisely where it's going. The beginning is the end and we double back to begin again as Morley and his accomplices wait for an ailing freighter to be repaired for its delayed sailing to Africa, where there are mischiefs to be done—uranium deposits to be snatched from unsuspecting natives. Bogart has been hired as a kind of free-lance consultant on governmental bribery. It was Bogart at his sardonic best. "Without money I become dull, listless, and have trouble with my complexion," he says, explaining his association with Morley.

Gina is his wife, pneumatic and Anglophilic, with eyes for those lovely English lawns, and for Edward Underdown, who seems to own acres of them. Underdown is the stuffy husband of Jennifer Jones, in a blond wig to match her talky dumbness. (At a Hollywood gathering some years ago, she told me, "When John was trying to recruit me for the part, he said, 'Sweetie, they'll remember you longer for *Beat the Devil* than for *Song of Bernadette.*' I think," she added bitterly, "that he may turn out to be right.")

Nothing and no one in *Beat the Devil* is what it/he seems to be, and the sniffings and the spyings and the counterplottings advance in vivid and unforgettable dialogue, which I presume to be largely Capote's work.

Miss Jones suspects Morley & Co. to be the desperate villains they are because they are all too preoccupied to admire her swell legs. Morley is the soul of pompous evil. Leading his crew on a constitutional around the ship, he cries, "Breathe deep, me hearties, every breath a guinea in the bank of health!" Ivor Bernard as a murderous little cashiered major delivers a bar-side harangue in favor of Hitler. "This generation has had its chance. The world is going up in smoke, and let it come, I say. Not a moment too soon." Lorre does a set piece on time: "The Swiss manufacture it," he tells Bogart, "the Italians squander it, the French hoard it, the Americans worship it. . . ."

Saro Ursi as the drunken ship's captain and Mario Perroni as the cheery purser are minor and fleeting figures raised to colorful cameo status through the magic of casting and scene construction. Manuel Serrano as the head of police in an unnamed Arabian state puffs dreamily on a water pipe and commands the captured Bogart, "Tell me more of Rita Hayworth. Tell me everything."

It is nutty and preposterous from start to finish, but Bogart and the cast give no winks and nudge no ribs. It is all played with a lovely solemnity, a sort of calm seriousness which lets the audience (the "laymen," in *Films and Filming*'s patronizing word) get the jokes, rather than share them.

History, as always, has had the last reviews. When I found *Beat the Devil* in 1956 (as others before me found mah-jongg and others after me have found TM), it was already an underground enthusiasm. There were cells of true believers at *Life* in New York and at the *World-Telegram* (the movie has outlived both publications, I realize), and they can still recite great savory chunks of the dialogue. (The Fascist major's speech, building as it does to incoherent ramblings about Rosicrucianism and hidden powers of the mind, is an excellent device for repelling conversational bores in almost any social situation.)

Over the years, a cablegram which figures importantly in the plot—NO CHELM ESTATE GLOUCESTERSHIRE. NO LANDED GENTRY CHELM. THE COMMITTEE—has become a kind of change-of-post or-status greeting among certain of the *Beat the Devil* faithful.

I love the film for itself and as well for the associations it obviously now holds for me. And yet, with as much critical detachment as I can still master, *Beat the Devil* still seems to me to possess an absolute if limited perfection. It is a film whose intentions are realized with marvelous professional efficiency, invention, and control. (The photography by Oswald Morris and Freddie Francis glistens even through the torn and battered prints I have often had to watch.)

It has an inspired absurdity which may well have been precocious. But even now it strikes me as leagues better than some of the self-conscious romps which have come along since. It was a beginning, but it was also, as Bogart has occasion to say in the film, the end.

[1975]

# CAT BALLOU
### Judith Crist

Well, let's get those old superlatives out again, this time for a small package of enormous delight labeled *Cat Ballou,* a western to end all westerns (or at least our ever looking at another with a straight face) and a comedy that epitomizes the sheer fun of moviemaking and movie watching.

Producer Harold Hecht and director Elliot Silverstein, with a Walker Newman–Frank R. Pierson screenplay in hand, have cast a satiric eye on every sacred aspect of our western mythology—i.e., every cliché of character and plot—and laughed it to bits by way of one piece of nuttiness after another and by means of a poker-faced reverence on the part of everyone concerned. And everyone concerned manages to hit perfection every sprightly step of the film's lovely love-ridden way, with Lee Marvin practically putting his brand on an Oscar with the top comedy portrait of the year.

*Cat Ballou* is a pristine pure western. It's a hanging day in Wolf City, Wyoming, in 1894, a couple of banjo-strumming shouters named Nat King Cole and Stubby Kaye tell us in trite-and-true title-song balladry, and they're getting ready to hang that angel-devil killer-outlaw, Cat Ballou. There she is, pacing her prison cell, blond and beautiful and pensively starting the flashback that will tell us how it all began.

Here's Catherine Ballou lovely girl-graduate-schoolmarm, heading home to her Pa and the ranch and the loyal Indian retainer, meeting a drunken preacher and a licorish-eyed cattle rustler en route, and coming home to find that the vile Wolf City Development Company is trying to run Pa off his ranch. The company's instrument is the vile black-clad silver-nosed gunslinger Tim Straun (he got his nose bit off in a fight); finally Cat gets herself a gunslinger of her own, importing the great and good Kid Shelleen, whose feats have been immortalized in the penny dreadfuls Cat has secreted in the pages of her Tennyson. And when local justice fails her, Cat has to turn outlaw, with a showdown between Straun and Shelleen on the agenda and Sir Harry Percival, lecherous head of the development company, as Cat's personal target.

But wait a minute. Scarcely have those shouters walked off camera and their sweet balladry blended into the score before we see something slightly out of kilter, a tinge of lunacy to the color film. It's around the edges of Cat's literary discussion with the preacher, it's coming into focus as Cat cringes in her lower berth with the rustler-on-the-run winning her affection, and it pops right at us as Pa and Jackson Two-Bear, the faithful Indian, argue about Indians being one of the Lost Tribes of Israel.

And we're in a wildly daft West where outlaws refuse to fire at anyone in anger, little boys refuse to hold hands with little girls at a hoedown, sheriffs consider the "ramifications to peace-officering" and Kid Shelleen turns out to be the biggest soak in the West. Everything isn't what it should be and every disillusion and misadventure that doesn't feaze Cat brings hilarious twists and turns and take-offs, with those shouters coming back on screen after each fun foray to tell us what hasn't been happening. They sing it pure and sweet and kill the western ballad with kindness.

Lee Marvin does the same for Shane in his dual portrait of gunfighters. His Straun is just lovely straight menace in the Marvin manner we know so well, but his Shelleen is a work of art, a marvelously rheumy-eyed guzzler who straddles a horse in a stupor and comes up statuesquely as "End of the Trail," a reformed character who prepares for a gunfight with a ritual right out of *Blood and Sand,* a eulogist of the Day of the Gunfighter to set the old nostalgia salivating, a gunslinger who actually manages to miss the side of the barn— in short, a cliché gone mad—and marvelous.

Jane Fonda is marvelous too as the wide-eyed Cat, exuding sweet feminine sex appeal every sway of the way—and so is everyone else listed in the cast or just caught on camera. And Stubby Kaye and the late Nat King Cole—well, if somebody doesn't put out a complete sound track of the movie, and soon, we'll picket—or gunsling.

Beyond the imaginative wit that turned Roy Chanslor's dead-serious novel into a brilliant film satire, the moviemakers have applied all the ingredients of good rousing fun, from camera tricks to slapstick to madness to rib-cracking dialogue. This *Cat Ballou* is just a honey.

[1965]

# UP FROM UNDERGROUND

## LONESOME COWBOYS
### Richard Schickel

> Show me a cowboy who rides sidesaddle, and I'll show you a gay ranchero.
> —Ernie Kovacs

That one-liner, which I heard the late great comedian throw away one time, is as accurate a summary of Andy Warhol's new movie, *Lonesome Cowboys,* as one can make. But the point of one of his films is never to be found in its content, but simply in its existence, whether it happens to be twenty-four hours long, as one of them is, or twenty-four minutes, as one of them might perfectly well be. None of the matters usually brought up when we talk about films— story, style, technique—has any relevance to his work. Indeed, I have no hesitancy in admitting that I left *Cowboys* ten minutes before it was over, on the grounds that since it had no beginning and no middle it probably didn't have an ending either. It seemed to me at least as important to get to my lunch appointment on time as it did to hang around and see whether Viva, his current superstar, got debagged one more time.

Do not misunderstand; the film did not suddenly reach some new low in "tastelessness" or stupidity. I will not pretend that walking out was any kind of critical gesture. As an act it was neither more nor less significant than any of the gestures one observed on screen. Like them—like the entire movie—it was just something one felt like doing that day. Indeed, the only important act we make regarding a Warhol film is walking in; after that it clearly makes no difference to him what we do, how we respond.

In the profoundest sense, therefore, Warhol is impervious to criticism. Implicit in the act of reviewing any work of art is the assumption, shared by critic, creator, and audience, that the work is always potentially a "question for further discussion," as a study guide might have it. One assumes that the artist may want to engage, if only in the privacy of his own mind, in some sort of dialogue with his auditors, while they in turn may wish to observe the "development" in his technique and sensibility from work to work. But clearly Warhol engages with no one outside his coterie (he lives—and eventually will die—on the quality of his publicity, but that is another matter), and there is no development worth speaking of in his thing.

To be sure, *Cowboys* was shot in thirty-five millimeter (a first for him) and had an unprecedented four-day shooting schedule, but he remains firmly rooted, technically and aesthetically, to a point in film history around 1904–1905, when the first American story films were being shot. Like the primitives, all he does is borrow a real setting, place amateur actors in front of it, and instruct them to improvise dialogue and action based on a rough outline. A genius can stretch this technique to masterwork lengths (e.g., Griffith's *The Birth of a Nation*), but Warhol cannot or will not.

It is fair to say that he knows only one thing, for, as Robert Mazzocco has shrewdly pointed out, his works in all media are repetitions of a single simple juxtaposition, that of "the mindlessly banal and the haphazardly corrupt, or of the totally outrageous and the totally bloodless." It is, he notes, a peculiarly American juxtaposition, and I would venture to say that is the basic mix in about nine-tenths of our popular culture. Warhol's virtue, if he may be said to have one, is that in his essential stupidity he makes the contrast between the two very stark, stripping away the platitudes and hypocrisies with which we customarily attempt to unify these contradictory elements.

There is something basically funny in *Cowboys,* for instance, about skinny, androgynous Viva, so obviously the creation of the Now Culture, impersonating a frontier hooker, something weirdly engaging about the cowboys being fruitcakes—borrowing mascara from one another or using the hitching rail as a barre. What Warhol has done is to place faggery in the context from which we have drawn our traditional sustaining masculine mythology—a corruption and a banality together again, you will observe—and we are surprised and annoyed to find genuine laughter being jerked from us. Surprised because it occurs in the midst of the acute fatigue Warhol's lack of intelligence and technique (and his aggressive desire to administer shocks to the bourgeois sexual sensibility) customarily engenders; annoyed because one wishes to return his very real contempt for us with contempt for him. Our laughter spoils the perfection of our disdain and has, for some critics, created a problem: how to explain away that laughter?

Some have leapt to the conclusion that he is beginning to emerge as a self-conscious rather than unconscious satirist, and *Cowboys* has been here and there written up as a genuine spoof—sort of *Support Your Local Sheriff* in drag. That is, I think, rather too long a leap to make on the basis of the evidence before us. Indeed, I would say that he is still considerably less an artist than Kovacs, who found a form for the same basic juxtaposition (or absurdity or insight) more appropriate to its importance than a two-hour movie. The most you can say for Warhol is that he is, as Mr. Mazzocco says, "sophisticated by default."

Specifically, he has lingered long, and one suspects for want of a better idea, at this business of corruption and banality endlessly combined and recombined, as a child out on a nature walk will linger over some small thing—an odd-shaped stone, a dandelion gone to seed—while the adults have hurried on in pursuit of larger quarries. Returning to hurry the laggard, we are interested to observe that, yes, the thing is pretty or interesting in its humble way and, yes, one is pleased to see the child using his eyes. But it is a nuisance when he keeps pausing, slowing one down with observations of similar trivia dozens of times.

To this, one might add another point. Obviously, his sensibility was formed entirely by the media culture, so by practicing journalism on himself he can also, in a way, journalize the entire culture that made him. But, in the nature of things, a journalist cannot transcend his subject, while the artist can—and must. Which is another way of saying that journalism is not art, although increasingly the distinction eludes us, since both now confuse the mere assertion of self with the creation, in the one case, of a genuine report on an event observed, in the other, of an art object.

There is, of course, something delicious about a mass culture that gave Warhol his subject and the ready-to-wear sensibility he applies to understanding it celebrating him as if he were an exemplary rebel against it instead of the model prisoner of it. But there is something frightening about it, too. People are always asking critics about the so-called underground film, and it always turns out they're asking about Warhol. He has pre-empted the field, leaving no audience for the more serious independent artists who work below our normal sight lines. Indeed, it is risky to attempt to criticize him, for criticism is instantly converted into still more publicity, the piece that attempts to understand him becoming, all disclaimers to the contrary, an endorsement.

So let me be very clear. I don't think Warhol or *Lonesome Cowboys* is any good. I don't even think he is an artist, avant-garde or conventional. He is just very, very important—too important to go on mindlessly denigrating or trying to ignore, as if he were just a fad like hula hoops. He may, like them, quietly disappear. But like his soup cans he is endlessly replicable in this culture of ours.

[1969]

## TRASH

### Vincent Canby

The opening credits (ANDY WARHOL PRESENTS TRASH . . .) appear as words spelled out in little light bulbs of the sort still used on old theater marquees. On the sound track can be heard some breathless, tinny movie music taken from Josef von Sternberg's *The Blue Angel*. Even if you don't get the point immediately, you will soon after *Trash* begins. This second film by Paul Morrissey (his first was *Flesh*, described as a tribute to John Ford) is a relentless send-up of attitudes and gestures shanghaied from Hollywood's glamorous 1930s and 1940s.

The joys of *Trash* are not inexhaustible, but compared to things like the pretensions of *Cover Me, Babe* and the calculating heart of *Sunflower*, *Trash* is true-blue moviemaking, almost epic, funny and vivid, though a bit rotten at the core. I'm writing this on Monday and I'll say, quite simply, that it's the best American film made in New York that I've seen all day.

Like *Flesh*, to which it is a kind of moralizing sequel, *Trash* is a circular odyssey, only this time Joe (Joe Dallessandro), the male hustler of *Flesh*, is a heroin addict. In spite of pimples on his rump and face, his physique is still so magnificently shaped that men as well as women become disconnected at the sight of him, all of which does no one any good, since Joe is impotent.

*Trash* is the story of Joe and his lover-protector Holly (Holly Woodlawn) who, in real life, is a female impersonator, though in the film the matter of Holly's sex is ambiguous. Joe and Holly try to make a go of things in their Lower East Side basement, from which Holly goes forth from time to time to cruise the Filmore East and to scavenge garbage cans, while Joe's journeys are in search of real junk. The film takes its shape principally from his encounters, which have the style (and the substance) of grotesque grass fantasies.

There is a sweet, absolutely round-breasted go-go dancer (Geri Miller) whose philosophy sounds as if it could have been learned at Judge Hardy's knee: "If you're sexy, you can be sexy doing anything. Sex is from the inside." There's a soft-headed girl from Grosse Pointe (Jane Forth), whose apartment Joe intends to rob. Instead, he gets propositioned for a rape.

"I'm only a rich newlywed with no furniture," she says by way of introduction. Later, while the camera is in a tight close-up on Joe's arm as he gives himself a fix, Jane whines at her husband, "Oh, Bruce, we don't have fun any more. Do you know how long it is since I slept with another man?"

All feelings, all values are turned upside down and played for laughs, with the result that it's difficult for me to take *Trash* more seriously than it takes itself. In spite of the grubbiness of the scene and the ineffectuality of the various disguises and escapes employed by Joe and Holly and the rest, there is no sense of despair. At heart, the film is a kind of exuberant exhibition of total apathy.

Mr. Morrissey is, I think, a talented moviemaker, even though much of the effect of *Trash* depends on outrageous shock or on rather curious plays on pathos. I assume that the performers have been handled with skill, in spite of the fact that it's not always possible to tell—in this sort of movie—just what the performers themselves have brought to their roles.

Holly Woodlawn, especially, is something to behold, a comic-book Mother Courage who fancies herself as Marlene Dietrich but sounds more often like Phil Silvers. I shall also remember for some time the very funny performance by Michael Sklar as a welfare investigator who comes to call on Holly and becomes enchanted by her silver shoes, which, he thinks, would make a marvelous lamp.

*Trash* is alive, but like the people in it, it continually parodies itself, and thus it represents a kind of dead end in filmmaking.

[1970]

## PUTNEY SWOPE
### Vincent Canby

Robert Downey's *Putney Swope* more or less details the rise and rise of a black Madison Avenue ad agency called Truth and Soul. To be as precise as is possible about such a movie, it is funny, sophomoric, brilliant, obscene, disjointed, marvelous, unintelligible, and relevant. Its humor is in the tradition of the new American frontier, a land whose pioneers are hung up with all kinds of guilts about race relations, sex, money, and the politics of success.

*Putney Swope* also has some dull patches, but if anybody, including Downey —who has a way of fooling around with his movies after they've gone into release—tries to improve it, he should be sentenced to watch "Laugh-In" for thirteen weeks or *The Maltese Bippy* once, from beginning to end. The same should go for anybody who tries to improve Downey. His manic attacks on all things absurd must be cherished for just what they are, movies whose vulgar, chaotic style defines their content. I'd hate to think of a Downey movie that had a logical narrative and characters, and that didn't use dirty words for shock effect.

To the extent that *Putney Swope* can be described with any coherence, it's about a moribund ad agency that elects Putney Swope, its black musical director, to the post of board chairman. Putney (Arnold Johnson), a handsome, bearded, cool-eyed gentleman who talks in a frog-throated monotone, transforms the agency into a mad, black brotherhood that rocks to success with such accounts as Face Off (an adolescent skin cream), Lucky Airlines, Ethereal Cereal, and the Get-Out-Of-Here Mousetrap.

Truth and Soul also has scruples. It refuses to promote cigarettes, booze, or war toys (the Audie Murphy Toy Company), and only agrees to handle the Bormann Six, a sports car with strobe headlights and the Star of Israel on its hood, after being pressed by the President of the United States, a pot-smoking midget named Mimeo.

The movie has all the form of a feature-length collection of television commercials, and, indeed, quite a lot of footage is devoted to the commercials produced by Truth and Soul. Several of those, like the vignettes that make up the real life of the film, depend simply on the abrupt use of four-letter words in pious contexts. Others are fully realized conceits, of which my favorite is the paean to Face Off in which a black boy and a white girl run arm in arm through sylvan settings, singing a sweet, gentle ballad that begins: "It started last weekend / At the Yale–Howard game. . . ."

The continuity of the movie is tenuous and its point of view rather all-purpose put-down. Everything gets rapped—pushy nuns, orphans, integrationists, militant blacks—much of the time in terms that I associate with college humor. Downey loves crazy proper names like Wing Soney (the Chinese mousetrap manufacturer), Dr. Alvin Weasley (a motivational-research specialist), Miss Redneck, N. J. (a beauty-contest winner), and the odd association of names. "In the nineteen-forties," says someone, apropos of nothing very much, "it was Victor Mature and Judy Canova. In the fifties, Christine Jorgenson and James Dean. In the sixties, Smith and Wesson."

Technically, *Putney Swope* is much superior to Downey's first two features to receive commercial release, *Chafed Elbows* and *No More Excuses*. It is extremely well photographed mostly in black and white, with color for the commercial interludes. Spiritually, it is a continuation of those two films. That is, it's a view of the world distorted just enough to look as contradictory, open-ended, and nonsensical as it really is.

Downey is, as he likes to call himself, a prince.

[1969]

# MEL BROOKS

## THE PRODUCERS
### Andrew Sarris

Mel Brooks's *The Producers* did not make me laugh as much as I had anticipated, and perhaps anticipation is part of the problem. Let us suppose that an acquaintance stops us in the street with the announcement that he is going to tell us the funniest joke ever told. But first, he tells us, he is going to synopsize the joke, describe its high and low points, analyze the style of its telling, compare it with other jokes in the same genre from other eras, and psychoanalyze those listeners who will laugh at it and those who will not. Then and only then does he tell us the joke. Do we laugh? Not likely. The element of surprise is gone because we listen with too many preconceptions. In short, we listen more to the how of style than to the what of content. By now I don't think there is anyone in the Greater New York area who does not know that *The Producers* is concerned with two relatively unscrupulous theatrical promoters (Zero Mostel and Gene Wilder) who decide to bilk their backers by oversubscribing a show that is bound to fail. And what is more bound to fail than a show called *Springtime for Hitler,* acted by a hippie Hitler (Dick

Shawn), directed by a fag failure of a director (Christopher Hewett), and written by an iron-helmeted Village Nazi (Kenneth Mars). The combination of Brooks, Mostel, Shawn, and Wilder added to all these wild, irreverent premises would seem to promise an unending succession of belly laughs. Unfortunately, the capacity of the motion-picture medium for realism, social contiguity, and generalized experience confounds the expectations of *The Producers*.

The idea that two Jewish producers would engage in a project called *Springtime for Hitler* even as part of a swindle is more a cabaret idea than a movie idea. Even on the Borscht Circuit, a Jewish comedian can assume a Nazi role as a temporarily shocking point of departure to arouse black laughter in his audience. Actually Nazis are the political equivalents of fags in these mandatory bad-taste-put-the-children-to-bed-first entertainments. Cabaret characterizations are entirely hypothetical. If you accept such and such a premise, such and such will occur. Screen characterizations are historical. The characters played by Zero Mostel and Gene Wilder are obviously if not blatantly Jewish, and they carry their pasts around with them while they humor a psychotic Nazi author to the point of singing "Deutschland Uber Alles" and wearing swastika armbands. Here Brooks tries to play it both ways by having Wilder spit on the swastikas after they are deposited in a trash basket, but it is too late. The hypothesis contradicts the history. There are supposed to have been producers on Broadway like *The Producers* insofar as the fraudulence of the situation is concerned. (An old Reed Hadley "Racket Squad" sequence on television some years ago had almost the identical plot, but of course without the added *frisson* of *Springtime for Hitler*.) No matter. I simply cannot believe that any Jewish producers would involve themselves in such a project even for a million dollars when there is such a wide range of other possibilities.

However, even if we assume that there were two Jewish producers greedy enough to do something so distasteful, it is difficult to laugh, however blackly, at a plot device that has received so much advance publicity. As it turns out, the whole movie is based on this one plot premise that is supposed to attest to the New Audacity in movies. Instead, everything in *The Producers* attests to the New Vulgarity.

Except for two or three expert sequences, the direction of Mel Brooks is thoroughly vile and inept. Everyone in the film down to the least extra mugs with an extravagance not seen since the most florid silent days. When *Springtime for Hitler* is finally staged, the audience looks with collectively wide-eyed, wide-mouthed shock and amazement at a hilariously professional mixed chorus of boys and girls in black jackets and swastikas tapping, kicking, and prancing away. But why should an audience be so shocked at a show called *Springtime for Hitler*? What did they expect? the realistic conscience of the medium keeps whispering in my ear. To make matters worse, the audience within the film begins roaring with laughter at precisely that instant when the spectacle on the stage within the film ceases to be amusing. Dick Shawn makes a funny hippie singer and writher at the audition, but an unfunny hippie Hitler in the play proper, and then everything goes downhill.

There is a lilting moment when Gene Wilder walks around the suddenly gushing Revson Fountain in Lincoln Center as a manifestation of his ecstatic corruption, but on the whole I thought that Wilder and Mostel played too much footsie and feelsie for my taste. This is the kind of movie where the only formal gown is worn by a female impersonator who enters the scene with complete gratuitousness. Gone is the *Charley's Aunt* convention of involuntary impersonation by farcical but virile victims of plot twists. Female impersonation is now an end in itself, and just so we don't miss the point, Mostel mugs and leers for our benefit. At a time when film aestheticians are solemnly debating the merits of looking directly at the camera to talk to the audience, Mel Brooks indulges in asides too stagy even for the stage. With no grading in the direction, the performances are all grating. Zero Mostel rolls his eyes on the screen as if he were running a bowling alley in his skull, while Gene Wilder skitters and jitters even before the plot begins.

*The Producers* resembles *Enter Laughing* both in its conceptual and directorial crudity and in its isolated moments of hilarity with stage-struck mediocrities. *The Producers* is in a class by itself as a movie that completely ignores the existence of women except as props, toys, or old bags. I hope this isn't a trend in the bright new world of sophisticated cinema.

[1968]

## BLAZING SADDLES
### Gary Arnold

In *Blazing Saddles* Mel Brooks squanders a snappy title on a stock pile of stale jokes. To say that this slapdash western spoof lacks freshness, spontaneity, and originality is putting it mildly. *Blazing Saddles* is at once a messy and antiquated gag machine.

Brooks is so preoccupied with the idea of acting outrageous that he neglects to give the material any style or unity. Moreover, I don't think he realizes that he's acting outrageous about a moribund, irrelevant subject. *Blazing Saddles* is probably the western spoof Brooks has wanted to make for twenty years, and he's had to wait too long. If his jokes were any older, they'd be pushing up daisies in some backlot Boot Hill.

*Blazing Saddles* may seem especially dismaying if you happen to regret Brooks's recent absence from the screen. Evidently, it took him three years to line up another film project after the commercial failure of *The Twelve Chairs*. I think it's disgraceful that the studios have been letting the comic resources of people like Brooks or Renée Taylor and Joe Bologna lie fallow. Now, irony of miserable ironies, it appears that Brooks's worst picture might become his big box-office breakthrough.

The best outcome one can hope for in these circumstances is that Brooks won't take the success of *Blazing Saddles* to heart and start serving up more of the same. Some part of him must recognize what a strained, derivative entertainment it is, and despite those early box-office figures from New York

City, a large percentage of the audience may also feel the strain. *Blazing Saddles* is heavily indebted and markedly inferior to *My Little Chickadee,* the Marx Brothers' *Go West,* Bob Hope's *Paleface* movies and the Hope–Crosby Road series. It's not even as witty or consistently funny as the last hit western spoof, *Support Your Local Sheriff,* which no one considers a classic.

When people claim that a comedy like *Blazing Saddles* broke them up, I like to believe they've gone a long time between movies. Brooks imagines he's being killingly funny when he's just painfully facetious. Instead of creating funny characters or even caricatures, he merely makes up jocular names—Hedley Lamarr, Lili von Shtupp, etc.—and considers the job done. His carelessness leaves many of the actors stranded, condemned to belabor the single schtik they've been assigned, like Harvey Korman's prissy irritation when people keep calling him "Hedy Lamarr" and Madeline Kahn's ponderous impersonation of Dietrich in the Lili role.

The relationship of the title to the movie as a whole is constantly repeated: if you've heard the funny labels you've heard the whole joke. There's no continuity or variety or momentum in *Blazing Saddles.* It's a collection of inadequately rejuvenated wheezes, and a staggering number of punch lines depend upon surprise profanities, the shock effect of Bad Words. These are evidently the source of the film's R rating, and they're at once foolish and offensive.

There's no reason, either practical or artistic, why Brooks should risk alienating a potential family or kid audience on a picture as fundamentally trivial and old hat as *Blazing Saddles.* He has risked it, and all for the thrill of swearing on the screen. Brooks writes naughty punch lines in the same way little kids try out naughty expressions on their parents, and what makes you wince is not the expressions themselves but the ignorant, indiscriminate way they're being used.

The profanity is the only "new" element Brooks brings to the old western-spoof formula, and this is scarcely a novelty in contemporary movies. The film was originally called *Black Bart,* so one assumed that the more or less new angle would be an interracial angle. Richard Pryor worked on the screenplay at some point, and Cleavon Little has the nominal starring role, as a black lawman in a mildly bigoted frontier town, but the racial yocks are as moldy as the western yocks. It's as if Brooks hadn't even caught up with *Putney Swope.* His conception of daring and outrageous racial humor might have lifted a few innocent eyebrows a decade ago, but it's all stock-in-trade at this late date.

The two characters who should dominate the movie, Little as Bart and Gene Wilder as his deputy, a serene, alcoholic ex-gunfighter called The Pecos Kid, have very little to do. They haven't been endowed with abundantly funny personalities, and they haven't been placed in the thick of the action. Wilder's benign detachment is rather endearing in the crude, overbearing context of this film; it's as if Brooks didn't have the heart to subject him to the indignities he had in store for the other clowns.

Nevertheless, one wonders what *Blazing Saddles* might have been like if Richard Pryor and Gene Wilder had been paired in full-bodied comic roles and

Brooks had given the material some pertinence and control. Westerns are no longer the staples they once were, not even on television, but Brooks might have used the decrepitude of conventional westerns with old stars like John Wayne or the decadence of westerns in the Sergio Leone–Clint Eastwood style as the starting points of satire. He might even have kidded something we've had too much of recently—cop melodramas in the *French Connection* style.

The point is that it's pointless to kid a tradition that doesn't have much vitality left. The horse opera as people once knew and loved it is virtually dead, and all Mel Brooks is doing in *Blazing Saddles* is beating a dead horse.

[1974]

## BLAZING SADDLES
### Richard Schickel

A certain number of sissies are bound to go around condescending to *Blazing Saddles* as a comedy of less than perfect form. They will note that it lacks the careful construction and polished wit that are often evoked by essentially humorless people—usually to justify the minor cultural sin of having a good time at a movie that is less than thirty-five years old and does not star either the Marx Brothers or W. C. Fields.

It is easy to forget that a lot of the old comedians' gags did not quite come off either. Their movies too might have been even funnier had their scripts been edited more rigorously and directed more artfully instead of being produced on the everything-but-the-kitchen-sink principle of comedy. Like its many raucous predecessors, *Blazing Saddles* is a thing of bits and bits—some good, some awful—pinned carelessly to a story line that sags like a tenement clothesline. The movie tends to improve in the retelling, as memory edits out ineptitudes, the better to dwell on moments of glory.

*Saddles* is about a hip black sheriff who must overcome racial prejudice and the machinations of a corrupt frontier political machine. With very little help, he manages to save the citizens of Rock Ridge from being driven away so that a railroad may pass more cheaply through their land. But so what? The important thing is that the chief villain is named Hedley Lamarr and that the actors insist on mispronouncing his name; that a black labor gang, ordered to sing a Negro spiritual by their straw boss, respond with a nice arrangement of Cole Porter's "I Get a Kick Out of You"; that ex–football tackler Alex Karras, on hand to play a homicidal moron, gets in a fight with a horse and fells it with a single roundhouse blow; that Cleavon Little, as the heroic sheriff, has saddlebags by Gucci.

And so on. And on. Very often the film is too fast and furious for its own good. Still, the scene where everyone is grouped around the old chuck wagon enjoying a good old-fashioned bean supper is in itself a high point in the short history of screen scatology. Even more flamboyant is the ending in which the entire cast, engaged in a classic western brawl, breaks through the wall of an adjoining sound stage where a campy musical—tails, top hats, and lots of white platforms—is being shot. In the ensuing effeminate uproar, hearty Slim Pickens punches out the jodhpur-clad director of the film next door, while Cleavon Little ducks out to Grauman's Chinese Theater and watches . . . *Blazing Saddles*.

The whole raveled sequence is the work of men desperate for an ending. It is also in bad taste, though it cannot stand comparison to Brooks's most egregious caper, the "Springtime for Hitler" number in *The Producers*. But gol-durned if it doesn't work. Gol-durned if the whole fool enterprise is not worth the attention of any movie-goer with a penchant for what one actor, commenting on another's Gabby Hayes imitation, calls "authentic western gibberish."

[1974]

## YOUNG FRANKENSTEIN
### Colin L. Westerbeck, Jr.

The Frankenstein story, as we all know, is about a creature made up entirely of misappropriated and mismatched parts. That's pretty much the way Mel Brooks has made his new film, *Young Frankenstein,* too. Since all comedy has to be based on some sort of incongruity, this approach works out pretty well for Brooks. Most of the parts he has misappropriated come out of other people's movies. Besides having stolen the whole idea for this movie from James Whale's *Frankenstein* (1931), Brooks has, for instance, stolen the hairdo for one of his stars, Madeline Kahn, from Elsa Lanchester in *The Bride of Frankenstein* (1935). At times, as when Miss Lanchester's streak job is set atop Miss Kahn's head, the stolen parts hardly look out of place at all. At other times, as when Brooks's monster (Peter Boyle) clomps his way through a Fred Astaire number of about the same vintage as the hairdo, Brooks is purposely letting all the sutures show.

Many of the film's parts which Brooks has not stolen from other movies his characters have stolen from each other. This results, first and foremost, from the need to outfit the monster, a need which sends Frederick Frankenstein (Gene Wilder) off to the cemetery while his assistant, Igor (Marty Feldman), is dispatched to the brain repository. For the most part, however, the people in Brooks's story prove to be of higher moral character than he is, and restrict themselves merely to swapping parts rather than swiping them.

The wholesale exchange begins innocently enough with the name Frankenstein itself, in which a couple of vowels show a tendency to trade places. At first Frederick insistently pronounces his name with a short "a" and a long "e" for the diphthong, but after a while he pronounces it just as insistently the other way around, with the short and long vowels reversed. Then there's the hump on Igor's back. Like the phonemes in his employer's name, the hump keeps shifting from one side to the other. (Even Frederick remarks on it.) And the unruly prosthesis worn by the local police chief does the same thing, switching from his right arm to his left and back again.

Once you start permitting parts to circulate this way, there's no telling where it will lead. It leads the characters here to entire exchanges of identity. For example, another part of those interchangeable parts in the film is the police chief's right forefinger and the monster's thumb. In a couple of parallel scenes, these detachable digits are each lit on fire in the attempt to light a cigar, a happenstance which leaves the monster howling but doesn't even make the chief flinch. As this suggests, it is really the chief, not the monster, who is the unfeeling brute. In like manner, Frau Blücher (Cloris Leachman), at whose name horses start and stamp, reveals herself to be a sentimental old sweetie in the end. But Frederick's fiancée (Miss Kahn), who is early in the film too cold a fish to kiss Frederick for fear of mussing her make-up, ends up being raped by the monster, and loving it.

Eventually Frederick and the monster even trade a few parts. Before the monster comes into being, Frederick is caught one night with a coffin from which an arm is protruding, so to disguise his grave robbing, Frederick passes the arm through an armhole of his cloak as if it were his own. Later on, when the monster falls victim to yet another of those misappropriated, mismatched parts—the abnormal brain Igor has procured for him—Frederick does a little transmutation, swapping part of his own brain for part of the monster's private parts. A very even trade.

The effect of all this on the monster, as on the whole Frankenstein myth, is to domesticate it. Just as contemporary racism finds a home in the Old West in Brooks's *Blazing Saddles,* and Nazism plays on Broadway in *The Producers,* so Frankenstein and his monster are made a part of modern American kitsch in his film. "Pardon me, boy, is this the Transylvania Station?" Frederick inquires when his train first arrives after his journey from the States. "Yeah," says a smart-aleck shine boy in lederhosen, "Track 29." Later that night at the castle, Frau Blücher archly offers Frederick brandy before he retires. The offer refused, she begins to turn away but then has a second thought. "Warm milk?" she asks, archly. Refused again, she starts to turn away but then has a third thought. "Ovaltine?" she asks in her heavy German accent. By the end of the film the monster is propped up in bed reading the *Wall Street Journal* at his home up in Westchester County somewhere.

A good deal of Brooks's energies in *Young Frankenstein* have been devoted to keeping up our awareness of his movie as a movie. He realizes that the culture on which his insanity really feeds is not Mary Shelley's England nor Transylvania nor even America at large, but just Hollywood. For this reason, *Young Frankenstein* is, from its over-all composition to its isolated details, a comedy of production errors. The whole movie has been thrown together from spare parts of other movies as if it were a bin full of outtakes, a face off the cutting-room floors where Hollywood's campiest films were made. The migration of Igor's hump and the switch-hitting the chief does with his prosthesis look like the mental lapses of some script girl who should be maintaining continuity in such details, but isn't quite up to her job. In vowel shifts that occur in a single one-liner, as in the execution of entire sequences, movie conventions fly through the air in this film in a mad jugglery that never lets us get down to earth for a moment.

[1975]

# WOODY ALLEN

## AN ALLEN OVERVIEW
### *Joseph Gelmis*

"I will take fate by the throat," said young Ludwig Beethoven, who was going deaf at the time. Tough talk, but check out his late string quartets. A stone-deaf composer of sublime music. It's all in the mind, right?

Woody Allen is all in the mind, too. One apocryphal tale told of him is that he spends up to five hours a day with his analyst and then uses those innermost confessions of anguish as the basis of his comedy. He cannibalizes his neuroses. He seizes his fate as an anxiety-ridden, aging adolescent and makes fun of himself. What bravado. What courage. What time is it?

Pierre Auguste Renoir, an heroic artist who painted with gnarled, arthritic stumps of hands in his old age, detested Beethoven. In *My Father, Renoir,* by Jean Renoir, the humanist filmmaker (his *Rules of the Game* is my favorite adult movie), the painter complains that Beethoven was indecent for putting so much suffering into his music. On his deathbed, Beethoven said, "Friends, the comedy is over."

Comedy proceeds out of suffering. Usually somebody else's suffering. They slip on banana peels. They want something they can't have. Woody Allen's humor is based on suffering. He is his own fall guy, and his own hero. He's silly, he's sad, he's a loser—because he's so sensitive, so aware, so ineffectual. He's funny because he makes fun of himself and the odds against him, while suffering openly. Two emotions striking simultaneously produce a heightened effect, a resonance that tickles our funny bones while tapping into our own private sorrows. It's a more potent effect than just farce or just tragedy.

Woody Allen is no Chaplin—that Dickensian waif whose millions couldn't protect him from the fear of poverty or the memory of a mother gone mad and a childhood hustling on London streets and stages and/or in bleak orphanages. Chaplin incorporated suffering as the leitmotif of his slapstick comedy.

What was it the *Times* obit writer said of Picasso? That in the twentieth century he never found a subject equal to his talent? I guess I feel that way about the great movie clowns. W. C. Fields was paranoid. He stashed money in banks all over the country under aliases he later had trouble remembering. He was a boozer, a hard case. But he created his own universe, as William Blake would say, so that he didn't have to live in a universe created by another. Fields mocked that amalgam of buffoon, flimflam, drunk, suffering, ineffectual Everyman who was his screen persona. But we recognized his rascality, his cynicism for what it was. Fields had a hammer lock on fate. He took the red-nosed middle-America town drunk and made him a contender. He thumbed that bulbous nose at propriety and created a comic hero out of his private experience.

The rich don't make public shows of their suffering. The poor, or the driven, cultivate showman skills to sell themselves, to earn their fortunes by their wits. We should not, as Brecht warned, confuse character with talent. But the talented comic who knows the score from personal hardships is tuned in to more than pratfalls. He has a survivor's grasp of human behavior, and his very character expresses the dynamic balance of the agony and the ecstasy of life. The careers of Buster Keaton and the Marx Brothers—vaudevillians whose youths were shaped by life at its sleaziest—embody this struggle to laugh and endure in adversity.

Woody Allen got his early education in Brooklyn movie houses. He was a comedy writer who became a comedy director to protect his material. Chaplin and the others started as performers. Allen got close to pure slapstick in *Sleeper.* Yet basically he remains a writer, a talker, a monologuist who gets laughs selling himself short.

He can create vivid images with his words. Once on television, Allen described how, when he was drowning, his entire life flashed before his eyes. He went into a detailed recounting of the farm where he was born, how he milked the cows, wrestled girls in the hay, went fly-fishing for trout . . . before finally realizing that, even at death's door, "it was someone else's life flashing before my eyes."

There was a time, perhaps before I got a few lumps myself, when I might have felt disappointed by Allen's new movie, *Love and Death.* Not up to par, blah, blah, blah. Why didn't he do this? Why do that? I gladly leave the carping, for whatever its merit, to others. Is it thin, or thick? Too episodic? Check elsewhere.

I like the comic's take-off on *War and Peace.* I like his receding hairline. I like the Grim Reaper showing up at intervals throughout the movie and then taking a pirouetting Allen off to his fate in a long final shot. I like his close-up sequences, those long takes when he rambles on and gives us his philosophy of life.

I like the way he can't wear a uniform properly and can't murder even Napoleon when he's got the gun and the privacy. I like the way Diane Keaton keeps up with him. I like the way Allen makes serious things silly and silly things serious.

If you need a laugh, you know you are going to see *Love and Death,* whatever the critics say. Go back and look up some of the reviews of the Marx Brothers and W. C. Fields movies and you'll be instructed in how the nit-picking critics of the thirties demanded perfection. But the films come down to us as classics from larger-than-life, flawed characters, the likes of whom we have not seen in motion pictures since. Now, we have Woody Allen and Mel Brooks, another frail kid from New York who grew up with cockroaches for playmates and learned to make being a psychological underdog pay at the box office. (Gene Wilder, who is now directing himself in *The Adventures of Sher-*

*lock Holmes' Smarter Brother,* may also move into their league, with luck.)

Woody Allen's *Love and Death* is a costume epic with a battlefield spectacle, a Russian priest with beard so long it's impossible not to tread on it, a duel in which the life-reverencing Allen shoots up in the air rather than at his rival —and gets hit by his own bullet returning, courtesy of gravity, to earth.

*Love and Death* is more diffuse than *Sleeper* and more of a unit than *Everything You Always Wanted to Know About Sex.* Despite the wise-guy parody of *War and Peace,* Allen's appeal is that even his grossest insults and punkiest snide comments never for a moment camouflage his genuine concern about the issues that obsess him—love and death.

[1975]

## BANANAS
### Roger Greenspun

It seems apparent in *Bananas* that Woody Allen is pushing for something like classic-comedian status, and if he keeps making movies as good as *Bananas* he is going to deserve it. Everything about the film feels classic—from the title, which is pure Marx Brothers, to Woody Allen's impenetrable bearded-revolutionist's disguise—which is also pure Marx Brothers. *A Night at the Opera,* to be specific.

Actually, the disguise is only ninety-nine per cent impenetrable. I mean it fools the FBI and the State Department, but when Woody shows up as the leader of the newly liberated island of San Marcos, who should he run into but his old flame Nancy, whose burning ambition has always been to make a great liberator, and he screws her, and then confesses that he is none other than Fielding Melish, native of New York City and no stranger to her parts, either. She is shocked into recognition: "Oh my God! I *knew* something was missing."

Nancy (Louise Lasser—ex–Mrs. Woody Allen) is one of the chief glories of *Bananas.* But behind her plump blond Jewish protest-freak characterization, who finds her friend Fielding "emotionally, intellectually, and sexually immature," there lies the tradition of Chaplin's homeless waifs and Buster Keaton's dumb broads, and it is good to find a descendant of those ladies brought up to date and made—Nancy would approve the notion—relevant.

Actually, she shows up only at the beginning and the end of *Bananas,* and the all-important middle has Fielding at first the victim and then the personal victor of a revolution on a Caribbean island lying somewhat to the wilder side of both Castro's Cuba and Hitchcock's *Topaz.* Having been invited there as a potential incident by the revolutionary dictator (Carlos Montalban), who meant to kill him—by hand—blame it on the guerrillas, and then cash in on American aid; he stays to serve freedom and finally to personify it when the guerrilla leader turns out to be more power crazy (I mean crazy: he proclaims himself the nation and Swedish the national language) than the dictator he replaced. But when Fielding returns home for a little aid-grubbing of his own, he is, of course, finally unmasked as a no-good New York Commie Jewish intellectual, and he is brought to trial. At his trial, testimony is given against him by, among others, J. Edgar Hoover in disguise (a young black woman) and also by Miss America, who sings an Italian opera aria before marshaling her thoughts.

Though not the best thing in *Bananas,* Miss America's offering in the talent competition is typical of the best that gets into *Bananas,* and that qualifies it as comedy of ideas. I don't mean great ideas—but good ideas, ideas that work, that might make a joke, and that are closer to the springs of a truly political satire than most of the pseudo insight that passes for political satire in the media these days. The Woody Allen persona, though relatively indistinct and as yet without the feeling for comic gesture that characterizes both Chaplin and Keaton, makes sense and becomes funny (when it becomes funny) in terms that always imply a location in the political spectrum (lower left-hand corner) and an allegiance to at least the nebbish fringe of current thinking.

I don't want to claim too much, or to claim the wrong things for *Bananas,* but it does seem to me closer to the quality of life in America than a good many more serious movies that have "the quality of life" as their aim in view. Maybe half the ideas in the film don't come off (which leaves half that do—a very good percentage), but even those include some fantastic tries—like the finale, a TV-sportscast wedding night for Fielding and Nancy, complete with postcoital interviews in which Fielding modestly admits he was in top form but Nancy still notices something missing. But much better, because more thoughtful and less mechanically extended, is the other night of combat—in San Marcos—when the dictator mistakenly requests American intervention not from the CIA but from the United Jewish Appeal (UJA)—so that when the revolutionary troops advance through the capital city, they are met only by a force of black-coated, bearded, fund-raising rabbis.

[1971]

## SLEEPER
### Gary Arnold

Woody Allen's *Sleeper* is fast, inventive and delightful: a slapstick chase comedy set two centuries in the future, the better to satirize the present. *Sleeper* confirms Allen's position as our first distinctive, all-around film comedy star since Jerry Lewis, whose talents began to decline sharply almost a decade ago. It is the fourth picture in which Woody Allen has functioned in the multiple roles of star, screenwriter, and director, and it demonstrates Allen's increasing confidence and range as a movie clown.

Like the recent shortage of starring vehicles or good leading roles for actresses, the recent shortage of regularly employed movie clowns has given American filmmaking since the late sixties a peculiarly distorted, cheerless image. This apparent failure to encourage and develop a new generation of women stars or comic artists is unprecedented in the history of the business. I don't believe there's ever been another period in which movie-goers suffered from a lack of either female or comedic companionship.

It's probably too late for the movies to take advantage of the clowns they neglected to recruit during the past decade—for example, Carol Burnett, Jonathan Winters, and Tim Conway. However, Allen's breakthrough would seem to bode well for the comedians a little younger than he is, like the wildly imaginative Richard Pryor. Allen has proved that all it takes to rejuvenate the slapstick tradition is some fresh, hip, committed new talent. Woody Allen comedies are one of the few reliably bright prospects facing the American movie industry in the decade ahead, and perhaps their popularity will open the door for other gifted, ambitious, movie-loving clowns.

In *Sleeper*, Allen plays a modern Rip Van Winkle named Miles Monroe, a Greenwich Village health-food store owner (and part-time clarinetist) who enters the hospital in 1973 to correct a gastric upset and wakes up two hundred years later to confront a regimented, computerized utopia. It appears that the twentieth-century doctors made Miles an involuntary subject for cryogenic research. The twenty-second-century scientists who discover his capsule and thaw him out prove to be kindly, enlightened types, but they're also political subversives, members of an underground determined to overthrow the ruling technological dictatorship.

Miles's benefactors protect him as long as they can, but the authorities close in and Miles is forced to take it on the lam, in hopes of reaching rebel headquarters somewhere in the West. Thinking fast to avoid capture and lobotomy—"Not my brain! It's my second favorite organ!"—Miles pretends to be a robot in domestic service.

In this disguise he becomes houseboy to the heroine, Luna, a futuristic adaptation of the spoiled, dilettantish society girl played by Carole Lombard in *My Man Godfrey* and embodied with a similar kind of agitated but winning high-spiritedness by Diane Keaton. At first Luna is no help at all; she thinks she's living in the Best of All Possible Worlds, what with such wonders as the Telescreen, the Orb (a sphere which gets you high after a little rubbing) and the Orgasmatron (an electrical appliance that produces instant sexual gratification). It takes a little persuasion, but Miles eventually wins her over to his side, and they are assigned key roles in the upcoming *coup d'état*.

*Sleeper* has some of the acceleration and momentum of a Mack Sennett comedy. The situations and gags accumulate and snowball for stretches of ten or fifteen minutes, usually climaxed by a renewal of the chase. Then Allen seems to take a breather for a few minutes before resuming his all-out, head-long comic attack. His machine doesn't have a classic, smooth-running hum, but it gets you where you want to go, and I think the brief rest stops are necessary in feature-length slapstick.

Despite occasional lapses—Allen shortchanges a few sight gags after setting them up quite nicely—*Sleeper* impresses me as the most incisive and consistently funny Woody Allen comedy to date. Allen has acquired a cameraman —David Walsh—who gives him a look that harmonizes with the crisp, clean-cutting style of editor Ralph Rosenblum. Allen's gags are now visualized with far more assurance and dispatch than they were in his first picture. The technical improvement in his movies has been steady and remarkable, and while some of his jokes may misfire, there are no lingering duds in *Sleeper.*

There has also been remarkable improvement in Allen as a movie performer. He uses his body with far more comic skill than he used to. His pantomime in the opening reel, when Miles is coming out of his two-hundred-year coma, is particularly good. Allen demonstrates a marvelous backward stagger when he tries to take his first unassisted steps, and he gets better in the next stage of the recovery process, as Miles roams around the lab behaving like a mischievous chimpanzee. Allen is becoming almost as much fun to watch as he is to listen to. The laughs in *Sleeper* seem to derive from outrageously funny situations as often as they derive from outrageously funny lines.

If Woody Allen continues to leave certain segments of the mass audience cold, it won't be because he's seriously deficient as a funnyman but because his sense of humor offends some conventional tastes. On his part, Allen has reached out to a large public and met it more than halfway—symbolically, by slipping on a giant banana peel. *Sleeper* is a hip popular comedy, uniting broad slapstick gags with a tart, satirical, up-to-date point of view.

I don't want to spoil the better jokes in the show, but in hopes of whetting the general appetite, let me mention such highlights as Allen's encounter with robot Jewish tailors, his coronation as a beauty queen, his interpretation of Blanche du Bois (Miss Keaton contributes a pretty good Brando–Kowalski), and his interrogations, during which Miles supplies researchers with choice bits of misinformation about the present, which they're trying to reconstruct from fragmentary records. For example, the best minds of 2173 are mystified by tapes of Richard Nixon and Howard Cosell. Miles gladly settles their place in history for an inquiring posterity. Now and two centuries from now, Woody Allen gets the last laugh.

[1973]

# SLEEPER
## Molly Haskell

First, the Consumer Index Rating. For movie-goers who want to know whether to hire a baby-sitter and stand in line for Woody Allen's *Sleeper,* and whether to eat after or before the show (for fear of stomach-muscle strain), the new comedy, pitting Woody against brainwashed bullies living in the year 2173, has a fair share of laughs—four uproars, seven or eight knee-slappers, fifteen chuckles; or, more than *Play It Again, Sam* and *Everything You Always Wanted to Know About Sex* and fewer than *Take the Money and Run* and *Bananas.* In other words, enough to justify a baby-sitter, but not enough to keep you from feeling hungry afterward. As likable and intermittently funny as Allen is, there is little connection between gags and nothing to take up the slack when a joke fails. [. . .]

There are those who think we reviewers should take our chuckles and run, but I happen to believe that we have an obligation to go beyond the first hedonistic reaction to a movie to an analysis of the aftertaste, and that we also can (and cannot help but) react to other stimuli—to books on which movies are based, to other movies in the genre (to say that a movie based on *Death in Venice* or *The Long Goodbye* should be analyzed in isolation from the original is like asking us to look at Cézanne's mountains without considering our experience of real mountains—or of other paintings of real mountains), to other critics. Reviewing, being an essentially comparative task, inevitably becomes polemical: if a book is praised as the best novel of the year it is, willy-nilly and implicitly, raised over the dead or at least battered bodies of other novels—books that failed to achieve the monumentality of this one, the stylistic perfection of another, the up-to-dateness of still another. The oversell is part of a campaign to get people to buy books and go to movies, but who among us can help but react to overreaction?

Woody Allen, by treating the film medium as his private sandbox—to play in, to dump on, to ignore—has become the darling of critics who jeer at other critics for taking movies too seriously and of audiences, represented by these critics, who find the attempt to develop an idea into some kind of complete and cohesive work (heaven forbid we should use the word "art") heavygoing. The strained ambitiousness of so much contemporary filmmaking has induced in critics a neophilistinism that is as intolerant of aspiration as Harry Cohn's bellwether ass.

Woody Allen plays to this, elevating sloppiness to a governing principle. This can be hysterically funny, as when, at the opening of the film, he emerges from a cryonics tube, his feet wrapped in booties of Reynolds Wrap like some hastily frozen product. Or the idea of his going into St. Vincent's for a minor operation (and having found a parking place right in front, at that) and emerging two hundred years later. But as soon as it becomes necessary to establish his surroundings—the doctors who are sponsoring him and their conflict with the authorities—Allen is at a loss.

Allen the director can't turn away from Allen the performer and Allen the performer is not always interesting enough to sustain the mutual-admiration society. He mugs, nudges his audience, plays to them rather than to his fellow actors, alters the roles of his characters to suit the whim of the moment (Diane Keaton, for example, goes from screaming enemy to silent partner to active ally, all ineffectively, and is denied the consistency, even rigidity, that would give her comic plausibility), uses sight gags that would have as much, possibly more, impact in verbal form—as incidental humor pieces in *The New Yorker*, for example, where Allen and his screenwriter Marshall Brickman do time as writers; and displays a contempt for logic that is less grand than gratuitous. The initial Swiftian conceit of Woody as Miles Monroe, a proprietor of a Greenwich Village health-food store, thrust among the dehumanized Brobdingnagians of tomorrow, becomes anti-Swiftian in its indifference to scale, and its failure to define the natives with any detailed consistency. The sight gag of a garden of giant-sized fruits and vegetables, for example, has nothing to do with the physical proportions or any other characteristics that we know of the master race, and hence falls flat after its momentary shock value.

Allen, with four films and considerable cultural chic to his credit, can hardly claim the figurative definition for the title of his new film, and yet he presumably means for us to do so. He has cannily promoted the idea of not taking himself too seriously into a first principle of business. He distributes his films in what appears to be a hit-or-miss fashion so that most people haven't seen all four (now five), has systematically withheld them from television, where closer scrutiny might expose his limited skills and durability as a performer, and has encouraged a "just fun" attitude toward his films while stealthily adding more elaborate sketches to his repertory in order to invite comparison with the great comedians of the past. Critics have noted the influences on him —Roger Greenspun has mentioned Chaplin; and Richard Corliss, Langdon as superior to, but recognizable in, Allen's white-face, robot-servant impersonation in *Sleeper,* and Stuart Byron has suggested an affinity with Jerry Lewis.

But Allen's sense of his own identity is too strong and too obtrusive for him ever to successfully camouflage himself as a mechanical man, the way Chaplin does in *The Circus,* the way Keaton enters animistically into harmony with other organisms. Nor can he quite envision a world of "normal" people as Lewis does in *The Nutty Professor.* Allen clings tenaciously to the worm's-eye view which is the source of his humor and of his success, and which defines the limits of his vision. It is the humor of a stand-up comic, wit that plays off a given world, rather than inventing it. It is a verbal, parochial, ratty, ethnic, bargain-basement humor, sexist, conservative, self-centered, and the funniest lines in *Sleeper* are hangover lines, when the "morning after" happens to be two centuries later: "I haven't seen my analyst in two hundred years . . . *(pause)* . . . I might have been cured by now." Or, to Keaton's exclamation, "You haven't had sex in two hundred years," Miles's answer: "Two hundred and four if you count my marriage."

In alien territory, Allen can just about survive. He lacks the ability of a Chaplin or a Keaton to turn expediency into poetry, and his overconcrete personality—Jewish ethnic, New York—is a cross he brandishes with bravado (unlike Lewis who, in the Establishment fifties, was obliged to sublimate his). In this, Allen is very much in tune with the contemporary *Zeitgeist,* the vision of the alien as insider, the underdog as top banana. Whereas most comedians suggested, by their smallness or obesity, the plight of outsiders looking in, longing to join the beautiful people (and thus were universal), Allen, to his disadvantage and advantage, comes at a time when little of the decorum and ritual of an elitist society remains for the comedian to sabotage, and when the WASP establishment has been demoted, in movie mythology, with the ethnic occupying centerstage. Actors and actresses who normally would have played character parts or supporting roles (Al Pacino, Dustin Hoffman, Robert De Niro, Bruce Dern, Dennis Hopper, Barbra Streisand) are leading men or stars; the WASP has become a figure of ridicule. Note the paper-doll imbecility of the smart-set girls in *The Way We Were,* or the conversion of the Durk character in *Serpico* into the lightweight Lindsayite played by Tony Roberts (the actor, incidentally, who played the womanizer opposite Allen in *Play It Again, Sam*). Perhaps we could trace a parallel trajectory between the declining fortunes of Mayor Lindsay and the loss of potency of the screen WASP.

At the same time, Allen—and this is the source of the reactionary side of his wit—wants *in*. Like the traditionally upward-mobile Jewish kid, part of him wants to join the dumb goyim, the smiling blond middle-Americans whose surrogates are the lobotomized futuristic race of *Sleeper* who say "Green-witch Village" and never heard of Norman Mailer. But Allen never develops the tensions, and contradictions, inherent in this situation beyond showing a disinclination to become involved in a radical plot, by a group called Aries, to overthrow the government, and by showing a marked contentedness once he has been reconditioned as a member of the Establishment. He tries to have it both ways—the vernal paradise of the revolutionaries recalls *Fahrenheit 451*, but it also plays on the negative image of carnivores in Godard's *Weekend*.

Allen is too much a product of his own biography to make the leaps of association of which the great comedians were capable, or—and this is a more serious failing—to envision an adversary as a worthwhile opponent. Allen's vision of a futuristic society, despite the elaborateness of the sets under Dale Hennesy's art direction, makes one appreciate the authority of a Stanley Kubrick. The comedian lives in a symbiotic relationship with his enemy, and this is where we appreciate the genius of Chaplin and Keaton, not just in the sublime grace (or deliberate gracelessness) of their mimetic art, but on the conceptual level, in the instinct for investing the opponent with strength—the towering mass of the bully in *Easy Street,* the numerical advantage of the cops or the army of women in Keaton's films, which give rise to feats of grace and ingenuity and intimations of the spirit's immortality that are beyond the considerable talents of Woody Allen.

[1974]

## LOVE AND DEATH
### Joy Gould Boyum

Over full-bodied strains of Prokofiev and behind images of a wind-swept, thickly clouded sky, the voice of a condemned prisoner explains that he is about to be executed for a murder he did not commit. Now we shall hear the tragic story of his life, which promises to be a tale of pulsating passion and epic conflict in a nineteenth-century Russia threatened by Napoleon's hordes. But wait. There's something very familiar about that voice, something antiheroic, something schleppy, if you will. It's not the voice of a Myshkin or a Bolkonsky; it's the voice of a Woody Allen who has just introduced his current opus, *Love and Death.* And as we shall shortly see, it is Allen's own special version of a *War and Peace* in which Tolstoy has collaborated with Dostoevski, Voltaire, and Margaret Mitchell; which has been adapted for the screen by Sigmund Freud, Jean-Paul Sartre, and Jules Feiffer; which has been directed by the team of Sergei Eisenstein, Ingmar Bergman, and Cecil B. De Mille; and which boasts a star-studded cast with some forty-five speaking parts, thirty-nine of which seem dubbed by Akim Tamiroff.

And it's an epic for our time—at least, our time as perceived by an erudite and nutty little comedian who happens to have an extraordinary gift for locating intellectual pretensions and satirizing sacred cows. The title itself here makes the point. For while it plays with *War and Peace* (no more, no less pretentious a title after all), *Love and Death* also suggests the contemporary intellectual's preoccupation with psychoanalytic theory (e.g., Professor Leslie Fiedler's study, *Love and Death in the American Novel*).

But *Love and Death* also translates into another preoccupation—that of movies in general, and in particular the swashbuckling romance which devotes itself chiefly to love and the art film which preoccupies itself with death. Allen, in other words, operates on many levels at once. He can be clown enough and slapstick enough so that his movies will be entertaining to kids; he can build jokes on popular culture and so reach a mass audience (think of the use he makes of *Casablanca* in *Play It Again, Sam*); and he can also satirize a very special literary and film culture for the *cognoscenti*.

And while one can imagine many other comedians pulling off *Sleeper*'s flying sequence or kidding around with Bogart's trench-coated image, there doesn't seem to be another comedian working today who could put together the Antonioni parody in *Everything You Always Wanted to Know About Sex* or any other comic writer who could create a critical pastiche on Scandinavian playwrights like Allen's *New Yorker* piece, "Lovborg's Women Considered" ("Lovborg's work can be divided into three periods. First came the series of plays dealing with anguish, despair, dread, fear and loneliness—the comedies; the second group focussed on social change—Lovborg was instrumental in bringing about safer methods of weighing herring").

Never before *Love and Death,* though, has Allen in a *movie* made so many references to monuments of man's intellect. And this may have something to do with the fact that here, for the first time, he is working without any collaborators. His script for *Play It Again, Sam,* for example, was directed by Herbert Ross; and although Allen directed himself in *Sleeper,* Marshall Brickman shared credits with him for the screenplay. *Love and Death,* however, cites Allen alone as its writer, its director, its star, and he has made of it not only his richest film but also his most carefully structured and consistently successful one. For while there are fewer boffo laughs here than in his other movies, it also seems to me to have fewer quiet spaces. It's a movie in which Allen and his costar and straight man, the wonderfully appealing Diane Keaton, as well as the rest of a perfect cast, keep you giggling all the way through.

It's good-natured laughter, too, deriving in large part all from simply sharing in Allen's sheer pleasure in travesty, in being slightly disrespectful to what we have learned to revere. Playing with Bergman and Dostoevski, Allen reduces to absurdity such philosophic agony as the crisis of faith, such lofty concepts as spiritual rebirth, and often by introducing some farfetched and ridiculous association into a serious context. Sometimes, though, Allen gets us laughing by simply making reference to a cultural behemoth, presenting it uncaricatured, absolutely straight. And in these instances, especially, the joke ricochets, making us its butt and not what's up there on the screen.

For when Allen inserts a reference to the Odessa Steps sequence from Eisenstein's *Potemkin* which every film student has analyzed frame by frame, or recites a line from T. S. Eliot which every college freshman has committed to memory, he is not really playing with Eisenstein or Eliot. He is playing instead with our educated awe, poking fun at the deadly earnestness with which we have learned to approach these artists. And because Allen went to school with us, we know that if he is asking us to laugh at ourselves, he is laughing at himself as well. He endears himself to us then by being one of us. We don't laugh at Woody Allen—despite his often absurd appearance—the way we laugh at Groucho or Harpo Marx, that is, from a distance. Our laughter is instead a matter of recognition, of seeing in his absurdities our own.

When, in *Bananas,* for instance, he plays a revolutionary leader who is invited to dinner at the home of a Latin-American dictator and arrives carrying a little white cakebox, he makes us laugh less because of the incongruity than because we, too, have carried little white cakeboxes—mostly forced into our hands by our mothers—to dinners where such gestures seemed to us inappropriate, ridiculous.

The hilarious voice of that well-behaved, embarrassed child, as well as of the girl-crazy, bespectacled goof-up who is also the underdog in all of us, Allen speaks with even more wit for those serious students of culture who took on the challenge of *War and Peace*'s massive length, who pondered the godless universe proposed by Sartre and Camus, who worked to unravel the symbolism of Bergman's *The Seventh Seal.* And if there's something of you in that student, it's a good bet not only that Woody Allen may be your favorite funnyman but that *Love and Death* may be your favorite Woody Allen film.

[1975]

# BROOKS VS. ALLEN

## FOR WOODY
### Gary Arnold

[. . .] On the basis of their first directing efforts, one wouldn't have been able to guess that Woody Allen would develop a flair for movie comedy that was impossible for Mel Brooks. If anything, *The Producers* seemed more promising than *Take the Money and Run.* But Allen's fourth feature, *Sleeper,* is the work of someone who has mastered a considerable amount of technique, while Brooks's *Young Frankenstein,* also a fourth feature, reveals a director whose visual imagination and technical resources remain elementary. Allen has difficulty ending his movies, but he no longer struggles to sustain his ideas over feature length. Brooks, on the other hand, can't seem to think past a single gag or punch line. Evidently, strategic considerations don't enter into his thought processes. His only system of organization is One Wheeze After Another. The choppy continuity and static situations wouldn't be so bad if the wheezes were still fresh, but Brooks has worked them into the poorhouse. He may be an example of a great funnyman who got a chance to create for the screen too late—after his comic conceits had hardened into clichés.

[1974]

# FOR MEL
## Andrew Sarris

[. . .] I have experienced a mini-*auteur*ist epiphany of sorts vis-à-vis the movies of Mel Brooks and Woody Allen, movies that are so alike in some ways, and yet so radically different.

Actually, I am indebted to Stephen Gottlieb for his review of Mel Brooks's *The Twelve Chairs* a couple of years ago. I had written off Brooks as a film director after *The Producers,* and I hadn't even bothered to see *The Twelve Chairs* when it came out. As for *Blazing Saddles,* the coming attractions on television were enough to discourage me, and the lines at the Sutton kept me away for weeks and weeks. Finally, I decided to brave the madding crowd and saw the movie under what movie publicists insist are the ideal conditions for watching a yock-yock comedy. For the first half hour, my mind kept mumbling such tentative first-draft adjectives as "imbecilic," "idiotic," "inane," "moronic," "sophomoric," and "retarded." Indeed, some of the adjectives were spilling over from the movie onto the audience that was guffawing it. When Brooks uses a slow camera movement to make sure that every last person in the theater, including the village idiot with an IQ of zilch, catches the Howard Johnson ice-cream shoppe in the Western town, I decided that Brooks had directed *Blazing Saddles* for subway riders who read the ads with their lips. Similarly, the close-up of the Gucci bag on Cleavon Little's saddle constitutes comic direction of an unspeakable vulgarity.

Still, people laughed and laughed and laughed. Why? Perhaps they came prepared to laugh, and Bergson's notion of surprise as a criterion for laughter has to be modified. Perhaps viewers refuse to believe that they are looking at a witless farce when they have stood on line so long for what seems to be a sure-fire word-of-mouth hit. Most important, most members of the audience tend to look at television longer and more often than they look at movies. Although I look at an enormous amount of television myself, I keep up with all the new movies as well. What this means is that I am not likely to be shocked into laughter by such expressions as "crock of shit" or "up your ass," whereas television audiences still seem to react to these taboo-on-TV outbursts as if demons of repression had been exorcised from the at-home psyche. Hence, movies have a great deal to gain by bucking the ratings restrictions at least where language is concerned. This may well be the most lasting moral of the box-office success of *The Exorcist.*

Toward the last half hour of *Blazing Saddles,* however, my whole attitude toward the movie changed profoundly. People around me had stopped laughing at the idiot gags and they were beginning to get restive, but the movie suddenly came alive for me. Another step remained. I had to check out *The Twelve Chairs,* which was being thoughtfully revived at bargain prices. I did so, and everything suddenly clicked into place. Mel Brooks, the comic artist, was dead and buried, and in his place was Mel Brooks, the lyrical artist.

If one were to contemplate *Blazing Saddles* and *Sleeper* from high enough up in the sociological stratosphere, one might be tempted to subsume both films under the subgenre of Jewish Humor. After all, both Mel Brooks and Woody Allen are Jewish, and they both tell jokes with more than a soupçon of Jewish self-mockery. Hence, when Mel Brooks himself (as an unlikely Yiddish Indian in the Old West) exclaims, *"Schwartze,"* at the strange sight of black-skinned pioneers in the white, white West, he is ridiculing racism on two levels, the first and more superficial in terms of the genre's white chauvinism, the second and more scathing in terms of growing Jewish-American alienation from the black community. The deep, knowing laugh at this joke erupts on the second level rather than on the first, which is to say that the joke is not so much on Randolph Scott as on Molly Goldberg. (Incidentally, I cannot vouch for the spelling of any Yiddish words on the sound track of *Blazing Saddles.* Rumor has it in *Variety* that Brooks intends to redub Yiddish words into English for middle-American audiences. I would advise him instead to provide English subtitles for the benefit of American gentiles who believe that the only way to make it in New York is to pick up a working familiarity with Yiddish.)

By the same token, when Woody Allen confesses in *Sleeper* that as a schoolboy he was regularly beaten up by Quakers, he is very laboriously resurrecting the pre-Israeli stereotype of Jewish squeamishness in the face of physical combat. The added kicker to the joke is Allen's implied disavowal of the pugnacity of the JDL as if to counter their "Never Again" with his own "Over and Over Again."

The trouble with most sociological criticism, however, is that it negates stylistic nuance. Also, sociological critics tend to be aware more of the audience's history than of the artist's. *Blazing Saddles* and *Sleeper* have evolved out of previous experiences in filmmaking by the artists gropingly involved. But whereas Brooks has adjusted his methods to correct previous failures, Allen has enlarged his canvas to exploit previous successes. By all the portents of critical fashion, Allen should now be riding high, and Brooks should be in bankruptcy, but in New York at least, *Blazing Saddles* seems to have become a bigger audience success than *Sleeper.* More than one paradox is involved here. Most critics tend to treat Allen as the merry pundit, and Brooks as the mindless prankster. My own reading is that Allen's filmmaking is more cerebral, and Brooks's more intuitive. In a strange way, Brooks is more likable than Allen. Thus, even when Allen tries to do the right thing, he seems very narrowly self-centered, whereas even when Mel Brooks surrenders to the most cynical calculations—as he does so often in *Blazing Saddles*—he still spills over with emotional generosity.

It is not so much a matter of funny lines as of the moody intersections of time and space on the screen. Brooks falls into moodiness effortlessly; Allen struggles hopelessly to show feeling through the impenetrable shell of his ego, but all he can do is wobble grotesquely across the screen in all his egg-shaped eccentricity. Actually, both Brooks and Allen derive their verbal cadences and cadenzas from roughly the same sources. Both started out as media gag writers, and both are noted for their improvisations. Among the four other writers with whom Brooks collaborated on *Blazing Saddles* is Andrew Bergman (who also wrote the original story), an alternate with Woody Allen in the "humor" pages of *The New Yorker,* yes *The New Yorker,* in the course of that august publication's shift of its socio-satiric axis from Columbus, Ohio, to Goodbye, Columbus.

As they have evolved, however, Allen has a clear edge in the development of appropriately idiosyncratic expressions for an established comic persona. Allen's best gags are consistent with the wryly recalled misadventures of a punk kid from Brooklyn with mother, wife, sex, and analyst problems that are like everyone else's and then some, and it is the "then some" which constitutes Allen's unique wit—like the time he tried to learn Spanish on long-playing records, and got the wrong speed, and would you like to hear his torpid Castilian. By contrast, Brooks has spent a great deal of his life writing either for other comedians, or for fanciful buffoons (like the thousand-year-old man) he invented for himself. What is strange is that whereas Allen seems to lack the feeling to direct himself and others in his own movies, Brooks seems to lack the most rudimentary skill in making a funny joke on paper come out funny on the screen. On a ha-ha level, Brooks is nothing short of a directorial disaster. Carl Reiner, Brooks's long-time crony, is a veritable genius by comparison in rendering both the uneven material of *Enter Laughing* and the extremely dangerous material of *Where's Poppa?* Neither of Reiner's projects came close to the comic premises of *The Producers* and yet Reiner got bigger and lustier laughs on both occasions.

Why then, aside from eminently understandable human vanity, doesn't Brooks turn over the directorial reins to Reiner, and concentrate all his creative energies on the screenplay? Quite simply, I suppose, because Brooks enjoys making his own movies, badly executed jokes and all, and this enjoyment shows through in his lyrical expression of the joys of collaboration. In *The Producers,* it was Zero Mostel and Gene Wilder finding their fountain of happiness at Lincoln Center. In *The Twelve Chairs,* it was Frank Langella and Ron Moody working out their pseudo-epileptic routines in the land of Dostoevski amid the dead bureaucratic souls of Gogol. And, finally though not ultimately, it is Cleavon Little and Gene Wilder in *Blazing Saddles,* lazing and charming their way through a mock western to the final reward of a studio limousine, thus obeying Zero Mostel's long-ago admonition: "Flaunt it, baby, while you've got it." Production story gossip has it that big cuts were made in *Blazing Saddles* (originally entitled *Black Bart*) and mostly in the Busby Berkeley finale. I have mixed feelings about this gossip, partly because I am almost certain some good stuff was lopped off, and partly because a little bit of Dom DeLuise goes a very long way with me.

Still, I'll take Brooks any way he can be made accessible to a mass audience.

*The Twelve Chairs* is clearly his best film, and it turned out to be his biggest commercial failure. In *Blazing Saddles* he has written in too much idiot laughter for my taste, but I cannot quarrel very strenuously with his strategy for survival. Besides, his lyricism, like Renoir's, depends upon a disconcerting broadness for its full impact.

That Brooks has celebrated on each occasion the collaborative ecstasy of two males for whom all women seem to function as the silliest of sex objects would seem to add a grotesque dimension to contemporary sexism. Who needs another boy-meets-boy romancer? Should we not encourage instead Woody Allen's relatively constructive relationship with Diane Keaton? The trouble is that Allen goes through all the motions of a civilized love affair, but the magic is missing, the feeling is contrived. What Allen lacks is the reckless abandon and careless rapture of Brooks. Indeed, Brooks reminds me in his most serious moments of artists like Renoir and Sternberg. But, alas, in his most comical moments, he reminds me of the Ritz Brothers. Allen reminds me of no one at all, mainly because he cannot escape from himself long enough to become a universal presence on the screen.

[1974]

# 4

# SEX AND MARRIAGE

Presixties comedies generally did not follow amorous couples right into bed, but the boudoir has become a favorite setting of late. Two new types of films which have centered on the particulars of seduction and of life after the wedding are the stud comedy and the marriage comedy.

Considering its popularity in literature, it's a bit surprising that the Don Juan or Casanova story was rare in films before the sixties. Roués and ladies' men were not unknown in the cinema before then, but, except for some Chevalier roles, they usually were secondary characters. Only after the relaxation of the Production Code allowed more sexually realistic pictures and ushered in an era which its critics at the National Catholic Office for Motion Pictures referred to as "the post-pill paradise" did the stud and his relations with women become the subject of films as popular as *Tom Jones, The Easy Life, Alfie,* and *Shampoo.*

Whereas earlier films might have discreetly portrayed a roué who would show up in each new scene with a new girl on his arm, now the films would go with him during his sexual exploits. The result was a new structure, called "picaresque" by its defenders and "episodic" by its critics, in which a film consisted of a series of brief encounters between an amoral hero and his various women.

Even the new films would not allow the stud to escape without suffering. But there was a curious ambivalence in the genre. On the one hand, the ostensible message was that the hero, pathetically substituting "sex" for "love," was unable to sustain a "mature relationship." On the other, he was always the audience identity figure, and his conquests over the opposite sex were presented as titillating heroics or subtle seductions. He was played by a charming Albert Finney, not a greasy Bruce Dern.

Feminists have argued that the genre was an inevitable result of the

"Playboy Philosophy" and the chauvinistic age it represented; the women were stereotypes seen only from the point of view of the stud hero. Entering and leaving the movie only as they entered and left his life, they were inherently dehumanized—even when, the argument goes, an attempt was made to portray them sympathetically as exploited by the stud. Certainly the sexual revolution in films never completely revolved as far for women as for men. Despite the liberation movement of the seventies, women have never had roles as equivalents to normal film "bachelors." Except for a few happy hookers *(vide Never on Sunday),* most of the women who have slept around have been the subjects of tragedy, not comedy.

Perhaps the progenitor of the stud genre, René Clément's *Monsieur Ripois (Knave of Hearts),* now strikes us, like *Beat the Devil,* as a quintessential "film ahead of its time." To many critics in 1954, it was scandalous that a movie should present as its main character a man who coldly seduces and dumps woman after woman—even if his actions were ultimately condemned—and the film was largely misunderstood as being "immoral." More than ten years later, the same charge was widely applied to the far more commercially successful *What's New Pussycat?,* perhaps because it quite openly refused to condemn the one-night-stand philosophy of its era and did not take seriously its hero's betrothal at the end. Richard Schickel's pan is representative of the fact that this box-office phenomenon was one of the most critically reviled of movies.

Ironically, the movie which gave the stud genre its greatest impetus, *Tom Jones,* shared the amoral philosophy of *Pussycat;* but the fact that it was a costume drama based on a major novel perhaps accounted for widespread acceptance of its stand. *The Easy Life, Alfie,* and *Shampoo,* though they take place in different countries and within differing social and political milieus, are more classic in their delineation of the stud story: Gassman, Caine, and Beatty are pleasure seekers who, learning too late the consequences of their love-'em-and-leave-'em attitudes, are left tragically alone at the end. If only a handful of films were pure stud comedies, nevertheless overtones of the genre were frequent in films of the sixties, particularly in series like the James Bond films and in so-called youth comedies like the American *You're a Big Boy Now* and the British *The Knack.*

In the revisionist look at love in the sixties, marriage was regarded as only slightly less frustrating than being single. It's obvious that court-ship, like war, is more dramatic than (a stable) marriage or peace. Since comedy includes—indeed, requires—as much conflict and suspense as most dramas, this situation has applied to comedy, too. The Hollywood past includes only very occasional comedies about adultery (Stroheim's early silents *Foolish Wives* and *Blind Husbands*), divorce (Leo McCarey's screwball comedy *The Awful Truth*), incompatibility (George Cukor's *The Marrying Kind*), and career conflicts (Cukor's *Adam's Rib*). In these films, if only for dramatic reasons, the institution of marriage itself was sometimes questioned, and maybe even challenged, but always in a moneyed or bohemian social context and always as a radical idea. And only occasionally, as in the *Thin Man* series, would a comedy-drama not about marriage use married couples as its main characters.

The spate of marriage comedies in recent years sometimes deals with the same plot situation—Paul Mazursky's *Blume in Love,* like *The Awful Truth,* is about the rewinning of an ex-wife—but with an important difference. The new films take place in a society where lifelong fidelity to a single partner is no longer the norm, where having sexual relations without benefit of license is generally acceptable, and where advances in birth control have made marriage less necessary and adultery less dangerous. In this new society reverence for marriage is as eroded among all classes as it once was only for fantasy figures who dominated the thirties roles and with whom the audience did not identify sociologically. When these recent films question the institution of marriage they don't do so in the abstract but treat it as a living issue —in fact, as the most important question of our time. Inherent or stated in many of the reviews that greeted recent marriage comedies was a critical delight with the fact that Hollywood was producing films that for once touched upon the lives and problems of their viewers. Whereas the existence of an entire life style as an alternative to marriage was hardly implied in *Two for the Road* and *Divorce American Style,* the films of Paul Mazursky have advanced to the stage where marriage is at war with some very seductive and institutionalized alternatives. His films, like *Bob & Carol & Ted & Alice,* certainly come out in favor of marriage, but so defensively and with such consciousness of its being almost a rear-guard point of view as to seem to confirm that in the brave new world the marriage comedy will perforce have to join its subject as a thing of the past.

Mike Nichols, Elaine May, and Neil Simon are as interested in sex and marriage as everyone else. What differentiates their films from the episodically structured stud and marriage comedies is their more classical approach to film structure. The interrelated film careers of Nichols, May, and Simon seem to represent a last stand for order amidst the open-ended disarray of such contemporaries as Mel Brooks, Woody Allen, Paul Mazursky, Robert Downey, and Michael Ritchie. The films of Nichols, May, and Simon, almost geometrically structured, are dependent on precise plot developments and well-scripted characterizations which don't leave actors much room for elaboration. At first glance this is surprising. As opposed to former gag men and television script writers like Allen and Brooks, Nichols and May come out of cabaret humor with its supposed emphasis on improvisation. But this gap between reputation and realization was always a bit of a problem with Nichols and May—indeed, such classic albums of the late fifties as their "Improvisations to Music" contained nothing but impeccably constructed playlets which belied the title.

As far as improvisation goes, any tendency in that direction on Nichols's part was in any case superseded by his tenure as a director of a string of Broadway hits, the career to which he turned immediately following the breakup of the Nichols-May act. But it was not only the idea that he was largely limited to interpreting a previously existent text which was new for Nichols. Far more drastic was his decision to specialize in the comedy of Neil Simon, whose middle-class humor was directed to another audience entirely from the collegiates who supported Nichols and May. But the application of cabaret timing to bourgeois jokes made for a fruitful tension and in retrospect provides the key to Nichols's success as a comedy film director. In Nichols's films a strong text is often structured so theatrically that it seems to divide into acts. At the same time, Nichols directs so obliquely that the inevitable result is an ambiguity which sparks debate.

In *The Graduate,* is Dustin Hoffman's Benjamin rebelling against his parents' life style, as the film's multitudes of young fans thought, or will he, as Nichols insisted in every interview, end up exactly like them? Is *Carnal Knowledge* chauvinistic toward its female characters, as Roger Greenspun believes, or is it sympathetic to them as part of a put-down of male chauvinism, as other critics have argued? Similarly, is Stockard Channing, the intended murder-victim in *The Fortune,* an innocent young thing for whom we fear or a loquacious spoiled brat whose doom is almost welcome? Nichols's ambiguity is not a matter of creating characters who are complex as, say, the title character in Mazursky's

*Blume in Love* is complex; in Nichols's films the characters suggest possibilities that are mutually exclusive. In a sense, his films are unsolved mysteries.

There is only one other recent comedy director who has been mysterious in a similar way. Unsurprisingly, it is Elaine May. Viewers and critics of *The Heartbreak Kid* seemed equally divided on whether Lenny had fulfilled his dreams, however wrongheaded, with his second marriage at the film's end, or whether he would go through the same fast change of mind that he had with his first wife. Again, a *Blume in Love* where we can say that the future of the main character "doesn't matter," is different; clearly, the future of the Heartbreak Kid *does* matter, but two opposed predictions of it seem equally plausible.

It is the measure of the success of the contrapuntal technique of these directors that they practice it against strong, self-contained texts, most often by important writers with independent reputations. Indeed, the challenge would be lost if the original text were to be radically altered by the director. Andrew Sarris, who notes the word-for-word fidelity of *The Graduate* to the original novel by Charles Webb in his favorable review (one strongly opposed here by Pauline Kael), perhaps hit on what was to be the key to Nichols's films; *Carnal Knowledge* retained the three-act structure, including even the "curtains," of the unproduced play by Jules Feiffer that it was at first. May's *Heartbreak Kid* had two celebrated names connected with its text: Neil Simon "scripted" it from a story by Bruce Jay Friedman. Molly Haskell sees conflicts between Friedman's story and May's direction, while Colin Westerbeck, Jr., sees Simon's screenplay as dominating over May's quite different directorial aims.

But such is the way with three such strong personalities as Nichols, May, and Simon. Indeed, Simon's plays, turned into films after their Broadway runs, remain Simon's completely, as they have without exception been entrusted to weak, impersonal directors. Perhaps the only other playwright previously discussible as a movie *auteur* is Tennessee Williams, whose plays were transferred into "photographed stage plays" practically scene by scene and word by word. The films of Simon's plays can be analyzed only in terms of Simon, which is why the general debate about this most successful of Broadway dramatists is as applicable to movies as it is to the stage.

Collectively, Nichols, May, and Simon represent the Broadway theatrical sensibility in present-day Hollywood; and in its concern for form and craft, in the importance it places on precision and ambiguity, it is as foreign to Hollywood as was once the Viennese cynicism of Lubitsch and Ophüls. The loose behaviorism of Southern California seems currently ascendant, even in the films of an unregenerate Gothamite like Woody Allen. It remains to be seen just how much this Broadway sensibility can survive following the move to the Coast of Simon, so much the *éminence grise* behind the recent careers of Nichols and May. So far, the outlook is problematic: *Bogart Slept Here,* an original Simon screenplay being directed by Nichols, was canceled abruptly after less than a month of shooting in 1975.

# STUD COMEDY

## *TOM JONES*
### *Arthur Knight*

Now that Tony Richardson has brought the venerable *Tom Jones* so thunderingly to life, the only question is why it had not been done earlier. Certainly Henry Fielding's novel contains all the elements necessary for a good movie. It has lovers' misunderstandings, it deals with the very rich (albeit of two centuries ago), it has comedy, chases, action, sex. In fact, it is so completely suited to cinema that one must perforce be grateful that, having been long in public domain, it never fumbled into lesser hands than those of producer-director Richardson and his skilled scenarist, playwright John Osborne. And grateful, too, that no less an actor than Albert Finney essayed the title role.

For this *Tom Jones* is a stunning job. Nothing is more difficult in the movies than a re-creation of the past—not in the genteel sense of paintings brought to life, the canvas and even the curlicued gilt frames still sticking to them, but in the purely cinematic sense of the camera burrowing in and, like a newsreel, capturing all the feeling of unpremeditated movement snapped on the fly. Richardson's England resembles Rowlandson's England rather more than Hogarth's. Caricature is subordinated to verisimilitude; elegance is to be found even among the most bumptious of rustics. But Hogarth's robust appetite for the brawling, teeming life of eighteenth-century England is here as well, and the combination is irresistible.

Most of all, however, it is Henry Fielding's England, a country viewed through the wryly critical eyes of a man who knew all too well the hypocrisies of his people and his age. And Osborne's screenplay, telescoping the early years, quickly has Tom dishonored and off on the road to London, so that Fielding's social canvas is opened to the full almost from the start. En route, there are encounters with beauties and brigands, with soldiers and scoundrels —and, as Tom dines with the copious Mrs. Waters, the funniest and lewdest eating scene ever set to celluloid.

In London, where young Tom's fortunes take an unexpected turn for the better, we are introduced into the world of fashion—of elegant ladies and their frivolous intrigues, of elaborate masked balls while the poor starve, steal, and murder on the streets. The backgrounds are etched in delicately but indelibly as Tom makes his way from Lady Bellaston's genteel bed to the foot of a roughhewn gallows. The gulf between the classes has never yawned more ominously.

But no yawns from the audience. Richardson has pitched his picaresque comedy at breakneck speed, whisking his viewers from a glimpse of the swinish table manners of a country squire to the blood-lust pleasures of a cross-country hunt, from milady's rarefied drawing room to a street brawl of Homeric proportions. In all of this, he has been masterfully aided by Walter Lassally's color cameras. Often hand-held, for the hunting sequence apparently deployed from a helicopter, constantly in motion, they swarm in for close-ups, track through the streets, or ride the carriages as if they, too, were part of the eighteenth-century scene. Lassally's work adds immeasurably to the verve and intimacy of the film, just as England's stately homes and timeless landscapes contribute the sense of a living past.

Curiously, neither Richardson nor Osborne has been willing to settle for merely a capturing of the past. Repeatedly, even before the main titles come on, they seem to be insisting that their *Tom Jones* is indeed a movie; and they play constantly with such effects as silent subtitles, stop-motion camera, and undercranking. It makes for a strange mixture of styles as the film shuttles between long passages of newsreel reality and typical presound techniques, with an occasional aside directed to the audience thrown in for good measure. But, more curious still, the effect is exhilarating because the filmmakers are so obviously having a good time. Besides, the technique permits them to get in with the utmost compression many a Fielding plot point that has long since become cliché, while, with a wink, they eliminate all feeling of cliché.

So felicitous is the ensemble playing of the large, inspired cast that it is not only difficult but downright unfair to single any out for special praise. Hugh Griffith's Squire Western, however, is cut from the same cloth as Laughton's Henry VIII—funny, full-blooded, and authentic. Susannah York is properly all sighs and stormy tears as Sophie; while Joan Greenwood plays superbly that aging feline, Lady Bellaston. And Albert Finney, in the title role, is wondrous to behold—roisterous, ribald, romantic, human.

While such mundane matters as money should be the least of a critic's concerns, I find it impossible not to add as a footnote that this sumptuous, satisfying production cost only $1,300,000. In this age of superbudgets, such a modest statistic might prove sobering. The race is not to the rich, it seems to imply, but to the talented.

[1963]

# WHAT'S NEW PUSSYCAT?

## Richard Schickel

What's new pussycat? I'll tell you what's new. Nothing's sacred any more, that's what's new. Everything's got to be insy, funsy, hippy, zippy, and, as one of our currently fashionable journalistic wordweavers would have it, everything's got to go Biff, Bam, Pow, Whoosh, and Zonk. What's happening man? It's happening man. Watch ouuuuuut belooooow.

This outburst of nonwords is occasioned by a star-filled, expensive, vulgar nonmovie called *What's New Pussycat?* It is a witless attempt to cash in on the spirit of camp which now blights our land. Camp, in case you have been wandering in the wilderness lately, has been defined as the esthetic view that something is good precisely because it is awful. But as Susan Sontag, the pioneering lexicographer of camp, puts it, "One must distinguish between naïve and deliberate camp. Pure camp is always naïve. Camp which knows itself to be camp is 'camping,' which is usually less satisfying."

You said it, lady. *Pussycat* was written by Woody Allen, our leading neurotic comedian, who also appears in it. He faithfully follows one of the cult's favorite subnotions, which is that it is wonderful fun to resurrect the almost-forgotten, just-too-much popular styles of other eras. What he has chosen to do over in the latest decorator colors is the old French bedroom farce. Peter O'Toole, who plays each scene as if he has just been violently ill off camera, is a fashion editor (what else?) afflicted with satyriasis. His problem is that, try as he may, he cannot avoid nymphomaniacs. Peter Sellers is his analyst, more eager to join him than to cure him. No plot whatever develops out of this situation—just more situations, each less logical and connected than the last, until the whole thing collapses into a lengthy unmotivated chase of excruciating ineptitude.

Being very, very hip, Mr. Allen has heard that the sex impulse is only the reverse of the death wish, so he stirs in some Freudiana about that, too.

That is the first strike against *Pussycat.* It knows too much. But on another level, it knows too little. It labors under the impression that speed is the essence of screen comedy. Its makers have obviously appreciated the works of such masters as the Marx Brothers. Who hasn't? But what they missed therein was the relentless internal logic, the compulsive concern for sticking to the truth of the basic characterizations that was the real strength of the old-timers. When they engaged in a chase, they chased *for* something, they did not run aimlessly around, hoping to stumble on the reason for their activity while it proceeded.

*Pussycat* has no internal rationale or logic. It wants only to be externally fashionable. Although it would like to be the *Dr. Strangelove* of sex, it merely ends up resembling nothing so much as an awful home movie in which a hopelessly indulgent father (or father figure?) has allowed his camera to run and run, while his smug and bratty children grow sillier and sillier, naughtier and naughtier.

At which point it precisely catches the very worst elements of the camp spirit, which is, at bottom, an exercise in self-love and self-indulgence. Camp's only real value is to its practitioners, allowing them to demonstrate to their own satisfaction their cultural superiority to those who don't dig what they dig, to those who persist in the square notion that style is merely a tool, not an end in itself. Camp is, in the end, regressive in its self-assertiveness. It is juvenilia. [ . . . ] So, *What's New Pussycat?* is, for the adult viewer, a double disaster. Not only is it camp, it is bad, self-consciously imitative camp. And there is, perhaps, another point worth raising. Camp as a matter of private taste—a Tiffany lamp in the living room, a collection of Batman comics under the bed—is a fairly innocuous matter. Who cares what *they* want to waste their money on? But deliberate camp, offered in a public medium, which we are asked to pay our money to witness, is a deliberate insult. The final triumph of camp is that moment when we masochistically put down our money at the box-office window and pay for the privilege of being scorned by children. Since *What's New Pussycat?* is a big, expensive effort in this direction, it may be a strategic place to begin the revolt against this latest form of cultural tyranny. Nothing could be a better corrective for camp than a big expensive flop.

[1965]

## ALFIE
### Richard Schickel

You may hate yourself for it in the morning, but I think you are going to enjoy *Alfie* very much. It is an exuberant movie on a savage subject—the contemporary antihero, a coward, ne'er-do-well, and mighty fornicator, a man who uses people—mainly women—and when he is finished with them throws them away like Kleenex. The trick that writer Bill Naughton (adapting his own play) and director Lewis Gilbert have brought off is to show you this all-too-familiar modern character whole, without blurring sentiment or crowd-pleasing dishonesty, and make you like both him and the process of discovering all the twists and turns of his disconcerting personality.

Several factors contribute to their unlikely achievement. There is the sheer joy they seem to find in the business of making a movie. They don't indulge in a lot of fashionable camera and editing tricks, but there is a zing in the language, a zip in the pace which give the film the sort of life that technique alone can never impart. The principal novelty devices—old-fashioned theatrical asides, interrupting the action and delivered directly to the camera—are no annoyance here; indeed, they function perfectly to draw us into Alfie's conspiracy to expose and thus undermine the conventional moral wisdom. Along with him, we joyfully discover that we are all brothers in our moral incapacity.

Then there is the pleasure of watching Michael Caine, late of *The Ipcress File,* make something wonderful out of the title role. His is a portrait in which the hard bright primary colors of his basic characterization are blended and shaded into the most subtle designs. Somehow he manages to engage our sympathies without ever once asking for them outright. Finally, and most important to its success, this is the first in the long, honorable tradition of English working-class films that does not blame its protagonist's stunted growth on the sociology or politics of postwar Britain. Alfie is not a poor Midlands lad trying to cut his way up through the unfeeling Establishment. On the contrary, he is content with life on the lower rungs of the ladder—so long as he can indulge his penchant for petty graft. Nor does he appear to be particularly afflicted by the new life of swinging London, an atmosphere that in recent fictions seems mainly to engender tedious demonstrations of the rebellious rootlessness of the young and equally tedious (and ostentatious) searches for true values on the part of one or more frightfully sensitive leading characters.

Alfie never searches for anything more complicated than a new bird. He remains, exactly as he describes himself in the first reel, a man whose only article of faith is a belief that love in any form makes you vulnerable and in the end is bound to lead to unsupportable disappointments and rejections and is therefore to be avoided at all costs. The film is, then, on the simplest level simply a string of anecdotes demonstrating Alfie's skill at getting what he wants without giving anything.

Prominent among the many women he tricks into succumbing to his very special charm are a homebody who becomes his common-law wife and bears him a son, a fancy woman, a masochistic beatnik, even the wife of the man who shares his room in a TB sanitarium. Indeed, if the film has a fault, it lies in the overabundance of evidence it lays before us to demonstrate the deadliness of Alfie's aim. But this has its uses, for it shows us how widespread and desperate is the need to love, for surely no one would fall for Alfie's ersatz product if the real thing were more readily available.

But there is more to *Alfie* than that unexceptionable point. At the end of all this his sometime victims are given the opportunity to turn on him when he needs them. Not viciously or even very dramatically, merely as casually as he left them when it appeared they were about to make unreasonable demands on him, distractedly, offhandedly. The irony is that by now he has learned from some of his experiences—the lost love of the son he loved without even knowing it at the time, the terrors of an abortion that is the wages of his adventure with his roommate's wife—that he was wrong, that worse than the dangers of love is its total absence. As he wanders away from the camera, his last aside cast aside, he knows—and we know—that he has condemned himself to the worst sort of exile, outside the circle of warmth and light which only love can create.

It's a simple message, but it is delivered with respect for the small truths of modern life as most of us live it, and with an awareness that Alfie is not the product of a special time and place but is, instead, a timeless character all of us emulate some of the time and some of us emulate all of the time. That he has been placed before us on the screen in a style that blends sympathy, savagery, and satire in such satisfyingly lifelike proportions is a small, gaudy, but at heart authentic boon. Michael Caine's Alfie is somebody you are going to carry around with you in your mind for a long time, as you did Laurence Harvey's Joe Lampton or Julie Christie's Darling.

[1966]

# SHAMPOO
## Janet Maslin

*Shampoo* is a home movie of sorts, albeit a troubling and provocative one. The leading man, a hairdresser, is an incurable lady-killer. One of his lovers, with whom he apparently had a long, steady relationship at one time, is played by Julie Christie. Politics are central to the film's attitude, if not to the hairdresser's. *Shampoo* is not Warren Beatty's baby for nothing, and in some ways it feels like a purgation of private tensions as well as a rationale for foibles that may be as much Beatty's own as his alter ego's.

I laughed during *Shampoo*'s first hour, which pivots on a series of multiple-bed mix-ups, but the film as a whole left me annoyed and disappointed. George the hairdresser, who blow-dries his way from woman to woman with neurotic aplomb, is never a very sympathetic character, and his rotating bed partners —Lee Grant as a wealthy matron, Christie as the mistress of Grant's financier husband, Goldie Hawn as the model and flibbertigibbet who is supposed to be George's steady girl—are hardly any more likable. Yet the film suddenly turns serious in midstream, with Paul Simon humming his fifty-thousand-dollar two-minute theme as George's inability to love assumes centerstage. By then, however, I was finding the coitus interruptus aspect of George's sexual style (he is always being discovered *in flagrante delicto* by one jealous interloper or another) exhausting, his numbness benumbing, and his self-pity too consuming for any further pity to be necessary.

Ah, but then Warren Beatty came to town, and before I knew it my brains were being washed and set. I should explain that Beatty's fabled charm has nothing to do with this, and neither does the sullenness of which interviewers are always (unjustly, it seemed to me) accusing him. Rather, it was his mastery of the art of circular reasoning that was overpowering. You see (his argument goes roughly like so), the critics didn't understand *Bonnie and Clyde* (the other film Beatty produced) when *it* first came along because they were too eager to pigeonhole it and too programed in their thinking to accept it for the ground- and convention-breaker it was. *Bonnie and Clyde* was a synthesis of different genres, and so (remember, this is *his* story) is *Shampoo*. Why can't a picture be callous and also compassionate? Why must a character be conventionally ingratiating to be liked? Just because a person is promiscuous, does that mean he or she can't have feelings? Are we really so committed to monogamy that we aren't ready to understand people for whom monogamy has proved unworkable? And if you don't like the characters in *Shampoo*, doesn't that say as much about you as it does about them? Well, doesn't it?

This picture is unsettling, said Beatty, because it dares to accept sexual promiscuity as a given and to treat its concomitant problems seriously. It dares to equate sexual and political apathy—the film is set on and about election eve, 1968, and its sets are plastered with Nixon–Agnew posters, yet none of the characters votes. Younger audiences can watch it and just laugh; they were brought up promiscuous, and so they take the pitfalls of that kind of life for granted. But older audiences, people just like Beatty, have a tougher time. They were caught between generations; they had the freedom and perhaps even exhausted it, but they were weaned on the Puritan ethic and have never quite reconciled their behavior with their backgrounds. They share all the liabilities of excessive liberty along with those of moral failure. Whoever they are, *Shampoo* is their movie.

Needless to say, I had to see the thing again to give my brains the figurative comb-out they so badly needed after all this rationalizing. Certain things were objectively clear immediately, one of them the appalling ineptitude of Hal Ashby, the director (he was also responsible for *The Landlord, The Last Detail,* and—Lord have mercy—*Harold and Maude*). Ashby's style is generally described as adequate but anonymous, yet he is more of an *auteur* than even his relatively enthusiastic admirers let on. Ashby envisions a profoundly cute world in which parties are fragmented into series of flip interchanges, where eyebrows are constantly being raised, where deadpans are truly dead. It's not the audience's inability to slide from comedy into contemplation that hampers *Shampoo;* the awkwardness is Ashby's. He is incapable of directing with any consistency from scene to scene.

And he is cheap, occasionally in dramatic moments, and always when it comes to humor. *Shampoo*'s comedy is utterly devoid of wit; it's the kind of picture where an "Oh, shit" is played as a laugh line. The first hour's funny moments are all of the will-X-find-out-that-Y-is-sleeping-with-Z? variety, and the casting of Jack Warden—who does very nicely, though the role to which he gives depth is better suited to a Neil Simon opus—as the philandering husband is a major mistake. He's good but, like the jokes he delivers, damagingly crude. If *Shampoo* couldn't be two pictures in one, then the story Beatty wanted to tell was far more original than the comedy at which Ashby plugs away. The guffaws do the whole thing a disservice. (Beatty admitted to a certain uneasiness over Pauline Kael's rave, which hails *Shampoo* as the "farce" he never intended it to be.)

Still, the film's basic problem lies with George, whom Beatty describes as a "dumb blond" and whom he plays brilliantly. Though the women are major characters too, George is *Shampoo*'s focal point, and as such he is taken for granted. Beatty and coscenarist Robert Towne like George, but we never find out enough about him, and he disappoints us too often. Though preconceived audience expectations are Beatty's avowed idea of a cardinal sin, the film plays so readily with our comic reflexes and political hindsight (must Nixon portraits be used to draw laughs?) that it can hardly plead innocent to charges of manipulation. *Shampoo* finally loses its grip and crosses into the realm of the exasperating when, after a wearisome spate of sexual mix-and-match, Beatty and Julie Christie finally seem to be experiencing a renewed and genuine-looking tenderness for one another. Accompanied by Simon's soothing lullaby, they leave a party and sequester themselves in a clubhouse where Beatty declares a certain limited devotion, Christie offers an understanding smile, and the two begin to make love. We are caught almost as unawares as they when a refrigerator door swings open in mid-passion, its light exposing them to three other principals who just happen to be standing outside a window.

*Shampoo* was meant, then, to be frustrating and unsatisfying, but I'm not sure the nature of the frustration dovetails with the intent. Certainly the grimly nihilistic cast it lends modern sexuality is enough to qualify it as original and to make it perversely fascinating; certainly its inability to distinguish sexual freedom from prostitution is disturbing. But the ways in which this is ultimately Beatty's home movie and apologia, the way his private insights linking sex and politics are never successfully generalized, the way in which George is more important as a Beatty alter ego than he is on his own, are all shortcomings *Shampoo* never successfully rinses away.

[1975]

# MARRIAGE

## MARRIAGE COMEDIES
### *Penelope Gilliatt*

WIFE *(near tears):* Something's wrong.
HUSBAND: Look, honey, I've had a heavy day on the Long Island Rail Road.
WIFE: I know, but we're not *relating.*

Sometimes the couple will be living in the suburbs, sometimes on Central Park West, sometimes in a converted brownstone, and sometimes the wife is the one who has had the long day, worn out with appliances and taking the children to dancing class, but in any case this piece of dialogue is roughly what all marriage comedies now produce as the crisis of the marriage and of the comedy. Congreve's descendants have decided to confine themselves to the bedroom, wit has declined into complaints about brand names, society has been thrown out of the window, and the sound of sheets rustling over huffy bodies fills the air (a sound that the miracles of recording manage to reproduce as something like the immensely amplified noise of a fly's feet clambering over the wrinkles inside a brown paper bag). The action of the typical comedy will take place mostly in bed, with excursions to the icebox, the electric toothbrush, and the electric washing machine, and to the dining area for some frenzied family meal that badly needs the sour presence of Clifton Webb. There will also be a sortie into the living room for the ritual nightmarish party that is generally the nub of the plot and the climax of the fun. Apart from the central married couple, one or other member of which will probably be mustering the courage to go into therapy (never mind the mustering of the cash), the cast will include at least two dishearteningly superior children and two sets of in-laws equipped with wry common sense and born a class lower than the young marrieds, America being (God save the language) upwardly mobile. The acting in these pieces requires technical skill of a special sort. The male lead has to be able to look manly though mother-smothered. The female lead has to be able to seem woebegone when she is actually being vicious, and she has to make you feel moved for her in dilemmas the size of a pin. Both have to be able to deliver lines on the run, and both have to be able to flounce out of bed, which is not an easy place to flounce out of.

[1970]

## TWO FOR THE ROAD
### Joseph Gelmis

*Two for the Road* is a romance of hard, shiny surfaces and of affectionately gentle ironies and paradoxes about that most hazardous of modern trips—marriage.

The film says, without having to say it outright, that marriage is a trip, that you're always on the road, and that one for the road is not enough. The film is continuously shifting time gears, moving back and forth from Audrey Hepburn and Albert Finney's meeting on the road as naïve young hitchhikers falling in love to their present trip as a disillusioned couple trying to save a shaky marriage.

"Did we get married?" Finney taunts. "Yes," Miss Hepburn replies wearily, "don't you remember? When sex stopped being fun?" "Oh yeah," he recalls, "when it got official."

*Two for the Road* is not a very deep look at real people. But its gimmick, a series of flashbacks of previous trips interspersed with their present one to make it seem like a single journey, works beautifully.

The screenplay is an original by Frederic Raphael, who wrote the script for *Darling.* It has more bite and zing and expletives than you'd normally expect to find in a film playing the staid Radio City Music Hall.

Their first trip is an adventure. Audrey, in jeans and a sweater, looks like a Maypole Twiggy (or, maybe, Twiggy, a mannequin-come-lately, looks like a runty Audrey Hepburn). She's touring Europe with some girls. When the girls get chicken pox, she continues her trip hitchhiking with Finney, a young architect who's studying old buildings.

They have an affair, almost part, but decide to get married instead. There are several more trips, with the cars reflecting their increasing affluence. On the first trip after their marriage they are more involved with their secondhand MG than each other. In a later trip, they travel with a boorish American couple and a child who is a monster because the parents are raising her permissively. The father is an efficiency expert with a stop watch for a soul. He does things like stopping abruptly in the middle of nowhere because by his calculations it's precisely Finney's turn to drive the next two hundred miles.

On another trip, they have a flashy red convertible, a child, and no time for one another. On the latest trip, they have been married perhaps ten years and they snap at one another and keep reopening all their old wounds and toting up each other's sins and shortcomings and discussing the possibility of divorce. And yet, always, they hold on, moored by that vital bond of shared experience, affection, and private tenderness which is the basis and justification for marriage after the first attraction of sex and novelty are ancient history.

One instance of the effective shifting of time planes will do. Hitchhiking on their first trip, they are ignored by so many indifferent motorists they swear that if they ever get a car they will never pass a hitchhiker by. Suddenly a car whizzes by them, and it is *them* in their snazzy white Mercedes sports coupe and the camera holds steady until the car passes and the faces of the hitchhikers are now another romantic young couple like they were.

The director of *Two for the Road* is Stanley Donen, one of the best in the business. Credit him and Raphael for a movie which, while not profound, is continuously entertaining, absorbing, and often poignant and moving.

[1967]

## DIVORCE AMERICAN STYLE
### Richard Schickel

*Divorce American Style* is a rarity among comedies American style in that it actually has something truthful to say about the way we live now and says it with a savagery of tone that runs completely counter to the warm, babbling, socially meaningless flow of our comic-movie mainstream. If you are looking for the sort of chuckly little situation comedy usually associated with stars like Dick Van Dyke and Debbie Reynolds, you may find the film a bit disconcerting at first. But if you believe that an occasional plunge into a cold needle-sharp spray of wit has a therapeutic effect, I think you may find this picture uncommonly refreshing.

It is mid-marriage time, and the Harmons (Van Dyke and Miss Reynolds) find their life together has become one long low back pain—not unbearable, but not much fun either. Marriage counseling of the professional and the over-the-back-fence varieties proves to be equally unanalgesic, and before you know it he's moved out and she's called her lawyer. So far, so routine, though the awful banality of their squabbles indicates that scriptwriter Norman Lear has observed marriage à la mode with an eye more observant and an ear more sensitive than most, while director Bud Yorkin has choreographed a door-banging, drawer-slamming nonverbal fight that is as intricate as a Chinese puzzle.

The film does not get down to cases, however, until man, woman, and their lawyers start divvying up the community property. She gets the house, he gets the mortgage; she gets the car, he gets the payments on it; and so on, until Van

Dyke begins to get the point of this exercise in legalized larceny and cries, "She gets the stock in the uranium mine, and I get the shaft."

Enter—shambling—one Nelson Downes (Jason Robards), hairy and harried, a frightful vision of the penury that is to come when the law has finished with poor Harmon. So disastrous was Downes's settlement that he cannot afford even a two-bit shave and a haircut. He drives a rusting hulk of a car, he limps horribly because the operation he needs on his leg is beyond his now-ridiculous means, and he has taken to hanging around public places looking for someone to marry his ex-wife and thus lift the alimony burden from shoulders you can hear creaking.

Alas, Harmon is absolutely the wrong man for his purposes. So, of course, the former Mrs. Downes (Jean Simmons) falls in love with him. Which means that all must now try to find a mate for the former Mrs. Harmon so he can be relieved of *his* alimony. They come up with a pip—a mother-fixated used-car salesman (Van Johnson) of surpassing smarminess—and for a moment it looks as if we are about to witness something truly unprecedented: a comedy that actually leaves its principals worse off than when it began.

Unfortunately for truth, but perhaps fortunately for our already jangled expectations, Lear and Yorkin cop out and tack an ambiguously happy ending on the film. You can't complain too much, however, for they have by this time made their point—that there is something wrong with a legal system that intervenes in a situation where normally the guilt is equally divided to punish excessively only one of the errant parties. That they dare to make jokes about it seems a minor miracle of courage. That they are often such good, gutty jokes is an astonishment.

I particularly liked the way in which Harmon is divested of his goods and chattels in a series of casual asides as the lawyers attend to the really serious business of comparing country clubs and setting up a golf date. It is a perfect gem of comic writing. It is matched on the sight-gag level by the cautionary scene in which squads of children from just one couple's string of marriages and remarriages are sorted out on a suburban front lawn and handed around to natural and stepparents whose visitation hours have accidentally coincided one sunny Saturday. It is hilarious—and it is also poignant.

The performances match the script's best moments and, indeed, easily compensate for its occasional lapses into vulgarity, its more frequent signs of strain. Miss Reynolds finally acts her age, and she has never been better than she is as the housewife who can't stand to see the magic fading from her marriage. Van Dyke proves again that he is less self-conscious as a comic actor lost in a role than he is as a straight comedian lost in himself. As for Robards, his natural gift for the grotesque gesture here shines as it has not previously had the opportunity to do in a movie career that has been a very mixed blessing.

But the best thing about *Divorce* is what it says about divorce. It animates those depressing statistics and proves that what was once a scandal—or at least an anomaly—is now firmly established as a way of life. By holding up to an unsparing, unblinking satirical light the almost universal customs that have grown up around this most peculiar of institutions, the film suggests that it is time to make it into a psychologically less desperate, more humane thing. The cliché is that divorce is hard on the children. The truth is that it is even harder on the parents and that the kind of spiritual contortions *Divorce American Style* so expertly captures is no good for anyone, be he participant, innocent underage bystander, or just a member of a society which tolerates such absurd goings on.

[1967]

I overpraised this movie. Usually there is no time for me to see films twice, but because I thought my wife might enjoy it and we were on vacation and this drive-in down the road was playing it . . . Anyway, it seemed pretty thin the second time around. What was good—notably Jason Robards's performance—was still good, but the banalities I had originally overlooked loomed distressingly large now. The thing is, I'm always looking for American movies that reflect what seems to me the most common experience in our daily lives —namely, plain ordinary middle-class desperation—and there were a few passages in *Divorce* that got that quality just right. I was apparently so delighted (and amazed) that I chose to overlook a lot of material that was merely slick and comfortable. No great harm done, I suppose, since the movie at worst was not unbearable, but I'm still looking for the film that accurately reflects the sadness (no, it's not quite a tragedy) of a class just a little too dumb and numb to rule a great nation or even to raise a family properly.

[1971]

# PAUL MAZURSKY
## *Richard Corliss*

The American political system, which expanded in the late sixties to the point where it almost cracked from excessive heat, is now contracting and consolidating. The Left has renounced righteous masochism for dextrous activism ("work within the system"), and has realized that the way to power, and thus change, is by proving not its superiority to the electorate but its similarity to it ("the system works").

Hollywood, as ever the soft-focus image of America, has reflected this change. The heady era of easy riders and cute campus radicals gave way to the acid indigestion of *Zabriskie Point, Brewster McCloud, Alex in Wonderland,* and that aptly-named epitaph, *The Last Movie:* personal statements shouted into the void of viewer apathy. But having passed through a turbulent adolescence, during which the requisite dirty words were spoken and funny cigarettes smoked behind the woodshed, America's most interesting filmmakers may be approaching the Hollywood equivalent of political maturity, whether sensible or eccentric. While Robert Altman and Richard Lester have recently muted their talent to outrage and produced the oddly academic *Thieves Like Us* and *Juggernaut,* Paul Mazursky keeps tugging away at the lunatic fringe of American comedy.

Except for the tentative happy endings, Mazursky's career could serve as a paradigm of the New Hollywood: arrival of the poor boy from Brooklyn as the star of a low-budget independent feature (Kubrick's first film, *Fear and Desire*); apprenticeship as actor *(The Blackboard Jungle),* revue performer (the Second City troupe), and TV gag writer ("The Danny Kaye Show"); modest success as a novice screenwriter *(I Love You, Alice B. Toklas);* big hit about sexual life styles *(Bob & Carol & Ted & Alice);* narcissistic, postlinear flop *(Alex in Wonderland);* unemployment (two years); retrenchment and regeneration *(Blume in Love);* modest success as an established director *(Harry and Tonto).*

Mazursky even fits that moldiest of stereotypes, the Easterner who changes his name (from Irwin Mazursky!) and goes Hollywood. But with a difference. He seems to have realized that California is merely a sprawling suburb of Hollywood, and that the rest of the country has spent the past decade trying to "go California." So he got inside Hollywood—and vice versa—the better to report, satirically but sympathetically, from the front lines. Mazursky has become that contradiction in terms, the liberal satirist: closer to an indulgent Horace than to a bitter Juvenal. He implicates himself in the general decay even as he falls in love with the would-be objects of his might-have-been scorn. Ignoring the satirist's first rule ("keep your distance"), he instead embraces his loners and swingers, hustlers and chanters, as crazily wonderful characters whose idiosyncrasies are a precious natural resource.

In many respects, Mazursky is an updated model of those pre-eminent Hollywood satirists of the fifties and early sixties, Frank Tashlin and George Axelrod—but a Tashlin after years on the analyst's couch, an Axelrod after the Esalen experience. His protagonists, like those of his mentors, are insecure, guilt-ridden, obsessive, middle-aged, middle-class males, seeking escape not into Tashlinian breast fixation or Axelrodian infidelity but onto a level of self-awareness that accepts and forgives everything. In the end, their flights are grounded, and they ruefully accept matrimony the way Churchill accepted democracy: as the worst system, except for all the others.

Each Mazursky film ends in an image of escape, either from Chayefskian reality *(Alice B. Toklas)* or into Fellini fantasy: the climactic camaraderie of *8½* in *Bob & Carol* and *Alex,* the recognition of the sea as rejuvenating life force in *Blume in Love* and *Harry and Tonto.* These resolutions are rarely satisfying, because they don't resolve anything; they simply end successive chapters in Mazursky's free-form autobiography, not with a bang but with a beatific "Oh wow!" He's a little like one of the bit players in *Blume:* a blissed-out, pansexual cutie who smiles and says, "That's O.K.," to everything from a broken date to a misfired orgasm. Having cauterized his victims, Mazursky also wants to give them final absolution.

Mazursky's first three scripts were written with Larry Tucker (who had followed much the same journeyman's road as his partner, including a Second City stint and some movie acting, as in Fuller's *Shock Corridor*), and in these films the appropriate golden-age analogue was Preston Sturges. As authors, Mazursky and Tucker had the same kind of caustic fondness for their characters—all searching for ultimate answers in head-shop fortune cookies—as

Sturges had for the fast-talking shysters and shills in his nonpareil rep company. As director, Mazursky allows plenty of room in which his own stock company of Beautiful People can wander: the middle-aged hippie waiter who looks into your soul as he describes the menu; the curly-haired teen-ager whose father freaked out in an Oregon commune ("I have to send him some bread every once in a while"); the with-it studio executive with visions of a heart-transplant love story; the Indian chief who explains his genuine healing powers with a modest "I like my work."

But Mazursky's spacious, even spaced-out *mise en scène* is the polar opposite of Sturges's visual congestion. In this relaxed atmosphere, Mazursky's actors are freer to put themselves into their characters, to collaborate in setting the film's tempo, to see their director as a fellow adventurer instead of a dictator. You might call it "encounter filmmaking." Whatever the mood may be on the set, it has helped Mazursky draw from Robert Culp, Dyan Cannon, Ellen Burstyn, George Segal, Kris Kristofferson, Marsha Mason, Art Carney, and Chief Dan George their finest movie performances. If Sturges sets in motion a determinist tornado that carries the actors willy-nilly, Mazursky lets his film float on a grass-scented California breeze.

Sturges's influence can be seen in all three Mazursky–Tucker films (with *Toklas*'s Peter Sellers retreating, like *The Lady Eve*'s Henry Fonda, from the seductive corruption of two different social worlds, and with the merry *ménage à quatre* of *The Palm Beach Story* repeating itself with hip variations in *Bob & Carol*), but most specifically in *Alex in Wonderland.* The schizophrenic ambivalence of Donald Sutherland's Alex—should the successful young director sell out and make a commercial hit, or chance ruining his career with a personal project?—itself reflects the gap between *8½* and *Sullivan's Travels,* the authors' obvious sources of inspiration. It also reflects the ambivalences within the Fellini and Sturges films. Ultimately and fatally, *Alex* opts for *8½*'s circus surrealism over its everyday ironies, and for *Sullivan's Travels'* ambitiousness over its slices of apple-pie-in-the-face Americana.

For all *Alex*'s acuity in defining the pretensions of Nouveau Hollywood, and its wry empathy with the struggling, loving couple played by Donald Sutherland and Ellen Burstyn, the film was nonetheless a critical and box-office failure. It ended the Mazursky–Tucker partnership, and was instrumental in reducing the M-G-M roar to a bankrupt purr. But perhaps Mazursky, and the American commercial film, had to get the worst of the European influence out of their systems, while retaining what was best: the recognition that movies should be made by people and not by committees. Certainly Mazursky benefited from the purging. His most interesting work lay ahead.

With *Blume in Love,* Mazursky took the hip moviemaker's biggest risk: being romantic, even corny, about love. (It was also, of course, a risk the moguls could understand.) Lionel Trilling's famous comment—that *"Lolita* is not about sex but about love . . . This makes it unique in my experience of contemporary novels"—could be said to apply, on a less rarefied but no less intense level of achievement, to Mazursky's film; for *Blume* is about a man obsessively in love. About his ex-wife Nina, Blume says, "She's the only woman I will ever love. Ever. I will die if I don't get her back. I don't want to die. Therefore, I have to get her back." The rigidity of this syllogism is matched by the cunning of his desperation. Blume tries to tiptoe back into Nina's life, but his soul squeaks pathetically. He's a kind of cartoon werewolf —a cross between Droopy Dog and Loopy de Loup—who feeds as much on her obstinate rejection of him as on her sainted presence. No contemporary actor can touch George Segal for klutzy charm or a seriocomic capacity for suffering (he's the Tom Ewell of the seventies), and no film has used his manic copelessness as well as *Blume in Love*.

At first, Mazursky seems closer in spirit to Kris Kristofferson, who plays the minstrel-bum Nina takes under her social-worker's wing as Blume's successor. As the pattern of a moralistic *Design for Living* emerges from the strands of an interrupted marriage, Blume discovers that "I still loved Nina, but I liked Elmo, too." But if Nina's character verges on caricature—the blond California wraith with translucent teeth who's too stubborn to notice how much her ex-husband loves her, and the living embodiment of the contradictions within California liberalism—it's because she exists not as a butt for Mazursky's satire but as the focal point of Blume's obsession. Mostly, we see Nina reflected in the double vision of Blume's star-crossed eyes.

Blume is not your average romantic hero. He rapes his ex-wife, listens through a keyhole while she talks to her analyst about him, and, when he has to fire his secretary (for sleeping with him), takes her to bed in order to cushion the blow—and still retains our sympathy. But Blume *is* very romantic, and so is *Blume*. The Venice of your summertime dreams may be a trite romantic symbol, but it's also a romantic city; and if it had not existed Mazursky could easily have invented it, as a floating stage on which to reunite his estranged lovers, as a Shangri-la of consummated love where even Tadzio and Aschenbach end up walking arm in arm into the Piazza San Marco. The Southern Cal mysticism of Mazursky's endings is less forced here, so it hardly matters whether Nina's unheralded appearance in the Piazza, nine months pregnant with Blume's child, represents reality or fantasy—the fulfillment of Blume's obsession or his final surrender to it. This ending, like those of *Letter from an Unknown Woman* and *An Affair to Remember,* must be taken or rejected as a secular movie miracle. Cynics need not apply.

After the vagrant but visible narrative line of *Blume in Love* comes the episodic *Harry and Tonto* (which Mazursky wrote with his long-time friend Josh Greenfeld). And after all the hints dropped in the earlier film about a Joycean odyssey (the names of Stephen Blume and his expected daughter Molly), one might wince at the prospect of Art Carney as the King Lear of Manhattan's Upper West Side, who travels across America with way stops at the homes of each of his three disappointing children. Mazursky, to his credit, doesn't seem to take these classical citations very seriously. Much more important are Old Harry's references to Russ Columbo, Maurice Chevalier, Arthur Godfrey—touchstones of a gentler age to which Harry enjoys returning. Returning but not retreating: for Harry is a domesticated Zorba, with an unquenchable thirst for life in a world of social drinkers. "I know, life is confusing," he tells his sapless elder son, "we're just trying to get on with it."

Of all Mazursky's heroes, Harry is the only one who isn't a tortured, middle-aged, vaguely Jewish, love-craving, sex-crazed lawyer or filmmaker. So for Mazursky *Harry and Tonto* seems like an itinerant vacation from his preoccupations. It's full of incidental felicities that in fact function as the vertebrae of the film's spine. As Harry keeps moving west (toward Hollywood) with his informal caravan of runaway youths, health-food peddlers, hundred-dollar whores, and a Sancho Panza tomcat named Tonto, it becomes clear that *Harry and Tonto* is a road picture: the road to an accessible utopia, which is the one Mazursky has been traveling in each of his films. It's probably just as well that the road keeps turning back on itself, and ends up not on the Via Veneto but on Sunset Boulevard; for in the hands of American utopians like Paul Mazursky, Hollywood—not just the place, but the state of mind—survives.

[1975]

# BOB & CAROL & TED & ALICE
## Rex Reed

*Bob & Carol & Ted & Alice* sounds like two 1945 radio soap operas running back to back. Don't let the title fool you. It's really a fascinating skinny dip into the psychotic state of today's modern marriages, with particular emphasis on all the wife-swapping, head-shrinking, and free-thinking phenomena indigenous to modern marriage Beverly Hills–style. It's a story of modern swingers trying to get their thing together, told with vigor and crispness, directed by a young man named Paul Mazursky in a style that is a cross between Fellini and the Maysles Brothers, and acted with such a documentary-like honesty by Natalie Wood, Robert Culp, Dyan Cannon, and Elliott Gould that I often felt like I was intruding on their most private moments by peering through their most private keyholes. There is one fabulous trip to a nudist group-therapy camp in the San Gabriel Mountains (the kind of weekend spa where all the disturbed swingers in California are going these days, the way New Yorkers go to the Hamptons) that is one of the most involving sequences I've seen on film lately. Mazursky allows the camera to linger on his subjects in this and other scenes until they all but drop dead from humiliation before the scene changes.

I don't know whom to discredit for the uneven sections of the movie; in any other film, they might not seem so strident. But *Bob & Carol* is such a fine, personal statement that it becomes annoying when it begs for laughs with situations right out of Saturday-night television comedy. At the precise moment when the two couples reach the moment of truth in a Las Vegas hotel-room orgy that will finally test the bond of their friendship, the camera lingers much too long on Elliott Gould in the bathroom, preparing his toilet like a corny routine from some prehistoric night-club act by Pinky Lee. It's a desperate attempt to inject comic relief into a tense scene that doesn't need any comic relief. All it does is destroy the scene. Other sections of the film are formless and actionless, with an ending that has everyone in Las Vegas streaming symbolically out onto the Strip in twos, like stuffed animals on their way to some psychedelic Noah's Ark. The effect, like a pale imitation of *8½,* is so pretentious and silly it is embarrassing to watch.

Fortunately, the weak things about the picture are eclipsed by other moments of wit, intelligence, and insight. And even when things get clumsy and self-conscious, everything is redeemed by the vivid, throbbing sensitivity of Natalie Wood. A criminally underrated and often badly used actress, she is one of the few Hollywood-trained stars still working in films today who, with each successive role, seems to learn from the camera instead of trying to compete with it. In *Bob & Carol & Ted & Alice,* her portrait of a groovy upper-middle-class wife combines layers of humor, subtlety, and flowering beauty in a performance of hair-raising candor. She makes the screen bigger than it really is, which, after all, is what great movie acting has always been about. Unashamedly, I must confess I find her one of the wittiest and most hypnotic screen presences since Carole Lombard.

[1969]

## BOB & CAROL & TED & ALICE
### Richard Schickel

Bob and Carol are the swingers. He's a documentary filmmaker, and one weekend they journey out to the Esalen-like institute which is to be his next subject, there to participate in an encounter group. Result: they see the future and discover that it works—for them at least.

Ted and Alice are the squares. They are the kind of old, old friends whose companionship is so taken for granted that neither couple has noticed they really have nothing in common any more except the history they have shared.

Anyway, Bob and Carol (Robert Culp and Natalie Wood) want to introduce Ted and Alice (Elliott Gould and Dyan Cannon) to their new state of grace. The latter are appalled and titillated by that prospect—appalled when Carol follows a restaurant waiter all the way into the kitchen in an attempt to relate to him as one human being to another; titillated when they discover that Bob has casually slept with a girl in San Francisco, confessed, and found his wife ever so modern and understanding about it. To be sure, he has to work a little harder when he discovers Carol exercising the same freedom in his very bed with the local tennis pro. But he manages—mixing a round of drinks and serving them, amid strained small talk, right in the bedroom they all now share.

In the retelling it sounds, perhaps, a little sour. But on the screen it is not. Neither is it black, farcical, desperately chic. To put the matter simply, *Bob & Carol & Ted & Alice* is as sweet and charming and funny and, above all, *human* as any comedy that has been made in the United States in this decade. Indeed, one has to delve much deeper in movie history to find apt comparisons to it. In the thirties, Myrna Loy and William Powell gave us our first believable vision of a sophisticated modern marriage. A little later Hepburn and Tracy revised and expanded that vision in the lovely series of marital comedies they gave us.

But in the fifties and sixties the movies have proved to be neither very funny nor very helpful when they tried to report to us from the front lines of the battle between the sexes. We have been too preoccupied with kinky kicks, not enough concerned about what Benjamin DeMott calls "the texture of domestic dailiness." And that, really, is the basis of this film's success. Its people look, act, talk like real human beings, and they move through an achingly familiar suburban world. If, perhaps, the majority of us are not yet putting the new morality into everyday use, these four people make us realize how genuinely tempting it is, how easy it can be for the people DeMott calls "competent, caring, functioning" to experiment with it. And it is perhaps a measure of how far we have come from the great days of Kate and Spence to note that it now requires a team of two couples to fully recount our follies and troubles.

There are scenes in *B&C&T&A* that will come to seem, in memory, the perfect measures of our contemporary domestic desperations in this "transitional" era. The best of them is an inbed quarrel between Ted and Alice that may be the longest—and is surely the funniest—such scene in Hollywood's history. It summarizes so many issues that cause us anguish and anxiety—the statistics of Kinsey and Masters, the psychological by-products of the pill and the pursuit of prosperity, the half-explained (and half-digested) news and advice we have received about the new ways men and women are supposed to relate to one another. It is a great scene—at once hilarious, discomfiting, and, finally, a little sad and more than a little thought-provoking. Other sequences are almost as good. For example, there is Alice head to head with her analyst—a maddeningly nondirective type who offers little more than monosyllabic encouragement (but no real assistance) in her struggle to understand herself. At long last she surfaces with a precious insight—only to have her doctor turn very directive indeed. It seems her hour is up and he firmly directs her right out the door. It seems to me a perfect paradigm of the way our calendars and schedules defeat almost every attempt to understand ourselves and the world.

But I mustn't give the impression that all the humor in the picture stems from the struggles of the squares to get with our brave new world. The smugness of the swingers—so sure they have hitched a ride on the express train of history, so endlessly understanding of everything and everybody, so earnestly helpful to each other and to their friends as they try to make it to the promised land—that is a joy, too.

In fact, one of the great pleasures of the film lies in the way all four principals keep surprising us with their excellence. One has no sooner decided that Miss Wood is doing the best job than one changes his mind; clearly Mr. Gould is best. But no—here is Miss Cannon being brilliant. And now look here—Mr. Culp has topped her. One finally gives up. They are all marvelous—wonderfully contrasting types, always in control of themselves and their material. When, finally, the movie reaches its climax in an abortive spouse swap during a Las Vegas weekend ("First the orgy, then we'll go hear Tony Bennett"), one leaves them with real regret. And with real admiration for the beautifully observed, very original script by Paul Mazursky and Larry Tucker and for the former's superb direction. If there is a criticism to be made, it is of the very last sequence, an expressionistic business out of tone with the rest of the film and quite unnecessary. It is, however, a very small regret and one quite overshadowed by the memory of the first film that has dared to be intelligently witty yet decent and compassionate about people caught up in a sexual revolution no one fully understands.

A false reputation precedes *Bob & Carol & Ted & Alice*. The night I saw it the audience was determined for a reel or two to treat it raucously, as if it were another heartless, mindless satire of an increasingly familiar type. In time, however, the boyish shouts and girlish giggles died down, replaced by another kind of laughter—the thoughtful kind which accompanies at least a degree of rueful self-recognition.

[1969]

# BLUME IN LOVE AND A TOUCH OF CLASS
## Joy Gould Boyum

Once upon a time, our male movie stars were mostly lovers. They were such Adonises as Robert Taylor, Tyrone Power, and Errol Flynn. Self-contained, self-absorbed, and courageous, they seemed to us even in their cruelty and neglect the very essence of manhood. Women could never quite possess them, for they were always departing for new and exciting adventures, inevitably committed to some manly way of life like sword-wielding, bull-fighting, jousting, even racketeering.

Today, our movie stars tend more and more to be husbands. They are reasonably attractive but quite unexceptional men like Richard Benjamin, George Segal, and Elliott Gould. Frequently cast as slightly awkward types, given to nail-biting and perspiration, and involved in such mundane professions as accounting, insurance, and the law, their chief virtues in these roles tend to lie in their reliability and conscience and, above all, in their familiarity. Lovers, after all, appeal to fantasy; husbands to our sense of reality.

And so it is no surprise that we find these husbands in films which attempt to set themselves securely in our world and which demand for their total effectiveness a considerable degree of identification on the part of their audiences. Take, for example, two current George Segal vehicles: *Blume in Love* and *A Touch of Class*. Both are romantic comedies—films, that is, about people in love which ask us alternately to laugh and if not to cry, at least to be rather moved. *Blume in Love* is not too successful in effecting either of these ends, although we can feel it trying very hard to achieve them throughout. *A Touch of Class* does a good deal better and while it's a bit too predictable, a bit too obvious in its sentiments to pull on the heartstrings of us all, most of the time it does manage to be funny enough to take in almost anyone. And a good part of its humor derives from the comic incongruity of a husband trying to make of himself a lover.

It's hardly a new gimmick—clumsy spouse playing at cool Don Juan—and has in fact been used before by the very writing team, Melvin Frank and Jack Rose, who put together this current film, most notably in their 1959 movie, *The Facts of Life,* where a husband tries unsuccessfully to consummate an extramarital affair. But in *A Touch of Class,* which Frank has also directed with an absolutely impeccable sense of comic timing, the idea has been carried further, as has the wit, to more inventive extremes. It's not simply that husband George Segal, an American insurance adjuster living in London, does in this case finally make it with his mistress, Glenda Jackson, a divorced English fashion designer—although not, of course, without a prelude of complications including a spasm in Segal's back at a very delicate moment. It's rather that, once the affair has begun, Segal carries his intrinsic domesticity over into his extradomestic life. He becomes a lover with such a developed sense of duty, with such decency and constancy as to make us feel he has taken himself not a mistress but a second wife.

And so we watch him potentially wearing himself to a frazzle by running from bed to bed, while also fulfilling his many obligations—taking his children to the park, walking his dog, writing insurance reports, playing in a Sunday-morning baseball game—but maintaining his weight, after all, by running straight from one carefully prepared and considerately accepted meal to another.

Never, in other words, has an affair looked so much like a marriage. Even the love nest the two make themselves in Soho, what with the effort both have put into it through painting, paper hanging, and building bookshelves, and with its plants and art books and spice-filled kitchen cabinets, reeks of home and hearth, and naturally, then, of the recognizable. For the clever visual and verbal gags and their consistently adroit delivery aside, what really makes *A Touch of Class* work is the degree to which George Segal's would-be lover persuades us to acknowledge in *his* comic fallibility and all-too-human limitations, our own—or, at least, those of our husbands.

*Blume in Love* tries to exact from us a similar kind of identification. Mr. Segal once again is cast as a husband who cheats on his wife—only this time he's less discreet, and when his wife catches him in bed with his secretary, she promptly divorces him. He is also, this time out, more miserable, more guilty, and decidedly more Jewish. (The issue here seems not merely that, as some aestheticians would suggest, all comedy is at base ethnic; it is rather that the particular brand of Everyman we keep confronting in these films bears considerable resemblance to that stereotype known as "the Jewish husband.")

In any case, the plot here (put together by Paul Mazursky, who also produced and directed) ostensibly concerns Blume's efforts to win his wife back —in other words, to once more play the lover. But these efforts, as well as Blume's memories which constantly interrupt them, carry us with such completeness through the very-world-that-we-live-in—we visit yoga classes, spend fifty-minute hours at the analyst's, watch people take meals at health-food restaurants, join protests by California farm hands, sit around while Mrs. Blume (Susan Anspach) and her hippie boy friend (Kris Kristofferson) sing folk songs and spout homespun words of wisdom and universal love and a woman's right to be herself—that the film almost loses sight of poor Blume and turns into a social satire. As such, however, it fails to expose very much or to take a very clear stand toward the social trends it dramatizes. For the most part, these little contemporary vignettes seem merely thrown in either for the purposes of a gag (which more often than not turns out unworthy of the trouble) or to provide for instant recognition.

This we get aplenty. But like so many other instant artifacts in our time, ease of production comes only at the expense of substance. Still, I suspect there are many who will agree to see themselves and their world in Blume and his—not least of all, all those nail-biting, slightly dishonest husbands among us.

[1973]

---

# NICHOLS & MAY & SIMON & THE MOVIES

## THE GRADUATE
### Andrew Sarris

*The Graduate* has been adapted by Mike Nichols, Buck Henry, and Calder Willingham from a novel of the same title by Charles Webb. I like the movie much better than the book, but until I had read the book I had no idea how literally faithful the screenplay was to its source. Charles Webb seems to be the forgotten man in all the publicity even though eighty percent or more of the dialogue comes right out of the book. I recently listened to some knowledgeable people parceling out writing credit to Nichols, Henry, and Willingham as if Webb had never existed, and as if the quality of a film were predetermined by the quality of its script, and as if the mystique of the director counted for nought. These knowledgeable people should read the Webb novel, which reads more like a screenplay than any "novel" since John Steinbeck's *Of Mice and Men.*

Webb's book is almost all dialogue, with the intermittent straight prose passages functioning as visual tips for the director. That is not to say that Nichols, Henry, and Willingham are not entitled to their credits, but merely that their contributions pertain more to nuance than substance, more to the how than the what.

*The Graduate,* more than *Who's Afraid of Virginia Woolf?*, is Mike Nichols's diploma as a director. Whereas Nichols merely transferred Albee, he actually transcends Webb. *The Graduate* is a director's picture not because Nichols wrote all the dialogue and acted out all the parts and sang and composed all the songs under the double pseudonym of Simon and Garfunkel and directed the cinematography under the alias of Robert Surtees, et cetera, ad infinitum, ad credit sheetum. *The Graduate* is a director's picture because even its mistakes are the proofs of a personal style.

Style is more an attitude toward things than the things themselves. It can be a raised eyebrow or a nervous smile or a pair of shrugged shoulders. It can even be an averted glance. By playing down some of the more offensive qualities of the book, Nichols expresses his own attitude toward the material. The main trouble with the book is its reduction of the world to the ridiculous scale of an overgrown and outdated Holden Caulfield. The catcher in the rye has been perverted by time and affectation into a pitcher of the wry. Charles Webb's Benjamin Braddock expresses himself with a monosyllabic smugness that becomes maddeningly self-indulgent as the book unravels into slapstick passion. Ben even goes "on the road" for a brief period to demonstrate his beatification at the expense of the beatniks. He is superior to his pathetic parents and adults generally. He is kind to the wife of his father's law partner even though she seduces him with cold-bloodedly calculating carnality. Ben then falls in love with Elaine, his mistress's daughter, and makes her marry him through the sheer persistence of his pursuit.

The screenplay has been improved by a series of little changes and omissions constituting a pattern of discretion and abstraction. The hero is made less bumptious, the predatory wife less calculating, the sensitive daughter less passive. The "on the road" passage is omitted from the movie, and the recurring parental admonitions are reduced in number and intensity. The very end of the movie is apparently the result of an anti-cliché improvisation. In the book, Ben interrupts Elaine's wedding (to another) before the troths have been plighted or the plights have been trothed or what have you. In the movie, the bride kisses the groom before Ben can disrupt the proceeding, but the bride runs off just the same. And this little change makes all the difference in dramatizing the triumph of people over proceedings. An entire genre of Hollywood movies had been constructed upon the suspenseful chase-to-the-altar proposition that what God hath joined together no studio scriptwriter can put asunder. The minister could turn out to be an impostor, the bridegroom a bigamist, but once the vows were taken, that was the old ball game. *The Graduate* not only shatters this monogamous mythology; it does so in the name of a truer love.

The emotional elevation of the film is due in no small measure to the extraordinarily engaging performances of Anne Bancroft as the wife-mother-mistress, Dustin Hoffman as the lumbering Lancelot, and Katharine Ross as his fair Elaine. Nichols is at his best in getting new readings out of old lines and thus lightening potentially heavy scenes. The director is at his worst when the eclecticism of his visual style gets out of hand. The opening sequence of bobbing, tracking, lurching heads in nightmarishly mobile close-ups looks like a "homage" to Fellini's *8½*. A rain-drenched Anne Bancroft splattered against a starkly white wall evokes images in *La Notte*. The languorous lyricism of Ben at Berkeley seems derivative of Varda's *Le Bonheur* and even some of John Korty's landscape work in the same region. Unfortunately, the cultural climate is such that the intelligent prose cinema of Mike Nichols tries to become the intellectual-poetic cinema of Michelangelo Nichols. Still, I was with *The Graduate* all the way because I responded fully to its romantic feelings, and my afterthoughts are even kinder to a movie that, unlike *Morgan!*, didn't cop out in the name of "sanity." Some people have complained that the Bancroft–Hoffman relationship is more compelling than the subsequent Ross–Hoffman relationship. I don't agree. As Stravinsky once observed, it is easier to be interesting with dissonance than consonance. Similarly, it is easier to be interesting with an unconventional sexual relationship than with a conventional love pairing. *The Graduate* is moving precisely because its hero passes from a premature maturity to an innocence regained, an idealism reconfirmed. That he is so much out of his time and place makes him more of an individual and less of a type. Even the overdone caricatures that surround the three principals cannot diminish the cruel beauty of this love story.

[1967]

## THE GRADUATE
### Pauline Kael

Part of the fun of movies is in seeing "what everybody's talking about," and if people are flocking to a movie, or if the press can con us into thinking that they are, then ironically, there is a sense in which we want to see it, even if we suspect we won't enjoy it, because we want to know what's going on. Even if it's the worst inflated pompous trash that is the most talked about (and it usually is) and even if that talk is manufactured, we want to see the movies because so many people fall for whatever is talked about that they make the advertisers' lies true. Movies absorb material from the culture and the other arts so fast that some films that have been widely *sold* become culturally and sociologically important whether they are good movies or not. Movies like *Morgan!* or *Georgy Girl* or *The Graduate*—aesthetically trivial movies which, however, because of the ways some people react to them, enter into the national bloodstream—become cultural and psychological equivalents of watching a political convention—to observe what's going on. And though this has little to do with the art of movies, it has a great deal to do with the appeal of movies.

An analyst tells me that when his patients are not talking about their personal hang-ups and their immediate problems they talk about the situations and characters in movies like *The Graduate* or *Belle de Jour* and they talk about them with as much personal involvement as about their immediate problems. I have elsewhere suggested that this way of reacting to movies as psychodrama used to be considered a preliterate way of reacting but that now those considered "postliterate" are reacting like preliterates. The high-school and college students identifying with *Georgy Girl* or Dustin Hoffman's Benjamin are not that different from the stenographer who used to live and breathe with the Joan Crawford–working girl and worry about whether that rich boy would really make her happy—and considered her pictures "great." They don't see the movie as a movie but as part of the soap opera of their lives. The fan magazines used to encourage this kind of identification; now the *advanced* mass media encourage it, and those who want to sell to youth use the language of "just let it flow over you." The person who responds this way does not respond more freely but less freely and less fully than the person who is aware of what is well done and what badly done in a movie, who can accept some things in it and reject others, who uses all his senses in reacting, not just his emotional vulnerabilities.

Still, we care about what other people care about—sometimes because we want to know how far we've gotten from common responses—and if a movie is important to other people we're interested in it because of what it means to them, even if it doesn't mean much to us. The small triumph of *The Graduate* was to have domesticated alienation and the difficulty of communication, by making what Benjamin is alienated from a middle-class comic strip and making it absurdly evident that he has nothing to communicate—which is just what makes him an acceptable hero for the large movie audience. If he said anything or had any ideas, the audience would probably hate him. *The Graduate* isn't a *bad* movie, it's entertaining, though in a fairly slick way (the audience is just about programed for laughs). What's surprising is that so many people take it so seriously. What's funny about the movie are the laughs on that dumb sincere boy who wants to talk about art in bed when the woman just wants to fornicate. But then the movie begins to pander to youthful narcissism, glorifying his innocence, and making the predatory (and now crazy) woman the villainess. Commercially this works: the inarticulate dull boy becomes a romantic hero for the audience to project into with all those squishy and now conventional feelings of look, his parents don't communicate with him; look, he wants truth not sham, and so on. But the movie betrays itself and its own expertise, sells out its comic moments that click along with the rhythm of a hit Broadway show, to make the oldest movie pitch of them all—asking the audience to identify with the simpleton who is the latest version of the misunderstood teen-ager and the pure-in-heart boy next door. It's almost painful to tell kids who have gone to see *The Graduate* eight times that once was enough for you because you've already seen it eighty times with Charles Ray and Robert Harron and Richard Barthelmess and Richard Cromwell and Charles Farrell. How could you convince them that a movie that sells innocence is a very commercial piece of work when they're so clearly in the market to buy innocence? When *The Graduate* shifts to the tender awakenings of love, it's just the latest version of *David and Lisa*. *The Graduate* only wants to succeed and that's fundamentally what's the matter with it. There is a pause for a laugh after the mention of "Berkeley" that is an unmistakable sign of hunger for success; this kind of moviemaking shifts values, shifts focus, shifts emphasis, shifts everything for a sure-fire response. Mike Nichols's "gift" is that he lets the audience direct him; this is demagoguery in the arts.

Even the cross-generation fornication is standard for the genre. It goes back to Pauline Frederick in *Smouldering Fires,* and Clara Bow was at it with mama Alice Joyce's boy friend in *Our Dancing Mothers,* and in the forties it was

*Mildred Pierce.* Even the terms are not different: in these movies the seducing adults are customarily sophisticated, worldly, and corrupt, the kids basically innocent, though not so humorless and blank as Benjamin. In its basic attitudes *The Graduate* is corny American; it takes us back to before *The Game of Love* with Edwige Feuillère as the sympathetic older woman and *A Cold Wind in August* with the sympathetic Lola Albright performance.

What's interesting about the success of *The Graduate* is sociological: the revelation of how emotionally accessible modern youth is to the same old manipulation. The recurrence of certain themes in movies suggests that each generation wants romance restated in slightly new terms, and of course it's one of the pleasures of movies as a popular art that they can answer this need. And yet, and yet—one doesn't expect an *educated* generation to be so soft on itself, much softer than the factory workers of the past who didn't go back over and over to the same movies, mooning away in fixation on themselves and thinking this fixation meant movies had suddenly become an art, and *their* art.

[1969]

## CARNAL KNOWLEDGE
### Roger Greenspun

The conflict that often exists between film truth and film style is usually resolved in favor of truth by movie-goers—partly because most of them wouldn't recognize style if it came up and shook hands with them; partly because, as somebody once said, film *is* truth twenty-four times a second. That is, it is a collection of photographs strung together. And photographs don't, or at least shouldn't, lie.

I happen to share everybody's preference for truth in movies. But I should have to point out that there is *always* style (though it is not always assertive; great movies especially seem to tend, as if by natural instinct, toward a remarkably plain style) and that the distinction between style and truth is, like the distinction between form and content, worth holding in mind. When actually seeing a movie the distinction may or may not matter much. In the best movies it is supposed to disappear, at least according to that organic metaphor of the wholeness of the work of art in which I was trained, and which is still largely current, but which begins to look less and less useful—at least as an aid to actually saying something about the poem or the picture or the play or the song or the movie that happens to be at hand.

The movie that happens to be at hand is Jules Feiffer and Mike Nichols's *Carnal Knowledge.* You will have noticed that the title promises truth—and of an especially satisfying kind. But the film moves chiefly in the artifices of its style—which in turn serves a satiric impulse of the sort that movie audiences, or audiences in general, commonly equate with "insight." I don't mean to put down audiences. Insight is the name of the game with movies of this sort, and it is the very best and most reassuring substitute for the recognition that everybody's fate is somehow part of everybody else's, which is the ultimate demonstration of great drama.

It therefore follows that the heroes of *Carnal Knowledge* are "typical," rather than universal—or individual. Some critics have complained that they are rather too specifically typical of a country of the spirit running, geographically, from Manhattan's Upper West Side to the Bronx High School of Science, to serve even the purposes that Feiffer and Nichols have in mind. I think that for the purposes, they are recognizably representative enough, but I don't much like the purposes.

We meet Jonathan and Sandy (Jack Nicholson and Arthur Garfunkel—who is good, but not very exciting) as undergraduates at Amherst in the late forties, and we leave them, respectively a successful New York accountant and doctor right about now, in the early seventies. *Carnal Knowledge* covers twenty-odd years in the lives of these two friends—but sketchily. For example, Nicholson, who looks a good forty, is never made up to look any less, while his college, which does look like Amherst, is made to sound rather more like CCNY. The coverage is also sketchy in the sense that it doesn't include whole lives but only parts of lives, relationships, male-female relationships—or, to be more exact, fucking, and certain of its ramifications. That is what the title means. *Carnal Knowledge* follows two more or less normally messed-up American males from the problems of their early twenties to the problems of their early forties from the drama of getting it in to the trauma of getting it up.

At Amherst, Jonathan and Sandy share a dormitory room and they share a girl, a bright Smithie named Susan (Candice Bergen, a beautiful and beautifully accurate performance) with whom they both make out—though Sandy doesn't know it, and he goes on to marry her, after which we don't see Susan again. Some years later, with Sandy deposited in dull suburbia, Jonathan, who has always been a breasts and buttocks man, meets Bobbie (Ann-Margret, an even more beautiful performance), who is mostly breasts and buttocks, and after some prodding he shacks up with her. More years pass. Sandy has apparently left Susan—or she might have died, for all the movie says about her. He has now married Cindy (Cynthia O'Neal), a cool competitive castrator whom Jonathan also fancies, now that he has tired of Bobbie. But Bobbie attempts suicide and Jonathan, trapped, marries her—as we learn some time later, after their divorce, and after Bobbie has dropped out of the movie.

Many years pass. Jonathan is almost gone in impotence, and Sandy, on a youth-and-young-girl kick, is slipping into a middle-aged parody of Consciousness III. They meet and talk a couple of times. Jonathan visits a whore (Rita Moreno) in her apartment, and, according to a prearranged script, she agrees with him that all women are ball-breakers. She pockets a hundred dollars and, extolling his self-sufficiency and inner strength, urges him on to yet one more late, pitiful erection. The movie ends with the recall of an earlier image—a lovely, blond, firm-breasted young figure skater who for a moment flashes into Jonathan's mind, pure and unobtainable, until she fades into a general whiteness.

The film is wholly episodic, generally without connecting links, oblivious to the fate of its women, unbalanced in the treatment of its men, apparently formless as a whole but rigidly structured in detail. That rigid structure appears in a decision, very nearly absolute, to allow no more than two principal characters on screen at any one time. Where that limitation might be violated, where there really are three people involved in a scene, then one or two will be off screen speaking, and the person on screen will react. Occasionally a character will be held in view only for a reaction (some of Ann-Margret's best moments occur this way), and occasionally only for confession directly into the camera.

The result is a kind of closet drama consisting mainly of close-ups. Some people have seen in this a weak imitation of the more anguished up-against-the-wall Antonioni (as the white-on-white figure skater is pretty clearly a weak imitation of Fellini's ambiguous image of innocence); but others, more logically, see in it an extension of the Jules Feiffer newspaper cartoon panels—a satiric enterprise of a special brilliance, but one that does not translate very effectively into live movies.

Every scene in *Carnal Knowledge* has a kind of formal unity, and every scene is a routine—from the meeting of Sandy and Susan at the college mixer with which the film begins ("I'm an act." "I know. I'm an act too . . .") to the deadly serious fantasy-making with which it ends. Some of the routines derive from domestic reality, like the really vicious arguments between Bobbie and Jonathan (tantrums are becoming a Jack Nicholson specialty, and he's good at them) as their affair dissolves into boredom before marriage. Some derive from the traditions of sexual comedy.

And some merely transfer the self-serving confession that makes up so much of Feiffer's nonpolitical satire. That satire tends toward simplifications that are (usually) redeemed by the sophistications of the Feiffer cartoons. But the lines without the line drawings don't sound like much. And when they are put into the mouths of real people, or of people in such a "reality medium" as film, they become uncomfortably reductive and subversive of what we know to exist right before our eyes.

Perhaps in spite of themselves, Jonathan and Sandy generally speak the truth when they are with women (actually, after the Amherst episodes, the movie really becomes "The Affairs of Jonathan"—and in more than one way it suggests Schnitzler gone sour and a trifle witless), and they speak crap when they are confiding in one another. I am not at all sure that this is intentional, and I am not at all sure it does not result as much from the healthy need to produce real dialogue in the man-woman situations as it does from any special appreciation of women. Some critics have said that *Carnal Knowledge,* because of the humiliations its dumb heroes impose on their women, is really, in subtle ways, demeaning to men.

I don't think that is true. I think that *Carnal Knowledge* is really, in its own terms, demeaning to women—not because it sees them and talks about them as sex objects but because, in the particular ways it values them, it never allows them the time or the freedom to make self-deluded fools of themselves. And the drive to self-delusion is, perhaps more than a sex drive, the impulse that keeps *Carnal Knowledge* going. If this weren't the case, Sandy would still be screwing Susan on the living-room floor in Westchester, and Jonathan would have accepted his bliss in Bobbie's bosom.

If for nothing else, *Carnal Knowledge* would have to be honored for undressing Ann-Margret and at the same time perceiving in her such a profound depth of pathos. From beginning to end, from sex kitten to booze hound, Bobbie is pure movie fantasy, and it is amazing just how responsible and true that fantasy seems. I can't imagine a better performance than Ann-Margret's, but I also can't imagine a performance that good with lesser material. Of course, the movie has to get rid of her, as it has to get rid of each of its individual complexities—in Susan and Cindy—though taken all together they might have made a work of less fashionable but more interesting potential.

As it is, a good deal is gotten rid of, or is slighted: from the youth make-up that might have been on Jack Nicholson's college-boy face, to the social history that is generally confined to period popular songs on the sound track and the most cursory clichés of the day in the dialogue, to the scene design that is accurate but ordinary, to the actual fucking—of which there is very little beyond a few grunts, a few rhythmic heaves, and a few sighs of satisfaction when it is over.

Such self-denial can't be less than wholly intentional. Mike Nichols's previous movies—*The Graduate, Catch-22,* etc.—haven't exactly avoided clutter. But intention doesn't guarantee achievement, and I think that *Carnal Knowledge* becomes good, when it does become good, more or less by default—as if in spite of its main design. That design—according to which Susan emerges out of the darkness to attend the mixer dance that gets things going, and Bobbie swings into view while sitting at a rotating bar to the sound of the waltzes from *Rosenkavalier,* and the gracefully circling skater in white remains the image of an ideal receding into a blanketing brightness—that design has as its basis the notion of constancy in change, a round dance for which each end figures a new beginning that is always a little nearer the end. It might have been an elegant, if rather simplistic, design, and *Carnal Knowledge* might have been a movie about the fullness of life rather than about its barrenness. But the film really lacks elegance, lacks even the sense of proportion necessary to support its own formal artifice.

Therefore it is left with only its contents: the neuroses of its men and the frustrations of its women, the insufficiency of its ideas, the predictability of its observations, and the futility of its insights. What I want to say is that life isn't like that—nothing is that simple, nobody is that available, that unapproachable, that stupid. But what I ought to say is that somebody hasn't thought long enough or hard enough about the shape a movie might take—and that a great deal of valuable energy and quite marvelous talent could have been put to better uses.

[1971]

# THE HEARTBREAK KID
## Molly Haskell

Unlike the Jewish antiheroes and alter egos of Philip Roth, Bruce Jay Friedman's protagonists have no past. They invent themselves from moment to moment, and their Jewishness is a matter of style rather than soul, a weapon turned outward in ruthless pursuit of the gag (or success), rather than inward as an instrument of persecution and self-discovery. As they ascend in a spiral of upward mobility, they erase the tracks that would have given us the clues to their future; dazzlingly unpredictable, they nevertheless lack consistent characterizations, and as such are the unscrupulous agent-victims of situation comedy that is often funnier to read than see.

Lenny, the hero of *The Heartbreak Kid*, played by Charles Grodin, seems more the progeny of Friedman, who wrote the story on which the film is based, than of Neil Simon, who wrote the screenplay, or Elaine May, who directed. But May has softened the edges, making Lenny more enchanting than he has any right to be, and brought into dramatic, if not completely resolved, focus, the surrounding characters: Jeannie Berlin, Elaine May's look-alike daughter as the briefest First Wife on record; Cybill Shepherd as the Sun-and-Snow Princess Minneapolis (the WASP Ideal, the female equivalent of Joe Namath, and as easily acquired as her predecessor is dumped); Eddie Albert as her fierce watchdog father ("I'm a brick wall, a rich brick wall," he says, just before he crumbles); and Audra Lindley as the smiling, conciliatory, and obtrusively self-effacing mother.

Elaine May's second feature is a funny and sometimes sidesplitting film whose whole never approaches the success of its best moments in which the two levels of romantic fantasy and satire are reconciled. It falls prey to the kind of tonal inconsistencies, or rather irresolutions, that one might expect from the collective effort of such similar, wittily urbane, but not identical sensibilities as May's, Simon's, and Friedman's.

The first half hour, and weakest section of the film, sets up in derisive, skit-like fashion, the marriage from which Lenny will be at least partially excused from wishing to escape. The steps leading up to (and down from) marriage are established, inadequately, through a montage of quick-cut vignettes: Lenny dressing nattily; meeting Lila in a singles bar (why couldn't we have a conversation between them to parallel the later bar scene with Kelly?); trying unsuccessfully to persuade her to make love before marriage; the Jewish wedding (a repeat of the one in *A New Leaf* minus the romanticism); and the trip to Miami in the course of which Lenny discovers enough repugnant personality traits in his wife to have her committed.

The minute Kelly comes into view, or, more properly, eclipses the sun on a deserted Miami beach, the movie picks up—not just because of Cybil Shepherd's Amazon beauty and slyly comical self-awareness, but because the WASPs are treated with hardly a trace of the caricature lavished on the Jews. They belong to a fantasy world and the question the film asks, without being able to answer, is, What happens when a fantasy comes true?

It plays on a reversal of the usual expectations: that fantasies don't come true, and that the Jewish hero will slink back, chastened, to his ethnic bride. The problem—and this brings us back to the equivocal nature of the hero, who is beautifully played by Grodin as a kind of young, Jewish Teddy Kennedy— is that the film is predicated on the compelling nature of that fantasy, without any clear understanding of what is behind or ahead of it. He is not the usual intellectual hero or poor boy, driven by social or economic motives to reach beyond himself, and the whole notion of marriage loses its urgency. However else May, Simon, and Friedman may differ, they begin with the common assumption that marriage is ridiculous, an idea that not even society is at great pains to contradict these days. Hence, there is no real reason to make marriage crucial to the narrative except to make satirical points. But the fact is, there *is* a strong impulse to marry (astonishingly, the *Times* recently reported that a larger percentage of Americans marry than any other nationality, and more now than ever before!), and if May and company had approached it with curiosity instead of derision, they might have come away with more satisfying (poetically and logically) reasons for its failure. She came closer to suggesting a feeling of complementary needs among the romantic oldsters of *A New Leaf* than she does here, where the egotistic male fantasies prevail.

The best scenes seem to bear her mark—scenes which combine satire, dead-pan humor, and sheepish vulnerability, often with little or no dialogue, long takes, and three or four people in the frame: the Miami night-club scene in which Grodin stares stupidly at Albert while Albert tries desperately, but hopelessly, to avoid his gaze; the scene in the seafood restaurant when Berlin dissolves in croaking sobs over Grodin's decision to leave her (a scene in which Friedman's cruelty seems to meet May's pathos head on); the delicious comic-erotic nude game Shepherd and Grodin play on their first "date"; and the confrontation in which Grodin "lays his cards on the table" for Albert while Cybill looks beyond them with elaborate boredom. And there are wonderfully accurate touches of décor, like the interior of Kelly's archetypally WASP Minnesota house, whose expensively tasteful furnishing is marred, characteristically, by an execrable portrait of their daughter. For such touches and minor enchantments *The Heartbreak Kid* is well worth seeing.

[1972]

## THE HEARTBREAK KID
### Colin L. Westerbeck, Jr.

A typical Neil Simon comedy is about some guys who couldn't make it in a million years, no matter what *it* is. Simon's hero is always completely out of it—out of his element like the men trying to keep house in *The Odd Couple* or the father of the bride in *Plaza Suite*, permanently out to lunch like the restaurateur in *The Last of the Red Hot Lovers*, out of a job like the advertising executive in *The Prisoner of Second Avenue*, or just out of town like the

Midwesterners visiting New York in *The Out-of-Towners.* And Simon's latest script, *The Heartbreak Kid,* which has been directed by Elaine May, begins as if it's going to run true to formula.

This time the nice Jewish boy, Leonard (Charles Grodin), is out of his mind. He marries an appropriate girl, Lila (Jeannie Berlin), and sets out from New York for a honeymoon in Miami. By Virginia, however, Leonard is finding the former girl of his dreams revolting. When a burn confines her to the hotel room for their first couple of days in sun city, he begins chasing a blonde from Minneapolis, Kelly (Cybill Shepherd), whom he meets on the beach. After a few casual encounters with this icy goddess, Leonard finally takes his newly molted wife out to dinner—so he can tell her he's leaving her and moving to Minneapolis.

Up to this point *The Heartbreak Kid* is the usual Simonizing. It makes Simon's earlier script look like *The Second-to-Last of the Red Hot Lovers.* In fact, Leonard has a lot in common with Barney (Alan Arkin), the last "last" lover. Like Leonard, Barney is schlepping after a woman who is out of his league. Actually, he's schlepping after several. His first two times at the plate he strikes out with a fast ball (Sally Kellerman) and a screwball (Paula Prentiss), so his last time up he goes for a change of pace (Renée Taylor). But even with the neighbor's wife, Barney has no more chance than we would give Leonard with Kelly.

Barney's attempted seduction of Jeanette (Ms. Taylor) is the kind of scene that Simon can write from memory—and usually does. He has written it again in *The Heartbreak Kid* when Leonard takes Lila out for dinner in Miami. (That Barney's purpose is to get Jeanette into his bed, while Leonard's is to get Lila out of his, only demonstrates the algebraic quality of Simon's mind; whenever a formula proves valid, he assumes that its converse must be valid too.) In such classic Simon scenes, each character pursues his or her own line of reasoning without listening much to the other, except to misconstrue something from time to time. Through years of practice Simon has learned to include a distracting side issue in every scene of this sort. In Barney's case, it is a bathrobe of his mother's that he happens to be wearing. At Leonard and Lila's farewell dinner, it is a piece of pecan pie Leonard orders for dessert.

If *The Heartbreak Kid* ended here, it would be as soggy a matzo ball as *Red Hot Lovers.* At the very most, when it does continue, we expect Leonard to return to Lila the way Barney returns to his senses. But Simon surprises us, for once. Leonard goes through with the annulment, moves to Minneapolis, outwits Kelly's ape of a boy friend, outlasts her bear of a father (Eddie Albert), and woos her into marriage. Perhaps if Elaine May weren't directing this time, or Simon weren't adapting a Bruce Jay Friedman short story instead of one of his own plays, things would have turned out differently for Leonard and Lila. But I doubt it. One of the disappointing things about this movie is that Simon's writing clearly dominates Ms. May's direction. The Simon touch is so deadening in the first half of the movie, it's impossible to believe he hasn't still got the upper hand in the second half.

Situation comedy is an attempt to domesticate one's nightmares, and so far Simon's nightmares have been a stock assortment: violence and social alienation *(The Out-of-Towners)*, homosexuality *(The Odd Couple)*, and, especially, sexual humiliation *(Plaza Suite, Red Hot Lovers, et al.)*. True to the function of comedy, Simon's plays are written only to make our fear of such things laughable, not to overcome it. This is why the out-of-towners flee New York defeated, Barney remains an unadulterated schlemiel and Simon's heroes generally fail to score. One way to account for Leonard, then, is to suppose that he's not a nightmare at all, but a wish fulfillment: a *gemütlich* David from New York who triumphs over the Aryan Goliaths of the Midwest.

But it seems just as likely that Leonard reveals a deeper, spookier level of Simon's unconscious. In the last scene of the film Simon and May finally begin to work harmoniously. Having opened with Leonard's marriage to Lila, the film closes with his marriage to Kelly. At the reception Leonard makes the rounds of her father's friends, handing them all the same bull about his future plans. Finally there's no one left to tell except a couple of little kids, who sit through Leonard's spiel uncomfortably and run away as soon as he's finished. Alone now on the couch, Leonard glances around with a peculiar, restless look on his face. Is he looking for new worlds to conquer, or is he looking with apprehension and dismay at the world he has conquered and must now live in? Perhaps the one possibility that Simon fears more than being put down by the Sally Kellermans and Paula Prentisses and Cybill Shepherds of the world is being accepted by them.

[1973]

## THE ODD COUPLE
### Charles Champlin

My not very fearless forecast is that *The Odd Couple* will cause more people to do more laughing than any film you are likely to see all year.

Like *The Graduate, The Odd Couple* is set in the here and now. The difference is that the here and now of *The Odd Couple* is a holdover, in both form and content, from a fondly remembered yesterday and day before yesterday. No small part of the comforting delight of Howard W. Koch's production for Paramount is its trouble-free, four-square, nostalgia-inducing, peg-joined traditional solidity. *The Graduate,* with its edgy technique reflecting and emphasizing an edgy here and now, owed to yesterday only an undated respect for craftsmanship.

As a play, Neil Simon's account of compulsively neat Felix and compulsively untidy Oscar setting up joint housekeeping in the wake of their ruptured marriages was not just foolproof, it was shockproof, dustproof, waterproof, and has proved to be serenely unaffected by translation into Italian or Swahili and hardly fazed by incurable ham acting.

As a movie, with screenplay by Simon himself and with stellar performances by Jack Lemmon as the suicidal Felix and Walter Matthau as the sardonic

Oscar, *The Odd Couple* is in some ways even more effective and sure-fire than the play.

The play, for example, has not been opened up much but it has been opened up to maximum advantage: to show Lemmon seeking out and finding the fleabag in which he aims to end his marital and sinusoidal miseries once and for all; to show Matthau (who is a sports writer) missing the rare sight of his beloved Mets pulling a triple play against the Pirates; and, most of all, to show Oscar's apartment in its entirety and in detail.

That apartment is itself a character in the proceedings, and in its pre-Felix days it is a soaring masterpiece of dusty debris, of smoldering ashtrays and aromatic cigar butts, of gray-green bread crusts and sour milk, unwashed dishes and unmade bed, yellowing newspapers and blotchy melted candy bars. It is revolting and only the miracle of cinema could show us just how revolting. Art directors Robert Benton and Ray Moyer served Simon and director Gene Saks very well indeed.

In its post-Felix days, the apartment is no less a triumph of squeaky-clean orderliness.

As he did (far less effectively) in *Luv,* Lemmon gives a very straight and earnest performance as tormented Felix. In fact, he sets up Matthau for the pay-off lines in precisely the way he did in Billy Wilder's *The Fortune Cookie.* It is a kind of brinkmanship—risky, as *Luv* proved—but here I think it mostly works, laying a base of seriousness and reality on which the comedy builds and which lets it pay off. The usual critic's term is "finely judged" and I judge the Lemmon–Matthau relationship to have been finely judged for maximum laughs by Saks and by Simon (who sat in on the several weeks of rehearsal which preceded filming).

Comedy is serious business and anyone watching *The Odd Couple* is likely to have a startled and uneasy moment at the outset, realizing that he's laughing at the difficulties a man is having committing suicide. The secret of comedy as Simon understands it is that those involved must not think they are being funny and, indeed, that their problems must seem real and the stakes high. (In confirmation, *Odd Couple* seems funnier than *Barefoot in the Park* because the problems in *Barefoot* are frivolous relative to the problems and stakes in *Odd Couple.*)

The support is at the same high level of expertise as the two principals provide. John Fiedler, David Sheiner, Larry Haines, and Herbert Edelman fill out those poker games. And Monica Evans and Carole Shelley are the English sisters who conspire with our heroes in the movie's longest sustained comic sequence (one of the high points in all of film comedy).

Neal Hefti's score is sophisticated and never overly obtrusive.

*The Odd Couple* is an old-fashioned film, solid and straightforward. The camera is a recording device, not an interpretive or impressionist device. Saks's prime concern is with the effective delivery of Simon's lines, which are the strength of the movie. It remains to be seen what Saks would do with a movie which starts from scratch. But he has been just right, I think, for Paramount's purposes in *The Odd Couple.*

I saw the film at a preview attended by an audience eager to laugh at the Western Electric trademark in the credits. But I've watched failed comedies fail before similar audiences. For what it's worth, I clocked 208 laughs, and I may have missed a couple.

I don't know that it's a relevant movie, just damned funny.

[1968]

# 5

# SOCIAL SATIRE

On the screen black comedy almost always used to mean murder made funny. As in *Arsenic and Old Lace, Monsieur Verdoux, Kind Hearts and Coronets,* and *The Trouble with Harry,* the contrast was between a bucolic or domestic setting and some most involuntary deaths. Despite the many mass slaughters in the history of war, an individual murder was until quite recently still considered an atrocity. But the nuclear bomb, the Holocaust, and the recent spate of political assassinations have had the effect of making your routine homicides look like what Jules Feiffer has famously called "little murders." Actually, 1947's *Monsieur Verdoux* was a transitional movie. Chaplin's protagonist murders individual women—but justifies his action by reference to the quite legal mass murders made possible by modern munitions.

With Stanley Kubrick's *Dr. Strangelove* (1964), black comedy entered the modern age. Not one murder, but the end of the world, became the subject of humor. Far from being domestic, it was almost epic in scope, the scenes taking place a half world apart. Ever since *Strangelove,* an expansive vision of a world going mad, implying a spiritual if not physical apocalypse, has come to lend itself to comedy. More or less traditional black comedies are still made *(Where's Poppa?, Nothing but the Best),* but the emphasis now is on large-scale horror, even if that is largely symbolic and metaphorical. Some critics have considered *Phantom of the Paradise* and *Nashville* to be apocalyptic films because, however narrow their ostensible subjects, they imply that the situations portrayed symbolize the end of a civilization.

In such an era as this, past wars as well as future ones are treated as absurdities, as in *Catch-22* and *M\*A\*S\*H.* But there's a difference. *Catch-22* clearly uses the entire World War II experience to suggest an apocalyptic end to civilization; *M\*A\*S\*H,* for all its blood, has a narrower vision. Many critics called it a black comedy inasmuch as it juxtaposed raucous humor with scenes of death. But inasmuch as it jokes not about death but about the military mentality, it may be, as William S. Pechter argues, really a service comedy.

If mass insanity is a new subject for American comedy, the individual kind is not—but there has been a significant change in the sixties. Historically, American comedy has been of two minds about clinical insanity. On the one hand, the certified crazy was often an object of fun —for example, the religious fanatic, an asylum escapee, in *Twentieth Century*. On the other hand, few figures so much became a cliché of American comedy than did the "Viennese" psychiatrist spouting incomprehensible jargon, as in *What's New Pussycat?* If comedy—especially satire—is always somewhat subversive of established order, it had to wait until psychiatry *was* the order before the subject could be met head on. It was the Age of Anxiety, with psychiatrists the unacknowledged legislators of the world, which brought forth something of a new film genre, the crazy-is-sane comedy.

Before the Freudian era, it wasn't exactly unknown to suggest that eccentricity and nonconformity were preferable to the presumed lot of most people leading lives of quiet desperation. Frank Capra's Oscar-winning *You Can't Take It with You* (1938), with its family of antimaterialistic weirdos, is undoubtedly the archetype of this sort of story, in which the world's problems are seen largely in social terms. The heroes want to escape the nine-to-five routine, the "rat race"—all those ideals of responsibility rather than sanity. It is this older tradition which continues in the sixties with such films as *A Thousand Clowns, Get to Know Your Rabbit,* and *Harold and Maude.*

But *Morgan!, King of Hearts,* and *One Flew Over the Cuckoo's Nest* are something new. The psychiatrist is seen as the creator and enforcer of society's definition of sanity—a definition that leads to war, sexual repression, and the suppression of creativity. In some ways these films reflect the work of such radical therapists as R. D. Laing and Thomas Szasz, who suggest that those whom society considers insane may be the truly sane. More indirectly, they reflect the general anti-Establishment movement among students during the sixties.

It was students who made hits of most of these films. Few were smashes when first released, and most were absolute flops. But they became "cult" films in areas around campuses, celebrated phenomena. *Harold and Maude* lasted several years at a small theater in Minneapolis and *King of Hearts* had a five-year run in a tiny house in Cambridge, Massachusetts. Boston-based social critic Andrew Kopkind has suggested that since Cambridge, home of Harvard and M.I.T., has more psychiatrists per capita than any other city in the country, the success of *King of Hearts* represents their patients' revenge on the shrinks. Inasmuch as cult success often harbingers mass success in America, it's not really surprising that *One Flew Over the Cuckoo's Nest* has finally brought gigantic commercial acceptance to the crazy-is-sane genre.

# BLACK AND APOCALYPTIC COMEDY

## DR. STRANGELOVE
### *Judith Crist*

*Dr. Strangelove, Or: How I Learned to Stop Worrying and Love the Bomb* is one of the most cogent, comic, and cruel movies to come along in many a year, and one of the best. Don't miss it—provided that you have the wit and stamina to withstand a savage satire on any number of our society's untouchables, the courage to hear a howl of outrage at the supersonic supersecurity idiocies of our time and the readiness to share Stanley Kubrick's realization that ironic laughter and ferocious caricature are the only possible responses of a sane man to the insanities of the international race toward nuclear self-destruction.

In this age of superautomation there has been the general suspicion that fool or madman could trigger the atomic holocaust on whose brink we hover; Kubrick has chosen to have it triggered by a madman—General Jack D. Ripper, of Burpelson Air Force Base, who sends a missile-laden wing of Strategic Air Command bombers off to attack the Russians, declaring his own war against the triple-pronged threat of communism, fluoridation, and sex. "Well, boys, I reckon this is it—nuclear combat toe to toe with the Ruskies," drawls the airborne wing commander, Major T. J. "King" Kong, swapping his flight helmet for a Stetson as the Red Alert Go-Code is transmitted—and off they go into the big-boom yonder.

And there's not a thing anybody can do to stop them—not with all the supersecurity, chain-of-command, automated secrecy that is the order of the day. And there's not a facet of the civilian and military involvement in this order on which Kubrick does not cast a scathing eye as Ripper's war sets off an American counterattack on Burpelson, international intrigue in the Pentagon's War Room, and intercontinental defensive plotting to have the Russians destroy the planes before they reach their targets.

For there are fools, bigots, and madmen in high places, Kubrick points out, and men of good will are at their mercy and at the mercy of the push-button scientific know-how that controls our future. And so a well-intentioned President Muffley copes with a besotted Premier Kissoff on the hot line ("Now, then, Dimitri, you know how we've always talked about the possibility of something going wrong with the bomb—the bomb, Dimitri, the hydrogen bomb . . ."); General "Buck" Turgidson urges a follow-up on Ripper's attack ("It is necessary to choose between two admittedly regrettable but nevertheless distinguishable postwar environments: one where you've got twenty million people killed and the other where you've got one hundred and fifty million people killed"); Ripper's executive officer, arrested by Burpelson's conquerors as a "deviated prevert [sic]," is finally allowed to phone the President with the Stop-Code, only to find that he hasn't the right change for the toll call—and Kong's plane, sole survivor of the mission, goes bravely on, dodging missiles and radar detection, heading for its target in the grand tradition, because "There's folks back home is a-counting on you, and, by golly, we ain't about to let them down."

Know-how, something that "bunch of ignorant peons," the Russians, haven't got, Turgidson points out, will undoubtedly enable Kong to get his disabled plane through to target, and that will trigger the Russians' "doomsday" machine. And here, emerging in pure admiration of the nihilism of this ultimate weapon, comes Dr. Strangelove, the "kraut" scientist with the artificial arm that has a will of its own as it swings to a Nazi salute or gropes for its owner's throat. Strangelove has the scientist's sunny hope for the future, for the survival of several hundred thousand people, carefully selected, of course, in some of the country's deeper mine shafts, with males polygamously repopulating an earth that would be fit for human habitation in about a hundred years. . . .

For this is the way the world will end, in a welter of mechanical failures, human bloopers, jargon, and gobbledygook. And the sheer insanity of it all bubbles forth as Ripper babbles on about the purity of life fluids, a gum-chewing Turgidson grapples with the camera-clicking Russian ambassador ("Please—gentlemen—you can't fight here—this is the War Room," the President protests), an officer who has blasted his way into an Air Force base questions the propriety of breaking open a soft-drink machine, and Kong's crew cheerfully checks survival kits, from pep pills to tranquilizers to a combination Russian phrase book and Holy Bible.

And behind the flashing needles and knives that Kubrick wields against the sacred cows, there is a gripping suspense thriller, sharply unfolded, tightly told, neatly cut from climax to climax. And beyond the laughter and the tension there is as bitter a little morality tale for our times as we have had to face in a long time, neatly tucked between the opening bars of "Try a Little Tenderness" as an airborne B-52 is refueled, and a grand finale of "We'll Meet Again (Don't Know Where, Don't Know When) . . ." as mushroom clouds fill the sky.

Kubrick earns further distinction as a model of self-discipline in his triple roles as coauthor, director, and producer, maintaining a fine balance throughout the film's taut 93 minutes. He has, of course, a superb cast at hand. Peter Sellers tops his past record for versatility in three diverse roles, as Mandrake, Ripper's British aide, embodying understated sanity in the face of madness; as President Muffley, a man made neither fool nor hero but simple and decent; and as Strangelove, the fascist supreme feeding on even the possibility of annihilation. Sterling Hayden, as the pleasantly paranoid Ripper, and George

C. Scott, as the military mind of Turgidson at large in a civilian world, are perfection; and Slim Pickens, as Kong, Keenan Wynn, as the officer hunting "preverts," and Peter Bull, as the Russian ambassador, are outstanding.

*Dr. Strangelove* is irreverent to a point of savagery; it is funny and it is engrossing. And it's heady stuff for movie-goers, for Kubrick, boy genius that he is, assumes that we're grown-up enough to share his bitter laughter.

[1964]

## DR. STRANGELOVE
### Andrew Sarris

The great merit of *Dr. Strangelove* is its bad taste. It is silly to argue that we have the right to say anything we want but that to exercise this right is the height of irresponsibility. Responsible art is dead art, and a sane (no pun intended) film on the bomb would have been a deadly bore.

Given the basic premise of nuclear annihilation, the zany conception of Stanley Kubrick, Terry Southern, and Peter George has much to commend it. Where my critical fallout with most of my colleagues occurs is in the realm of execution. Aided by the tightest scenario since *Rashomon,* and the most deceptive as far as directorial exercises go, Kubrick has been hailed in many quarters as the greatest director since D. W. Griffith. This despite a career that has consisted of six near and far misses.

Why not? *Dr. Strangelove* seems so audacious at first glance that even its faults have been rationalized into virtues. To take a crucial example, no one to my knowledge has commented on the fact that Peter Sellers was supposed to play the pivotal role of Major "King" Kong, commander of the ill-fated bomber (named "Leper Colony") that destroys the world. Because of an injury, Sellers was replaced at the last moment by Slim Pickens. Sellers was already involved in three roles—President Merkin Muffley, RAF Group Captain Lionel Mandrake, Dr. Strangelove alias Merkwürdigichliebe, formerly one of Hitler's V-2 rocket researchers at Peenemünde—so that almost everywhere you turn there is some version of Peter Sellers holding the fate of the world in his hands. The satiric symmetry of this mass casting, cribbed from *Kind Hearts and Coronets,* makes comic sense only if Sellers closes every escape hatch with his mimicry. By dropping Sellers out of the Kong role, Kubrick creates a fatal gap in his scenario between the War Room–Air Force Base sequences, where everyone is horsing around, and the bomber sequences, where an antistereotype Negro bombardier (James Earl Jones) evokes a Hawksian nobility that reminds us that "our boys" once destroyed Hitler with the same courage and professionalism now deemed ridiculous. Kubrick does his best to hoke up the actual bombing with anticowboy whoops and hollers, but the bomber has long since eluded him as it has the combined surveillance of the Pentagon and the Kremlin. Sellers playing three out of the four parts originally assigned to him is comparable to Guinness's having interpreted only six of the eight D'Ascoynes in *Kind Hearts*. Not that Sellers is any Guinness. More a mimic than an actor, Sellers starts brilliantly with President Muffley but ends badly; starts badly with Strangelove but ends brilliantly; and just muddles through with Mandrake despite some of the choicest lines in the script.

I suspect that most of the clever touches in the script can be credited to Terry Southern, author of such "underground" classics as *Flash and Filigree* and *Candy*. The nomenclature is particularly ambitious in its unrelenting expressiveness. Mandrake and Jack D. Ripper make a particularly mythic pair of misfits. Turgidson and DeSedeski read better than they sound, while Dimitri Kissoff and Bat Guano sound better than they read. Merkin Muffley is about perfect as a representation of a Stevensonian cipher.

Since Kubrick's major shortcoming, like Kurosawa's, is in structuring (or rather in failing to structure) his films with a consistent camera viewpoint, a scenario like *Dr. Strangelove* comes as a godsend. All the action is divided neatly and plausibly into three main sections, separate in space and concurrent in time. With the fate of the world riding on every twist and turn of the plot, suspense is virtually built into the theme of the film. Kubrick could sit back and let the clock tick away without reducing the tension in the audience. In this context the feeblest jokes gain added vibrations from the nervous relief they provide. Still, Kubrick's direction is, on the whole, efficient without ever being inspired. Where I think he has miscalculated most grievously is in directing George C. Scott's Air Force Chief of Staff, General Turgidson, like a saber-rattling hillbilly. Scott, who can play very quietly given half the chance, is encouraged to chew up his lines and any spare scenery lying around the War Room. By contrast, Sterling Hayden's General Ripper comes over as a tortured, psychotic, but never unintelligent fanatic. Whereas Scott masquerades as a general as if there were nothing sillier than exercising authority, Hayden captures the pathos of the man of action perverted by the contradictions of his calling. With the pathos, Hayden captures more of the comedy as well.

Kubrick can be faulted occasionally for blatant overstatement. The sign reading PEACE IS OUR BUSINESS has an ironic kick, however obvious, the first time it is shown in a strife-torn Air Force base, but when repeated a half dozen times more, the effect crosses the thin line between satire and propaganda. It is also hardly necessary to have General Turgidson lead the War Room dignitaries in prayer when all seems saved. This is even bad propaganda, since it confuses the argument. If the Pentagon is ruled by monstrous hypocrites, the audience can assume that a more reasonable set of chieftains might avert such a disaster.

Some of Kubrick's most admired effects are not quite as original as they may seem to the unschooled eye. The aerial copulation-fueling introduction is hardly a patch on the rampant jet-propelled sexuality of Josef von Sternberg's *Jet Pilot* some seven years ago. (Of course, an anti-Communist farce with John Wayne could never hope to be taken as seriously as an anti-American farce with Peter Sellers.) The trick of using popular songs as an ironic counterpoint to monstrous images may be relatively new in feature films, but people like Stan Vanderbeek have been turning out shorts like this for years. The Hiroshima and Christmas Island explosions constitute the most dog-eared footage for "peace" movies on both sides of the Iron Curtain. Consequently it is never clear whether Kubrick's "doomsday" ending is actually representational or merely rhetorical in the time-honored symbolism of antibomb movies.

*Dr. Strangelove* is more effective, if less consistent, when it probes the irregular sexual motivations of its crazy generals. It is hilariously unfair to ridicule one officer for keeping a tootsy on the side and then ridicule the other for conserving his precious fluids from hordes of women seeking his depletion.

Ultimately, *Dr. Strangelove* is not a bad movie by any standards, and I would feel much more kindly toward it if it were not so grossly overrated. Yet aside from questions of critical perspective, I think the whole subject is about a year out of date. It is just Kubrick's bad luck that he instituted this project before the signing of the test-ban treaty and the Kennedy assassination. The agitated apocalyptic mood of the Cuban confrontation is long gone. Today we read about natives with bows and arrows shooting down American helicopters flying under an alleged nuclear umbrella that is becoming more and more nebulous. What Walter Lippmann calls polycentrism is infecting both hitherto monolithic concentrations of power in the Cold War. Each day local satraps taunt the moguls in the Kremlin and the Pentagon with greater and greater impunity. Indeed, as I write, a Russian negotiator at Geneva has apparently defected to the West with all the secret Soviet strategy for conducting disarmament negotiations. Maybe Kubrick, Southern, and George can now turn their talents to a satire on all those people who were subconsciously disappointed when the world was not obliterated at the time President Kennedy had the impudence to affirm America's interests in the world. As it is, *Dr. Strangelove* can serve as a comic testament to the death wish of many American intellectuals. The world may still come to an end, of course, but the current odds are not with a bang but a whimper.

[1964]

## *MONSIEUR VERDOUX* AND *NOTHING BUT THE BEST*
### *Judith Crist*

With the dog days yapping at our heels, the time has come to seek the coolth of crime, with the relaxing chill of murder available in hammock with paper-back mystery or movie house with murder-for-laughs.

Murder for our pleasure is, of course, a movie staple, with murder for high comedy one of its rarer but more delightful aspects. The embarrassing or befuddling corpse or, preferably, corpses in the closet—or, better yet, in the open—have been high points of hilarity in a number of films, from *A Slight Case of Murder* to *Charade*. But much rarer is the comedy provided by the killer; the lesser criminal as clown can be a laughing matter (as the Europeans most often demonstrate in the *Big Deal on Madonna Street* or *Lavender Hill Mob* sort of story), but clowns are close to our hearts, and who, besides his mother, can love a murderer, let alone laugh at his on-the-job activities?

It has been done, of course, with such classics as *Arsenic and Old Lace* and *Kind Hearts and Coronets*—but there was the touch of madness for mitigation. And now we are offered two comedies—*Monsieur Verdoux* and *Nothing but the Best*—that offer us the murderer as hero amid slapstick and social comment.

*Verdoux* is a classic that we are at last privileged to appreciate after its abortive debut seventeen years ago. Some say that the cool reception accorded this Chaplin movie reflected the public's reaction against the great performer's private life and political activities; others, claiming objectivity in separating the man from the performer, feel that the temper of the times (of 1947, with war wounds still fresh) was wrong for equating a Bluebeard who murders to support his loved ones with a war hero—that the temperament and sophistication of the general public were not yet attuned to the particular brand of satire and the relatively "sick" humor of the plot.

Whatever the reasons for its initial failure, Chaplin's Bluebeard story is ours to revel in for the sheer brilliance of performance, the cinematic excellence of his direction, and the simplicity that shines in all its latter-day naïveté. The naïveté is clearer now, for Chaplin's genius is as performer and creator of performance; as ideologist he tends to oversimplify and to harangue. If only, one wishes, he had constantly had in mind the absolute perfection of the final scene between the tramp and the flower girl in *City Lights*—a wordless scene, with the pantomime underlined only by music. This would have precluded the endless harangue that mars the conclusion of *The Great Dictator,* and in *Verdoux* it would have led to sentences rather than paragraphs in the serious scenes.

If one can—well, not even quarrel—simply point to Chaplin's writing as a flicker of a flaw in the jewel that is *Verdoux,* one can proceed to the declaration that seldom has murder been made more delicious in all its various stages— the exquisite courtship of a reluctant prospect, the single shot of the smoking furnace, the hilarity of the attempted drowning of Martha Raye in the rowboat, the insane sequence of switched peroxide bottles and wineglasses. Has there ever been a comedy partner to compare with Miss Raye in all her hideous bellowing vulgarity? Here indeed is a dame who goes fishing with silver-fox stole and pompon chapeau. And the slapstick, the delicate timing of ringing doorbells and tinkling telephones, the face after face of the venal grotesques who deserve all they are to get at the murderer's hand. And there's cruelty in Chaplin's making Verdoux's wife and child so romantically sweet—and the young refugee widow so openhearted—a cruelty whose calculation is just right, for the murderer has won our hearts through them and we become a part of his nightmare in all its fantastic comedy, its biting ironies (where is there a precedent for Verdoux's gentle, "What can I do for you?" to the priest who comes to his prison cell?) and its crushing social satire.

*Monsieur Verdoux* stands as a work of art—and as, perhaps, the prototype of the lovable-murderer comedy. The latest effort in this direction, a successful one, [Clive Donner's] *Nothing but the Best,* does not *have* a "lovable" hero, only one who charms us completely because he's our kind of anti-Establishment success story.

The hero of this offbeat British film, Jimmy Brewster, is not an angry young man; he's just a horribly clear-eyed one with ambitions, who knows that in England's postwar society it's still the old school tie that counts, regardless of your inner talents and outer charm, when it comes to getting the "smashing" things of this world. So Jimmy sets out to make himself upper-U under the tutelage of a down-and-out but still teddibly upper-upper-U remittance man. But his tutor, alas, who has done a perfectly fine job on Jimmy, who's whizzing his way to the top, has had the bad taste to see Jimmy plain as one more "ambitious yob," and so, like anyone who has outlived his usefulness or has impeded Jimmy's progress, he's "got to go." But this time, instead of having the metaphorical dagger deftly stuck in his back, the victim is all too literally strangled by the old school tie and stuffed into his own old school trunk. "The trouble with living in digs is there's no place to put things," Jimmy remarks as he struggles sloppily down the stairs of his rooming house to stow the trunk in the basement. And from this point on it's a case of body, body, who's got it and who'll find it—and when it does pop up, does it drag Jimmy down?

The answer is left in your lap, and if you like, you can decide that the most offbeat feature of this film is that it suggests that crime might pay—at least for Jimmy Brewster. You may even want it to pay for him, because the beauty of the film is that its various victims usually deserve what they get, that his invasion of the upper echelons succeeds because underneath their veneer the old guardsmen are just as venal and shrewd as Jimmy, and that all he's doing is playing their own game in their own style, albeit his style is acquired rather than inbred.

And the joy of this jazzy, stylish, dashing film is its ruthless satire on the Establishment Jimmy is joining—the university phonies, the gaping and hesitant young men who've been mannered into a near-catatonic state, the doting dowagers and their rapacious daughters, the stultified clubmen, and the young set with a jargon and jive all its own. ("You've done something facetious to your hair," the playgirl sighs. "I've cut it," her fiancé explains.) It's all too obvious that once Jimmy has acquired the polish there's nothing that separates him and the elite—beyond the fact that Jimmy's handsomer, far more charming, and the smartest of the lot. Get away with murder? Maybe yes?

A cooling thought—or is it chilling? Monsieur Verdoux walks in resignation to the guillotine and Jimmy Brewster is left preparing himself for the crucial test of his masquerade and we are left to ponder our affections for the murderers.

[1964]

# WEEKEND

## Pauline Kael

Only the title of Jean-Luc Godard's new film is casual and innocent; *Weekend* is the most powerful mystical movie since *The Seventh Seal* and *Fires on the Plain* and passages of Kurosawa. We are hardly aware of the magnitude of the author-director's conception until after we are caught up in the comedy of horror, which keeps going further and becoming more nearly inescapable, like *Journey to the End of the Night*. The danger for satirists (and perhaps especially for visionary satirists) is that they don't always trust their art. They don't know how brilliantly they're making their points; they become mad with impatience and disgust, and throw off their art as if it were a hindrance to direct communication, and they begin to preach. When Godard is viciously funny, he's on top of things, and he scores and scores, and illuminates as he scores. When he becomes didactic, we can see that he really doesn't know any more about what should be done than the rest of us. But then he goes beyond didacticism into areas where, though he is as confused and divided as we are, his fervor and rage are so imaginatively justified that they are truly apocalyptic. It is in the further reaches—in the appalling, ambivalent revolutionary vision —that *Weekend* is a great, original work.

*Weekend* begins with a callous disrespect for life which is just a slight stylization of civilized living now; it's as if the consumers of *The Married Woman* had become more adulterous, more nakedly mercenary, and touchier. The people in *Weekend* have weapons and use them at the slightest provocation, and it seems perfectly logical that they should get into their cars and bang into each other and start piling up on the roads. By the time the bourgeois couple (Mireille Darc and Jean Yanne) start off on their weekend trip—to get money out of her mother—we have been prepared for almost anything by the wife's description of a sex orgy that moved from bedroom to kitchen and went so far she doesn't know for sure if it really happened, and by a couple of car collisions and the violence with which people responded to having their cars injured. And then the larger orgy begins, with a traffic jam that is a prelude to highways littered with burning cars and corpses. As long as Godard stays with cars as the symbol of bourgeois materialism, the movie is superbly controlled; the barbarousness of these bourgeois—their greed and the self-love they project onto their possessions—is exact and funny. But the movie goes much further—sometimes majestically, sometimes with brilliantly surreal details that suggest a closer affinity between Godard (who is of Swiss Protestant background) and Buñuel than might have been expected, sometimes with methods and ideas that miss, even though the intentions are interesting. The couple wreck their car, and as they wander the highways, lost among battered cars and bleeding dead, they have a series of picaresque adventures, encountering figures from literature and from films, until they meet a new race of hippie guerrillas—revolutionary cannibals raping and feeding on the bourgeoisie. It is both the next step and a new beginning.

The movie has extraordinary sections: the sequence of the wife's erotic confession, with only very small camera adjustments slightly changing what we see; a long virtuoso sequence that is all one or two tracking shots of the cars stalled on the highway and the activities of the motorists, with the car horns sounding triumphantly, like trumpets in Purcell—a masterly demonstration of how film technique can itself become the source of wit—until we get to the accident that is the start of the congestion, and the principals drive by and out of frame; a discussion seen through the windshield of a moving car when the couple are grilled by an "exterminating angel" who promises them miracles but refuses to give them anything when he finds out what they want (a big sports Mercedes, naturally blond hair, a weekend with James Bond).

But not all the big scenes work. There is respite in the story, a musicale sequence (which might be one of the cultural programs outlined in *La Chinoise*) in which a pianist plays Mozart in a farmyard while a few peasants and farm laborers listen or walk by. We are so alerted to the technical feat of this sequence (another long single shot, this one a 360-degree tracking pan around the pianist, taking in the action in the area, and then returning to the pianist and circling *again,* catching the same actions at their next stage) that the actions caught seem too mechanical. And the meaning of the sequence is too ideological and too ambiguous (like much of *Les Carabiniers*); Godard may possibly believe in that musicale—that is to say, Godard may believe that art must be taken to the peasants—but more likely he's satirizing the function and the place of art, of himself along with Mozart. This might be clearer if it were not for another, and worse, ideological sequence—a big symbolic garbage truck manned by a Negro and an Algerian, who empty the refuse of our civilization and make speeches directly at us. The more "direct" Godard is, the more fuzzy and obscure he is. Who can assimilate and evaluate this chunk of theory thrown at us in the middle of a movie? Probably most of us blank out on it. And there is the embarrassment of the thirties again because artists are not as well equipped to instruct us in political decisions as, in the intensity of their concern, they may suppose. Though the movie slackens during this agitprop, the horrors soon begin to rise again, and they get higher and higher. Some of this doesn't work, either: Godard has been showing us life going wild and depraved into nightmare, beyond totem and taboo, but his method has been comic and Brechtian. Characters become corpses and the actors reappear as new characters. We are reminded that the two principals are moving through the landscape of a movie; the fields are unrealistically green, and the blood on faces and bodies is thinly painted and patterned (like the blood on the peasant-prostitute's face in *La Chinoise*), and when the heroine kills her mother, the mother's blood splashes over a skinned rabbit like cans of paint being spilled. But then Godard shoves at our unwilling eyes the throat-cutting of a pig and the decapitation of a goose. Now, when people are killed in a movie, even when the killing is *not* stylized, it's generally O.K., because we know it's a fake, but when animals are slaughtered we are watching life being taken away. No doubt Godard intends this to shock us out of "aesthetic" responses, just as his agitprop preaching is intended to affect us directly, but I think he miscalculates. I look away from scenes like this, as I assume many others do. Is he forcing us to confront the knowledge that there are things we don't want to look at? But we knew that. Instead of drawing us into his conception, he throws us out of the movie. And, because we know how movies are made, we instinctively recognize that his method of jolting us is fraudulent; he, the movie director, has ordered that slaughter to get a reaction from us, and so we have a right to be angry with him. Whatever our civilization is responsible for, that sow up there is his, not ours.

The excellent score, by Antoine Duhamel, is ominous and dramatic; the pulse of the music helps to carry us through some of the weaker passages (such as the witless movie jokes, and the prattling of the figures from literature, who are feeble and seem fairly arch—rather like the book people in Truffaut's *Fahrenheit 451*—though Emily Brontë has a good, flaming finish). The astonishing thing is that, with all these weaknesses, the nightmarish anger that seems to cry out for a revolution of total destruction and the visionary lyricism are so strong they hold the movie together; they transcend the perfectly achieved satire. The most hideously flawed of all Godard's movies, it has more depth than anything he's done before. Although by the end his conscious meanings and attitudes are not at all clear, the vision that rises in the course of the film is so surreally powerful that one accepts it, as one accepts a lunar landscape by Bosch or a torment by Grünewald. *Weekend* is Godard's vision of Hell, and it ranks with the visions of the greatest.

*Weekend* is the fifteenth of Godard's feature films, which began with *Breathless* in 1959, and he has also made sections of several omnibus films. At thirty-seven, he is in something of the position in the world of film that James Joyce was at a considerably later age in the world of literature; that is, he has paralyzed other filmmakers by shaking their confidence (as Joyce did to writers), without ever reaching a large public. He will probably never have a popular, international success; he packs film-festival halls, but there is hardly enough audience left over to fill small theaters for a few weeks. His experimentation irritates casual movie-goers, but those who are more than casual can see that what may have appeared to be experimentation for its own sake in a movie like *Contempt* is validated by the way he uses the techniques in *Weekend*. It's possible to hate half or two-thirds of what Godard does—or find it incomprehensible—and still be shattered by his brilliance.

Again like Joyce, Godard seems to be a great but terminal figure. The most gifted younger directors and student filmmakers all over the world recognize his liberation of the movies; they know that he has opened up a new kind of moviemaking, that he has brought a new sensibility into film, that, like Joyce, he is both kinds of master—both innovator and artist. But when they try to follow him they can't beat him at his own game, and they can't (it appears) take what he has done into something else; he's so incredibly fast he always gets there first. He has obviously opened doors, but when others try to go through they're trapped. He has already made the best use of his innovations, which come out of his need for them and may be integral only to his material. It's the strength of his own sensibility that gives his techniques excitement. In other hands, his techniques are just mannerisms; other directors who try them resemble a schoolboy walking like his father. Godard has already imposed his way of seeing on us—we look at cities, at billboards and brand names, at a girl's hair differently because of him. And when others pick up the artifacts of his way of seeing, we murmur "Godard" and they are sunk. At each new film festival, one can see the different things that are lifted from him; sometimes one can almost hear the directors saying to themselves, "I know I shouldn't do that, it's too much like Godard, but I've just got to try it." They can't resist, and so they do what Godard himself has already gone past, and the young filmmakers look out-of-date before they've got started; and their corpses are beginning to litter the festivals. For if Godard can't save himself how can he save them? If he is driven, like his self-destructive heroes, to go to the limits and beyond, to pursue a nonreflective art as though fearful of a pause, to take all risks and burn himself out, it's partly because his imitators are without this drive—this monomaniac's logic that carries him beyond logic to mysticism— that his liberation of film technique and content becomes mere facility when they attempt to follow him. Michelangelo is said to have observed, "He who walks behind others will never advance." Jean Renoir has been a different kind of movie influence; with his masterly simplicity and unobtrusive visual style, he has helped people to find their own way. You don't have to walk behind Renoir, because he opens an infinite number of ways to go. But when it comes to Godard you can only follow and be destroyed. Other filmmakers see the rashness and speed and flamboyance of his complexity; they're conscious of it all the time, and they love it, and, of course, they're right to love it. But they can't walk behind him. They've got to find other ways, because he's burned up the ground.

[1968]

## M*A*S*H
### Rex Reed

*M*A*S*H* treats war like some kind of painless mass suicide. It is a riotous farce about a surgical unit in Korea and most of it is totally ridiculous, yet the style of its zany good nature is so relentless in its insanity that I found myself laughing more hysterically than I've laughed in any Hollywood comedy since *Some Like It Hot* (which, I might add, it in no way resembles).

Director Robert Altman obviously decided to deal with the obscenity of war by pulling out all the plugs and leveling the audience to its knees with lunacy. The result is like mating Abbott and Costello with the Ace Trucking Company. People step on each other's toes and have flat tires in the rage of battle. Nurses flirt outrageously over the operating table and use clamps to scratch their noses before applying them to erupting blood vessels. "I can't really see —it's like the Mississippi River in there," says a surgeon, peering into an open chest wound. When the electricity goes off in the surgical ward, all the personnel instinctively forget their dying patients and hum a snappy chorus of "When the Lights Go Out All Over the World." The blood bank is full of cold beer. The helicopter landing strip for emergency wounded is used as a golf course.

Blood donations are taken from unsuspecting commanding officers in their sleep. Elliott Gould and Donald Sutherland are two hot-shot surgeons who, at one point, operate in golf shoes and Japanese kimonos.

It is all totally offensive, of course, but after a while it all makes a very heavy point about American humor and where it is right now. I found myself angry at first for having such a good time watching such irreverence. Then I got with it and I *knew*. War *is* obscene. War *is* offensive. War *is* a charade of vulgarity, an endless variety act of uncompromising stupidity. In short, war is a joke, and unless we can laugh at it, the joke's on us. The routines in *M\*A\*S\*H* are outrageous; only the corpses keep changing.

I've never held to the theory that the theater of war could also conceivably be a theater of comedy. I took it all very seriously, because I grew up with bitter doses of the kind of patriotic slush people like General Patton had dished out. *M\*A\*S\*H* is the kind of film that will hopefully change that kind of thinking for today's youth. They will like the Super Nuts in Ring Lardner, Jr.'s script because they are so full of impudent, anti-Establishment sass! And they will probably also accept the platform of ideas in *M\*A\*S\*H* because it is chock-full of the human goofs that make real life funnier than fiction. (There is, for example, this intercom, see, that gets so confused all the time that it keeps having to spell out words between Japanese renditions of "Darktown Strutters' Ball." I can't tell you how refreshing that is, after all those endless Tyrone Power war movies in which the intercom systems always sounded as though they were being emceed by Harry Von Zell!)

*M\*A\*S\*H* topples the American system of cornball idealism so perfectly that Korean War veterans are likely to picket the movie houses where it plays. But thank goodness for all those army football players smoking grass on the bench, all those nurse cheerleaders yelling "Sixty-nine is Divine!" and all those idiots sitting around the mess-hall table in a Second City re-enactment of the Last Supper. And thank goodness for Sally Kellerman, all passion and squeak in her ironed khaki uniform as an officer named Hot Lips. With all these ingredients at the front, America may go down for the count, but it will go down grinning.

[1970]

## M\*A\*S\*H
### William S. Pechter

Carping at *M\*A\*S\*H* is inevitably carping at its critics. The film deserves its immense popularity, and even (given the competition) its Grand Prize at Cannes; it is immensely likable, funny, and free of straining to pretend to be something it isn't. But what is it? From the critics, one might assume an impassioned antiwar protest, outrageous black comedy, some sort of "cinematic breakthrough." The army-surgeon heroes crack jokes as they cut into chests and saw off legs, and more than one critic has seen in this levity amidst gore the evidence of the characters' attempt to preserve sanity in an insane world. And, though the film keeps its mouth shut on this score, the case can be made for it, even if the evidence seems circumstantial enough to make one suspect the critics' insight may owe more to a press handout than to the film itself. The preservation-of-sanity idea *might* be valid, if the film had characters; characters, at least, would be the minimum required to support it. But, though Donald Sutherland has a wonderfully mobile, goofy face and Elliott Gould is here to register a much stronger and more mysterious screen presence than in *Bob & Carol & Ted & Alice,* the film remains as much as that one an animated cartoon, with the cartoon figures played by real people.

Which still needn't be bad, if it weren't for how much was being claimed for it. Like *Bob & Carol,* etc., *M\*A\*S\*H* is not so much allied with the new youth-culture movies as it is in the hip, left wing of commercial entertainment films having a more general appeal. Though the kids can dig it for its scabrous language and relaxation, it seems geared essentially to an audience bred on Committee-style, fast fade-out, revue humor, which means a slightly over-thirties-age, college-educated, professional audience, capable of assuming a mocking attitude to "Establishment" values while to some extent sharing in them. The Committee is, in fact, represented in the cast of *M\*A\*S\*H,* and the film is, like that satirical theater company, essentially a writer (Ring Lardner, Jr.)–actor collaboration; the director's role, in such an enterprise, being mainly to direct traffic, a job which Robert Altman, the director of *M\*A\*S\*H,* does deftly and with self-effacement. If *M\*A\*S\*H* often leaves one feeling, as do Richard Lester films, that things are flying by so thick and fast that one must strain to keep up and even then not take everything in, it is not so much for Lester-style quick-cutting directorial pyrotechnics as it is for the unstressed, occasionally inaudible, overlapping dialogue and the speed at which this is played.

There is, however, the ghost of a director conjured by *M\*A\*S\*H,* and even in shadow form his figure carries more force than the substance which evokes it. Though it may owe only to the hallucination of an imagination overbred by movies that the sight of the army chaplain blessing a jeep calls to my mind Simon of the desert distractedly blessing a lost tooth, I think there can be no doubt that the Last Supper given the suicide-bent dentist in *M\*A\*S\*H* inevitably recalls not Leonardo but that previous movie memento of him in Buñuel's *Viridiana.* But the Buñuel, in both instances, is not only far funnier than the echoes of it in *M\*A\*S\*H;* it is also genuinely and disturbingly blasphemous. Though the chaplain in *M\*A\*S\*H* is the object of good-natured ridicule throughout, the irreverence is strictly varsity-show variety; despite the film's slightly self-conscious show of having something to offend everybody, all is undercut by its desire to please: it is naughty, but nice. And, of course, since everyone really does like racy language, sexy jokes, enlisted men's (in this case, junior officers') deflation of military brass, and gentle pokes at the clergy, *M\*A\*S\*H*'s offensiveness is really a safe bet. When Buñuel gets this innocuous, even he will get an indulgent parent's pat on the head, as witness Stanley Kauffmann's commendation of *The Milky Way.*

Which is still to speak less of the film than of its reception. I think, black comedy and antiwar protests aside, that *M\*A\*S\*H* is best seen as a genre film with certain of its formulaic elements slightly askew, and Pauline Kael is, as usual, right when she describes it as a service comedy. (Though it might also be seen as a war film, with the operating room substituting for the battlefield; certainly films such as *Battle Cry* have demonstrated how few actual combat scenes a war film need contain.) Placed in the line of service comedy (and the film tapers off into a more conventional instance of this genre as it progresses), *M\*A\*S\*H*'s chief anomaly is its bloodshed, whose function seems to be mainly to create the illusion of a greater contact with reality than the bloodless antics of the film will themselves sustain, and, conversely, to sell the audience on this notion by extracting the price of its occasional discomfort; the actual "offensiveness" of these sequences is of the sort (subspecies, "sick humor") described above, and the details sufficiently restrained so that I, as at least one member of the audience with a fair tendency toward squeamishness, could find them less unpleasant than the sight of some oozing chipped beef on toast.

Service comedy turns essentially on the fantasy of beating the system, and it is here that *M\*A\*S\*H* really comes into its own. From the very first, the surgeon heroes set about putting their superior officers in their places, unstuffing shirts, turning up dry martinis and moist nurses, and generally running the show; and never before has it all looked so easy. Usually, as in *Operation Mad Ball,* an amusing if also overrated example of this generally impoverished genre, one is kept aware that one is knocked down nine times for every tenth time that one triumphs. There is, that is to say, the presumption of some reality principle against which the fantasy takes on its meaning and its satisfactions, a reality principle whose absence in *M\*A\*S\*H* cannot be adequately explained away by the fact that its heroes are officers and doctors; even officers and doctors don't *begin* by calling their commanding officer Henry. But the fantasy of service comedy masks a fantasy of another kind in *M\*A\*S\*H,* the fantasy of professional expertise as moral armor. This is seen most nakedly in the self-congratulatory sequence of the golfing expedition (as comedy, the flattest episode of the film), in which the heroes' medical prowess enables them to lord it over a virtual microcosm of the military establishment with impunity, but is already latent in the "Haven't-I-seen-you-somewhere-before, stranger?" introduction of the two doctor heroes to one another toward the film's beginning. This fantasy—a translation of "the fastest gun in the West" into "the fastest knife in the East"—of the doctors' skills as both empowering them to beat the system and providing them with immunity from the system's values is fundamentally a devious rationale for "simply doing one's job." And, of course, since the job of these men is saving lives rather than taking them, they are acceptable to their audience as heroes in a way that soldiers wouldn't be. Yet, ultimately, their job is the army's, and their saving of lives an activity which makes that of taking lives run more smoothly; and, as medical resisters to Vietnam participation have shown, doing one's job may not be the only alternative.

Of course, *M\*A\*S\*H* is set in Korea, not Vietnam, which may make such issues irrelevant, yet one hardly needs Stanley Kauffmann and the other critics to point out that *M\*A\*S\*H*'s Korea *is* Vietnam, in a way that redounds to the film's credit for boldness without touching on any of the unpleasant questions that an actual setting in Vietnam might raise. *M\*A\*S\*H* is punctuated periodically by fatuous announcements, over the company's public-address system, of the showing of various guts-and-glory war movies, and ends, self-mockingly, with the announcement that "tonight's movie has been *M\*A\*S\*H*." No doubt, there will be people in the film quarterlies to cite this as a stroke of Brechtian alienation; I think, rather, it is an admission that, for all the film's pointed ridicule, *M\*A\*S\*H* ends up—with its fun and games, pretty nurses and easy sex, and final sentimentality in depicting one of the doctors reluctant to accept his discharge papers—as a species of what it is mocking. And though the closing send-up may argue further for the film's unpretentiousness, I think at this point unpretentiousness has become indistinguishable from equivocation. Artistically achieved fantasy can help put one in closer contact with reality. One leaves the theater at the end of *M\*A\*S\*H* lulled by assurances that, with one's professional skills as protection, beating the system is laughably easy; and, insofar as I thus left the theater at the end of *M\*A\*S\*H* even less in touch with reality than I was when I went in, I think the film, for all its affability, charm, and real accomplishment is to be resented.

[1970]

## *PHANTOM OF THE PARADISE*
### Frank Rich

Ten years ago the horror of an age seemed to have reached its penultimate expression in Stanley Kubrick's *Dr. Strangelove, Or: How I Learned to Stop Worrying and Love the Bomb,* a bitter comedy about mad militarists hell-bent on transforming humanity into a mass of Silly Putty through the modern miracle of nuclear explosives. For a society that had long since lost its grip on a wildly proliferating technology, Kubrick provided a swift kick in the balls. His vision coincided precisely with what was probably our last truly collective, bipartisan national nightmare—a nightmare full of such tangible, accessible elements as mushroom clouds, Barry Goldwater, strontium 90 and jargon like "first-strike capability" and "better dead than red" (or was it "better red than dead"?). But that was in 1964. In the time since, a funny thing has happened on the way to the apocalypse: for better or for worse, neither the Yankees nor the Commies have ever gotten around to pressing that tiny red button which promised to blow us all to kingdom come. We traded in the Cold War for a generation of ersatz peace, and, as of this writing, civilization—or at least what passes for civilization—is still very much with us. These days no one spends too much time talking about the fallacy of fail-safe or about whether ill-prepared neighbors should be allowed to crash in one's fallout shelter. We're beyond all that. We have learned to stop worrying and love the bomb.

Just how much we love it, and just how that love reveals itself, is made indelibly clear by Brian De Palma's new rock-horror movie, *Phantom of the Paradise*. It's a picture that explains with traumatizing and often hilarious accuracy what the real effects of nuclear fallout have been during the decade since Kubrick made his classic satire. What De Palma understands—and I believe he is right—is that the bomb, once perceived as the number-one threat to our culture, has now been enshrined by that culture. Americans have grown impatient in their wait for the end of the world and have taken to acting out that frustratingly delayed climax in the here and now—even to the extent of turning the specter of nonsensical mass murder into a basis for mass entertainment. While De Palma, like Kubrick, tells the story of a monomaniacal crazy who controls the imagery as well as the actual hardware of holocaust, his updated Strangelove is not a creature of the Pentagon but a titan of show business: a hip-looking cretin by the name of Swan (Paul Williams), whose fabulously successful media complex, Death Records, trades in the music of mutilation and humiliation. As De Palma sees his time (the movie is set in December 1974), the noise and gore of nuclear violence have been effectively sublimated into rock violence; an Alice Cooper is nothing more than Kubrick's General Jack D. Ripper dressed up in drag and quadraphonic sound.

Actually, *Phantom of the Paradise* is about a lot of things, some of which are more interesting than others. At its most juvenile level, the film is, as the title indicates, a modern reworking of that old horror war horse *The Phantom of the Opera*—with touches of *Faust* and *The Picture of Dorian Gray* grafted on for good measure. Beyond that, De Palma (who both wrote and directed) has packed his project with a fair amount of highly detailed spoofing of current rock stars—satire that, high-grade as it often is, may well date as quickly as last year's issues of the *National Lampoon*. Where the film pays off, and what makes me feel it is the most original American film comedy I have seen this year, is in De Palma's grotesque depictions of an America intent on killing itself—bloody visions that he has devised entirely within the context of his metaphor of record-industry-as-doomsday-machine. In *Phantom of the Paradise,* a rock composer is permanently disfigured by getting his own hit album's grooves pressed into his face, a rock star is fried on stage via a hurled neon lightning bolt that short-circuits his electronic paraphernalia, and a real-life assassination is staged within a televised rock wedding because, as Swan puts it, "That's entertainment!" Meanwhile, of course, the fans sing and dance and cheer in the aisles.

De Palma's smartest move in terms of crystallizing this rather unruly film's principal concern is to make Swan, the promoter of death entertainment, an actual killer himself. In his lust to find the perfect music to open a dream rock palace, the Paradise ("his own Xanadu, his own Disneyland," explains a narrator), Swan rips off a prized rock cantata, *Faust,* from its composer and attempts to have the poor gaga-eyed musician (William Finley) murdered; when the composer survives and comes back to haunt the Paradise in the guise of the proverbial phantom, Swan then buys up his soul. De Palma's portrait of his villain may not sit too well with the reigning boy geniuses of our record industry—or with the rock-publishing magnate whose well-chronicled personality traits Swan seems to share—but the character proves to be a perfect vehicle for forcing us to recognize the ultimate import of an environment where brutality and merchandising are hopelessly intertwined; Swan's own actions parallel those of a business which can find in yesterday's seeming dance of planetary death the inspiration for tomorrow's gold record. Death Records, housed in a steely black skyscraper full of sterile white corridors, denim-clad hired thugs, and reel upon reel of clandestinely recorded video tape, is in a sense the corporation of Coppola's *The Conversation* recast in specific terms. Even such intrinsically harmless artifacts as the company's logo (an upturned dead bird) and its stock pile of *Faust* record jackets (black with silver lettering) seem to be quintessential manifestations of a shell-shocked moral universe in which living no longer qualifies as a legitimate human endeavor.

Such stuff may not be immediately identifiable as sure-fire laugh material, but then again I never found Kennedy assassination theories so amusing until De Palma had a go at them in his centrifugal sixties comedy, *Greetings.* This filmmaker has a sensibility worth caring about; he informs his work with a sweetness of spirit that is not only ingratiating in and of itself but which also serves to lighten the ideological load of his theme. In *Phantom,* De Palma has envisioned an evil Swan Foundation that funds prisons for nefarious purposes —but the substance of that evil has its whimsical side: the inmates are forced to have their teeth replaced by silver dentures and are then required to manufacture tiddlywinks on an assembly line. The director's victimized heroine, a diminutive singer named Phoenix (Jessica Harper), looks (like many of this director's leading ladies) as though she were a refugee from a Charles Addams cartoon, but underneath her dark physical demeanor beats a giddy heart. When Phoenix steps in, *42nd Street*–style, to substitute for a vanished concert headliner, she literally shakes away her ghostly pallor and metamorphoses into a bouncing figure of bracing eroticism. (Harper herself, by the way, is a real find.) There's also something gentle about the way De Palma handles his parodies of rock entertainers—he never lets these sequences slip into the obnoxious, generalized clowning of, say, a Carol Burnett–Harvey Korman routine—and, in Beef (Gerrit Graham), a glitter-singer outfitted in iridescent red scars and meticulously set spit curls, he has the funniest rock-and-roll send-off since Dick Shawn danced the cockamamie in the pre-twist era. Beef is just a shade too beefy to prance around with the delicacy of a David Bowie, and he can't quite handle his platform shoes; he looks and talks like a tired stripper who hasn't heard that burlesque is dead. ("I'm a pro-*fes*-si-o-nal," he shrieks. "I've been in the business a long time.") But De Palma stops short of drawing the character so broadly that he might be construed as a put-down of homosexuality. Beef is vulnerable and self-aware, insisting on his ability to distinguish between "drug real" and "real real," even as he presides over an act whose chorus of ghoulish backup men throws around members of the audience while simulating acts of dismemberment and necrophilia.

De Palma has pulled off a number of other risky tactical decisions as well. Certainly Paul Williams—the Carpenters' slick songwriter–turned–Vegas crooner—can be a lamentable, even downright offensive, personality, but in *Phantom,* De Palma has smartly chosen to capitalize on his star's negative qualities. With his lengthy, too-too platinum hair, tinted eyeglasses, and gratingly silken voice, Williams makes a swell, insidious creep—a literal and figurative agent of the devil with a briefcase full of multicolored pills and a burning desire to have the whole world "under contract," as long as those contracts are signed in blood. Much to my surprise, Williams has also written a good score for the picture, and De Palma has had the good sense to have him perform it on the sound track but not on camera. Regrettably enough, the director has been less successful at curbing his own worst excess—his predilection for mimicking other film directors. The passions of a cultist, I guess, die hard. Although *Phantom* in no way revives the slavish, dead-end Hitchcock paraphrasings of De Palma's last film, *Sisters* (a reasonably fun picture that was as empty as a copybook exercise), it does contain some camera flourishes borrowed from old horror movies and the apparently obligatory (in American films this year) references to *The Manchurian Candidate* and *Psycho* (though on this occasion, I'm happy to report, De Palma reworks the shower scene from the latter picture to his own self-mocking advantage). *Phantom* also suffers slightly from that undertone of tackiness which is endemic to De Palma's career; thanks to some bad lighting and a lack of attention to detail (e.g., New York's City Center's identifying sign appears in one shot where that landmark is meant to serve as the exterior of the Paradise), the film occasionally calls attention to its less than lavish budget and, in so doing, unravels its spell.

If you are on De Palma's wavelength, however, I doubt these minor gaffes will matter too much. The real issue here is whether you will be on that wavelength. I suspect that *Phantom* is going to pass some audiences by completely, for it unfolds within a parochial cultural idiom—one that denies the film the reach of a greater postnuclear comedy such as Kubrick's own *A Clockwork Orange*. Even so, there are times when *Phantom* transcends its idiosyncratic milieu and takes on a persuasive life of its own. Especially so in the case of De Palma's most frequently used and, as it turns out, closing image: that of the Phantom, a mangled bundle of flesh enclosed in a grasshopperlike costume, banging away at his piano in a glass cage adrift in a pool of darkness. Like Strangelove's bomb pilot, who insists on riding his own "nuke" to earth, the Phantom, too, is locked eternally into a fatal embrace with technology— for Swan has taken away the composer's natural voice and wired him for a new one that can be manipulated by an infinity of space-age consoles, amplifiers and filters. Through this hideous electronic Phantom, De Palma does paint a scathing and lasting portrait of mechanized murder, which is, as this filmmaker recognizes, the only growth industry we still have left.

[1974]

## NASHVILLE
### Colin L. Westerbeck, Jr.

Early in Robert Altman's *Nashville* there is a chain-reaction freeway crash that is, except for an assassination at the end, the only time the film's twenty-four characters all get together. And in the thick of this crash a boat being trailered by a car proves to be full of water, which it sloshes all over the highway. That boat, though only a momentary detail, suggests quite well what sort of movie *Nashville* is: the sort where water in a boat is a more likely occurrence than a boat in water. One way or another, all the characters in *Nashville* have things backward like this. Their lives are all transposed, upended, turned inside out. At the beginning country-western star Barbara Jean (Ronee Blakley) is convalescing, and at the end, after her condition has deteriorated steadily for the film's whole two and a half hours, she is shot and wounded. Everybody else's life seems to move that way—in reverse—too.

Basically, however, the life style of these characters is not so much neat reversal as haphazard interruption. After all, that's what a freeway crash really is, isn't it? An interruption. Throughout the film people constantly walk out on each other, hang up on each other, and run into each other's cars. Even the songs of this so-called Opry Land seem to compete in a continuous game of Stop the Music. While a young soldier is trying to listen to Barbara Jean sing, Mr. Green (Keenan Wynn) insists on talking about how his son died. (But later, just after Mr. Green hears that his wife is dead too, the soldier comes up and starts talking about how his mother saved Barbara Jean's life.)

At a party given by Opry star Haven Hamilton (Henry Gibson), a journalist (Geraldine Chaplin) coaxes Haven's shy son into singing her his only song, but then she runs off to interview Elliott Gould before the song is over. At a stag smoker run by a political-campaign manager, the hooting of the audience finally silences the evening's entertainment, who was not told she's supposed to strip rather than sing. At a stock-car race, another aspiring singer (Barbara Harris) has her performance completely drowned out by the roar of the engines. From the film's first recording session, which Haven walks out on, to its closing concert, which is called on account of assassination, people and events butt in on each other all the time.

In fact, the very form of the film is one which butts in on itself as Altman tries to keep track of his twenty-four characters. When Haven cues the control booth at the recording session for another take, Altman cuts to the booth; but it turns out to be the booth in another studio where a singer named Linnea Reese (Lily Tomlin) is working, not the booth in Haven's studio. Similarly, Mr. Green's cry of anguish at his wife's death segues into the campaign manager's chuckle as he inspects the night club where the smoker is to be held. And the night of the smoker, there's another drama being played out in another club across town, where Linnea has come for a rendezvous with a pop singer (Keith Carradine). Altman cuts back and forth between these two clubs in such a way that we are sometimes unsure which drama we are reacting to.

For at least the last two or three films, interruption has been very much the style of the action in Altman's work. The murder at the end of *The Long Goodbye* interrupts a conversation between the murderer and his victim. The prison break in *Thieves Like Us* is interrupted by another conversation, an argument which causes one of the thieves to put another out of the getaway car in mid-escape. The end of *California Split* seems, to one of the two gamblers in the film, an incomprehensible interruption of a streak of luck. When you look back a couple of years, *Nashville* seems to follow Altman's recent work as a logical (which is to say, screwball) development.

Yet in *Nashville* this style of action becomes something more than what it has been before. In the earlier films the action is forever being interrupted by something. In this film, the action *is* interruption: interruption becomes the main event. This is so partly because there are so many characters there can be no main plot line. The film has a good half dozen plot lines that repeatedly overlap, obscure, intrude on and interrupt each other like the cars in that freeway accident. One of these plot lines deals with a Presidential candidate very like George Wallace, a grass-roots candidate whose party is called the Replacement Party. "Replacement" is what interruption becomes in this film, too: a permanent condition, a usurpation rather than a momentary distraction. When Barbara Jean is felled by the assassin in the end, the woman who couldn't get a song in edgewise at the stock-car race picks up the microphone and goes right on with the show. It's as if she were an expected stand-in rather than an interloper.

Altman's films have always given the impression that he was trying to distill the metaphor out of his plots, to boil off pure images from ordinary reality. With *Nashville,* he perhaps succeeds. Where *M\*A\*S\*H, Brewster McCloud, Images,* and *California Split* are each films organized around some central, controlling metaphor, *Nashville* simply is a metaphor. To Altman the place itself, Nashville, is in some vague, urgent way a metaphor for the whole country; and since he feels himself to be dealing with a metaphor rather than a fact, there is no need to restrain his fantasies. The last thing he intends *Nashville* to be is a documentary on the Nashville scene. If Altman succeeds more completely than before, perhaps it is because he has been able to carry his ideas to such extremes. In *Brewster McCloud* or *Images,* the disruption of reality with images seems a listless, even aimless effort. Like the dialogue in *McCabe and Mrs. Miller,* at times the visual language of Altman's films has seemed to be mumbling. But in *Nashville,* this is no longer the case.

[1975]

# ODDBALL HEROES

## *MORGAN!* AND *GEORGY GIRL*
### Pauline Kael

Like just about everything else at the moment, movies seem to be out of control. Is it possible that, as we increasingly hear suggested in discussions of civil rights or air pollution or Vietnam or education, "nobody's minding the store"? At *Georgy Girl* you may find yourself laughing, but intermittently, in discomfort or even stupefaction, asking yourself, "What are they doing in this movie? Do they know what they're doing?" They're obviously very clever, very talented, but what's going on? To get at the peculiar nature of *Georgy Girl,* let me go back a bit to *Morgan!*, which probably just because of the way it's out of control has touched a nerve for this generation.

Thirty years ago in *My Man Godfrey*, when Mischa Auer, as the parasitic left-wing artist, imitated a gorilla to entertain the rich family who kept him as a pet, the meaning and relations were so clear no one had to signal us that it was symbolic. In *Morgan!* David Warner isn't nearly as good at the gorilla act, which is plastered with so many tags and labels that all we can be sure of is that it's meant to be symbolic. He's not just a parasitic left-wing artist with a gorilla act, he's the misfit as hero, and a childlike romantic rebel, anarchist, outsider, nonconformist, etc.; he's also crazy, and in his pop fantasy life he's King Kong. *Morgan!* is Ionesco's *Rhinoceros* turned inside out: the method of *Rhinoceros* may have been absurd but its meaning was the conventional liberal theme—the danger of people becoming conformist-animals. *Morgan!* is a modernized version of an earlier, romantic primitivist notion that people are conformists, animals are instinctively "true" and happy and, of course, "free."

*Morgan!* was maddening to many older people because of its kids' notion of nonconformity as crazy fun, its way of giving adolescent confusion the borrowed significance of symbols, its maudlin, schizoid mixture of comedy and whimsy and psychopathology and tragedy and pathos. It seemed the ultimate in grotesque pop homogenization: Trotsky's death acted out in farce with a smashed eggshell went even farther than Edward Albee turning a great writer's name into a stupid joke.

I haven't bothered to say that *Morgan!* is a bad movie because, although that's implicit in what I'm saying, it's a minor matter. The point is that it's not an ordinary movie and whether it's good or bad is of less interest than why so many young people respond to it the way they do, especially as, in this case, they are probably responding to exactly what we think makes it bad. Sometimes bad movies are more important than good ones just because of those unresolved elements that make them such a mess. They may get at something going on around us that the moviemakers felt or shared and expressed in a confused way. *Rebel Without a Cause* was a pretty terrible movie, but it reflected (and possibly caused) more cultural changes than many a good one. And conceivably it's part of the function of a movie critic to know and indicate the difference between a bad movie that doesn't much matter because it's so much like other bad movies and a bad movie that matters (like *The Chase* or *The Wild Angels*) because it affects people strongly in new, different ways. And if it be said that this is sociology, not aesthetics, the answer is that an aesthetician who gave his time to criticism of current movies would have to be an awful fool. Movie criticism to be of any use whatever must go beyond formal analysis —which in movies is generally a disguised form of subjective reaction to meanings and implications, anyway.

Those who made *Morgan!* probably not only share in the confusion of the material but, like the college audience, *accept* the confusion. This indifference to artistic control is new. I think *Morgan!* is so appealing to college students because it shares their self-view: they accept this mess of cute infantilism and obsessions and aberrations without expecting the writer and director to straighten it out or resolve it and without themselves feeling a necessity to sort it out. They didn't squirm as we did: they accepted the grotesque and discordant elements without embarrassment. I'd guess that to varying degrees they felt they *were* Morgan. And that suited them just fine.

They may be shocked when they see that he really is crazy and in pain, but they can quickly accept that, too, because he's mad in a pop way they respond to—madness as the ultimate irresponsibility for the rebel, the only sanity for those who see what the "responsible" people supposedly did to this world, and all that. If flipness is all (as it is in so many of the new movies) the flipout is just an accepted part of life. Students liberally educated not to regard analysis and breakdowns and treatment as anything shameful refer to their own crackups casually, even a little proudly, like battle scars, proof that they've had *experience*. They even talk about breakdowns as "opting out"—as if it were a preference and a moral choice. And of course to flip out and then flip back again, that makes you a hero because you've *been* there. It also takes the fear away.

Georgy is a misfit heroine: it isn't that she doesn't want to conform but that she can't because she just about *is* a gorilla. She's a brontosaurus of a girl, with the bizarre problems of a girl who's too big to be treated as a girl, and she's childlike and "natural" and artistic and all the rest of the paraphernalia which now decorate characters designed to be appealing to young audiences. *Georgy Girl* is so shrewdly designed it will probably appeal to older audiences as well. The out-of-control thing is so bad you take it for granted from the beginning. What's offensive about it is that *Georgy Girl* is already a commercialization of what in *Morgan!* seemed a genuine split and confusion. Lack of control is made grotesquely *cute*. Although it's funny, it's tricky and anarchistically chic and on the side of youth (like *The Knack*)—as if the most important thing that the writers and director could imagine was to be "larky."

*Georgy Girl* is so glib, so clever, so determinedly "kinky" that everything seems to be devalued. It's the cleverness of advertising art, of commercials, of fancy titles—it's as if nothing really meant anything and nothing simple could work any more. It's "touching" one moment and weird the next, and like *The Knack,* it has evaporated before you're outside the theater.

Even that sense of discomfort, of puzzlement, evaporates, because it is all made trivial—Georgy's pain as well as her bright remarks. For example, without any preparation or explanation, there is a horrifying sequence in which she makes a monstrous fool of herself at a party, and then everything goes on as if it never happened. Will the episode or the lack of reactions to it be upsetting to a younger audience? I doubt it. I recently saw a famous professor make such a spectacle of himself on a public platform that I had one of those great feminine intuitions—a premonition that he would go home and kill himself. As it turned out, he gave a big party for his students later that night, and his students didn't think anything special about how he'd behaved on the platform, because he did it all the time. Maybe they liked him for it; it made him more colorful, more of a character. His lack of control brought him closer to them. And I assume that we're supposed to like Georgy more because she acts out her ludicrous and self-pitying impulses and doesn't think too much about it afterward. She has all the blessings of affect and of affectlessness.

Is *Georgy Girl* a good movie or a bad one? It just isn't that simple. To discuss the cast (Lynn Redgrave, Alan Bates, James Mason) or Silvio Narizzano's direction wouldn't help. It's a less important movie than *Morgan!* because it isn't so seriously confused; it doesn't touch a nerve, it only comes teasingly close. It's more enjoyable partly because it doesn't get at anything so fundamental.

These movies are not just symptoms that will go away. I think a pretty good case could be made for including *Lord Love a Duck* and *Who's Afraid of Virginia Woolf?* among the American works that are out of control, and this may suggest that here, as in England, some of the most talented people don't really quite know what they're doing. At best, we may get something that makes a new kind of art out of embarrassment; at worst, lack of control may become what art is taken to mean. There is already a generation for whom art is the domain of the irrational, of whatever can't be clearly expressed or clearly understood, and they have adopted film as their medium, their "religion."

The general public probably cares less about artistic control than has been assumed, or the public is also changing. One of the most surprising box-office successes of last year, *A Thousand Clowns,* laid some claims to being about nonconformity and it, too, went more and more out of control, becoming redundant and embarrassing and gross in that same they-don't-know-what-they're-doing way. It didn't take its hero as far as Morgan's romantic insanity but only to romantic crackpotism—harmless American nonconformity. The hero's idea of freedom was to wander in Central Park with a kid and make TV-style jokes about TV before going back to do it for money. Basically, it was about as nonconformist as Mom's apple pie, and it even fudged on that much daring by giving the Madison Avenue spokesman the audience-pulling speech, which the Motion Picture Academy promptly and gratefully honored with an Academy Award.

These movies are full of contradictions. Is part of their appeal the ancient, wheezing plot devices which crank them in motion? The kid is being forcibly taken away from the TV gag writer; the gorilla is being separated from his mate; Georgy gets a baby to mother only to have the authorities take it away. Underneath all the nonconformity gear are the crooked little skeletons of old Shirley Temple pictures. Heart-warming. *Georgy Girl,* like *The Knack,* is the story of the ugly duckling, and by beating *Funny Girl* to the screen it jumps the gun on the new exploitation of comic pathos. Somehow those who made *Morgan!* managed (instinctively maybe but certainly shrewdly) to alter the original TV-play hero from a tired adulterer to a monogamous free spirit— probably the purest-in-heart hero of recent years. The director Karel Reisz's method is so eclectic, in the most blatant sense of that word, that he has taken what he feels will "go" together; the last sequence, which so many people have tried to interpret, is borrowed from the end of Buñuel's *El,* where it made perfect sense. Here it supplies a "larky" finish. The obscenely "happy ending" of *Georgy Girl* is so off-beat we lose the beat.

[1966]

# A THOUSAND CLOWNS
## Judith Crist

*A Thousand Clowns* is that exceptional film version of a Broadway hit—the rarity that transcends the stage play not merely in dimension but in character and content. As a result, we have a mature, perceptive, and very funny film, exhilarating in spirit and delightful in its various excellences.

The film's success is due in large part to the retention of so much that was good in the Broadway production. Fred Coe, the play's director and the film producer, makes his debut as movie director, bringing his pre-theater television-bred sense of space and pace to the screen; Herb Gardner has adapted and expanded his stage play; and four of the six leading players have been retained in their roles.

Jason Robards is again on hand as the feckless, charming, middle-aged adolescent who has given up the television-writing ritual to devote himself to fun and games and noting how naked the emperors of our time are. A man who, urged in serious discussion to "return to reality for a moment," retorts "I'll only go as a tourist," he is finally forced to consider an extended tour when a welfare agency threatens to take away the nephew he has been rearing in his own image unless the boy is given a more stable environment. And Barry Gordon is once again the nephew.

Barry, who just might singlehandedly bring child actors back into fashion, is a twelve-year-old who looks like a middle-aged manufacturer after a bad season; one of their many uncle-nephew gags, in fact, involves his uncle accusing him of being a forty-year-old midget named Max. Certainly there are few forty-year-olds who can match young Mr. Gordon's mastery of moods; as the precocious child functioning on a sophisticated level and suddenly and devastatingly revealing all the childish heartaches and hopes and hungers below the surface, he is superb.

In beautifully breathless scenes, celebrating the national holiday Robards has proclaimed to mark Irving R. Feldman's birthday (he is the local delicatessen man par excellence), uncle and nephew roam the city and its environs. Through the laughter and the gags, the moments of wonder and of truth-seeking, we see the man's footloose exultations covering up self-centered evasions, the boy's hero-worshiping pleasures being tinged with doubts and discontents.

And then the two come smack up against a pair of social workers. Back at the mealy-mouthed grind is William Daniels, as square a square as ever hit the sociology "firing line," and with him is Barbara Harris, new to the cast as the worker in charge of the psychological side. Miss Harris's triumph, in this her screen debut, is that beyond her collapse as a case worker (her tearful "I hate Raymond Ledbetter—and he's only nine years old—I didn't like him, so I tried to understand him and now that I understand him I hate him!" is immortal), beyond all the glorious soaring moments of a romance that literally skims through the city, beyond all the fussiness that brings about a décor Robards can describe only as "kind of fun Gothic," there is the hard core of a real

Sandra Markowitz, with solid roots, who is going to see that the tablecloth is used regularly even while the games go on.

Just as Miss Harris adds a new dimension of realism and durability to her role, so Martin Balsam, also new to the cast, gives a remarkable warmth to that of Robards's brother who is caught between his affectionate enjoyment of Robards's life and his frustrated disapproval thereof; he brings a stringent dignity to his concession that he has "the talent to surrender" that his brother unhappily lacks. And finally, there is Gene Saks as the horrendous Chuckles the Chipmunk, star of a children's show, frayed nerves and slithery soul writhing in the realization that he doesn't get along with children, that he's surrounded by "finks, dwarfs, phonies, and frogs," and that he's right in there as one of them.

In the close-ups of the fine cast, so that every mood and nuance is captured, in the explorations of the city, lightning montages of midtown lunchtime and rush-hour lock steps, Mr. Coe has turned what was once an almost closed-room joke about oddballs into a throbbing expansive story of the rebellions and conformities and, more important, the concessions we make for loving and living.

*A Thousand Clowns* comes to the screen with a joyous vitality and a probing compassion that are irresistible.

[1965]

# KING OF HEARTS
## Vincent Canby

In the last scene of *King of Hearts,* the latest Philippe de Broca import from France, Alan Bates stands at the gate of a madhouse, seeking permanent asylum from the real world. He is holding a bird cage and is stark naked.

The image, like all the others in this beautifully photographed color film, is a funny one. The scene, however funny, is also dark and sad, which pretty much describes the mood of this extravagant and highly comic morality play.

Mr. de Broca has already proved himself an uncommon cinematic wit with such films as *That Man From Rio* and *The Five-Day Lover,* which showed that sheer frivolity could be a legitimate end in itself. Here his intentions are much more serious and he has seized on a theme that even Bizet might have found *vieux chapeau.*

That, briefly stated, is that the certified insane of this world are a lot less lunatic than the madmen who persist in making lunatic war.

Set in that long ago antique time of World War I, *King of Hearts* recounts the adventures of an amiable Scot who, during the last days of the fighting, is sent into a little French village to find and dismantle a giant booby trap left behind by the Germans. By the time the Scot arrives, the citizens have fled, leaving the village in the custody of the inmates of the local asylum.

They are a larky crew indeed, and it's not particularly surprising when the good, sane Scot, whom Alan Bates plays with such decent and funny intensity, finally succumbs to their logic. Of course, Mr. de Broca, the director, and Daniel Boulanger, the script writer, have loaded the dice, or have they?

There is not a catatonic in the lot of these charming lunatics—dukes, duchesses, generals, a marvelously compliant madam and a virginal whore—all of whom persist in regarding Mr. Bates's efforts to save them as totally incomprehensible.

Instead, they name him the King of Hearts and hold a coronation that might have been choreographed by the Marx Brothers. When, at the climax of their festival, two opposing armies fight to the death in the village square, the "duchess" turns to the "duke" and comments blandly: "I think they're overacting."

Mr. de Broca has added a curious and disturbing dimension to this theme. It isn't just that his lunatics are happy, but that they seem to have consciously chosen their vagrant lunacy.

As portentous as all this may sound, the director has managed to tell it in the terms of wildly raffish slapstick and satire. There is a hilarious coronation procession, including a carriage drawn by a white camel, getting mixed up with a German patrol, and the infectious exuberance of Mr. Bates, after he has defused the booby trap, doing gymnastic exercises on the face of the cathedral clock.

This is moviemaking, de Broca–style.

The cast is uniformly excellent, particularly Mr. Bates, Geneviève Bujold, the lovely little girl who is chosen to be his consort; Jean-Claude Brialy and Françoise Christophe, the mad "duke" and "duchess"; and Adolfo Celi, that fine Italian comedian who plays, of all things, a Scottish colonel with what must be a dubbed-in burr. The French dialogue is translated by acceptable English subtitles.

The physical production—shot in the little town of Senlis—is extraordinarily attractive, as is the haunting music by Georges Delerue, who scored, among other notable films, *Jules and Jim*.

No matter how simplistic, Mr. de Broca's parable is a funny and touching experience.

[1967]

## HAROLD AND MAUDE
### Rex Reed

*Harold and Maude* is a *Love Story* for necrophiliacs. Harold, twenty, likes to hang himself to Cat Stevens records, immolate himself with gasoline, slash his wrists, drown himself in the swimming pool, stab himself with a hara-kiri sword, and blow his brains out while his mother fills out computer-dating questionnaires. Maude, eighty, steals hearses and lives on licorice, ginger pie, and straw tea. Naturally, they are both insane. One day in a graveyard, they fall in love and Hal Ashby, the talented director of *The Landlord,* photographs them as though they were Daphnis and Chloë, having picnics in demolition and skipping through tombstones that look like ceramic coffee tables. But, alas, any audience with a strong enough stomach to watch a twenty-year-old boy in bed with an eighty-year-old crone, must be avenged. So Maude kills herself: "Yes, dear, I took the tablets an hour ago—I'll be gone by midnight."

This sick, demented little movie has little to recommend it except the chance it gives to watch the wonderful Vivian Pickles play an eccentric mother like a cobra dressed by Mainbocher. There are only vague hints of life in the character of Harold, and since Bud Cort only seems vaguely alive, I guess he's perfect for the part. Ruth Gordon is always alive. Too alive, in fact, to appear in obnoxious movies like *Where's Poppa?* and *Harold and Maude.* Her indefatigable charm and personal pizazz deserve better showcases. Miss Gordon, I love you. But these scripts have got to get better.

[1971]

# ONE FLEW OVER THE CUCKOO'S NEST
## Vincent Canby

In a certain kind of sentimental fiction, mental institutions are popular as metaphors for the world outside. The schizoids, the catatonics, the Napoleons and the Josephines inside the hospital are the sanes, while all of us outside who have tried to adjust to a world that accepts war, hunger, poverty, and genocide are the real crazies. It's the appeal of this sappy idea, I suspect, that keeps Philippe de Broca's *King of Hearts* playing almost continually around the country. In that film, you remember, the Scots soldier (Alan Bates) seeks asylum among the certified lunatics while World War I rages nuttily outside.

It's a comforting concept, and a little like believing in Santa Claus, to think that if we just give up, if we throw in life's towel, and stop thinking rationally while letting our wildest fantasies take hold, that we'll attain some kind of peace. No fear. No pain. No panic. The world becomes a garden of eccentric delights.

The thing that distinguishes *One Flew Over the Cuckoo's Nest,* Miloš Forman's screen version of the 1962 Ken Kesey novel, is its resolute avoidance of such nonsense. Although the film is not without its simplicities and contradictions, its view of disconnected minds is completely unsentimental. I'm not at all sure that the terrifying events Kesey describes so jauntily in his novel could take place, or would ever have taken place in any mental hospital ten or fifteen years ago, so one must accept the tale as a fictional nightmare of its time—the sixties. The mental hospital in *One Flew Over the Cuckoo's Nest* is, I suppose, a metaphor, but it is more important as the locale of one more epic battle between a free spirit and a society that cannot tolerate him.

There is always, of course, a certain sentimentality attached to this conflict, at least in our society. Twentieth-century Americans feel terrifically sentimental about—and envious of—nonconformists while knocking themselves out to look, sound, talk, and think like everyone else. The only good nonconformist is the fictional nonconformist, or one who's safely dead. We apotheosize Yossarian while electing Presidents whose public images have been created in advertising agencies.

Randle Patrick McMurphy (Jack Nicholson), the fast-talking hero of *One Flew Over the Cuckoo's Nest*, more or less has his nonconformism thrust upon him, out of bravado and ignorance and the demands of this sort of fiction. All that we ever know about Randle before he turns up in the Oregon mental hospital, where we first meet him and which is the scene of the film, is that he has been serving a six-month prison sentence for statutory rape. The girl was fifteen though she had told him she was nineteen, he says, probably lying. After two months on a prison farm, Randle has gotten himself transferred to the hospital for psychiatric observation, figuring that the loony bin would be a softer touch than picking peas.

Once Randle is in the hospital, however, the world shrinks to the size of his ward, which is the private domain of a singularly vicious character named Nurse Ratched (Louise Fletcher), a woman of uncertain age who is capable of understanding and sympathy only when they reinforce her authority.

The story of *One Flew Over the Cuckoo's Nest* is the duel between Randle and Nurse Ratched for the remnants of the minds of the other patients in the ward, a contest that starts out in the mood of a comedy on the order of *Mr. Roberts* and winds up, rather awkwardly, as tragedy.

*One Flew Over the Cuckoo's Nest* is indecently sentimental and simplistic if you take it as a serious statement on the American condition, which is much too complex to be represented by this mental ward. However, if you can avoid freighting it with these ulterior meanings—and Forman and his screenwriters have had the good sense not to bear down too heavily on them—*One Flew Over the Cuckoo's Nest* is a humane, loose-limbed sort of comedy containing the kind of fine performances that continually bring the film to explosive, very unsettling life.

Forman, the Czech director of *The Loves of a Blonde* and *The Firemen's Ball,* has made one other American film, *Taking Off,* in which the eye through which we saw the world was clearly that of an amused, sympathetic, sometimes appalled visitor. Perhaps because the locale of *One Flew Over the Cuckoo's Nest* is more particular than the middle-class and hippie milieus of *Taking Off,* the new film betrays nothing except the director's concern for people who struggle to bring some order out of chaos. It's a struggle he finds supremely funny and sometimes noble, even when the odds are most bleak.

Jack Nicholson is something more than the star of *One Flew Over the Cuckoo's Nest.* He is its magnetic north. His is the performance that gives direction to those of everyone else in the cast. I can't believe that a nonprofessional like Dr. Dean Brooks, who is actually the superintendent of the Oregon State Hospital (where the film was shot), could have been so comically speculative in a key moment had not Nicholson been setting the tone of the scene. Nicholson's flamboyance as an actor here is of an especially productive sort. It doesn't submerge the other actors. It seems to illuminate them. This is most noticeably true of Louise Fletcher, whose Nurse Ratched is much more interestingly ambiguous than the character in Kesey's novel, as well as of Will Sampson, another nonpro, who plays Nicholson's deaf-mute Indian sidekick, and Brad Dourif, as the ward's "kid" character.

There are some troublesome things in *One Flew Over the Cuckoo's Nest* that I'm not sure can be alibied by saying that it is, after all, a fiction and not a documentary. The ward that we see in the film is (most of the time) so spick-and-span that it seems to give the lie to horror stories we all know about the filth and overcrowding in so many mental hospitals. Also, can it be possible that shock treatments are (or were until recently) given out so arbitrarily as punishments, and could a single ward nurse ever have authorized a lobotomy without some second opinion?

These can be major factors in the way one responds to the film. But another is the extraordinary way that Forman has been able to create important, identifiable characters of psychotics, people who are most often represented in films as misfit exotics, creatures as remote from our experience as members of a Stone Age tribe in the Amazon.

[1975]

# EUROPEAN COMEDY

# FRANCE: OLD WAVES AND NEW

Paris is the international hotbed of film criticism, the place where there has never been any question that the cinema was an art form. It is natural, then, that there has been more re-evaluation of the French cinematic past than that of any other country. A decade or two ago, judgments of what were the high points of French comedy differed greatly from the judgments of today. Indeed, some movies which today seem to be seminal works would have been excluded, not on grounds of quality but because they weren't considered to be comedies! But when things go topsy-turvy in French criticism, as they seem to do every other year, little remains untouched.

Part of the problem undoubtedly stems from a certain French cultural tradition, cosmopolitan and anticlerical at its source, which takes winking pleasure in sin. At its most vulgar it is Maurice Chevalier's "ooh-la-la," at its most exalted the profound hedonism of Jean Renoir. But the relevant point is that works permeated with this attitude can express a thoroughly comic vision of life without ever being funny. There is no significant comedy director—Clair, Vigo, Renoir, Tati, Truffaut—of whom it hasn't been said, "But it's just not funny," and of whom the defensive reply wasn't, "But it's not supposed to be."

Without ever descending into black comedy, a French director is often harrowing under the guise of giving us a good time. Clair's dehumanizing factory *(À Nous la Liberté)*, Vigo's oppressive school *(Zero for Conduct)*, Renoir's aristocrats frolicking their way into oblivion *(Rules of the Game)*, Tati's useless skyscraper *(Playtime)*, Truffaut's angst-ridden pianist *(Shoot the Piano Player)*—all of these sober subjects are presented to us in films that, at one time or another, have been seen as comedy classics.

Nowadays, it's universally accepted that Jean Renoir has utilized this aesthetic to express an open vision of life with such conviction and invention that he is revered by film lovers of almost every persuasion. Renoir's mystical view of life encompasses laughter and tears so profoundly that it is too simplistic to consider his films as being in the service of such earthly notions as "tragedy" or "comedy." And that, paradoxically, is why films like *Rules of the Game* and *French Can Can* can be seen as both noncomedies and among the greatest comedies of all.

Renoir's popularity today is abetted not only by our current acceptance of his cross-genre approach but also by the ascendant preference for loose structures over "well-made" construction. In a sense, the New Wave of 1959–1960 was an affirmation of Renoir's stylistic preferences, and a reaction against the officially approved "tradition of quality"— the well-made films by such Old Wave directors as Julien Duvivier and Claude Autant-Lara. In creating the "mixed genre" that Pauline Kael defends in her article on *Shoot the Piano Player,* Truffaut was in a sense formalizing a technique that previous directors had performed nonchalantly. And eventually Truffaut was to make more homogenized movies like *Stolen Kisses* in which the generic divisions were much less clear-cut. From the beginning, in the best French films humor has not so much been imposed on an otherwise solemn set of situations as it has been a redeeming aspect of the visions of life they portray. It is perhaps relevant to remember that the French idea of comedy as a whole attitude toward life is incorporated into the very language. For in French, as in other Romance languages, the word *comédie*—as used in the theatrical company La Comédie Française or Balzac's *La Comédie Humaine,* for example—has far broader meaning than the simple ha-ha implied by its English cognate.

# SOME WAVES THAT CAUSED RIPPLES

## RENÉ CLAIR
### *Arthur Knight*

Of all the French directors of [the silent] era, none was more talented or original, or had a greater instinctive feeling for the medium itself, than René Clair. His very first film, *The Crazy Ray* (*Paris Qui Dort,* 1923), made on a shoestring, reveals his sharp eye for the absurd and his enormous appreciation of the comic possibilities inherent in the motion-picture camera. A group of travelers alight from their plane; atop the Eiffel Tower they discover that all Paris is in the grip of a mysterious paralyzing ray. They alone, being above the ray, have escaped its effects. As they pass through the city, they discover its inhabitants frozen into the most delightfully grotesque positions—a pickpocket caught in the act, two sandwich men bending over to pick up the same franc, a nursemaid with pram kissing a gendarme. Later, they come upon the source of the ray in the home of a mad inventor and prevail upon him to throw the switch that will start life moving again. He does so but, in a manner very reminiscent of the early French trick films, everything goes out of gear, first too fast, then too slow. For all its crudities, *The Crazy Ray* is still fresh and tremendously funny.

The next few years found Clair feeling his way—the brilliant and hilarious Dadaist comedy *Entr'acte* (1924); more fantasy in *Le Fantôme du Moulin Rouge* (1924) and *Le Voyage Imaginaire* (1925); an adventure film, *La Proie du Vent* (1925). Each contributed to the fine art of comedy that burst forth so joyously in his next picture, *The Italian Straw Hat* (1927). Drawn from a popular nineteenth-century farce comedy by Eugène Labiche, it betrays little of its theater origins. As adapted by Clair, it is completely movie, with the camera mobilized in a fashion clearly derived from the post-Murnau German film, its cutting as swift and precise as the best American productions, and all sparked by a crackling Gallic wit and exquisite sense of the ridiculous. In Labiche's story, a young man on his way to his wedding is so unfortunate as to have his horse eat the hat of a respectable married lady while she is embracing her lover, a fierce, mustachioed officer. Since the lady can not return home without her hat, the officer forces the apologetic bridegroom to search for its twin throughout his nuptial day.

Quite apart from making full use of Labiche's highly serviceable plot, Clair kept his picture moving swiftly forward through a veritable cataract of marvelous sight gags. First, there are the characters themselves, the members of the wedding, each endowed with his own comic quality—the bride's father whose new shoes are too tight, her deaf uncle with a wad of paper lodged in his ear trumpet, a very proper cousin who has misplaced one of his white gloves, an elderly gentleman whose tie keeps slipping down. Then there are the incidents —the mayor's florid speech after the ceremony (punctuated by glimpses of the little man with the slipping tie, so intent on every word that he fails to catch his wife's frantic signals which the mayor comes to interpret as being meant for himself), the frequent and abrupt disappearances of the groom from the midst of the wedding festivities, the delightful bit of theater pantomime through which he outlines his version of his predicament to the suspicious husband. And finally there is Clair's virtuoso use of the camera itself, photographing in dreamlike slow motion the officer's wanton destruction of the young man's apartment, in nightmarish fast motion the bridegroom's enforced participation in the dancing after the wedding banquet when he would rather be out searching for the all-important hat—each shot impeccably placed and perfectly timed. *The Italian Straw Hat,* using a minimum of titles, suggests the full fluency of the silent film by one of the most imaginative directors of comedy the medium has yet produced. [. . .]

Perhaps the first director to appreciate fully the implications of sound was René Clair. Originally opposed to the whole idea, he insisted on the predominant importance of the visual element, declaring that the sound film need not and should not be, to use his own term, "canned theater." This opinion, almost revolutionary among filmmakers at the time, was brilliantly confirmed in a trio of sparkling comedies that quickly made Clair the most admired and imitated director in the world. In *Sous les Toits de Paris* (1929), *Le Million* (1931), and *À Nous la Liberté* (1931), he worked with a minimum of dialogue, using music, choruses, and sound effects to counterpoint and comment upon his visuals. In this principle of asynchronous sound, sound used against rather than with the images, Clair discovered a new freedom and fluidity for the sound medium. Why show a door closing when it is enough merely to hear it slam? Or why listen to a clock's ticking just because it is shown? In *Le Million* there is a brief glimpse of a clock on a mantel shelf, a clock elaborately overdecorated with porcelain cupids blowing trumpets. Clair's sound track at that point carries a blast of trumpets. In *Sous les Toits* a fight takes place at night near a railway embankment. The fight is almost obscured by the shadows, but its force and fury are conveyed in the roar of the passing trains heard on the sound track. In *À Nous la Liberté,* Clair goes so far as to kid the whole notion of synchronous sound by showing his heroine singing away at her window while the hero admires from afar. Suddenly something goes wrong with the voice—it whines and whirs, then fades away. A moment later, while the young fellow is still looking up at the window, the girl appears in the street, the song begins again and we discover that what we have been listening to all along is a phonograph record from another apartment.

Because Clair's early sound films were both musicals and comedies, he could permit himself an impish audacity denied practitioners of the more serious forms, whose dramatic themes forced them to use more straightforward techniques. Their efforts at realism made it difficult for them to break with the conventional practices that quickly surrounded the microphone soon after it had made its appearance in the studios. Clair, on the other hand, could ignore conventional sound, omitting the characteristic noises of a street, a factory, or an opera house altogether unless they served his purpose. It was *his* world, and he did with it as he wished.

And because above all he liked music and the dance, his pictures flash along like ballets. The incessant chases, the scramble after the flying banknotes in *À Nous la Liberté,* the mad party that opens and closes *Le Million*—all are set to gay, infectious tunes. Choruses sing a witty commentary upon the action as it unfolds. While sequences are bound together by music alone. In the opening reel of *Sous les Toits de Paris* a street singer is vending the title song of the film. While the camera wanders up and down the street, peering into the apartments and shops, one by one the people of the neighborhood join in the song. In this way Clair quickly introduces the principal characters in his story and gaily sets the mood of the entire film. Throughout his pictures, music functions in dozens of bright and unexpected ways, playing an integral part in the development of his diverting stories.

What Clair had done, what creative directors everywhere were trying to do at the same time, was to discover how to control all the elements that went into the making of a sound film as completely as, in the simpler days of silence, one could control everything that went before the camera. He demonstrated to everyone's satisfaction that much of silent technique was still valid, that it was the image and not the word that kept the screen alive. Sound, and especially asynchronous sound, could add its own grace notes, its deeper perceptions, its enrichment of mood and atmosphere—but not independently of the visual.

Because René Clair had instinctively grasped this principle in his first three films, and turned them out with a flair and finish unmatched anywhere at the time, his pictures had a profound effect upon other directors. He had achieved what they were groping toward. He had brought back into films spontaneity, movement, rhythm. The extent of his influence is immediately revealed by a comparison of the opening reel of his *Sous les Toits* with the first sequences of Geza von Bolvary's *Zwei Herzen im Dreiviertel Takt* (1930) or the "Blue Horizon" number in Lubitsch's *Monte Carlo* (1930). But more important than imitation are the innumerable films of the early thirties that suggest his liberating spirit. In Germany Eric Charrell's *Congress Dances* (1931), in England Victor Saville's *Sunshine Susie* (1932), and in Hollywood films like Frank Tuttle's *This Is the Night* (1932), Gregory La Cava's *The Half-Naked Truth* (1932), and Lewis Milestone's *Hallelujah, I'm a Bum* (1933) all reveal not only a new freedom in the use of sound but also—as in the Clair films—a rhythmic structure imparted by the sound track.

Clair's work was especially valuable to those men in the American studios who were themselves seeking to liberate the talking film from the confines of "canned theater." More daring than they dared to be, the fact that such pictures had found considerable popular as well as critical success was helpful in encouraging them to go ahead—quite apart from any technical lessons they might have learned. In this respect the early sound period was very much like the first decade or so of the silent era. The medium itself was still in a highly experimental stage, and directors looked to the box office to tell them how successful they were with the new techniques, and to the works of one another for useful hints that they could incorporate into their own efforts. In this period of search and confusion, Clair's pictures appeared as beacons to the future. And if Clair had a tendency to overstress the silent techniques in his early films, they provided a healthy counterinfluence to the overaccenting of the sound track in the films made by almost everyone else.

[1957]

## LA RONDE
### Roger Greenspun

After seventeen years in the wilderness, and with the restoration of some footage idiotically cut for its first New York run, Max Ophüls's *La Ronde* has returned. *La Ronde,* made in 1950, is the first of Ophüls's last four movies (the others are *Le Plaisir*—1951, *Madame de . . .*—1953, and *Lola Montès*—1955), which, together with the fifties movies of Jean Renoir, constitute the two most sustained creative achievements in the history of film.

Last year saw the return of *Lola Montès,* virtually rescued from oblivion by the brilliant proselytizing of the *Village Voice* film critic, Andrew Sarris. This year we have *La Ronde,* which, if less great than *Lola Montès,* is, on the other hand, more gracious and a more accessible introduction to the style and vision of Max Ophüls.

Sometimes there seems to be so much style it is hard to accept the existence of a vision in Ophüls's movies. Undeniably, he is the greatest ornamentalist among directors. Not only in the decorative density and the spatial surprises of his sets (the first sexual game of *La Ronde* is played up and down tremendous flights of steps; the second is observed through a foreground profusion of shrubs and branches) but also in his dedication to elaborate camera movement, Ophüls complicates everything that happens in his films. The point to remember is that all of the grand gestures and arabesques indicate form and discipline—and not mere indulgence in sensual excess.

More readily apparent is Ophüls's unfailing gracefulness and delicacy. He never attempts to upset the vital balance of illusions in his opulent world (though the opulence may be no more than the play of a few lights on painted backdrops—as he openly shows it to be in *La Ronde*) and he never ridicules his often trivial characters. Something akin to deeply ingrained very good manners is at work here, and the reward, as always in Ophüls, is that the unbearable becomes bearable and for a moment even humanly attractive. It is no accident, and no inconsiderable virtue, that the loveliest kitsch movie music ever written occurs in the last four films of Max Ophüls.

*La Ronde* is an adaptation of *Reigen,* a play in ten brief dialogues written in 1897 by the Viennese dramatist Arthur Schnitzler. Each of Schnitzler's "dialogues" is essentially a blackout sketch—a seduction followed by disillusioned aftermath—and one of the partners in each sketch appears in the following sketch. At the end of the play, a count bids a troubled good-by to the same whore who welcomed a common soldier at the beginning.

Ophüls does not so much change as add to the original: a master of ceremonies, some of the paraphernalia of moviemaking, an elaborate program of transitions from episodes, a real carrousel to get things moving, and a sense of the past. Schnitzler wrote about his own time; the movie is about a time fifty years ago—and Ophüls is at pains to affirm the pastness of the past, and then to walk in and out of it as if it were the sound stage next door.

*La Ronde* is about passing time, change, process. Schnitzler's ironic round dance becomes, in the shaping hands of Ophüls, a circular image of wholeness that incorporates and supports ideas of disorientation and disintegration, even to the cutting up of his movie. Ultimately the great sweeps and turns of Ophüls's cameras must be understood as spinning out of the artist's mind— for he is most crucially involved with his own creation.

That is why Ophüls includes a master of ceremonies, who is surely himself, and is also a surrogate for the audience, and who both observes and promotes the action of his film. It is a difficult and not wholly honorable task, and though the master of *La Ronde* (Anton Walbrook) maintains his suave dignity throughout, he must pay a price for what he does and what he knows. He becomes in some measure responsible for the condition of a world that is falling apart at the seams.

But while the carrousel still turns (it is beginning to break down) it brings us wonderful images—as once when Danielle Darrieux, wavering on the way to her young lover's bedroom, pauses for a moment and does not quite smile but with a movement of her eyes and face, accepts the pleasure, the pain, the knowledge, and the grace that is the condition of her cursed and lovely life.

[1969]

## ZAZIE
### *Pauline Kael*

Movies are said to be an international language, but sometimes a film that is popular in one country finds only a small audience in another. This anarchistic, impudent comedy (from Raymond Queneau's novel *Zazie dans le Métro*), a great success in France in 1960, has hardly even been heard of in the United States. There is perhaps some major national difference in reactions to slapstick and wit: the film, which is like a Mack Sennett two-reeler running wild, has been peculiarly disturbing for American critics and audiences alike. To Americans, *Zazie* seems to go too far, to be almost demonic in its inventiveness, like a joke that gets so complicated you can't time your laughs comfortably. The editing, which is very fast, may be too clever: audiences here can't quite keep up. Some critics have suggested that, for Americans, this comedy turns into some kind of freakish, fantastic anxiety. Putting it as squarely as possible, Bosley Crowther wrote in *The New York Times:* "There is something not quite innocent or healthy about this film." Yet the film is like *Alice in Wonderland:* Zazie (Catherine Demongeot) is a foul-mouthed little cynic, age eleven, who comes to Paris for a weekend with her uncle (Philippe Noiret), a female impersonator, and nobody and nothing are quite what they seem. Louis Malle, who directed, includes satirical allusions to *La Dolce Vita* and other films, and a parody of his own *The Lovers.* Many of the latest styles in film editing, which are generally said to derive from Alain Resnais or Richard Lester, have an earlier source in *Zazie.*

[1965]

# JEAN RENOIR

## *BOUDU SAVED FROM DROWNING*
### *Pauline Kael*

Jean Renoir's *Boudu Saved from Drowning* was made in France in 1931, when talkies were new and subtitling had not yet become a standard procedure, and so, like many other films of the early sound period, it was not imported. Some of those talkies waited a few years, some a few decades; others are still waiting —and may go on waiting because of the New York press response to *Boudu*.

The four New York dailies agreed: to the *Times* it is "a second-rate antique"; the *Post* found that it "is easily dismissed"; the *World Journal Tribune* said it should not have been rescued; and the *Daily News* gave it two stars— an event which should have alerted everyone that *Boudu* was a movie of unusual quality, because the *Daily News* plasters almost every Hollywood dud with four stars. They fall harder that way.

One may suspect that many early classics of the screen would be given the same short shrift by the daily reviewers if they opened now—the 1931 *À Nous la Liberté*, for example, or Vigo's *Zero for Conduct* (1932) or *L'Atalante* (1934); Louis Jouvet's performance in the 1933 *Dr. Knock* would probably be patronizingly put down as a curiosity. Fortunately, most of the best work from France plays regularly at revival houses and at colleges and doesn't depend on the daily reviewers to find its audience. Books and magazine articles over three decades, a reference here and there, even affectionate parental memories send new people each year to the Carné-Prévert *Bizarre, Bizarre* (1937) or Pagnol's adaptation of Jean Giono's *Harvest* (1937), to Renoir's *A Day in the Country* (1936) or *La Grande Illusion* (1937), as well as to revivals of the French films of the forties and fifties.

Other works by Renoir have come late and are taking their rightful place: the great 1939 *Rules of the Game,* one of the key works in the history of movies, first seen here in a cut version and then restored in the sixties; and, a lesser but still important film, *The Crime of M. Lange* (1935), not subtitled for American audiences until the sixties. But with *Boudu,* it's different: it belongs to an earlier era, it gives a different kind of pleasure. The style and rhythm of *Boudu,* that whole way of looking at things, is gone, and so it may be a movie only for those who know and care about that way.

*Boudu* is a more leisurely film than we are used to now, not that it is long, or slow, but that the camera isn't in a rush, the action isn't overemphatic, shots linger on the screen for an extra split second—we have time to look at them, to take them in. Renoir is an unobtrusive, unselfconscious storyteller: he doesn't "make points," he doesn't rub our noses in "meaning." He seems to find his story as he tells it; sometimes the improvisation falters, the movie gets a little untidy. He is not a director to force things; he leaves a lot of open spaces. This isn't a failure of dramatic technique: it's an indication of that movie-making sixth sense that separates a director like Renoir from a buttoned-up-tight gentleman-hack like Peter Glenville or a genius-hustler like Sidney Lumet. Glenville suffocates a movie; Lumet keeps giving it charges to bring it to life. *Boudu* is a simple shaggy-man story told in an *open* way, and it is the openness to the beauty of landscape and weather and to the varieties of human folly which is Renoir's artistry. He lets a movie breathe.

Boudu is a tramp saved from suicide by a bookseller who takes him into his home and tries to do for him what decent, generous people *would* try to do —make him over in their own solid-bourgeois image, make him one of them. But Boudu is not a lovable tramp like Chaplin nor a Harry Langdon innocent nor a precursor of the artist-in-rebellion tramp like Alec Guinness's Gulley Jimson or Sean Connery's Samson Shillitoe. Boudu, bearded and long-haired like a premature Hell's Angel, is a dropout who just wants to be left alone. And this may help to explain why the movie wasn't imported earlier: he doesn't want romance or a job or a place in society (like the forlorn little hero of *À Nous la Liberté*), he isn't one of the deserving poor. There's no "redeeming" political message in *Boudu* and no fancy Shavian double talk either.

Boudu is the underside of middle-class life, what's given up for respectability. We agree to be clean and orderly and responsible, but there is something satisfying about his *refusal.* There's a kind of inevitability—like someone acting out our dream—about the way he spills wine on the table, leaves the water running in the sink, wipes his shoes on the bedspread. There's some disorderly malice in him. He's like a bad pet that can't be trained: he makes messes. If Boudu's character were reformed, that would be defeat. The bookseller, despite his mistress-maid, is unmanned by the female household—and by being a householder. Boudu is, at least, his own dog.

Michel Simon, who plays Boudu, is better known for his masochistic roles, as, earlier, in Renoir's *La Chienne,* and, later, in Duvivier's *Panique* and *La Fin du Jour.* But his Boudu, like his tattooed Père Jules of *L'Atalante,* which Agee described as "a premental old man . . . a twentieth-century Caliban," is a misfit loner. The loose walk, the eyes that don't communicate, the Margaret Rutherford jaw, and the Charles Laughton sneaky self-satisfaction are not those of a man who rejects society: rejection is built into him, he merely acts it out. This, too, does not make the film easy for audiences: it is so much nicer to respond to a *Georgy Girl,* knowing that a pretty actress is putting us on. One of those four reviewers complained that Michel Simon "misses completely. . . . He is gross where he should be droll. He does wrong all the things that Fernandel later was to do right." That's rather like complaining that Olivier in *The Entertainer* is no Tony Bennett.

Renoir's camera reveals the actors as if they were there naturally or inadvertently—not arranged for a shot but found by the camera on the streets, in the shop, on the banks of the Seine. The camera doesn't overdramatize their presence, it just—rather reticently—picks them up, and occasionally lets them disappear from the frame, to be picked up again at a later point in their lives.

Despite the problems of sound recording in 1931, Renoir went out of the studio, and so *Boudu* provides not only a fresh encounter with the movie past but also a photographic record of an earlier France, which moved in a different rhythm, and because of the photographic equipment and style of the period, in a softly different light. The shopfronts look like Atget; the houses might have modeled for Bonnard. It is a nostalgic work, not in the deliberate, embarrassing way we have become inured to, but in spite of itself—through the accidents of distribution. And because Renoir is free of the public-courting sentimentality of most movie directors, our nostalgia is—well—clean.

[1967]

## RULES OF THE GAME
### Penelope Gilliatt

Renoir's *Rules of the Game* is a work to be put with *Così Fan Tutte* and *The Marriage of Figaro*. Society is satirized in it with Mozart's own mixture of biting good sense and blithe, transforming acceptance. Like the operas, the film has a prodigality that is moving in itself. Fugitive moments of genius pass unstressed, because there is always infinitely more to draw upon, in the way of those Mozart tunes that disappear after one statement instead of spinning themselves out into the classic a-b-a aria form. The serene amplitude of Renoir's view floods the sophisticated plot and turns it into something else. He thought at the time—in 1939—that he was simply making a film about a contemporary house party. Mozart probably had an equivalent feeling when he was setting da Ponte's librettos. The script of the film—by Renoir himself, with Carl Koch—was written with actual memories of eighteenth-century plays in mind, and it opens with a quotation from Beaumarchais.

Even for a masterpiece (masterpieces generally have savage voyages), the film has had a hard and strange history. It was made in the conditions following Munich. The opening in Paris, during the summer of 1939, was received with fury. Renoir saw one man in the audience start to burn a newspaper in the hope of setting fire to the cinema. Because of the presence in the cast of the Jewish actor Marcel Dalio and the Austrian refugee Nora Gregor, the film was attacked by both the anti-Semitic and the chauvinist press. Butcher cuts were made. In October 1939, it was banned by the government as demoralizing. Both the Vichy and the German Occupation authorities upheld the ban throughout the war. Until 1956, it seemed that only the mutilated version of the film was extant. Then two young French cinema enthusiasts who had acquired the rights to the film found hundreds of boxes of untouched footage in a warehouse. After two years of editing, under Renoir's supervision, they were able to reconstruct his original film. When it was first shown again publicly, I saw someone who had worked on it in 1939 sitting there with tears running down his cheeks at the sight of it restored.

The plot is a pattern of three triangles—two of them abovestairs, one below —seen mostly at a château during a big house party for the shooting season. The Marquis de la Chesnaye, played by Dalio, is a dapper man who collects eighteenth-century clockwork toys. He has Jewish blood, as his male servants point out behind the baize door to demonstrate that he can't be relied upon always to know the rules of being an aristocrat. His wife, Christine, played by Nora Gregor, is a highbred Austrian woman, frightened to find herself fond of an aviator who has just flown solo across the Atlantic and let out an angry declaration of love to her at Le Bourget during a radio interview. This is one of the triangles. The second is made up of the Marquis, his wife, and his mistress, a dark, overanimated society girl whose most sober thought is that she wants to be happy; she says it sadly two or three times during the film, between spasms of social chatter. "How are your factories?" she gabbles brightly, blotting out pain to greet a moneyed woman at the château. The third triangle is formed by Schumacher, the Marquis's gamekeeper; his wife, Lisette, the Marquise's maid, who is based in Paris away from her husband and living a surrogate life because of her loyalty to her mistress; and a poacher who crosses the lines to respectability and becomes a bootboy, because the Marquis has been tepidly attracted by the fact that the man is more efficient than the gamekeeper at trapping the rabbits that lower the tone of the shoot. With Lisette's adored mistress in town so much, Schumacher feels he might as well be a widower. He tries to get the Marquis to pay heed to the problem, in a desolately comic scene on the château doorstep while they move between car and front door, but the Marquis has guests and rococo and rabbits on his mind. This ignored third triangle is to intersect fatally with the others when Schumacher, run amuck with loss and jealousy, mistakenly kills the aviator because he thinks it is Lisette rather than the Marquise who is with him. And through it all—through the bright welcomes and the glances and the melancholy accommodations to loveless social rules, through the shooting party and the amateur theatricals and the good-night scenes in long corridors where nobly born men horse around with hunting horns while a lordlier-looking servant walks impassively past them—through the whole intricate gavotte of the film wanders the solicitous figure of Octave, played by Renoir. Octave is the eternal extra man, the buffoon who really has both more sense and more passion than the others of his class, the one who best loves the Marquise and pines to look after her in memory of her father, who taught him music in Austria long ago. He would have liked to be a conductor. The man whom everyone idly holds dear for being the perfect guest suddenly speaks of himself with hatred for living the life of a sponger. How would he eat if it were not for his friends? The thing is to forget it and get drunk. Though then, after feeling better, he feels worse—that's the nasty part. But he will grow accustomed, as necessary. He used to dream of having something to offer. Of having contact with an audience. It would have been overwhelming. . . .

The house party's formal shooting scene has its double later on, in the desperately actual one when Schumacher runs among the guests and tries to kill the poacher. The amateur theatricals that everyone treats so seriously have their mirror image also in this drama, which the house party takes for play. The intrusion of the aviator into an alien society—the romantic hero thrust among skeptics trained in old rules, the pure among the impure—has its counterpart in the poacher, catapulted into a world of snobbery-by-proxy and of a chef's adopted airs about making potato salad with white wine. He accepted the Marquis's offer gratefully, because he had always dreamed of being a servant. Limited hopes, delusory debts. He had always liked the clothes. Julien Carette plays him wonderfully. When he is seen in the servants' hall for the first time, a vagrant corralled within the laws of the housebound, his right arm wheels with embarrassment as he introduces himself. There is a shot of him in front of a palm tree with the Marquis during the evening fête, straightening the master's tie. "Did you ever want to be an Arab?" asks the Marquis. They are both thinking about women. The Marquis, with two on his mind, envies Arabs for not having to throw out one for another. "I hate hurting people," he says, and he means it, in his fashion. "Ah, but a harem takes money," says the poacher. "If I want to have a woman, or to get rid of her, I try to make her laugh. Why don't you try it?" "That takes talent," says the Marquis.

*Rules of the Game* is delicately good to every character in it, even to the most spoiled or stilted. For the people who are driven to their limits, it has the special eye that Renoir always reserves for men nearly beyond what they can manage. There is a wonderful shot of Schumacher, the violent, rigid game-keeper, now sacked from his job because of the shooting affair, and thus separated completely from the lady's-maid wife he was trying to save for himself. She chose to stay with Madame. He stands with his forehead against a tree, stiffly, finished, like a propped scarecrow. The game has gone wrong. The rules—for him as for the aviator—were so much deadwood, but he was deceived in hoping to hack his way back to life by violent action. For the others the game still holds, although the idea of honor has petered out into the advisability of avoiding open indiscretion, and the idea of happiness into being amused. The *crime passionnel* of the plot, terrible for all three triangles, is given the labeling of his class by the Marquis. It is called "an unfortunate accident." He tells his guests that the gamekeeper, who was actually egged on by the poacher to shoot the aviator because they thought he was poaching Lisette from them both, "fired in the course of duty" on an intruder suspected of the only kind of poaching that gamekeepers are supposed to deal with. Renoir's formal command of his film is beautiful. During the last part of the picture, the camera moves about almost like another guest. It must be some quality of Renoir's that makes his camera lens seem always a witness and never a voyeur. The witness here communicates a powerful mixture of amusement and disquiet. *Rules of the Game* was made in 1939, after all; it is not only a wonderful piece of filmmaking, not only a great work of humanism and social comedy in a perfect rococo frame, but also an act of historical testimony.

[1969]

## THE GOLDEN COACH
### Pauline Kael

At his greatest, Jean Renoir expresses the beauty in our common humanity—the desires and hopes, the absurdities and follies that we all, to one degree or another, share. As a man of the theater (using this term in its widest sense to include movies) he has become involved in the ambiguities of illusion and "reality," theater and "life"—the confusions of identity in the role of man as a role-player. The methods and the whole range of ideas that were once associated with Pirandello and are now associated with Jean Genet are generally considered highly theatrical. But perhaps it is when theater becomes the most theatrical—when the theater of surprise and illusion jabs at our dim notions of reality—that we become conscious of the roles we play.

Jean Renoir's *The Golden Coach* (1953)[1] is a comedy of love and appearances. In her greatest screen performance, Anna Magnani, as the actress who is no more of an actress than any of us, tries out a series of love roles in a play within a play within a movie. The artifice has the simplest of results: we become caught up in a chase through the levels of fantasy, finding ourselves at last with the actress, naked in loneliness as the curtain descends, but awed by the wonders of man's artistic creation of himself. Suddenly, the meaning is restored to a line we have heard and idly discounted a thousand times: "All the world's a stage."

The *commedia dell' arte* players were actors who created their own roles. They could trust in inspiration and the free use of imagination, they could improvise because they had an acting tradition that provided taken-for-granted situations and relationships, and they had the technique that comes out of experience. *The Golden Coach,* Renoir's tribute to the *commedia dell' arte,* is an improvisation on classic comedy, and it is also his tribute to the fabulous gifts, the inspiration, of Anna Magnani. At her greatest, she, too, expresses the beauty in our common humanity. It is probably not coincident with this that Renoir is the most sensual of great directors, Magnani the most sensual of great actresses. Though he has taken Prosper Mérimée's vehicle and shaped it for her, it will be forever debatable whether it contains her or is exploded by her. But as this puzzle is parallel with the theme, it adds another layer to the ironic comedy.

Perhaps only those of us who truly love this film will feel that Magnani, with her deep sense of the ridiculous in herself and others, Magnani with her roots in the earth so strong that she can pull them out, shake them in the face of pretension and convention, and sink them down again stronger than ever—the actress who has come to be the embodiment of human experience, the most "real" of actresses—is the miraculous choice that gives this film its gusto and its piercing beauty. If *this* woman can wonder who she is, then all of us must wonder. Renoir has shaped the material not only for her but out of her and

1. Based on Prosper Mérimée's one-act play *Le Carrosse du Saint Sacrement,* which was derived from the same Peruvian story that served as source material for an episode in Thornton Wilder's *The Bridge of San Luis Rey.*

out of other actresses' lives. Talking about the production, he remarked, "Anna Magnani is probably the greatest actress I have ever worked with. She is the complete animal—an animal created completely for the stage and screen. . . . Magnani gives so much of herself while acting that between scenes . . . she collapses and the mask falls. Between scenes she goes into a deep state of depression. . . ." Like the film itself, the set for the film is an unreal world where people suffer. In *The Golden Coach* we see Magnani in a new dimension: not simply the usual earthy "woman of the people," but the artist who exhausts her resources in creating this illusion of volcanic reality.

The work has been called a masque, a fairy tale, and a fable—each a good try, but none a direct hit: the target shimmers, our aim wavers. *The Golden Coach* is light and serious, cynical and exquisite, a blend of color, wit, and Vivaldi. What could be more unreal than the time and place—a dusty frontier in Renaissance Peru. (You can't even fix the time in the Renaissance—the architecture is already baroque.) A band of Italian players attempts to bring art to the New World. Magnani is Camilla, the Columbine of the troupe; among her lovers is the Spanish viceroy, who, as the final token of his bondage —the proof of his commitment to love over position and appearances—presents her with the symbol of power in the colony, the golden coach. Through this formal "taken-for-granted" situation, life (that is to say, art) pours out— inventive, preposterous, outrageous, buoyant. And in the midst of all the pleasures of the senses, there is the charging force of Magnani with her rumbling, cosmic laughter, and her exultant cry—*"Mamma mia!"*

The script has its awkward side, and those who don't get the feel of the movie are quick to point out the flaws. Some passages of dialogue are clumsily written, others embarrassingly overexplicit ("Where does the theater end and life begin?"—which isn't even a respectable question). Much of the strained rhythm in the dialogue may be blamed on the fact that Renoir's writing in English doesn't do justice to Renoir the film artist. And, though Magnani herself, in her first English-speaking role, is vocally magnificent, some of the others speak in dreary tones and some of the minor characters appear to be dubbed. The "international" cast—in this case, largely Italian, English and French—never really seems to work; at the basic level they don't speak the same language. And Renoir allows some of the performers more latitude than their talent warrants; though Duncan Lamont and Ricardo Rioli are marvelous love foils, Paul Campbell is shockingly inept, and the scenes in which he figures go limp. Another defect is in the directorial rhythm. This was Renoir's second color film, and as in his first, *The River*—which was also a collaboration with his great cinematographer-nephew, Claude Renoir—static patches of dialogue deaden the movement; his sense of film rhythm seems to falter when he works in color. Instead of indulging in the fancy fool's game of Freudian speculation that he fails when he tries to compete with his father, it seems simpler to suggest that he gets so bemused by the beauty of color that he carelessly neglects the language of cinema which he himself helped to develop.

But in the glow and warmth of *The Golden Coach,* these defects are trifles. When the singing, tumbling mountebanks transform the courtyard of an inn into a playhouse, the screen is full of joy in creative make-believe. When, at a crucial point in the story, Magnani announces that it is the end of the second act, and the movie suddenly becomes a formalized stage set, we realize that we have been enchanted, that we had forgotten where we were. When the hand of the creator becomes visible, when the actor holds the mask up to view, the sudden revelation that this world we have been absorbed in is not life but theater brings us closer to the actor-characters. So many movies pretend to be life that we are brought up short, brought to consciousness, by this movie that proclaims its theatricality. And the presence of the artists—Renoir and Magnani—is like a great gift. When, in the last scene of *The Golden Coach,* one of the most exquisitely conceived moments on film, the final curtain is down, and Magnani as the actress stands alone on stage, bereft of her lovers, listening to the applause that both confirms and destroys the illusion, the depth of her loneliness seems to be the truth and the pity of all roles played.

[1961]

# JACQUES TATI

## *MY UNCLE*
### Penelope Gilliatt

There is a particular mutinous mumble in the ordinary course of events which can suddenly sound like W. C. Fields; there are debonair acts of stoicism which evoke Keaton; and there is an overweening electronic buzz which reminds you of the films of Jacques Tati as strongly as a particular kind of starched lope summons up Tati himself. When M. Hulot's author balances a sound track, the human voice plays a small and outclassed part in the din of the inanimate. A while ago, at some stiff dinner party on the beach in California, where the outdoor ping-pong table was made of marble ("Because marble doesn't warp in the sea air," said the owner gravely), I remember a nearly unnegotiable ten minutes when the roar of twenty-four people's chicken bones being ground up by the garbage disposal in the grandly enlightened open-plan living room was entirely victorious over the twenty-four brave souls who went on pretending to be able to hear each other. The sound track was Tati's, by any right, and so was the politely programed lunacy of the people ignoring the racket. No other director has ever pitted the still small voice of human contact so delicately against the nerveless dominion of modern conveniences. Some noisy hot-water pipes become a major character in *Jour de Fête.* In *My Uncle,* the buzzings and hissings and gulpings of peremptory gadgets are prodigious.

Tati's father originally wanted him to be a picture framer, in the family tradition. He riposted with Rugby football. Between games, he filled in with what were, by all accounts, some marvelous mimes of athleticism. It would have been fine to see him on the field: six-foot-four of him, apparently always with a way of being able to lean alertly in any direction, as though he were balanced against a gale. The tilt is generally forward, exposing an eager five or six inches of striped sock, but it has been known to go just as far to the side. There is a sweet minute in *My Uncle* when, without interrupting the talk he is having with someone ahead of him, he keels neatly to the side to hear his four-foot nephew mutter something into his ear, and then quickly straightens up again to get some money out of his pocket so that the boy can buy a supply of crullers. The famous figure with the umbrella makes the stances of other and more ordinary people—and, indeed, of other and more ordinary umbrellas —look rather peculiar after a time. The umbrella, which he sometimes holds like a low-slung rifle, can also suggest the taut string of an invisible helium balloon or the company of a thin aunt sprinting ahead. Now and again, he will hold it by the ferrule and seem to have to tug against it, as if it were a leash with a hidden dog straining on the end. For himself, he seems to have learned nothing from the gait and posture of others. He is not one of the upright bipeds, because he slants; he doesn't so much walk as get ready to dive. And he hardly ever seems to sit. There is too much leg around, perhaps. Or maybe his hip joints have never taken to the suggestion of the right angle. Sometimes—very occasionally—he will lie down, and the effect is spectacular. He tends to do it in his hat, with the jutting pipe remaining in the mouth. To my recollection, none of his films show him lying on anything so commonplace as a bed, although he has been seen supine on a road in *Mr. Hulot's Holiday,* and curved amazingly along the serpentine front of a tormenting modern sofa tipped over onto its back in *My Uncle.* This is no ordinary man. He can make asphalt look quite like an air mattress; on the other hand, he can make it clear that a modern piece of furniture feels uncommonly like asphalt.

*My Uncle* is an attack of blistering docility on the generally unadmitted discomfort dealt out by house pride, contemporary design, and high standards of dusting. Hulot's sister, called Mme. Arpel, who is seldom seen without a duster, lives in a balefully mechanized and hygienic house where a speck of dirt would be like an oath in the Vatican. Her husband, who is in plastics, is a quail-shaped man who wears thick clothes however bright the sun. They live a life of unvarying merriment and pep. The front gates open by remote-control buzzer, and at the same time, if the company merits it, a sculptured fish in the middle of the unnatural little garden starts spouting water. For trade deliveries, and for her brother, the fountain subsides. The Arpels live in a world of ceremony but no actual fun, of regal fuss with two convoluted chairs that are placed in throne positions for the Arpels to watch mere television, of flavorless steaks cooked in two seconds by infrared rays, of high heels clicking on polished floors. Clothes are like the poor in the New Testament—always with them, and quite a trial. A severe-looking guest whom Mme. Arpel casts as a splendid possible future wife for Hulot, and as a certain admirer of the house, is dressed in a sort of horse rug or table runner. A dog leash then gets impossibly tangled in one of her long earrings. The women in the Arpels' world are perpetually harassed by their bags and stoles and hobble skirts, and M. Arpel throws his wife into a panic by nearly forgetting his gloves when he drives to work. Hulot, on the other hand, is curiously absented from his clothes, which regularly include the familiar short raincoat and ancient hat whatever the weather. He also seems agreeably unemployable. His natural allies are mongrel dogs and dirty children, who follow him in droves. His nephew, Gérard, adores him. Gérard's chirpy mother tends to sterilize the boy out of existence; Hulot is a comrade, being muddle's natural kin. The uncle lives on the top floor of a charming, ramshackle house in an old part of Paris, with windows that he arranges carefully before leaving every day so that his caged canary will get the sun's reflection. Until the last shot of the film, one never sees the inside of this house. All one catches are glimpses through half-open stairways and hall windows of people's heads and feet, or a segment of a girl lodger in a bath towel waiting to scuttle across a corridor when Hulot's legs have disappeared downstairs. Tati is visually very interested in bits of people. If he were playing the game of pinning the tail on the donkey, I think he would tend to find the dissociated tail too engrossing to go any further.

Maybe all funniness has a tendency to throw settled things into doubt. Where most people will automatically complete an action, a great comedian will stop in the middle to have a think about the point of it, and the point will often vanish before our eyes. In *My Uncle*, Hulot has this effect very strongly about the importance of holding down a job. His sister, who is bothered by his life as if it were a piece of grit in her eye, has put him to work in her husband's plastics factory. The place produces miles of red plastic piping, for some reason or other. Various machines pump out rivers of it. Hulot is mildly interested. "Keep an eye on No. 5," says a workmate mystifyingly, wrapped up in a piece of cellophane like a sandwich in an automat, and taking no notice of the fact that Hulot is slumped over a table and half moribund because of a gas leak. No. 5, a rebel machine, starts to produce piping with occasional strange swellings in it, like a furlong of boa constrictor that has slowly eaten its way through a flock of sheep. The thing then takes it into its head to start tying off the piping every few inches, as if it were a sausage machine. Hulot goes on manfully keeping an eye on it, which is all he has been told to do, and quite right. Care for plastic can go too far. His sister is a living witness to that. For her wedding anniversary, she has given her husband an automatic and doubtless plastic garage door that opens when his car goes past an electric eye. M. Arpel is overjoyed, in his plastic way. "No more keys. Happy?" his wife chirrups. Their dachshund then sniffs the electric eye and shuts them in the garage, yapping amiably while they try to persuade him to sniff again. The new door, like the bedroom floor of the house, has two round windows near the top: the Arpels' disembodied faces appear, yelling inaudibly for help, and bobbing about behind the windows like air bubbles in a bricklayer's level.

Husband and wife are content, mostly. They represent a new order of happiness. Hulot represents the old disorder. The Arpels, who rather grow on you, are funny partly because they treat themselves as if they were machines and partly because they have lost the defining human sense of relative importances. Trotting around with their gadgets and their dusters and their plans for tea parties, they have no grasp of their scale in the universe; they are a counterpart of the sort of endearing great Danes who will try to fit all four legs onto a lap in the delusion that they are the size of Pekes. These proud owners of this awful model house, tripping around on an artistic but farcically unwalkable pattern of paving stones and being careful not to put a toe to the grass, conduct themselves with a sober sense of import and duty. When they entertain, they might be the President of the Republic and his wife welcoming the signators of a peace treaty. The difference that they are only having some neighbors to a paralyzingly difficult tea party at which everyone is spattered by a minor debacle with the spouting fish destroys no one's aplomb and no one's sense of occasion. It is part of Tati's humor that the Arpels' perception of things is fastidiously concentrated and only a trifle off the point. Who is to say, in fact, that their absorption is not the norm, even if it does screen out what seems more fascinating to the casual observer? They are in the same comic position as the plumbers in one of Robert Dhéry's films, who stalk backstage through hordes of stark-naked showgirls without paying them the slightest heed while talking only about tap washers. In *Jour de Fête,* the postman played by Jacques Tati is entranced by the idea of Americanization of the mails through speedier transport. Speedier transport means, to him, bicycling instead of walking. The bicycle suits Tati. He uses one in *My Uncle* —a rather dashing one, with a puttering little motor. The shape of the thing fits his legs, which are long enough to turn the bike at will into a quadruped. Bicycles also meet a certain stateliness in his style and a certain disinclination for any vehicle that outsizes the human frame. You feel that he much detests the shiny cars in *My Uncle.* He prefers doughnut carts and horse-drawn wagons. The failed plastic piping is hurriedly taken away in a cart drawn by a strong-minded gray horse that exerts a will of its own about going to the right when the driver wants the left; its mood is not so unlike the recalcitrance of the obstreperous plastics machine, after all. Hulot has his own rules about mess. When he trips his way through the rubble of his part of Paris into the antiseptic modern quarter, he is careful to replace exactly a dislodged piece of wreckage as he goes.

Tati's droll, elegant films establish that one doesn't have to be a comic to do a gag. There are plenty of professionally uproarious people who come on signaling that they are funny men, that they are the life of the party. Tati seems to believe that it is in the nature of all mankind to be funny. High dignitaries have committed some of life's greatest physical gags. Hulot himself—like Keaton's heroes but unlike Chaplin's—is the least patently comic character in his author's scheme. In fact, he is extremely serious. His style is the inversion of the circus tradition, and of that silent-film tradition in which a normal world is ravaged by a comic personality; in Tati's case, the world is made comic by the sobriety of Hulot.

The films express the subtlest sympathy for other people's moods. In the company of the decorous, Hulot is as correct as a furled umbrella. With someone scared—like the maid in *My Uncle,* who is petrified by the electric eyes in the place and backs away from them as if they were basilisks—you can see him slowly submerging in fellow-cowardice. With dogs, small shopkeepers, and kids, he starts to borrow jauntiness. Everything in the films is meticulous and spare; nothing is pushed, and there are no set pieces. Some of the prettiest moments in Tati's work vanish as fast as a scent, recollected but not recoverable. In *My Uncle,* there is a marvelous beginning to a comic sequence when a long, shiny car is trying to back into a space between a ramshackle lorry and a vegetable cart. An old, old man carrying a bag with a French loaf sticking out of the end of it shuffles backward and forward with the car two or three times to signal the driver in, courteously shifting the bag from the left hand to the right as he changes direction. And then he simply gives up, and shrugs a mild "the hell with it," and leaves the sequence gently in the air.

[1971]

## PLAYTIME
### Vincent Canby

*Playtime* is Jacques Tati's most brilliant film, a bracing reminder in this all-too-lazy era that films can occasionally achieve the status of art.

*Playtime* is a gloriously funny movie about a Paris so modern it does not yet exist, a Paris composed entirely of streets like our Avenue of the Americas, hemmed in by efficiently beautiful glass-and-steel towers in which, if we are quick about it, we may see momentary reflections of Sacré-Cœur, the Arch of Triumph, or the Eiffel Tower.

It is a city inhabited almost entirely by tourists and their shepherd-guides who are spreading a terrible pox among the natives. It is not an immediately fatal disease but it makes everyone behave with the kind of frigid competence affected by airline stewardesses and reservation clerks.

Not even nuns are immune. Their heels click importantly as they glide across marbleized floors. A receptionist—a man so ancient that he could be a veteran of Verdun—operates a complex of computer buttons designed to announce a visitor's arrival in an office building. The old man does his best and the machine bleeps and gurgles successfully. It is the world of Kubrick's *2001* without the metaphysics and without Richard Strauss.

*Playtime,* which was made in 1967, is Tati's most free-form comedy to date, as well as his most disciplined—even more so than *Traffic,* which was made in 1971.

It is virtually three major set pieces, or acts. The first act is set at Orly Airport, where we pick up some American tourists who arrive in a single, all-expenses-paid clump. The second is more or less devoted to a trade fair, where the tourists cross paths with Tati's Mr. Hulot.

The last act, a kind of neon-lit Götterdämmerung—is set in a posh night club whose opening night turns into the sort of chaos that civilizes. Everything goes wrong, including the air conditioning, but in going wrong, life is somehow restored to the tourists as well as the natives.

You may well recognize the shape of the film, which is a variation on the favorite comedy theme about the family that inherits a lot of money, tries to put on fancy airs, loses its soul, and only finds itself again when the fortune is taken away.

However, it is not the shape of the film or its cheerful philosophy that are important. Rather it is the density of the wit. It is the gracefulness of the visual gags that flow one into another, nonstop, in a manner that only Tati now masters.

Mr. Hulot is still the nominal focal point of the comedy, particularly in the trade-fair sequence, but he is less in evidence in *Playtime* than in any other Hulot feature. The film is even further removed from character than was *Traffic*. It observes not persons, but social clusters, in a manner that serves curiously to humanize group action and response instead of to dehumanize the individual.

However, don't waste time analyzing *Playtime* too much. It can easily withstand such critical assaults, but they serve to distract attention from the film's immense good humor, from, for example, the closing sequence that shows us a Parisian traffic circle that has been turned into a giant Lazy Susan, serving, among other things, the sacred cause of inefficiency.

In addition to everything else, *Playtime* is a reckless act of faith—by Tati in himself. He photographed it in 70mm (though it is being shown here in 35mm), and he invested not only huge amounts of time in it but also his own money. As anyone connected with films can tell you, this is certifiable madness.

The movie business is supposed to exist so that people other than its artists can lose their shirts in it, thereby to gain things that are called (by those who can use them) tax-loss carry-forwards. I hope *Playtime* will make Tati very rich so that at some future time he can use a tax-loss carry-forward.

[1973]

## TRAFFIC
### Jay Cocks

Jacques Tati has made three previous excursions into the amuck world of Mr. Hulot, upon whose heron head rain down all manner of comic disasters. *Mr. Hulot's Holiday* (1953), the first, still seems the best, the most genuinely poignant and inventively funny. Further installments—*My Uncle* (1958) and *Playtime* (1967)—have grown progressively more precious. Often the complexity of a Tati gag outweighs the punch line. In *Traffic,* it overwhelms it. Ingenuity, not wit, is the real point of the exercise, and laughter is strangled by machinery.

Virtually plotless, the film is a series of skits having to do with the efforts of Mr. Hulot and his fellow employees of the Altra Auto Company to get a new-model family camper from the firm's Paris plant to an auto show at Amsterdam. They are waylaid on the highways by a seemingly endless variety of motorized misfortunes, ranging from an elementary flat tire to an epic collision. Oddly, most of the movie is so slow that it seems to have been enacted under water. Watching Hulot (Tati) trying to make his way through mazes of automobiles is a little like watching a wayward eel float through a fleet of submarines.

As a comic actor, Tati has become over the years so closely calculating that he has lost all trace of spontaneity and humanity. His every gesture is self-conscious and self-congratulatory. As a director, he has become a great deal more elaborate but somewhat less inspired. *Traffic*'s set pieces, like a large pileup of cars in an improbable accident, all seem too cherished and worked over; they have a laboratory air about them.

Tati has obviously—perhaps too obviously—learned from the old masters. Keaton's mechanical virtuosity is on view, or at least attempted, as are Chaplin's timing and resilience and Langdon's scrambled innocence. Tati absorbs and assimilates each skill like a diligent pupil taking great care with his lessons, and that is the way they are applied. Watching Tati is like listening to the brightest kid in the class run through his homework, dogged, letter-perfect, and without inspiration. His movies since Mr. Hulot's debut have been very like the best scene in that film, where Hulot, out for a little recreation, finds himself slowly and inescapably folding up in a kayak, then sinking majestically into the sea.

[1973]

# FRANÇOIS TRUFFAUT

## *SHOOT THE PIANO PLAYER*
### Pauline Kael

The cover of David Goodis's novel *Down There,* now issued by Grove Press under the title of the film adapted from it, *Shoot the Piano Player,* carries a statement from Henry Miller—"Truffaut's film was so good I had doubts the book could equal it. I have just read the novel and I think it is even better than the film." I don't agree with Miller's judgment. I like the David Goodis book, but it's strictly a work in a limited genre, well-done and consistent; Truffaut's film busts out all over—and that's what's wonderful about it. The film is comedy, pathos, tragedy all scrambled up—much, I think, as most of us really experience them (surely all our lives are filled with comic horrors) but not as we have been led to expect them in films.

*Shoot the Piano Player* is about a man who has withdrawn from human experience; he wants not to care any more, not to get involved, not to *feel*. He has reduced life to a level on which he can cope with it—a reverie between him and the piano. Everything that happens outside his solitary life seems erratic, accidental, unpredictable—but he can predict the pain. In a flashback we see why: when he *did* care, he failed the wife who needed him and caused her death. In the course of the film he is once more brought back into the arena of human contacts; another girl is destroyed, and he withdraws again into solitude.

Truffaut is a free and inventive director—and he fills the piano player's encounters with the world with good and bad jokes, bits from old Sacha Guitry films, clowns and thugs, tough kids, songs and fantasy and snow scenes, and homage to the American gangster films—not the classics, the socially conscious big-studio gangster films of the thirties, but the grade-B gangster films of the forties and fifties. Like Godard, who dedicated *Breathless* to Monogram Pictures, Truffaut is young, and he loves the cheap American gangster films of his childhood and youth. And like them, *Shoot the Piano Player* was made on a small budget. It was also made outside of studios with a crew that, according to witnesses, sometimes consisted of Truffaut, the actors, and a cameraman. Part of his love of cheap American movies with their dream imagery of the American gangster—the modern fairy tales for European children who go to movies—is no doubt reflected in his taking an American underworld novel and transferring its setting from Philadelphia to France.

Charles Aznavour, who plays the hero, is a popular singer turned actor—rather like Frank Sinatra in this country, and like Sinatra, he is an instinctive actor and a great camera subject. Aznavour's piano player is like a tragic embodiment of Robert Hutchins's Zukerkandl philosophy (whatever it is, stay out of it): he is the thinnest-skinned of modern heroes. It is his own capacity to feel that makes him cut himself off: he experiences so sensitively and so acutely that he can't bear the suffering of it—he thinks that if he doesn't do anything he won't feel and he won't cause suffering to others. The girl, Marie Dubois—later the smoky-steam-engine girl of *Jules and Jim*—is like a Hollywood forties movie type; she would have played well with Humphrey Bogart—a big, clear-eyed, crude, loyal, honest girl. The film is closely related to Godard's *Breathless;* and both seem to be haunted by the shade of Bogart.

*Shoot the Piano Player* is both nihilistic in attitude and, at the same time, in its wit and good spirits, totally involved in life and fun. Whatever Truffaut touches seems to leap to life—even a gangster thriller is transformed into the human comedy. A *comedy* about melancholia, about the hopelessness of life can only give the lie to the theme; for as long as we can joke, life is not hopeless, we can enjoy it. In Truffaut's style there is so much pleasure in life that the wry, lonely little piano player, the sardonic little man who shrugs off experience, is himself a beautiful character. This beauty is a tribute to human experience, even if the man is so hurt and defeated that he can only negate experience. The nihilism of the character—and the anarchic nihilism of the director's style—have led reviewers to call the film a surrealist farce; it isn't that strange.

When I refer to Truffaut's style as anarchic and nihilistic, I am referring to a *style,* not an absence of it. I disagree with the critics around the country who find the film disorganized; they seem to cling to the critical apparatus of their grammar-school teachers. They want unity of theme, easy-to-follow transitions in mood, a good, coherent, old-fashioned plot, and heroes they can identify with and villains they can reject. Stanley Kauffmann in the *New Republic* compares *Shoot the Piano Player* with the sweepings of cutting-room floors; *Time* decides that "the moral, if any, seems to be that shooting the piano player might, at least, put the poor devil out of his misery." But who but *Time* is looking for a moral? What's exciting about movies like *Shoot the Piano Player, Breathless* (and also the superb *Jules and Jim*, though it's very different from the other two) is that they, quite literally, move with the times. They are full of unresolved, inexplicable, disharmonious elements, irony and slapstick and defeat all compounded—*not* arbitrarily as the reviewers claim—but in terms of the filmmaker's efforts to find some expression for his own anarchic experience, instead of making more of those tiresome well-made movies that no longer mean much to us.

The subject matter of *Shoot the Piano Player,* as of *Breathless,* seems small and unimportant compared to the big themes of so many films, but it only *seems* small: it is an effort to deal with contemporary experience in terms drawn out of this experience. For both Godard and Truffaut a good part of this experience has been movie-going, but this is just as much a part of their lives as reading is for a writer. And what writer does not draw upon what he has read?

A number of reviewers have complained that in his improvisatory method Truffaut includes irrelevancies, and they use as chief illustration the opening scene—a gangster who is running away from pursuers bangs into a telephone pole, and then is helped to his feet by a man who proceeds to walk along with him, while discussing his marital life. Is it really so irrelevant? Only if you grew up in that tradition of the well-made play in which this bystander would have to reappear as some vital link in the plot. But he's relevant in a different way here: he helps to set us in a world in which his seminormal existence seems just as much a matter of chance and fringe behavior and simplicity as the gangster's existence—which begins to seem seminormal also. The bystander talks; we get an impression of his way of life and his need to talk about it, and he goes out of the film, and that is that: Truffaut would have to be as stodgy and dull-witted as the reviewers to bring him back and link him into the story. For the meaning of these films is that these fortuitous encounters illuminate something about our lives in a way that the old neat plots don't.

There is a tension in the method; we never quite know where we are, how we are supposed to react—and this tension, as the moods change and we are pulled in different ways, gives us the excitement of drama, of art, of *our* life. Nothing is clear-cut, the ironies crisscross and bounce. The loyal, courageous heroine is so determined to live by her code that when it's violated, she comes on too strong, and the piano player is repelled by her inability to respect the weaknesses of others. Thugs kidnaping a little boy discuss their possessions with him—a conversation worthy of a footnote in Veblen's passages on conspicuous expenditure.

Only a really carefree, sophisticated filmmaker could bring it off—and satisfy our desire for the unexpected that is also *right.* Truffaut is a director of incredible taste; he never carries a scene *too* far. It seems extraordinarily simple to complain that a virtuoso who can combine many moods has not stuck to one familiar old mood—but this is what the reviews seem to amount to. The modern novel has abandoned the old conception that each piece must be in place—abandoned it so thoroughly that when we read something, like Angus Wilson's *Anglo-Saxon Attitudes,* in which each piece does finally fit in place, we are astonished and amused at the dexterity of the accomplishment. That is the way Wilson works and it's wonderfully satisfying, but few modern novelists work that way; and it would be as irrelevant to the meaning and quality of, say, *Tropic of Capricorn* to complain that the plot isn't neatly tied together like *Great Expectations,* as to complain of the film *Shoot the Piano Player* that it isn't neatly tied together like *The Bicycle Thief.* Dwight Macdonald wrote that *Shoot the Piano Player* deliberately mixed up "three genres which are usually kept apart: crime melodrama, romance, and slapstick comedy." And, he says, "I thought the mixture didn't jell, but it was an exhilarating try." What I think is exhilarating in *Shoot the Piano Player* is that it *doesn't* "jell" and that the different elements keep *us* in a state of suspension—we react far more than we do to works that "jell." Incidentally, it's not completely accurate to say that these genres are usually kept apart: although *slapstick* rarely enters the mixture except in a far-out film like *Beat the Devil* or *Lovers and Thieves* or the new *The Manchurian Candidate,* there are numerous examples of crime melodrama-romance-comedy among well-known American films—particularly of the forties—for example, *The Maltese Falcon, Casablanca, The Big Sleep, To Have and Have Not.* (Not all of Truffaut's models are cheap B pictures.)

Perhaps one of the problems that American critics and audiences may have with *Shoot the Piano Player* is a peculiarly American element in it—the romantic treatment of the man who walks alone. For decades our films were full of these gangsters, outcasts, detectives, cynics; Bogart epitomized them all —all the men who had been hurt by a woman or betrayed by their friends and who no longer trusted anybody. And although I think most of us enjoyed this romantic treatment of the man beyond the law, we rejected it intellectually. It was part of hack moviemaking—we might love it but it wasn't really intellectually respectable. And now here it is, inspired by our movies, and coming back to us via France. The heroine of *Shoot the Piano Player* says of the hero, "Even when he's with somebody, he walks alone." But this French hero carries his isolation much farther than the earlier American hero: when his girl is having a fight on his behalf and he is impelled to intervene, he says to himself, "You're out of it. Let them fight it out." He is brought into it; but where the American hero, once impelled to move, is a changed man and, redeemed by love or patriotism or a sense of fair play, he would take the initiative, save his girl, and conquer everything, this French hero simply moves into the situation when he must, when he can no longer stay out of it, and takes the consequences. He finds that the contact with people is once again defeating. He really doesn't believe in anything; the American hero only *pretended* he didn't.

*Breathless* was about active, thoughtless young people; *Shoot the Piano Player* is about a passive, melancholic character who is acted upon. Yet the world that surrounds the principal figures in these two movies is similar: the clowns in one are police, in the other gangsters, but this hardly matters. What we react to in both is the world of absurdities that is so much like our own world in which people suddenly and unexpectedly turn into clowns. But at the center is the sentimentalist—Belmondo in *Breathless,* Aznavour here—and I think there can be no doubt that both Godard and Truffaut love their heroes.

There are, incidentally, a number of little in-group jokes included in the film; a few of these are of sufficiently general interest to be worth mentioning, and, according to Andrew Sarris, they have been verified by Truffaut. The piano player is given the name of Saroyan as a tribute to William Saroyan, particularly for his volume of stories *The Man on the Flying Trapeze,* and also because Charles Aznavour, like Saroyan, is Armenian (and, I would surmise, for the playful irony of giving a life-evading hero the name of one of the most rambunctious of life-embracing writers). One of the hero's brothers in the film is named Chico, as a tribute to the Marx Brothers. And the impresario in the film, the major villain of the work, is called Lars Schmeel, as a disapproving gesture toward someone Truffaut does *not* admire: the impresario Lars Schmidt, known to us simply as Ingrid Bergman's current husband, but apparently known to others—and disliked by Truffaut—for his theatrical activities in Paris.

If a more pretentious vocabulary or a philosophic explanation will help: the piano player is intensely human and sympathetic, a character who empathizes with others, and with whom we, as audience, empathize; but he does not want to accept the responsibilities of his humanity—he asks only to be left alone. And because he refuses voluntary involvement, he is at the mercy of accidental forces. He is, finally, man trying to preserve his little bit of humanity in a chaotic world—it is not merely a world he never made but a world he would much rather forget about. But schizophrenia cannot be willed, and so long as he is sane he is only partly successful: crazy accidents happen—and sometimes he must deal with them. That is to say, no matter how far he retreats from life, he is not completely safe. And Truffaut himself is so completely engaged in life that he pleads for the piano player's right to be left alone, to live in his withdrawn state, *to be out of it.* Truffaut's plea is, of course, "Don't shoot the piano player."

[1962]

## STOLEN KISSES
### Roger Greenspun

A quiet ballad by Charles Trenet starts up on the sound track, and from the pleasant but not especially distinguished prospect of a tree-lined Paris street, the camera pans left and moves down to face the barred entrance to the Cinemathèque Française. It is spring, and this is a sight to be seen in Paris in the spring of 1968. So begins *Stolen Kisses,* François Truffaut's best, most relaxed, and most serious film since *Jules and Jim.*

The ballad starts up again. A pleasant young couple get up from a park bench. He is clean-shaven, and his hair is not too long. Her hair is long, but it is well-brushed and very clean. Her attractive spring coat, at the most conservative edge of modern fashion, comes down almost to her knees. As they walk away, the camera pans right to follow them down a pleasant but not especially distinguished tree-lined path. So ends *Stolen Kisses*.

A lot has happened, but nothing has been concluded except that everything may be continued. Truffaut need never make another Antoine Doinel movie, but another one exists somewhere waiting to be realized, and another, and another. This is domestic drama of a very special sort, and it is in the nature of domestic drama that it does continue no matter what its crises and that it never has the finality of aristocratic art.

*Stolen Kisses* takes Antoine Doinel, the young hero of *The 400 Blows* and the "Antoine and Colette" episode of *Love at Twenty*, from his less-than-honorable discharge from the army, through a series of jobs and a brief affair with a married woman, to incipient unemployment and an informal engagement to the daughter of a middle-class couple who have befriended him. Jean-Pierre Léaud has played Antoine since the beginning, and the role has grown with him from movie to movie.

*Stolen Kisses* has little to do with *The 400 Blows*, but it looks back closely enough at "Antoine and Colette" to reintroduce the heroine of that sketch (Marie-France Pisier), now accompanied by husband and baby, and to have her ask him why he never calls her any more. Nobody waits around for the obvious answer—but Antoine does rush off to telephone his present girl friend, Christine (Claude Jade), to make apologies for having left her in the lurch the night before. That kind of movement by afterthought propels much of *Stolen Kisses*, just as that kind of arbitrary injection of motivation limits *Stolen Kisses*, and that kind of happy resolution for a momentary problem makes *Stolen Kisses* so easy to like.

Too easy on certain levels, and some movie-goers, like some no-nonsense movie critics, will object on the grounds of sentimentality. They will not be wrong, but they will have to admit that Truffaut has gotten there ahead of them, has charted the territory, and has placed himself in affectionate but unmistakably ironic relation to his hero, to his setting, to his times, and even to his own role as maker of pleasant entertainments.

For the director's credit at the beginning of the film, Truffaut has superimposed his name over what must be *the* archetypal shot of the Eiffel Tower. The obviousness of the phallic symbolism should not obscure the banality of the image: a banality that Truffaut reintroduces and extends with a view of the Sacré-Cœur, as seen from Antoine's balcony some time later, and with the Charles Trenet theme song, and with the whole corny business of kids in love —which is almost, but not quite, what the film is all about. A slight unease at the center of this lightest of all Truffaut's films seems finally to rest with the director himself, aware that his world and his way of seeing it have been very nearly drained of credulity by events that, in essence, scarcely touch that world at all.

The clue to understanding the best Truffaut films lies in recognizing that they work not so much toward dramatic resolution as toward a natural balance of forces, and that when they describe failure, as they mostly do, it is presented not as defeat but as stasis, or discontinuity, or loss of vitality. In *Jules and Jim,* for example, the balance pursued (and lost) is literally universal, and its maintenance involves the proper ordering of the four elements of earth, air, fire, and water. In *Shoot the Piano Player* the idea of balance defines the movie in a plot of fantastic intricacy that takes its inspiration from the strict moral division of crime melodrama and concludes by equalizing black and white across a screen that is essentially divided in half.

But in *Stolen Kisses* the program is less arduous. Opposites attract, drift apart, come together again. Balance amounts to no less, but also not much more, than viable accommodation between the sexes. And with a theme apparently so commonplace, artistic decorum requires that the events supporting it mostly illustrate the vicissitudes of ordinary living.

When Antoine comes to see Christine one night and her mother tells him that Christine has gone out, and we at the same time see her slipping out of the side door to avoid him, we are admitted to a glance at a wayward moment in a youthful affair, which with great tact (as if its characters had private lives beyond the private lives it creates for them) the film never explains. But the film does match that moment with another moment—on a morning when Antoine is in bed with a client's wife, Christine comes to his room to call and then quietly leaves because no one answers the door. We are in on the mystery this time, but between Antoine and Christine there is no explanation, recrimination, misunderstanding, understanding, forgiveness.

These are among the most beautiful vignettes in the film, and in their restraint, their reticence, they seem true to a notion of successful love as not having *always* to know, not *always* to make contact, that closely expresses the moral program of *Stolen Kisses.* But at the same time one action is shown balancing or equalizing another related action, the film progresses and establishes the rhythm of its world—in which there is much motion but no void.

An example of such motion, a gesture that has already drawn some strong criticism, occurs late in the movie and puts the camera into a rather complicated lyrical movement to the right and up a flight of stairs into a bedroom in which Antoine and Christine are (for the first time, one assumes) sleeping together. Having lost all his other jobs, Antoine is now a radio-dispatched television repairman, and when he makes his call he starts a small device, something like a taximeter, that records the amount of time he has spent on the job. Christine has cheerfully removed part of her television set and has called Antoine's company for repair service.

The camera movement, which begins with a low track past the still clicking timer, then past the strewn-about insides of the television set before beginning to climb the stairs, does a number of things at once. It climaxes the film's slightly breathless exploration of young love; pays tribute to that greatest of romantic trope-manufacturers, the balletic camera of Max Ophüls; makes light of the passing time; and generally offsets a movement to the right and down a set of stairs with which the movie begins.

Up vs. down, right vs. left—an opposition so broad and so unremarkable as to pass almost unnoticed. But in a world that moves by the gentle accommodation of contraries, that is at the same time a world in which so many characters are obsessed either with finding out or taking a position, the little balancing acts of Truffaut's graceful sentimental camera contribute a note of sanity.

Throughout most of *Stolen Kisses* Antoine works as a private operative for the Blady Detective Agency, which boasts a humane and conscientious boss, a roster of dedicated and attractive employees, and a list of clients whose problems, without exception, stem from loving too much or from not being loved. Antoine never hits the right stance as a detective, and we continually see him either mugging the role, losing interest and therefore dropping the trail, or getting so bound up in his work that he fails to maintain the proper distance. For example, he ends up welcoming into bed the wife (Delphine Seyrig) of M. Tabard, whose problem is that nobody, including his wife, loves him. That last indiscretion loses Antoine his job, as sex in one disruptive form or another always loses Antoine his job, usually with his passive cooperation. At the very end, when they become engaged, Antoine and Christine promise to teach one another everything they know, and one feels that Christine isn't making such a great bargain.

But foolish Antoine learns a good deal nonetheless, and if he fails all courses in prudential wisdom, he passes in a more important quality—tact. Twice in the film he picks up a whore. The first time, at the beginning, to satisfy the request of his army buddies in the stockade he rushes to get laid at five p.m. sharp—but he doesn't rush so much that he can't reject one whore because she refuses to undress for him.

The second pickup occurs after the funeral of an old Blady detective who had befriended Antoine. The camera follows Antoine in the graveyard, walking through a city of tombs, and then sweeps over the cemetery wall to peer down at Antoine again picking up another whore. Making love, one of his colleagues had told him earlier on, is a way of compensating for, of balancing off, death. But on this occasion, Antoine doesn't insist that the girl strip, though he pays her enough extra so that she is willing to—and in return for allowing her the dignity of her clothes, she offers him extra time.

Enjoyment of the relaxed spaciousness of *Stolen Kisses* is complicated somewhat by the disquieting realization that its vistas look out either upon that Paris of the tourist's imagination I have already mentioned, or upon an outside world impressively going to ruin. Truffaut dedicates his film to Henri Langlois; delays the entrance of his heroine because she is away while the students of the Conservatoire (where she studies violin) strike to protest the replacement of an old head by a new man they don't like; removes her mother from the scene for a while because she is stuck out of town while the trainmen also strike; and finally brings his young lovers together over a television set on which we have seen the students' barricades of May.

Obviously, Truffaut has not ignored actual and disruptive events. On the contrary, he has introduced them when he has no dramatic need for them. But *Stolen Kisses,* after acknowledging the times in which it is made, turns quite resolutely away from them.

Jean-Luc Godard, in taking his characters off on a brief vacation in *Weekend,* manages to bring modern times, human history, prehistory, and finally the geological eras along with them; Truffaut places his characters in the very midst of current events in the capital city—and then succeeds in producing pastoral.

Truffaut is a less intellectual director than Godard, but he is not much less intellectually rigorous—and, by excluding the larger world, he has developed for *Stolen Kisses* a meaning structure almost as impressive as Godard creates for *Weekend* by bringing the larger world so overpoweringly in. To a large extent, our accepting the viability of that structure depends upon our accepting the viability of love, friendship, personal loyalty—all the human ties that count for so much in the rationalist society that Truffaut's pastoral reflects. In the films of Godard there are arrangements for living and contractual agreements (for example, marriage), but there is scarcely even a hint of nostalgia for the fact that in his world people no longer really matter to one another.

The friendships and loyalties, the many small and even casual decencies that make up the fabric of *Stolen Kisses* are not less real or less important than, say, the closing of the Sorbonne; but they are surely less insistent. Truffaut's decision to limit the attention of his film to private events suggests he feels there are now two worlds, encompassing on the one hand public and on the other private areas and degrees of response. And he has centered on one because he can make meaning in one—as indeed he might in the other—but not in both at the same time.

But in fact the two worlds don't exist in the same time. The times that encompassed and helped shape the happenings of spring 1968 are not the times by which each of us individually lives and dies. "The times" are finally slave to time, and time is what *Stolen Kisses* strives to earn its release from.

*Stolen Kisses* begins at exactly ten minutes before four in the afternoon. Antoine is to get laid at five sharp so his stockade pals will know just when to enjoy their vicarious experience. One of them won't have much fun; he needs to take a leak, and regulations forbid his taking it before six.

*Stolen Kisses* ends at no special time, though we know that its romantic climax in the consummation of young love is being accompanied by the continuous ticking of the metered clock that Antoine has set before beginning work on Christine's television set. But the next day, just before the movie ends, Truffaut's oddest invention—an utterly private private eye, who has been trailing Christine throughout the film with a professional determination that is a continual reproach to Antoine's sloppiness—advances and declares his love for her. This detective tells Christine that he has no occupation and no preoccupation except her. She will have all his attention, without distractions. He says he is permanent, *"définitif,"* while all other men are temporary, *"provisionnels."* Having made his declaration, he announces that he is very happy, and he strides off. Christine says that the man must be crazy, and Antoine thoughtfully agrees.

Between enforced submission to time and insane participation in eternity, *Stolen Kisses* must make accommodation with a world in which hours pass, old men die, fashions change, and nothing quite remains from one minute to the next. One night Antoine has a date with a tall girl; the next day he tells a colleague that the first part of the date was awkward but the second part was fantastic. A date in two parts is no way for a date to be. But that is how almost everything in *Stolen Kisses* turns out; a man must learn to accept his chances or go crazy trying to pin them down.

Christine's mysterious admirer is crazy because he thinks he can stop the flow of life in time the more perfectly to adore his love. Most of the Truffaut movies offer some way of keeping things still at the end (the famous frozen shot of young Antoine that ends *The 400 Blows* was merely the first, the most sensational, and the least interesting instance), and in that context the admirer's proposal is not without a certain maniacal grandeur.

Almost equally grand, and equally unsuitable, is Mme. Tabard's proposal to Antoine that they spend a few hours together and then never see one another again. Mme. Tabard is time's mistress (all Antoine's meetings with her involve late appointments, early awakenings, momentary interruptions), completely winning in her appreciation for the marvel of humankind, and disastrous in the results of her practical suggestion for safe sexual satisfaction. Her intelligence, her pathetic marriage, and the graciousness of Delphine Seyrig's performance shouldn't obscure the film's very profound ambivalence toward her.

The most glamorous and most humanly appealing of Antoine's misadventures, Mme. Tabard is also the most misused of the film's many love-starved creatures and the most sophistic of its pleaders for a better deal. A kind of mortal Calypso to Antoine's witless Odysseus, when she proposes sex she mentions death—her father's, whose last words were, "People are wonderful!"

But when M. Henri, the old detective (Harry Max), keels over at his desk and death really comes close to Antoine, he buys his sex in his second visit to a whore, and now he is prodigal with time. Such prodigality is typical of Antoine and Christine, who in their innocence know enough to throw away that commodity that everybody else tries to save, record, or freeze. The first we hear of Christine, she is off on vacation while her fellow students strike. The last we see of her, she has rejected a man who offers her permanence but accepted one who is bound to time, who comes equipped with a device for measuring hours and minutes—which he nevertheless chooses to forget.

One of the loveliest passages in the films of François Truffaut occurs at the end of *Fahrenheit 451* after the rebellious fireman Montag has escaped to the Book People, and we see them speaking their memorized books and passing them on orally from one generation to the next. The sense of nostalgia for a life of intellectual discipline is very great and constitutes a unique insight into the condition of humanistic scholarship, but it is no greater than an analogous sense of nostalgia that permeates the whole of *Stolen Kisses*. Although it is drenched with a sense of time, *Stolen Kisses* turns its back on "the times" to convey an appreciation for normative order, for seemliness, that is as moving as it is fragile.

The subject of *Stolen Kisses* is ultimately not so much young love as the conditions under which young love exists, and its profoundest valuation goes to the public prospects and private retreats of the great city of the rationalist tradition—in which individual destinies are possible and personal anecdotes may be told. So when Truffaut takes a moment out to pay tribute to the efficiency of the Paris *pneumatique* (Antoine is sending an untimely farewell note to Mme. Tabard, and there is a brief documentary showing how the note speeds under the streets of the city from his apartment to hers), he is doing something similar to what the Blady Detective Agency does by advertising itself on the back of the Paris telephone directory: he is recognizing that the city is an environment with certain needs and gifts, and with a history that is the sum of all individual histories by which its existence is made possible.

As for the great commune, the global village, the conflicting tribes of which will one day soon destroy the city or at least diminish its meaning—it is there, making itself felt around the edges of the film. And this, as surely as Godard's *Weekend,* is a film at the barricades; but on the other side of the barricades, just a few hours before the knowledge of disaster, while the old decencies seem to apply, the postal service still works, lovers still hold on to their names and memories and play a while longer at wasting time.

[1970]

# DAY FOR NIGHT
## Colin L. Westerbeck, Jr.

The English-language title for François Truffaut's new film is *Day for Night,* and whoever wrote it pretty well got the point. But the French title, *La Nuit Américaine,* is still better. *La nuit américaine,* American night, is a technical term used in filmmaking when a night scene must be shot during the day. (Dense blue filters are placed over the camera lens to darken the scene and make sunlight read as moonlight on color-film stock.) Truffaut's film is about a director named Ferrand, played by Truffaut himself, who is making a film on an outdoor set near Cannes. Before Truffaut's film is over, of course, Ferrand has had to resort to *la nuit américaine* to complete his own shooting schedule.

At the beginning of *Day for Night* we see the climactic scene from Ferrand's film being staged. A young man played by an actor called Alphonse (Jean-Pierre Léaud) emerges from a Métro station and slaps another actor, Alexandre, who plays Alphonse's father. The reason is that the father has had a love affair with the son's wife; and as Truffaut develops his film, this plot line in Ferrand's film becomes apparent to us. By the time Ferrand reaches the final phases of production, however, he must do a retake of that climactic scene. Now a look-alike stands in for Alexandre, summer is converted to a snowy winter with fire-fighting foam, and day is played for night, *la nuit américaine.*

Between the original scene and its retake, day is exchanged for night in Truffaut's film many times in many ways. Julie Baker (Jacqueline Bisset), the female lead, is a source of much concern to Ferrand. Because she has had a breakdown and married her doctor, she is considered a bad risk. But she turns out to be the most stable member of the cast, the one who holds all the others together. Moreover, because she does so, her role in Truffaut's film is a peculiar sort of day-for-night reflection of her role in Ferrand's film. In the latter she is seduced away from her husband, Alphonse, by his father. In the former it is the husband who is the older man, and Alphonse does the seducing, which she allows purely out of compassion for his naïve and love-forsaken state. Similar inversions occur in other areas of the plot. For instance, Alexandre, the actor who plays the father, is really the romantic lead in Ferrand's film, but in Truffaut's he turns out to be a homosexual.

As opposed to Ferrand's film, which is a tragedy, Truffaut's is a comedy, and he playfully saturates his directing with this theme of inversion. When a trained cat balks at lapping milk as it is supposed to in one of Ferrand's scenes, the studio's alley cat is desperately auditioned and performs without a hitch. When a script girl runs off with a stunt man, Ferrand's movie-mad assistant comments in amazement, "I can see leaving a guy for a film, but never a film for a guy." Like a vase that Ferrand swipes from his hotel, a car that belongs to a member of the crew seems better suited to a scene than the one provided by the property department. And when we see the rushes from the wrecking of that car in a stunt, they are being run backward on an editing machine.

At a press conference at the New York Film Festival, Truffaut said that one of his purposes is making *Day for Night* was to depict the daily reality of making films, just as Hawks always showed his mechanics actually fixing cars and his pilots flying planes. If this is so, then the aspect of making films that Truffaut must feel dominates all others is the acting. We might think that staging a stunt sequence requires the most patience and care, but this is just one more area in which Truffaut turns our suppositions upside down. While the car wreck in Ferrand's film is done perfectly in one take, a simple scene where Alphonse's mother argues with his father must be done a half dozen times.

In Truffaut's view, actors and actresses have a topsy-turvy perspective anyway, as he suggests with, appropriately enough, an anecdote told by Severine (Valentina Cortese), the actress playing the mother in Ferrand's film. At a farewell dinner after her shooting schedule is completed, she relates how a friend of hers was botching up *Hamlet* one night. Finally he got to the soliloquy, "To be or not to be," and the audience began to howl. "Why do you blame me," he protested, "I didn't write this crap."

On first viewing, *Day for Night* is so fast-paced and pleasant that it may seem a rather lightweight film. But Truffaut's theme of inversions, of surprised expectations and revaluation, is at the very heart of his recent development as a filmmaker. Four years ago Truffaut began in an almost programmatic fashion to review his career. In making *The Wild Child* he remade his own first film, *The 400 Blows,* except that this time he was more sympathetic to the adult than to the child. In light of *The Wild Child, The 400 Blows* looks a somewhat deceiving film, a film that plays day for night, as in Ferrand's melodramatic last scene. In *Two English Girls* Truffaut again reversed the premise of an earlier film, *Jules and Jim.* Now *Day for Night* fulfills the pattern. Since Truffaut has been thinking so intensely about his own early films the last few years—has been, in effect, remembering the experience of making films—what could be a more natural next step than to do a film about filmmaking itself?

Of *Day for Night* Truffaut says, "I am playing what I have written and what

I have personally experienced. I am being myself both behind and in front of the camera." The result is rather a richer commentary on the relationship of Truffaut's life to his art than is at first apparent. Like the car, the vase, and the alley cat in Ferrand's film, the filmmakers' very lives are commandeered by their art—and vice versa. (If Jean-Pierre Léaud is here seen as an actor who is immature, insouciant, even selfish and cruel at times, is it not because Léaud the man is in some ways the creation of the character Antoine Doinel whom he has played for almost fifteen years?) Art that has such unity and wholeness as Truffaut's now does, results from a kind of inspired monomania which touches only the greatest artists. Under this influence the artist himself seems to live in a thematic way, as Yeats did, and his work reflects that theme even in the most minute detail. Only then do life and art begin to interchange as they do in Truffaut's film.

The metaphor for moviemaking which finally emerges from *Day for Night* is not a mirror but a window. The crucial relationship in Ferrand's film is that between Julie and her father-in-law; and in all three of the scenes that we watched Ferrand direct between them, the camera frames the action by shooting through a window. Through these windows where Ferrand sees the scenario for his film taking shape, Truffaut sees the reality of his life doing the same thing.

[1973]

# 7

# BRITAIN

Britain's comedies of the immediate postwar period—the best of them made at Ealing Studios—were mostly concerned with "little folk." People in them were seen quaintly, seemingly as part of Napoleon's "nation of shopkeepers"—an appellation that Englishmen sometimes seem to have taken to heart. Robert Hamer, Alexander Mackendrick, Charles Crichton, and other Ealing directors depicted a country of amiable eccentrics comfortable with their insularity. Mackendrick's *Tight Little Island,* about a liquor-smuggling operation undertaken by the entire population of an island off the Scottish coast, was almost a literalization of an idea of Britain as an isolated paradise, an idea which many Englishmen wanted to believe. An exception to all this—though insular in its own way—was Ealing's masterpiece, Hamer's *Kind Hearts and Coronets* (1949), a black comedy in which Alec Guinness (a frequent Ealing star) played all eight of the lords and ladies with whom Dennis Price must do away in order to succeed to a title. For various reasons, mostly having to do with the inability of the low-budget Ealing films to compete with the more aggressive Hollywood of the late fifties, British comedy was largely in eclipse until the "swinging London" era.

Some early Peter Sellers comedies were exceptions, particularly the anti–trade-union farce *I'm All Right, Jack* and the political fantasy *The Mouse That Roared* (1960), which, being based on the idea of a tiny country succeeding in world affairs by guile alone, was a fitting farewell to the insular comedy tradition. After the cultural revolution triggered by pop music, the British comedy became absurd, outgoing, fast-paced. A main influence was the nonsensical, structureless "Goon Show" of the BBC. "Goon Show" humor is aptly summed up by the title of its popular short, *The Running, Jumping, and Standing Still Film,* starring Peter Sellers and directed by Richard Lester.

Lester, an expatriate American, became the characteristic British comedy director of the sixties with his fast-paced action, *non sequitur,* almost plotless structure and flamboyant stylistics, which seemed especially appropriate for his two Beatles films, *A Hard Day's Night* and *Help!*. But his films, as well as the stud comedies—such as *What's New Pussycat?* and *Alfie*—at which the British became specialists (see Chapter 4), were also the products of an England that suddenly felt itself the trend-setter of a world where the word "mod" was "what was happening"—to use the lingo of the era. As Alexander Walker makes clear in his book *Hollywood, England,* the big irony was that most of this boastful creation was financed by U.S. interests. After the short-lived renaissance of the internationally popular English film, American financing was largely cut off. The only important British comedy success in the last few years is the work of the television-trained group which calls itself Monty Python's Flying Circus.

## THREE ALEC GUINNESS COMEDIES
### Pauline Kael

*Kind Hearts and Coronets.* This tart black comedy on the craving for social position and the art of murder has a brittle wit that came as a bit of a shock: such amoral lines were not generally spoken in forties movies. We were surfeited with movies that try to move us and push us around; *Kind Hearts* is heartless, and that is the secret of its elegance. Ninth in line to inherit a dukedom, the insouciant young hero (Dennis Price) systematically eliminates the intervening eight—a snob, a general, a photographer, an admiral, a suffragette, a clergyman, a banker, and the Duke—all, by a casting stroke of genius, played by Alec Guinness. Secure in the knowledge that Guinness will return in another form, the audience suffers no regret as each abominable D'Ascoyne is coolly dispatched. And as the murderer takes us further into his confidence with each foul deed, we positively look forward to his next success. With purring little Joan Greenwood as the minx-nemesis Sybilla, Valerie Hobson as the high-minded Edith, Miles Malleson as the poetasting executioner. Based upon the 1907 novel *Israel Rank* by Roy Horniman, adapted by Robert Hamer and John Dighton, Hamer directed. 1949.

[1956]

*The Lavender Hill Mob.* As the prim, innocuous little bank clerk with a hidden spark of nonconformity, Alec Guinness carries out the universal dream of larcenous glory: robbing a mint. A man who steals three million in gold bullion may be permitted to coin a word: Guinness describes his gleaming-eyed, bowler-hatted little man as the "fubsy" type. (Would it be stretching the point to suggest that, in the modern Western world, this sneaky, paper-weighted civil servant is the new image of Everyman?) T. E. B. Clarke's script, Charles Crichton's direction, and Auric's music contribute to what is probably the most perfect fubsy comedy of all time. Stanley Holloway is the genteel, artistic accomplice; Alfie Bass and Sidney James the professional assistants, and one of the beneficiaries of Guinness's wrongdoing is a bit player, Audrey Hepburn. Academy Award for Best Story and Screenplay. 1951.

[1956]

*The Man in the White Suit.* As a comedian, Alec Guinness has always been best in the role of an ordinary man with an obsession; who, in the modern world, could be so ordinary and so obsessed as a scientist? In an economy based on rapid replacement of consumer goods, Guinness is the quirky idealist fixated on the long-range benefits to humanity of a cloth that will stay clean and last forever. The impersonal, bland monomaniac scientist is beautifully matched with Joan Greenwood—all guile and scorn and perversity, and without any real aim or purpose. Alexander Mackendrick directed this deft social triangle (capital-science-labor) with a good eye for the tragicomic scientific mentality; the inventor is defeated not by economic storms but by a technical flaw. With Cecil Parker, and Ernest Thesiger as the half-dead industrialist. Screenplay by Roger MacDougall, John Dighton, and Mackendrick. (Item for collectors of ghastly movie memorabilia: the gurgling, bubbling squirts and drips of the hero's experimental apparatus were joined to a rhythm and issued by Coral Records as "The White Suit Samba.") 1951.

[1956]

# MONTY PYTHON AND THE HOLY GRAIL
## Joseph Gelmis

If the word "adult" can stand the strain of being associated with such anarchic lunacy, then *Monty Python and the Holy Grail* is an adult fairy tale.

A/D/U/L/T . . . A-d-u-l-t . . . (A)(D)(U)(L)(T).

If the word "sophomoric" can stand the strain of being associated with . . .

Actually, sophomores have been bum-rapped. It's a great mental age. It's childhood's end. It's a time when you still know what it means to play. And you're old enough to impersonate an adult if you have to.

*Monty Python and the Holy Grail* is a dazzling, 90-minute sophomoric blitzkrieg of some of 1975's most excruciatingly funny visual gags. It left me exhausted, but never bored.

There is so much sublimely outrageous visual humor that you could watch the movie silent and at least half the gags would still be boffo. In fact, there is no way to describe the movie adequately—giving a sense of how its humor works to back any claims for it—without describing entire gags. That's because there are so many episodic variations on the theme of King Arthur and his knights and their quest for the Holy Grail that any recitation of the plot is a giveaway of a string of gags.

So what do we do with a nonstop gag fest that can't be described without giving away the kickers and spoiling your fun? Well, we talk about the players first. Monty Python is a *nom de plume* for five British comics (Graham Chapman, John Cleese, Eric Idle, Terry Jones, and Michael Palin) and one American animator (Terry Gilliam). The movie resembles in style their series currently on public TV. But it's a more sustained narrative than anything they have done before. And, like Woody Allen and Mel Brooks before them, Gilliam and Jones seem to have become directors in self-defense to protect the group's material.

Next, we can describe the end of a gag without describing the build-up. Like, for example, the adventure in which the knight wipes out the wedding guests to rescue a damsel in distress who isn't a damsel at all.

Or we can talk about the monster rabbit guarding the sacred cave or the giant wooden Trojan rabbit built hollow by King Arthur's knights so they can sneak into a walled fortress.

We merely mention in passing primitive peasants who fish with wooden clubs, the burn-a-witch rally, Communist peasants who razz the king, insolent Frenchmen who empty chamber pots on royal British heads, the three-headed ogre, the chickenhearted Sir Robin, and a guest appearance by God.

One of the movie's episodes already has been shown on the Monty Python TV special.

An element of the Python humor is calculated excess, stylish bad taste, a plethora of gore as demonstrated by that episode. King Arthur finds a big black-armored knight in the forest fighting another knight. The black knight sticks his sword through the visor of his opponent. Blood spurts. Arthur asks the knight to join him. The knight refuses, and won't let Arthur pass. They fight.

Arthur lops off one of the knight's arms. Blood spurts. They fight more. Arthur lops off the other arm. Blood spurts. The knight insists it is just a scratch, calls Arthur a sissy, tries to kick him to death. Arthur lops off a leg. The knight hops around on one leg and chases Arthur. Arthur cuts off the other leg. The knight is now just a head and a torso on the ground. Arthur rides away. The limbless knight yells for him to come back and fight like a man.

We stake out as our own single excerpt from the movie, to make a point about how well it uses the medium, the horseless-rider running gag.

King Arthur and his knights "ride" the countryside on make-believe horses while their servants prance behind them producing the sound of hoofbeats by clapping coconut shells together.

The picture gets a lot of mileage in yocks out of this whimsical running gag. By quickly establishing an aura of fantasy in this horseless medieval horse opera, the movie has us seeing chivalry as a childish game in the midst of realistically photographed settings of mud, squalor, and death.

Silly, perhaps, but effective. Doubtless cheaper and more sanitary than using horses. And it serves as unspoken visual commentary on the folly of human behavior. We accept the gag in all its variations.

The troupe is one of those collective entities that is much more than the sum of its parts. Their work is dense with comic richness. The Arthurian chivalry legends are contrasted with the realities of medieval life.

The British comics get a lot of laughs from artful outrage, a genre that is simple tacky bad taste when practiced by inferior wits.

The movie seems to me least effective when it tries for a genre-exploding last laugh, like the ending of *Blazing Saddles,* where the action from one film seems to spill over to a wholly different film. But it's a minor reservation.

[1975]

# RICHARD LESTER

## *A HARD DAY'S NIGHT*
### *Penelope Gilliatt*

When some unsuspecting plodder asked why N. F. Simpson's play was called *A Resounding Tinkle,* the author said politely, "Because that's its name." In the same way, when a reporter in *A Hard Day's Night* asks one of the Beatles what he would call that hair style he's wearing, he replies blandly, "Arthur." Comedy never explains. Who knows why Robert Dhéry calls his brother-in-law Amsterdam, or why Beatrice Lillie in *Exit Smiling* wears a man's wrist watch on her ankle?

Like the slipped vowel in their own name, the way the Beatles go on is just there, and that's it. In an age that is clogged with self-explanation, this makes them very welcome. It also makes them naturally comic. They accept one another with the stoicism of clowns. None of them tries to tell you that his peculiarities are a sign of the traumas of modern man or because Mum did the wrong thing at six weeks. In Alun Owen's script, which has such a lynx ear for their own real speech that their ad libs are indistinguishable in it, they behave to one another with the kind of unbothered rudeness that is usually possible only between brothers and sisters.

I think it is really this feeling that you are looking at an enviable garrison of a family that is at the root of the Beatles' charm. I don't believe it is just the Lennon–McCartney numbers, good and sweetly odd as they are; when Richard Lester was shooting the numbers in this film the kids in the Scala Theatre were yelling so loud that they didn't even realize they were listening to six new hits months before anyone else. The only thing that would probably finish the Beatles with the fans would be if they split up as a family.

*A Hard Day's Night* has no plot. What it has instead, which is plenty, is invention, good looks, and a lot of larky character. The narrative is simply a day in the Beatles' lives and their situation when you think about it is pure comedy: four highly characterized people caught in a series of intensely public dilemmas but always remaining untouched by them, like Keaton, because they carry their private world around everywhere. Whether they are in a train carriage or at a press conference or in a television studio, the Beatles are always really living in a capsule of Liverpool.

As a piece of grit in the narrative Alun Owen has given Paul a scratchy old granddad (Wilfrid Brambell), about whom the nicest thing that anyone can say, and even this seems doubtful, is that he is clean. Granddad resents their unity and manages to create a fair amount of chaos. His gibes slide off Paul, John, and George, but they find a victim in Ringo, who is already worried enough about his shortness and the size of his nose. They are also the last straw for the boys' distraught manager (Norman Rossington), who is conducting a war of nerves with John that is lost from the start because John hasn't *got* any nerves.

Like Lennon's book, *In His Own Write,* and like Richard Lester's own *The Running, Jumping, and Standing Still Film, A Hard Day's Night* is full of slightly out-of-focus puns, both verbal and visual. For instance, a Beatle will make a dive for someone's square tie and ask vaguely, "I say, did you go to Harrods? I was there in 1958." Or John Lennon in a bubble bath will suddenly see a hand-shower as a submarine periscope and start playing war films. One of the best sequences, as in *The Running, Jumping, and Standing Still Film,* is a fantasy in a field. Lester obviously adores fields. This one inspires a jump-cut speeded-up sequence mostly shot from a helicopter in which the boys horse around, do a square dance, and lie down with their heads together in close-up as though they were swimmers in an old Esther Williams picture. There is a feeling of liberation about this sequence, like some of the dances in *West Side Story.* When the film sags, which it does a bit in places, there is a small part wittily played by Victor Spinetti as a television director, neurotic, queer, and implacably contemptuous: this is a new subdivision of social war, the camp against the hip.

The lighting cameraman on the picture was Gilbert Taylor, and the grainy blacks and glowing whites and freewheeling camera work are a minor revolution in a British pop film. *A Hard Day's Night* technically lifts a lot from *cinéma vérité:* in the use of hidden mikes, throat mikes, and hand-held cameras, for instance. But if you compare it with a real piece of camera truthtelling like Granada's Beatle film, *Yeah, Yeah, Yeah,* made by the Maysles Brothers in America, it's clear that Dick Lester's film hasn't very much to do with *cinéma vérité* in its character.

*A Hard Day's Night* is better described, perhaps, as a piece of feature journalism: this is the first film in England that has anything like the urgency and dash of an English popular daily at its best. Like a news feature, it was produced under pressure, and the head of steam behind it has generated something expressive and alive. If this is personality-mongering, which of course it is, it is also very responsive to temperament and eloquent about it. Ringo emerges as a born actor. He is like a silent comedian, speechless and chronically underprivileged, a boy who is already ageless with a mournful, loose mouth, like a Labrador's carrying a bird.

[1964]

# THE KNACK AND HELP!

## Pauline Kael

For some time, the "smart boys" had been saying that the future of movies was in TV commercials, that that's where the real experimentation was going on, where the real talents were working. They didn't mean it cynically: it was possible to try tricky shots and fast cutting—which looked like an advance over the sluggish big-studio methods. And then Richard Lester came along and demonstrated that movies could be made that were just like TV commercials; not too surprisingly, he was quickly acclaimed as a cinematic genius. He and other directors fill their time between movies by making commercials; as Lester puts it, "It's a year's free testing of tricks."

There's just one thing the matter with his genius, but it's a big thing: the content of his 1965 movies, *The Knack* and *Help!*, is the same as the content of TV commercials. At first, in *A Hard Day's Night*, it seemed to be different, because the Beatles were exhibited as joyful, anarchic, witty—that is to say, mildly rebellious. It almost looked as if the techniques of TV could be separated from and used against what was being sold.

The Beatles were thought to be anti-Establishment; but with astonishing speed, the advertising establishment has incorporated rebellion. Only the consumption patterns, the tokens remain: the long hair, the tight pants, the leather jackets, the motorcycles, the attitudes of indifference to adult values, contempt for adult hypocrisy. The outer forms of fantasy and rebellion become the new conformity. Youth is encouraged to be narcissistically youthful: it is cool not to let anything interfere with having a good time. Anarchism becomes just another teen-age pop fad, another pitch.

In the two-dimensional comic-strip world of *Help!*, everybody's in a rush. The movie can't slow down any more than TV commercials can. It (deliberately) has no depth. It is *nothing* but a chase, turning a structural device of early movies into the total substance, and without anywhere to go. *Help!* is all climax, but nothing is prepared for; finally it just exhausts itself and stops. In *The Knack*, the running jokes and gags never come off. In Mack Sennett comedies (to which Lester's work is often compared), an idea would be developed, and there would be the audience delight in watching it build, and as the two-reel format provided a quick cutoff point, the audience was quickly released from the surreal and restored, refreshed, to ordinary viewing. Lester doesn't build ideas; he picks up a gag and goes on to another. If there are enough gags, perhaps the audience, panting to keep after them, will not worry about why they don't go anywhere. The ingenuity becomes as tiresome as the pace; nothing is more fatiguing than things whizzing by too fast; after a while, you don't care how clever it all is.

Despite all the activity, or perhaps because of it, the main figures are rather flat. The more spurious the spontaneity around them, the more lacking in spontaneity they seem. Lester, perhaps aware of this problem, tries to manufacture sympathy by placing a Ringo Starr or a Rita Tushingham at the center;

but the center will not hold. In this advertising context, in which the first principle is that everything can be made beautiful, they are awkward survivors from an earlier kind of comedy who give the lie to the format. There really isn't any such thing as character in the world of TV commercials; there is only anonymous popularity: we are all models.

If there were an idea, if there were characters, the movie would risk being "square." In the current world of popular entertainment, the more pointless and nonsensical the plot, the more cool and sophisticated the movie may seem —an indication, perhaps, that the advertising world has made all feeling seem false. It's commercially safer to be deliberately foolish than to attempt something and be thought foolish.

These impersonal makeshift movies—inoffensive, pleasant-enough nonsense while you're seeing them—are all over with the seeing. The product is completely consumed. There is not even any roughage. By the time you're outside the theater, you've already forgotten the movie. You're hungry again. There is nothing to take home, no memory, hardly even an aftertaste.

[1965]

# THE THREE MUSKETEERS
## Jay Cocks

There is a certain giddiness that this movie instills, a sense of being royally entertained. *The Three Musketeers* is a surfeit of pleasures. It can be said, simply and with thanks, that it is an absolutely terrific movie.

It was fashioned with a wonderful skill and high humor. A translation of Dumas's story, even a fairly respectful one, it is simultaneously a satire, sometimes antic, sometimes serious, a send-up of the whole tradition of romantic fiction. Such an accomplishment seems paradoxical, but the movie successfully cuts both ways, largely because Richard Lester is a filmmaker who specializes in standing paradox on its ear.

A special joy is that this is Lester's first film since the wizardly but little-seen *The Bed-Sitting Room,* which played in the United States in 1969 for approximately the time it would take to soft-boil an egg. Lester made his reputation from his two gymnastic Beatles movies, but his later work (most notably *How I Won the War* and *Petulia*) disclosed a deeper, even more enterprising talent —one tempered by a pointed satiric force. *The Three Musketeers* is not so astringent; it is ebullient, full of roughhouse, and careens along on its own high spirits.

Lester has taken the tone of *The Three Musketeers* from scenarist George Macdonald Fraser, whose *Flashman* novels Lester once tried to adapt. The Fraser books are full of the kind of self-deflating braggadocio, the same sort of elaborate but inglorious combats one finds here. Heroics are mocked, survival is championed. The musketeers are made into creatures whose absurdities of conduct, florid codes of honor, and hollow protestations of heroism make them all the more recognizable and human. It is their own faint absurdity that makes them true.

The streets and taverns of seventeenth-century Paris here teem with vignettes of squalor (two men playing a seesaw game over a fire for a prize of food) that make their own comment set against the distant pomp of the royal court. The musketeers move through both these worlds with equal ease, yet are part of neither. Their sworn allegiance is to the King, Louis XIII, and against Richelieu, but they are men of pride. Their greatest battle and concern are simply to stay alive. For though they would call themselves their own men, they belong to Louis—pawns like the pet dogs he uses for his life-size games of chess in the gardens.

The musketeers—Oliver Reed, Richard Chamberlain, Frank Finlay, and Michael York as D'Artagnan—all perform admirably. When the casting threatens to become too capricious (Raquel Welch as the Queen's confidante, Faye Dunaway as the archvillainess, Charlton Heston as Richelieu), Lester exploits the absurdity. He made the discovery, for example, that Welch and Dunaway, for all their physical dissimilarity, are basically the same actress. So a climactic brawl between them is funny not just for itself but because of the two people playing them.

Cinematographer David Watkin has made the film ravishing to look at. There is even a happy ending: two of them, in fact. Everyone—musketeers, ladies, regents, and villains—receives his just deserts and retribution as the occasion demands. The rest of us get the promise of a sequel soon to be delivered. It seems that the producers decided to make two movies for the price of one. They cut *Musketeers* in half, and will release the parts separately. This one is subtitled *The Queen's Diamond;* the next will be called *The Revenge of Milady.*

[1974]

# 8

# IRON CURTAIN IRONIES

Russian tanks brought an abrupt halt to the brilliant series of Czech comedies made during the mid-sixties "Dubček era." The films of the so-called Czech New Wave, like those of the French New Wave, were mostly mixtures of genres, comedy-dramas, but the directors probably had more in common with the Italian neorealists. Though not as explicitly political, the Czech films related to doctrines of "socialist realism" in being concerned with the little man and with everyday experiences. Ivan Passer's *Intimate Lighting* and Miloš Forman's *The Firemen's Ball*, in fact, are among the most plotless comedies ever made, being little more than series of events that take place within a few hours. Unlike those of the Italians, the little-people films of the Czechs are marked by a sense of irony and a delicate, understated use of actors.

After the Warsaw Pact armies marched into Czechoslovakia in August 1968, Passer and Forman were among those artists who took refuge in America, where this same feeling for the common folk has persisted in their work. Jiří Menzel, director of *Closely Watched Trains*, elected to stay in Czechoslovakia and has made several films, none of which has achieved much of an international reputation. Forman's American *One Flew Over the Cuckoo's Nest* was highly acclaimed and is discussed in Chapter 5.

# YUGOSLAVIA

## *LOVE AFFAIR, OR THE CASE OF THE MISSING SWITCHBOARD OPERATOR*

### Roger Ebert

I am driven to desperation by attempts to describe the films of Yugoslavian director Dusan Makavejev. You've never heard of him, but never mind; neither have I. He has hardly any reputation. His *Innocence Unprotected* won this year's Chicago International Film Festival, and now comes *Love Affair, or The Case of the Missing Switchboard Operator,* an earlier film but unmistakably the work of the same bizarre, anarchist imagination.

The problem is this. Makavejev's films simply fail to connect with large segments of American audiences. *Innocence Unprotected* played to four capacity crowds at the Chicago festival, and I estimate at least half the ticket holders figured they wuz robbed. This wasn't because Makavejev is intellectual or anything horrible like that. His films are direct, candid, occasionally crude, and conceived in marvelously bad taste. They are also tender and funny.

No, Makavejev's problem at the Chicago festival was that he'd found the wrong audience. He got a theater full of earnest fans of serious films, and a lot of them were aghast at the way he messed around with continuity, cutting, color, and even the screen ratio. "The worst film I ever saw," said one young man with a fishing fly on his fedora. "Completely incomprehensible," testified a film-society treasurer. "A gas," said John the Garbage Man.

What Makavejev needs to reach is that specific American subculture consisting of old Bob and Ray fans, Marvel Comics readers, *Realist* subscribers, people who can recite scenes from *Catch-22,* and people who write obscene letters to large corporations. They will share Makavejev's vision of the real world, where the grotesque and the hilarious are identical.

This world existed in *Innocence Unprotected,* which was about an aging acrobat who believed his talents were unique and beautiful. But the film was also about an earlier film made by the acrobat in 1942. It was the first Serbo-Croatian talkie; it combined shots of the acrobat's stunts with a melodramatic tale of seduction and newsreel footage of Hitler's troops on the march. It was considered an act of underground resistance, and I guess it was. Any nation with its own talkie has something worth fighting for.

*Love Affair* is nominally about a switchboard operator who seduces a rat-control expert. He eventually does not exactly hurl her into a deep well. The story is told in an improvised style very much like early Godard or Buster Keaton.

But Makavejev pretends that he wants to do more. To tell the tale of the girl and her People's Rodent Control Hero is not enough; a film must inform the masses and be ideologically sound, right? So Makavejev spoofs those deadly-dull Russian morality films of the forties, where workers triumphed over capitalist-imperialist warmongers and ended the steel shortage while singing labor songs.

So we get a sexologist learnedly lecturing on ancient phallic cults, we get a grisly poem about rat extermination, we get a sanitation worker's marching song, we get more old newsreels, we get a detailed lecture on the methods of murderers, their weapons and the difficulty they have in disposing of bodies. And we get scenes like this: The rat fighter takes the girl to his home. They climb stairs to the roof of a building. "I live here, modestly," he says, indicating a cupola. "It reminds me of *Wuthering Heights,*" she replies sweetly.

You have to be the victim of a certain state of mind to appreciate the humor and truth of Makavejev. Last Saturday night at the Three Penny Cinema, perhaps two dozen people were in a state of rapture. We were weeping with laughter, we were gasping and wheezing and applauding. All about us, the rest of the audience sat in stony silence. I had the distinct impression they were there only to hear the Serbo-Croatian dialogue. There's that too.

[1969]

# CZECHOSLOVAKIA

## THE LOVES OF A BLONDE
### Bruce Williamson

*The Loves of a Blonde* is a boy-meets-girl comedy so fresh and unassuming that thirty-four-year-old writer-director Miloš Forman appears to have put it together without quite realizing the strength of his perceptions. The seeming simplicity conceals extraordinary skill: Forman observes small human aspirations very precisely, then borrows the style of a documentary to carve out a comic slice of life in swift, easy strokes.

The unglamorous blonde of the title is a pudding-faced little pretty (Hana Brejchová) housed with other unfortunates in a shoe-factory town where the girls outnumber the boys sixteen to one. To boost morale and expedite production, the factory manager gets some foot-slogging soldiers assigned to the area, most of them doggy, dumpy, and married. The blonde succumbs by default to a callow young piano player (Vladimír Pucholt) who has all but forgotten her when she shows up, a week or so later, at his parents' apartment in Prague.

Forman strews this commonplace tale with insights that are compassionate, painfully true, and almost continually beguiling. Instead of jokes, there is abundant, honest humor, erupting spontaneously in a dance-hall sequence that pits the man-hungry girls against a trio of loutish army Lotharios. One furtively removes his wedding ring, only to see it go spinning crazily off among the dancing feet. In an endearing seduction scene that avoids nearly every nudenik movie cliché, the shy blonde hasn't a stitch on by the time she reproachfully tells her playboy-pianist: "I don't trust you." He, in turn, observes boyish discretion by bounding up at intervals to tussle with a window shade that lets in too much light. The sly tone is sustained through a dormitory matron's wonderfully irrelevant lecture on morals to the film's bittersweet climax in Prague, where the boy's parents forcibly separate their wayward son from his unexpected guest by dragging him off to their own bed for a riotous family quarrel.

Using nonprofessional actors in all but the principal roles, Forman has collected a gallery of picture-perfect types. They not only look right; they smash the formulas of sex comedy. They sleep through situations that usually call for sobby sentiment, squabble when they should be snoring, sulk when they should be squirming. Altogether human, thus seething with quirky surprises, they satisfy the primal need of festival-goers who forever sit down in darkness hoping that small miracles may come to light.

[1966]

## THE FIREMEN'S BALL
### Roger Ebert

The firemen decide to have a ball. There'll be a drawing for prizes, a lot to eat and drink, a beauty contest, and a ceremony to honor the old retired chief. Everyone in town will come. The old chief should really have been honored last year, but the firemen didn't get around to it. They meant to, but something came up and they didn't. Now the old chief is dying, as everybody knows, and so it's obvious he will have to be honored this year or not at all.

Most likely he will suspect something. He may feel he's being honored only because everyone knows he's dying. Perhaps under the circumstances, the old chief would rather not be honored this year. But the old chief is not the only person to think about. It would be a terrible thing not to honor him at all. Not that he would care—but could the firemen look each other in the eye? So the old chief will be honored, even though it would be kinder to forget about it.

It's like that so often. We start out with the best of intentions, but we foul things up. And then we don't know whether to laugh or cry. And that is exactly the case with Miloš Forman's The Firemen's Ball, a small, warm jewel of a movie from Czechoslovakia.

Just about everything goes wrong at the firemen's ball, of course. People walk off with the raffle prizes, the young men drink too much, and the beauty contest is a shambles. A committee is appointed to choose the finalists from among the girls at the dance. There are a lot of pretty girls there, but the committee botches the job. Proud mothers force their daughters on the judges, while the pretty girls all have mothers who won't hear of a beauty contest. One fat girl gets selected by accident. An ugly girl is selected by misunderstanding.

When the judges look at the pathetic line-up of finalists, they hold their heads in their hands. What's worse, they have no idea how to run the contest. They'd like to see the girls in bathing suits, of course—but it's the middle of the winter. Any way you look at it, the local beauty contest is no match for the glamorous Miss Universe photographs the judges study for inspiration.

Forman (who also made the memorable *The Loves of a Blonde*) develops his material with loving care. He never laughs at his characters; instead, he sees them as victims of human nature. It's too bad that all the raffle prizes— even the glazed ham—are stolen. But if some of the prizes are already missing, isn't it only fair to steal one yourself since you bought a ticket? When the fire chief orders the lights be turned out so the prizes can be returned, isn't it only natural his wife will be caught with a prize in her hands when the lights go back on? Who is to throw the first stone?

This is a very warm, funny movie, and perhaps the best way you could spend an evening in a theater just now. It is a relief to find a director who doesn't force his material, who trusts us to understand what's funny without being told.

Some say *The Firemen's Ball* is an allegory of Czechoslovakia in the years before the Dubček reforms—and also the years after, as things turned out. Perhaps it is. But Forman is never obvious about it. And even if it's allegory, there's also something immediate and human about the advice the firemen give an old man whose house burns down. They arrive too late to save the house —they were at the dance—and now the old man is out in the snow and he's cold. Thoughtfully, they suggest he move his chair closer to the fire.

[1969]

## CLOSELY WATCHED TRAINS
### Richard Schickel

*Closely Watched Trains* is a film much simpler to enthuse about than to catch the flavor of on the printed page, so let's get the easy part out of the way quickly. This work, by a twenty-nine-year-old director named Jiří Menzel, is quite the best product of the celebrated renaissance of the Czech cinema that we have seen in this country so far, and it is also the best movie I have seen this year.

But the nature of the experience the film offers cannot be summarized nearly so neatly as one's response to it. When I say that it is mostly about the sadly comic attempts of a gawky, jug-eared, inarticulately sensitive adolescent to enter upon manhood, which he imagines to be simply a matter of losing his virginity, and when I add that he finally achieves this goal in the classic manner of such stories, through the understanding kindness of an older woman, I fear your silent, knowing withdrawal in the face of the clichés that have launched a thousand indifferent films and novels. One must look between the plot lines to discover the film's special distinction and delight.

The young man's misadventures occur for the most part in a provincial railroad station during the German occupation of Czechoslovakia during World War II. He is employed there as a trainee, a job that, unfortunately for him, fortunately for us, leaves him plenty of time to observe and misunderstand the life around him and to observe and only half-understand the life churning about in his own psyche. The station itself is observed in marvelous detail by Menzel's ever-questing camera. Its antique equipment and furnishings—including the most uncongenial sofa on which anyone ever attempted a seduction—perfectly symbolize the unyielding outlines and the drab coloration of the adult world as it so often seems on one's first innocent encounter with it.

The inhabitants of this microcosm are a cross section of humanity—a stationmaster dreaming futile dreams of promotion and spending far too much time with his backyard poultry farm; dispatcher Hubieka (beautifully played by Josef Somr), a shrewd womanizer whose successes belie his weird appearance and coarse manner; a girl telegrapher whose seduction by Hubieka is surely one of the great comic-erotic sequences in film history. Passing through, disturbing, and rearranging the relationships of these human particles as electric charges repattern a field of iron filings, are the outsiders—a railway supervisor who combines Quislingism, pomposity, and fatuity in a maddening manner; a girl from the resistance; a couple of girls with no resistance; a countess; an outraged mother; some German soldiery.

All of these characters are to some degree types, yet all are particularized by Menzel's uncanny eye for the telling detail, humanized by the spirit of compassionate satire that informs the entire film. A simple listing of those present indicates the wide, free range of the director's interest in the human animal under the stress of day-to-day existence, but it cannot begin to demonstrate his great gift for encompassing them all in his film without strain, without ever seeming to digress, without the slightest loss of dramatic tension. Again it is the brilliance of his selectivity that accomplishes this. He tells us all we need to know about all these people, but never one thing more than is necessary. His film is thus a miracle of compression, availing itself of the economies which modern film techniques offer the director, but never using them, as so many do, because their temptation is irresistible.

Menzel handles a variety of rapidly shifting moods with the same ease that he handles his throng of characters. He juxtaposes longing and laughter, despair and delight, rationality with absurdity, and the result is a movie that comes closer to capturing the texture of ordinary life as we ordinarily experience it than any contemporary movie I can readily think of.

That he does so without ever losing his sympathy—or ours—for the most befuddled or obnoxious of his characters is a measure of the warm, unsentimental humanism which is, despite his exciting technical mastery, Mr. Menzel's greatest strength. Perhaps I can best sum up the magic he works by noting that his film ends in sudden and shattering tragedy. Yet as I left the theater, my mood was one of peaceful happiness—as if I had been put in touch with man, with the world, in a way that is in the last analysis inexplicable, but which is extremely rare in this age of alienated and dehumanized art.

[1967]

# THE BRIGHT SIDE
# OF ITALIAN NEOREALISM

Comedy can be remarkably insular, basing its humor totally on customs, attitudes, or news events with which only certain initiates are familiar. Comedies that might be labeled provincial provide the backbone of most nations' film industries, and in almost every case are considered unexportable. Peasant comedies in Yugoslavia, carnival comedies in Brazil, sex comedies in Scandinavia, Cantinflas adventures in Mexico, the endless *Carry On* series in Britain, the "charming" maladroitness of Luis de Funès, the late Bourvil, and the Charlots in France—even such Hollywood cycles as the Elvis Presley pictures and the beach-party movies: all of these are what *Variety* calls "home items."

Only occasionally does a type of provincial comedy break through to the international market. The late French comedian Fernandel achieved a popularity with world audiences that was denied to such successors as Bourvil and de Funès. A group of comedies produced between 1948 and 1955 at Britain's independent Ealing Studios by a close-knit team under the supervision of Sir Michael Balcon also succeeded beyond their native borders.

And in the mid-sixties some earthy comedies from Italy were the international rage, though after a very few years they, too, once again became strictly for local consumption.

Under Fascism, almost no Italian films were exported to other countries, but it's well known that the film industry in Italy went through a "white telephone era," and apparently the comedies, like the other movies, were about the class of people who could afford white telephones. The neorealist movement, which stunned the world when it appeared after the fall of Mussolini, concerned itself with the kinds of people, urban and rural, who had black telephones or, more likely, none at all. Neorealism involved a change of style as well as of subject. The people in the dramas of Rossellini, de Sica, and Visconti were not only poor but often effusive, earthy, fulsome, demonstrative. Needless to say, this style rather easily lent itself to comedy. Needless to say also, it's a style guaranteed to have its critics—those to whom comedy based on broadness is tasteless. Lacking the precision of the silents, the wit of screwball or British comedy, the beguiling charm of the French, the Italian comedies were most frequently attacked as "vulgar."

Such a strong reaction was prompted in part by the fact that Vittorio de Sica, maker of such somber neorealist classics as *The Bicycle Thief* and *Umberto D.,* achieved his first real box-office success with *Gold of Naples,* its earthy boisterousness personified by a new actress named Sophia Loren. Its success kept de Sica occupied with follow-ups for years until the director again made "serious" films. But to most people, Italian comedy means Pietro Germi, whose Sicily of *Divorce—Italian Style* and *Seduced and Abandoned* was as many miles more effusive as it was south of de Sica's Naples.

Germi's comedies were directly concerned with social issues, particularly with the long debate which preceded divorce reform in Italy. And a great many, perhaps most, of the native comedies which continue to be highly popular in Italy are concerned with social problems so specific to that country (emigrant labor, Church reform) that by definition they are not for export. However, a director who combines farce with more general ideological questions has recently singlehandedly revived the Italian comedy in America. Lina Wertmüller's heroes, almost always played by Giancarlo Giannini, follow in the tradition by being Neapolitan or Sicilian peasants or workers. Their political beliefs—or lack of them—are put through allegorical trials, usually in the form of one or more women. Wertmüller is the most successful woman director in decades, and thus her frequent presentation of women in less than sympathetic stances has led to charges of sexism. She is also a former assistant to Federico Fellini, whose films always contain large comic elements, although his only true comedy features are the early *The White Sheik* and the recent *Amarcord.*

# VITTORIO DE SICA

## MIRACLE IN MILAN
### Pauline Kael

Part social satire, part fantasy, this Vittorio de Sica film suggests a childlike view of Dostoevski's *The Idiot*. A fun-loving old lady finds a newborn baby in a cabbage patch. The baby becomes Totò the Good, the happy man who loves everyone; when he is frustrated in his desire to help people, the old lady, now an angel, comes down and gives him the power to work miracles. Totò the hero, naïve and full of love, organizes a hobo shantytown into an ideal community; but the social contradictions are ludicrously hopeless—not even magic powers can resolve them. The failure of experience, as in *The Bicycle Thief* and *Umberto D.*, is tragic, but the failure of innocence is touchingly absurd—stylized poetry. Francesco Golissano is perfect as Totò; the heroine, Brunella Bovo, is what Chaplin's heroines should have been but weren't. The film provides a beautiful role for that great, almost legendary lady of the Italian theater, Emma Gramatica (many, many years ago, she took over Duse's roles and acted under the direction of D'Annunzio); as the supremely silly old woman of de Sica's fairy tale, she is as yielding and permissive as his Umberto D. is proud and stubborn. With Paolo Stoppa as the unhappy man. Cesare Zavattini adapted his own novel, *Totò il Buono*. Grand Prix, Cannes, 1951.

[1956]

## GOLD OF NAPLES
### Arthur Knight

Realism is a word that invariably creates a good deal of confusion in artistic circles, and especially when applied to the art of film. To be considered part of the realist tradition, a picture has generally got to be either terribly earnest or horridly sordid. And if the people it presents are drawn from the very dregs of humanity, oddballs who delight in torturing small dogs and children, then the sense of actuality is deemed to have been inestimably heightened.

A new film admirably captures a sense of reality without the slightest such overtone of sensationalism or shock. In fact, it's a comedy—although hardly of the slapstick or screwball schools. It has its funny lines, its amusing situations, its light moments. But there is also, and fundamentally, the awareness of people living, working, and reacting to a specific environment. Rather than dulling the humor of this picture, however, this very fact seems to heighten its appeal. In *Gold of Naples*, director Vittorio de Sica has attempted to capture the spirit of that teeming, brawling, colorful city in a series of vignettes of typical Neapolitans. Based on four short stories by Giuseppe Marotta, the episodes carry a slice-of-life conviction without turning completely serious until the final sequence. For de Sica has infused each of them with his own warm affection and enthusiasm for Naples, its people, and their ways.

It would be difficult to say which of the episodes in *Gold of Naples* is the best. Certainly, the final story has the greatest substance—and a truly extraordinary performance by Silvana Mangano as a prostitute who discovers on her wedding night that her husband has married her out of a twisted determination to expiate the wrong he did to another girl. But there is a wonderful gusto in the sequence of the beauteous pizza-maker (Sophia Loren) whose search for a misplaced ring takes her and her suspicious husband to the homes of all their morning's customers, a sentimental pathos in the story of a little street clown (Totò) bullied and victimized by a local racketeer, the suggestion of faded elegance in the portrait of an aging aristocrat (beautifully acted by de Sica himself) reduced to playing cards with the gatekeeper's son when he can no longer afford to gamble at his club. All of these aspects of the Neapolitan temperament and scene de Sica has captured with insight, delicacy, and humor —amiably abetted by the citizens and the sights of Naples itself.

[1957]

# PIETRO GERMI

## SEDUCED AND ABANDONED
### Judith Crist

*Seduced and Abandoned* is a hilarious and ferocious film, seething with anger and sparkling with scorn of the hypocrisies—nay, the crimes—that are committed in the name of honor and the sanctity of the family and society.

Pietro Germi, who gave us *Divorce—Italian Style,* has once again set his social comedy in Sicily and his sights on the moral and legal codes that sanction immorality and crime. His targets are broader than before and his aim truer; the result is a scathing mixture of high comedy and deep tragedy in a film distinguished by a number of stunning performances and by some exquisite camera work.

The story starts slowly, in siesta time, in fact, with the seduction of sixteen-year-old Agnese by Peppino, her elder sister's fiancé, a sleazy brilliantined swinger on whom she has a crush. And from there it proceeds, with gathering momentum and malice, through her father's discovery of her disgrace to his upholding the family face and honor regardless of cost—which includes the sanity, health, happiness, and even life of those involved.

Marriage is, of course, the immediate solution, and Don Vincenzo, getting Peppino's terrified agreement, even goes about saving the face of his elder daughter by buying her a destitute baron to replace Peppino as her fiancé. But then Peppino welches. "I won't marry a dishonored girl." "But you dishonored her." "So if I marry her that makes her less dishonored?" Every man, he argues, is entitled to a chaste wife—and his parents and the priest agree.

And so Don Vincenzo must resort to the law, that peculiar Sicilian legal code that permits anything and almost everything in the name of "honor." And "honor" is, in Germi's analogy, another false name for the false values we uphold.

Even murder is possible; the lawyer-cousin is consulted, and Agnese's brother, Antonio, is nominated by his father to clear her name—after all, he would face only a five-year maximum prison sentence for bumping off Peppino as part of a vendetta. But Antonio is no hero, the plot comes a cropper, and the problem remains, to force Peppino to marry Agnese without making Agnese's situation known to the world. She herself has committed a second and greater sin: she has gone to the police to prevent Peppino's murder—and the police, of course, about to prosecute Peppino on a morals charge, become the common enemy of the feuding families. We find ourselves—as Agnese and her father very literally find themselves—in a nightmare world of ghoulish comedy and fantastic morality.

Germi's malicious humor covers the gamut of Sicilian society with waspish characterizations and glitteringly ironic vignettes. There is the police chief, who can bear to look at a map of Italy only if he blots out Sicily; the undertaker, who serves as a Mafia-like intermediary and whose hobby is the invention of a portable electric guitar for serenading "but who serenades any more?"; the café habitués who seemingly swallow Don Vincenzo's version of the Peppino–Agnese affair but are perched, vulturelike, awaiting their prey; the lawyers, manipulating their clients but aware that no one is being fooled.

Above all, there are unforgettable performances from stars and bit players alike. Saro Urzi, who has a Raimuesque quality, makes the father a deeply human and somehow endearing villain in his single-minded slashing pursuit of surface propriety, skirting the edge of buffoonery with a passionate intelligence. Stefania Sandrelli is exquisite as the young victim, making the transition, in the course of the film, from temperish teen-ager to a madonnalike martyr. Aldo Puglisi is the epitome of a nasty mama's boy as Peppino, while Leopoldo Trieste gives the baron some glorious moments, whether he's attempting suicide before a gallery of street urchins or proving himself "not an expert—say rather a sensitive amateur"—when it comes to pasta. Lina La Galla is a pillar of domesticity as Agnese's mother, and Paola Biggio is a plump and stupid enchantment as the jilted elder daughter. And Carlo Rustichelli's musical score is perfection.

Germi has cloaked his fury in outrageous humor and gentle mockery; he turns from bloodcurdling to clowning and from heartbreak to hilarity with a master's deftness and, most important, he leaves his preachment to fester below the surface, to explode only in the cool irony of the film's brilliant conclusion. And that is the triumph of *Seduced and Abandoned.*

[1964]

# FEDERICO FELLINI

## *AMARCORD*
### Vincent Canby

*Amarcord* ("I remember" in the vernacular of Romagna) is Federico Fellini's thirteenth feature and as full of marvels as anything he's ever done. It takes place in the early 1930s in a small Adriatic resort town that seems to be Fellini's recollection of Rimini, where he was born and grew up, although it's sometimes as exotic as the ancient Rome of *Fellini Satyricon* and as familiar as the Rimini Fellini remembered in *I Vitelloni.*

*Amarcord* is a haunting, funny, beautiful work that makes most other recent movies, with the exception of Ingmar Bergman's *Scenes from a Marriage,* look as drab as winter fields without snow. What's more startling—and almost unforgivable—is the way in which it exposes the small, toll-taker souls of some critics (myself included) who have been fussing at Fellini about his last two films, *The Clowns* and *Fellini's Roma,* those visually spectacular, free-form memoirs that didn't seem to test his talents. A lot of us thought he was loafing —rerunning old scenes—and we expressed ourselves with the kind of sadness that usually accompanies a line like "this hurts me more than it does you." We needn't have worried as, I'm sure, he didn't.

Like *The Clowns* and *Roma,* Fellini's new film is a sort of memoir, and it is sometimes as splendid to look at as a light show designed simply to surprise, dazzle, and make the eyes blink. Yet *Amarcord* is often as emotionally implicating as *Nights of Cabiria* or *8½.* The free form has been combined with Fellini's insatiable curiosity about and fondness for the human animal, especially those who maintain only the most tenuous holds on their dignity or sanity.

*Amarcord* is not a single narrative in the conventional sense and thus, I'm sure, may be incorrectly described as a film without a story. It doesn't have a single narrative. It has dozens. There is one for nearly every character who turns up on the screen, plus the story of Fellini himself, not only the Fellini who is represented in the film by a firm-jawed, decently rebellious teen-ager named Titta (Bruno Zanin), nor the Fellini surrogate called the Lawyer (Luigi Rossi), who turns up in the film from time to time as a kind of tour guide.

Fellini himself is never actually in the movie, as he was in *The Clowns* and *Roma,* but he is all over it. *Amarcord* is his memory of a year in the life of Rimini, or a town much like it, and for Fellini memory has a lot in common with dream. It needn't be what literally happened but what he wanted to believe, or perhaps what time has forced him to believe.

One of the off-screen stories in *Amarcord* is that of the young man from the provinces who went to Rome to become a hugely successful film director. Forty years later he looks back, recalling the events of one year not as a novelist might but more like a poet, or a filmmaker who has enormous studio resources at his command and a small boy's love for the circus that provided Fellini with his sense of theater.

*Amarcord* has the circus's pace, drive, good spirits, fascination with costume and masquerade (sometimes grotesque), and abundance of events. The characters tumble onto the screen one after another, as if there weren't going to be enough time to get through all the acts.

Among these are Gradisca (Magali Noël), the town's pretty, romantic *femme fatale,* a hairdresser who so inflames the imaginations of every man and boy that on evening strolls around the piazza she must be escorted by two not-as-pretty women who act as human fenders; Titta's father (Armando Brancia), a construction foreman of terrible temper, abiding love for his family (which is constantly being tested), and hatred for the Fascists, who more or less force honor upon him; Titta's crazy Uncle Teo (Ciccio Ingrassia); his rummy old grandfather (Giuseppe Lanigro), who looks like something carved out of wood to be used as a bottle stopper; the tobacconist (Antonietta Beluzzi), a hefty woman with such formidable breasts that she almost smothers Titta in one of his initial forays into sex (he tries to lift her off the floor).

Some of the stories are both magical and funny, such as the one we are told about Gradisca and her encounter with an important prince to explain how she got her name (translated as "please do"). Some are bawdy and some elegiacal. Throughout the film, uproarious comedy is punctuated with images that foretell feelings of isolation and loss: a small boy walks stoically to school through a pea-soup fog, scared out of his wits; a terminally ill woman sits on a hospital bed and fiddles with her wedding ring that is now too big.

There are also images so mysterious that they defy simple categorization, such as the one of the peacock who comes out of the sky to land in the piazza during a snowfall, interrupting a snowball fight when he suddenly spreads his extraordinary tail.

One of Fellini's greatest gifts is his ability to communicate a sense of wonder, which has the effect of making us all feel much younger than we have any right to. Fellini's is a very special, personal kind of cinema, and in *Amarcord* he is in the top of his form.

[1974]

# LINA WERTMÜLLER

## LOVE AND ANARCHY
### *William S. Pechter*

Like many members of Lina Wertmüller's American audience, I saw *Love and Anarchy* before seeing any other of her films, though it wasn't the first film she'd made. I remember coming away from *Love and Anarchy* feeling both impressed by the obvious talent at work in it and vaguely troubled by the sensibility that the film seemed flickeringly to reveal. *Love and Anarchy* told the story of Tunin, a country bumpkin, who, in the Italy of the thirties, sets out to assassinate Mussolini. He goes to Rome, and, for the several days before the one on which he plans to strike, he's aided by a whore who shares his anti-Fascist sympathies, and who arranges (under the guise of his being her cousin) for him to hang about her fancy brothel, taking meals there and, through her, getting to meet the chief of Mussolini's security force, who happens to be one of her best customers. But, while waiting for the targeted day to arrive, Tunin and another of the whores fall in love, and they decide to spend the last few days before his deed in romantic seclusion. When the day of the planned assassination arrives, his lover deliberately lets Tunin oversleep, and is supported in this act by the other whore, who also declares her love for Tunin. Tunin awakes, discovers what's happened, and flies into a rage, lashing out alternately with words and with fists at the women for their interference, and cowering in terror when he mistakes a routine police inspection of the brothel's premises for a sign that the whores have betrayed him and that he's about to be captured. Crying, "Long live anarchy!" he runs amuck, shooting several policemen in the process, and finally breaking out into the street, where he shouts, "I wanted to kill Mussolini for all of you . . . so we could live in freedom. . . ." He's quickly and violently subdued by police and angry citizens. In the two brief scenes which end the film, we see him first being brutally interrogated by the security chief, and then, in a prison cell, as two of the security-force agents burst in on him and savagely beat him to death.

Now hard as it may be to believe from the foregoing précis, most of *Love and Anarchy* is played as farce, and quite successfully. Apart from the ending, the film's two most effective sequences are both quite straightforwardly comic ones: a long Sunday outing in the country with Tunin, the two whores, and the security chief (hilariously caricatured by Eros Pagni, something of a Mussolini look-alike); and a boisterous scene of Tunin having his first meal in the brothel. (The Fellini influence on the director's work—before making her own films, Miss Wertmüller served as Fellini's assistant—is perhaps most clearly to be seen in this latter sequence and in another, recalling *Fellini's Roma*, in which the whores display themselves for their customers to the accompaniment of a recorded rendition of "It's Delightful to Be Married," though the influence is pervasively evident in Miss Wertmüller's general fondness for the grotesque face and incident.) And though one's final impression of *Love and Anarchy* is of a work in a tragicomic mode, the film achieves this effect not so much by a true mixture of moods, but by their drastic alternation. Things in it aren't (as they are in, say, a *Seduced and Abandoned*, or the films of Buñuel) an inseparable fusion of the funny and the horrible; they are funny, and then they turn horrible. The ending of the film, in particular, is almost unbearably powerful: a sudden, swift, unrelenting outburst of sickening violence, the impact of which is such as to call into question the rampant use of prolonged slow motion as a means of intensifying the depiction of violence in films. And this stunning conclusion tends to leave one feeling that the film was all along more serious than it often seemed, a feeling reinforced by the work's being bracketed by, at one end, a photomontage of Mussolini and historical note on his rise to power and, at the other, a sober quotation from Enrico Malatesta to the effect that, though the use of murder as an instrument of political action is to be deplored, what will be remembered of the acts of assassins is not the acts themselves but rather the ideals that inspired them.

Yet the more one reflects on the film, the less satisfactory its swervings of moods and meanings seem to be. For one thing, Tunin really is portrayed throughout as too much of a comic figure to be dealt so savage a fate; it's rather as if *To Be or Not to Be* were to end with Jack Benny being dragged off, kicking and screaming, to face a firing squad. Moreover, though the closing quotation tends to impart a retrospective dignity and high-mindedness to all that's gone before, it seems singularly inappropriate to the case of Tunin, whose botched effort is made in the name of only the most generalized political sentiment ("Tyrants disgust me," he explains), and earns him only a newspaper obituary as an "unidentified" suicide. Tunin's "anarchism" seems never to have advanced beyond the moment (which we see in an opening flashback) when, as a child overhearing his father talking politics with his cronies, he asks, "Mama, what's an anarchist?" and his mother replies, "Someone who kills a prince or a king and is hanged for it." (The immediate cause of his resolve to kill Mussolini is the death at the hands of Fascist police of one of his father's friends, now an old man, who had announced his own intention to perform Mussolini's assassination; the whore's motive is revenge for the death of her fiancé, who was killed by a Fascist mob which mistook him for an assassin.) Indeed, throughout most of the film, the joke seems to be Tunin's absolute unfitness for the task he's set himself, and the film's point that politics in general and tyrannicide in particular had best not be left to amateur bunglers; at least, this might be the point were it not for the fact that, until the film's end, the security chief (who's given to laughable extolments of Fascist virility and boasts about Mussolini having "a pair of balls big enough to screw the whole world") seems to be, if anything, a bigger clown than Tunin, with the attendant suggestion that politics generally may be the province of clowns and simpletons. Then, suddenly, we seem to be meant to see Tunin as a noble martyr to some ideological cause that will survive him. Nor is it really a case of these apparent contradictions in meaning tending to combine with and enrich each other, any more than the tragic and comic elements in the film finally jell into true tragicomedy. Rather—and it's this which I found most disturbing about the film—such things seem ultimately to have the effect of canceling each other out.

[1976]

# SWEPT AWAY . . .
## Janet Maslin

You really have to watch out, when it comes to women directors, for the extent to which they tend to be overrated and for the venomous quirk that prompts some to treat their heroines more nastily than any male director might. Though Lina Wertmüller has made a couple of interesting pictures (notably *The Seduction of Mimi,* a good sex comedy that managed to triumph over its political pretensions), her negligible *Swept Away . . .* has been as irrationally overpraised lately as Joan Silver's blandly competent but hardly breath-taking *Hester Street.* And though Wertmüller's reputation as a radical would seem to imply a feminist bent, she inexplicably manages to handle Mariangela Melato about as charitably here as Elaine May did Jeannie Berlin in *The Heartbreak Kid.*

Melato is established as unappealing right from the opening sequence, which means to show the Italian elite splashing around in the Mediterranean but is shot so unimaginatively (and scored with such irritating Muzak) that it looks like a travelogue about Hawaii. Melato, who has a voice that can make one long for the sound of fingernails on slate, is screeching incessantly about mass sterilization and abortion and a lot of other things that don't quite go with the scenery. She continues to carry on noisily aboard the yacht, where we next see her, being particularly castrating and abusive to one unfortunate crew member, played by Wertmüller's other customary star, Giancarlo Giannini. After fifteen frenzied and excruciating minutes, the two of them finally manage to get marooned on a lovely desert island and begin to indulge in some wonderfully broad comedy, when the script does them in. Giannini, realizing he is suddenly in control of the situation, is called upon to starve, berate, beat, kick, rape (although he doesn't complete the act, for fear of her enjoying it), and generally abuse Melato. Even worse, *she* is called upon to like it.

"Now I'm going to show you what a real man is," cries Giannini, before the rape. A while after it, Melato is purring: "I feel crazy, drunk, as if I'd been ravaged [*sic*] by a band of pirates. . . . It was marvelous." Does it really matter that in the interim, as he slaps his prey, Giannini is shouting things like *"This* is for causing inflation, and for not paying taxes . . . *this* is for high bus and train fares, and the high price of gas"? The bearing of this whole little fable on the political issues it name-drops is dubious at best.

You can search until you're blue, but you sure won't find any evidence to support claims that this is meant to be funny, either. True, the whole situation is clichéd enough to suggest deliberate parody, what with its role-reversal and desert-island motifs, not to mention its startling naïveté in relation to Wertmüller's other films. But the would-be tragic ending is too dragged-out and maudlin to be the result of even a light touch, let alone a clever or ironic one. And despite the numerous and unpleasant ways in which she makes Giannini look foolish, Wertmüller is just sympathetic enough with her hero to throw off whatever balance her initial conception may have had. Hovering as it does between two genres as irreconcilable as overblown comedy and politically based cynicism, *Swept Away* . . . winds up being deeply annoying and not much else. Despite its wonderfully eye-catching poster shot of two bodies embracing in the surf, and despite a plethora of postcard sunsets and romantic-looking dunes, the picture is far too shrill to elicit any physical response except maybe a headache.

Giannini and Melato are better actors than this project warrants, and so their performances wind up feeling hammy yet vague; any thoughtful look from either of them is immediately framed in a cartoonish context that makes it ambiguous, hence irksome. Wertmüller's direction is no better than ordinary, with her few attempted bravura shots lavished on subjects that don't deserve them. (The fanciest one here swiftly circles a yacht, perhaps to show that it's surrounded by water.) And Wertmüller's abrupt cuts have an uncanny way of suggesting that the projectionist has slipped in the wrong reel.

[1975]

## SEVEN BEAUTIES
### Joseph Gelmis

Lina Wertmüller's specialty is serious comedy. In *Seven Beauties,* her newest and most ambitious film, for instance, she has an emaciated Italian prisoner of war in a Nazi death camp try to seduce the Amazonian female commandant so that his life will be spared. The prisoner is stubbled and rheumy-eyed. His pores are dust-choked. He adjusts his cap, slicks down his hair, adopts a heartsick expression, whistles like a fluttery bird stalking a mate. He is utterly pathetic and absurd. He circles near her, trying to coax with his caricature of male sexual rites a female King Kong who carries a riding crop and wears a carnivorous scowl.

There is, in the characteristic Wertmüller film, a conflict of biology and ideology. The two most clearly defined poles of her complex films are sex and power. It is within the matrix of sex and power that her men and women are imprisoned. In her last film, *Swept Away* . . . , Wertmüller marooned a Communist sailor and a capitalist shrew on a desert island and reversed their power roles. The female learned to submit to the male chauvinist and like it. And he insisted upon, and got, her passionate love, too. As long as he was the only game in town.

At forty-six, Lina Wertmüller is the world's foremost female writer-director of films. Her forte is the political comedy. Her political vision isn't doctrinaire leftist. In fact, she doesn't have a program so much as a vision of politics as sleeping accommodations. Politics is the bedfellow you choose or are forced to serve. Some feminist critics mistakenly assumed Wertmüller had betrayed the cause by having Mariangela Melato surrender to the arrogant Giancarlo Giannini in *Swept Away* . . . He is the same actor who has to crawl on his belly before the Nazi Valkyrie in *Seven Beauties* with his atrophied sexual prowess as a contemptible joke. Wertmüller plays no favorites.

She does have favorite targets, however. One is male supremacy. Another is the Mafia, as a sort of auxiliary of the free-enterprise system. For her, the Mafia is organized crime no different from the Fascists and the Nazis. In her movies, the Mafia institutionalizes and perpetuates for its own exploitative purposes the Italian male's violent code of personal and family honor as an ongoing means for recruiting new *soldati.*

The Nazi prisoner of *Seven Beauties* is a typical male egotist. He had collaborated with the Mafia in his civilian life to save his skin. And, as a deserter from the Italian army captured by the Germans, he is hoping to toady up to his Nazi masters. He complains that the Nazis "have made death an industry" in their work camp. It is one of the film's blackest jokes, because he himself has, if on an individual basis, been a "butcher"; he has not only murdered someone but disposed of his victim by carving the body into pieces and stuffing the results into suitcases.

The hero/victim of *Seven Beauties* is the quintessential Wertmüller prisoner —of economics (poor, uneducated, guardian of many unmarried sisters), of his macho prejudices, of the law, of the Mafia, of an insane asylum, of the army, and then of the Nazis. In each case, he cooperates with the power brokers to survive. For Wertmüller, survival at any cost is this character's politics. Wertmüller is most effective in this area of forcing her audience to recognize how little actual freedom of choice it has as prisoners of sex, caste, ideology, and, in her earlier films especially, as wage slaves, prostitute and/or consumer.

Wertmüller is a former playwright who got her filmmaking start in 1963, when Federico Fellini chose her to be his assistant director on *8½.* The same year, Fellini helped her get financing for her first film, *The Lizards,* a put-down of Italian bourgeoisie. Neither it nor her next film, *Let's Talk About Men,* made in 1966, were shown commercially in America. Her recognition in the United States as a major talent came two years ago, when *Love and Anarchy,* her fourth film, which had copped the best-actor award for Giannini at Cannes, attracted much attention and praise. Then her third film, *The Seduction of Mimi,* had a rush premiere to cash in on the attention and turned out to be even more interesting than *Love and Anarchy.* Her *Swept Away . . .* had its American premiere in 1975 and earned a place on a number of ten-best lists. And now, two more of her films are opening within a week of each other: *All Screwed Up,* made before *Swept Away . . . ,* and *Seven Beauties,* the new film.

Why the fuss? Simply because she is serious. A humanist, and a hell of a crowd-pleaser. Her culture—the profound polarization of Italy's Communists and neo-Fascists—is a rich source of pathological comedy. She is in vogue today because she uses Italian visual *élan,* comic eroticism, and outrageous black comedy in the service of political idealism. She is a moralist. But not a puritanical essayist like, for example, Costa-Gavras *(Special Section).* She is more the provocateur.

Born in Rome of Swiss ancestry, she is the daughter of a lawyer, the wife of a sculptor and set designer. She lives with her husband in a penthouse overlooking the roofs of Rome. She is small, vigorous, gritty. She wears an antihex amulet among a clinking assortment of charms that dangle from her neck. She gladly admits to cheerful vulgarity in her films. She thinks it is the one emotional outlet that the powerless proletariat whom she hopes to influence understands. In the United States, ironically, it is not the blue-collar worker but the cosmopolitan middle class that has enthusiastically adopted her.

Pivotal to the appeal of Lina Wertmüller's films are the performers she uses to embody her dialectical principles. She has had her biggest success with the team of Melato and Giannini, who is a Mastroianni for the seventies. When she doesn't use one or both of them (as in *All Screwed Up*), the film lacks emotional focus. With Giannini, she can make us sympathize in *Seven Beauties* with a man who committed ax murders, raped a bound madwoman, and was an accomplice of Nazis in choosing fellow Italian prisoners to be executed. We are provoked to nervous laughter in a scene where the nauseated *mafioso,* in a flashback, prepares to quarter a gas-swollen corpse in *Seven Beauties.* And the scene in which the Nazi commandant (the formidable Shirley Stoler of *The Honeymoon Killers*) calls the prisoner's bluff in her death-camp office is as grotesque and grossly funny as a sexual encounter with one of Fellini's gargantuan women in *8½* or *Fellini Satyricon.*

A minor frustration of all her films is the atrocious dubbing practice in the original Italian whereby virtually all the dialogue spoken during on-location shooting is rewritten and rerecorded in a studio. The bad lip-synch is especially noticeable in a dance-hall song in *Seven Beauties.*

*Swept Away . . .* is literally Wertmüller's sunniest film—having been shot on the Mediterranean—and *Seven Beauties* (which refers to a man who has a way with women in Naples) is her darkest film. *Seven Beauties* is the most terrifying comedy, or funniest horror film, you are likely to see this year. It is doomsday humor, *A Clockwork Neapolitan,* a dazzling epic of soul rot.

There is an imprisoned anarchist (Fernando Rey) in *Seven Beauties* who, presumably, speaks for Wertmüller when he explains to the hero/victim (Giannini) that in three hundred years there will be thirty billion persons on earth and families will be slaughtered for an apple. What can save us, the anarchist says, "is the New Man. Not the Intelligent Man, who ruined nature's balance. But the Civilized Man." Wertmüller hasn't given us a portrait of her civilized man yet. One feels reasonably sure she intends to at some point, as an alternative to innocents duped out of their humanity.

[1976]

# 10

# TWO OTHER MASTERS

Two celebrated European directors are very special cases.

Not only is Luis Buñuel not a part of a national movement, he is cinema's man without a country, making his films in Mexico, France, the United States, and even—twice in recent years—his native Spain from which he was exiled for twenty years. Still, his black humor is correctly termed Spanish, though his genius for risible *non sequitur* clearly derives from the surrealist movement in Paris with which he was associated in the twenties. Buñuel's humor is so based on derision and put-down, and yet comes across as neither condescending nor cruel, that penetrating its secrets has kept critics busy for years. William S. Pechter's essay here is probably the best attempt to explain not only why we laugh but also why we don't even feel guilty at laughing at what all our logic is telling us should not be funny at all in Buñuel's films.

As for Ingmar Bergman's *Smiles of a Summer Night*, what seems so striking today is that this great director has never again been able to make a successful comedy (with the special exception of *The Magic Flute*). The easy explanation is probably the correct one. He's gotten more somber and serious, and indeed the major criticism of *The Devil's Eye* and *All These Women* is that their tone was just too heavy for comedy. Bergman may be the type who can make a good comedy only before the natural lightness of youth has passed away. Such types often regain a sense of humor in old age, so there's a chance that Bergman may make us laugh again.

# LUIS BUÑUEL

## WHY WE LAUGH AT BUÑUEL
### *William S. Pechter*

[ . . . ] Far from there being, as Pauline Kael contends, "no way to get a hold on what Buñuel believes in,"[1] Buñuel's films constitute, with a singleness of purpose as unwavering as any to be found in art, a continually unfolding fiction in the form of an almost scientifically methodical testing of the proposition that we are living in the worst of all possible worlds—a belief if ever there was one. It is a world emblematized by its dislocations, whether inflicted by the folly of institutions, as in the saintliness of Simon[2] and bourgeois "virtue" of Don Francisco in *El;* or the cruelties of nature, as in the hopeless passion of the dwarf for his full-grown inamorata in *Nazarin,* or, as in the miseries of the Hurdanos in *Land Without Bread (Las Hurdes),* by the complicity of both.[3] It is a world evoked by an art in which loathing, a Swiftian revulsion and disgust, is a motive force, but an art in which, if one cannot really discover a recognizable sympathy or compassion in the "entomological" interest out of which a Francisco is explored, neither is there misanthropy.[4] Socially refined man may indeed be the monstrous creature which populates Buñuel's *Diary of a Chambermaid,* but the human needs on which society is based are depicted in Buñuel's *Adventures of Robinson Crusoe,* seen there undistorted by social institutions, as endowed with both dignity and a kind of beauty. If then, as Pauline Kael says, "Buñuel makes the charitable the butt of humor," it is not necessarily the impulse toward charity that is being ridiculed. The charitable impulse of Nazarin is never impugned (nor is that of the enlightened reformatory director in *Los Olvidados,* or that of Jorge toward the dog in *Viridiana*), but the main fact about Nazarin as about them all is that he's ineffectual, irrelevant to the plight of those to whom his charity is directed, *useless.* "You're thoroughly good and I'm thoroughly bad, and neither of us serves any purpose," the thief tells Nazarin in prison. Nazarin is as self-defeating in his charity as Francisco is in his jealousy; he is, like Simon of the desert and Archibaldo de La Cruz, like the young man in *Un Chien Andalou* and the husband in *Belle de Jour,* like Don Francisco (and all—church and state—that Don Francisco internalizes and exemplifies), obsessive: unyielding in the refusal to compromise with reality. They are not idealists but (like Cordelier, in Renoir's lone Buñuel-like black comedy) absolutists, and it is absurd, faced with a work so richly ambiguous as *Nazarin,* to say, as does

1. "Saintliness" in *Going Steady,* Boston, Atlantic Monthly Press–Little, Brown, 1970.
2. [ In *Simon of the Desert* .]
3. And, in the words of André Bazin: "It does not matter that they [the Hurdanos] are an exception; what matters is that such a thing can be."
4. Neither, however, is there always that "impression of incorruptible human dignity" which Bazin speaks of finding in *Las Hurdes* and *Los Olvidados.* Indeed, chief among Buñuel's charges against the world as it is made is precisely its power and propensity to strip man of his dignity and corrupt him.

Pauline Kael, that Buñuel is "so enraged by the unfulfillment of ideals that he despises dreamers who can't make their dreams come true," or that Buñuel fails to "give in" to the film's final gesture. For, though the specific effect on Nazarin of the woman's gift of the pineapple following his disillusionment with saintliness may not be knowable, the affective impact that the woman's mundane charity has on him is unmistakable in every detail of the scene's realization, from his stunned bewilderment to the final shattering roll of drums; indeed, it is a case of the final moment of the film (like the last line of Waugh's *The Ordeal of Gilbert Pinfold*) retrospectively transforming everything that we have experienced before. And, though it may be true that one cannot say with certainty that when Buñuel's obsessed characters "lose their faith" they become any more useful, it certainly would be false to assert that Buñuel is suggesting that human nature doesn't change, or that he holds a Grand Inquisitor's view of man's basic animality: false to the very essence of his films, which are nothing if not a demonstration that we must change human nature and change the institutions that at once distort and reinforce it in its present state—changes to which saintliness is irrelevant. And if it is true that Buñuel's films cannot be made to yield any programmatic definition of what a better human nature might be, it is clearly the implied injunction of his surrealist commitment and of the ribbon of dream which runs through his work that there can be no meaningful change which does not admit and dignify the irrational side of man's nature: this not as a surrender to animality but as a victory for a more whole humanity.

Apart from such things as the mock reformation of Archibaldo and mock damnation of Simon,[5] Nazarin's is the one serious instance of a Buñuel character brought in this world to at least the brink of some fundamental change of nature, though what lies over that brink we cannot know. Yet the importance with which Buñuel invests the critical moment in which that change hangs in the balance, the respect he accords it, is never in doubt. Buñuel's scorn is reserved for such change's substitute and counterfeit: for those anodyne half measures which serve to make clear consciences, of which the most troubling instance is that of the exploited dog which Jorge releases from his master, only to have yet another dog, bound to a cart in identical enslavement, follow in

5. Seldom can any sequence in films as straightforward as the ending of *Simon of the Desert* have been met with such obtuseness as that of most of the film's American critics. For, far from revealing to us Buñuel's vision of hell (and its impoverishment), *Simon* ends with a brilliantly insolent joke on the banality of "sin." Simon, unchanged in his "damnation," sits in a discotheque, sipping Coke, mechanically trading formulas ("Devil behind me!"—"Devil above you!") with Satan, both locked no less than before in their mutual irrelevance; it is, after all, the devil who describes the kids' innocuous dance as "Radioactive flesh . . . the latest and the last," and who earlier remarks to Simon, "We're very similar, you and I." Moreover, anyone reading the ending as originally written (published in *Three Screenplays,* New York, the Orion Press, 1969, with interpretive comments one takes on faith and reason not to be by Buñuel) can see that the ending as filmed has been made to emphasize just this joke, and that no shortage of money can, as has been alleged, be held accountable for the differences. But the strongest argument for one's understanding Buñuel's joke as I have described it is simply this: it, and not the moralistic interpretation of the critics, is totally in character with everything in the film (and in Buñuel's work) that has gone before.

its wake. For surely what Buñuel makes us see, and laugh at, in Jorge's act is not the particular kindness but its general inadequacy, and, more specifically, the vastness of its inadequacy in conjunction with Jorge's satisfaction in having acted virtuously. It is not the "saving one Jew from the ovens or one Biafran baby from starvation" that we laugh at, in Pauline Kael's emotionally charged comparison, but ourselves, and our ameliorative checks to the Biafra relief fund, which ameliorate, to be sure, while things go on essentially as before. Is Jorge only a realist who does what he can? But it is just this kind of realism, and the reality that shapes it, which Buñuel exposes to our shamed laughter. Yet Buñuel's scorn for our ameliorist liberalism comes not from the side of a Lawrence or Pound, as Pauline Kael misleadingly suggests, but from that of a surrealist anarchism.[6] And though we may be unable to appropriate him to any congenial reformism, the fact remains that his refusal to make the reformist statements is precisely that quality in his work which, in its denial of feelings to assuage ours, presses us to our own confrontation.[7] Upon our habitual numbness, Buñuel's films exert the terrible pressure of the noncommittal. And we laugh.

We laugh, in black comedy, at a vision of the world so intensely terrible that only our laughter can relieve its pressure; we laugh, at its very extremity, in order to endure it. (And it is no paradox that, but for the unflaggingly witty *Simon of the Desert,* Buñuel's deliberately light or playful films—*The Criminal Life of Archibaldo de La Cruz* or *Belle de Jour* or *The Milky Way*—are actually less funny than the darker ones.) It is the world of Modot in *L'Âge d'Or,* the Hurdanos, the forgotten ones of Mexico City, Nazarin, Viridiana and her Uncle Jaime, Celestine the chambermaid, and Joseph the fascist brute. It is a world at the very center of which lives Francisco in *El,* like a character out of French bedroom farce except that the farce is being played in his head. Whether prosecuting his paranoid legal suit (whose fortunes are so intertwined with those of his marriage) to redress some ancient grievance, straightening a picture or his wife's shoes, or scurrying around the house in his bathrobe with his queer assortment of implements, he is a figure as preposterous (in his sheer ineffectuality) as he is inescapably disturbing. Francisco is continually creating situations in which all alternatives confirm his suspicions; and it is in our sense of the discrepancy between things as they are, things as he imagines them, and the elaborate, self-defeating stratagems by which he attempts to deal with things as he imagines them, that the film's comedy lies. And yet, recognizably, his world is ours, and he its creation: almost, one might say, its purest creation. For the madman is also the model citizen and perfect Christian gentleman: the product of the institutions which sanction him. "Don't hurt him! He's my

6. ". . . In a world so badly made, as ours is, there is only one road—rebellion." (Buñuel, quoted in Ado Kyrou, *Luis Buñuel: An Introduction,* New York, Simon and Schuster, 1963.)

7. "I will let Friedrich Engels speak for me. He defines the function of the novelist (and here read filmmaker) thus: 'The novelist will have acquitted himself honorably of his task when, by means of an accurate portrait of authentic social relations, he will have destroyed the conventional view of the nature of those relations, shattered the optimism of the bourgeois world, and forced the reader to question the permanency of the prevailing order, and this even if the author does not offer us any solutions, even if he does not clearly takes sides.' " (Buñuel, quoted *ibid.)*

friend!" cries the priest, at the end, of the victim of that "friendship," and it is a cry into which Buñuel has managed to infuse not only his icy rage but also something surprisingly like compassion. If, then, we laugh, what is our laughter, the laughter of black comedy, but a strategy for preserving sanity while contemplating the intolerable? And, if the "entomological" interest can yield this, as it yields also the tortured Modot, the miseries of the Hurdanos and *los olvidados,* the agony of Nazarin, the convulsions of innocence in *Viridiana* and decadence in *The Diary of a Chambermaid,* then one must acknowledge that Buñuel's "coolness" is something which may contain passion: that it is, like the "coolness" of a Brecht or Bresson, an instance of the transformation of passion by art. And the sensitizing effect this coolness produces on us is a testimony to the degree of passion Buñuel's art truly contains. [. . .]

[1970]

# THE DISCREET CHARM OF THE BOURGEOISIE
## Stuart Byron

Luis Buñuel's *The Discreet Charm of the Bourgeoisie* has come as a shock, having had no plot or publicity "hook" to encourage anticipation. Born in Spain in 1900, collaborator with Salvador Dali on the classics *Un Chien Andalou* (1928) and *L'Âge d'Or* (1930), Buñuel earned his reputation very early for producing anticlerical, surrealist *succès de scandale.* A career as a producer in Republican Spain ended when Franco's forces won in 1939. Buñuel then endured a decade of silence, working as a dubbing expert for Warner Bros. in Paris and as a documentary archivist for the Museum of Modern Art in New York, all the while enjoying only an underground reputation. The "commercial" one has come about very late and very slowly, beginning with the first of his Mexican films in 1947, solidifying with respectable international successes such as *Los Olvidados* (1950), *Robinson Crusoe* (1952), and *El* (1952), and at last exploding with the Cannes grand-prize winner *Viridiana* in 1961. Buñuel's reputation as the world's great blasphemer was confirmed and extended in the last decade with such films as *The Exterminating Angel* (1962), *Belle de Jour* (1967), and *Tristana* (1970), among others.

But what was this *Discreet Charm*? Most expected a minor Buñuel, like the quickly forgotten *The Milky Way* of a few years back. All one knew was that it took place in Paris and had an all-star cast: Fernando Rey *(The French Connection),* Delphine Seyrig *(Last Year at Marienbad),* Stéphane Audran *(Le Boucher),* and Bulle Ogier *(La Salamandre).* And even after viewing, it remains indescribable in a few words—and perhaps unexplainable. But its impact was instantaneous, and on the following Sunday, for the first time in recent memory, *The New York Times'*s critical scoreboard recorded unanimous raves from the city's critics (fifteen favorable, no mixed, no unfavorable). The *Times'*s Vincent Canby called it the one must-see film "in years." Andrew Sarris of the *Village Voice* told everyone it was the best movie in "two or three years." To Norma McLain Stoop of *After Dark,* it was the best in a decade. Critics found themselves reaching back to describe its importance: the best since *Persona,* since *8½,* since *2001,* since *Blow-Up,* since Buñuel's own *Belle de Jour.* . . .

My own opinion? I think *The Discreet Charm of the Bourgeoisie* is the finest film made since Robert Bresson's *Au Hazard, Balthazar* (1966), and one of the ten greatest films in cinema history.

Rey, in the movie, plays the ambassador to France from the fictional South American country of Miranda, but his major activity in life consists of smuggling heroin, an enterprise in which he is joined by Pierre Frankeur—whose wife is Seyrig and whose sister is Ogier—and Jean-Pierre Cassel—whose wife is Audran. The three, then, are businessmen, and Buñuel indicates by his choice of their "product" just what he thinks of the "bourgeoisie"—for it must not be forgotten that in historical terminology bourgeoisie does not mean "middle-class" but "tradesmen," the class of manufacturers and sellers which became the ruling class when it was victorious over the landowning aristocracy in the French Revolution of 1789 and subsequent civil wars (including our own) in the other major industrial nations. In the West, we are still living in the bourgeois era.

The film's "plot" consists of no more than the six main characters gathering together, in different groups and, twice, with others. One episode is an illicit tryst between Rey and Seyrig, another a business conference between the three men; except for these, all involve dinner parties, at homes or in restaurants. In other words, the dinner party in the movie is a metaphor for the state of the world as ruled by the bourgeoisie. Each and every one of these gatherings is interrupted or otherwise ruined—sometimes logically, sometimes absurdly, sometimes surreally. For example, four of the group have arrived at the home of the other two on the wrong date. They go to a restaurant but the manager has just died. The three women are in a tearoom but the kitchen is out of tea, coffee, and everything else. A soldier comes over to their table and tells a story of his neurotic childhood. At the home of one couple, a bishop arrives and offers to become their gardener. Another dinner party consisting of all six is interrupted by *another* soldier who recounts a Baudelairean dream.

What does all this symbolize? In my opinion these interruptions and ruinations represent all those events and philosophies which for more than a century have been predicted to cause the downfall of the bourgeoisie. That class, Buñuel shows us, has survived it all—all the wars (the army maneuvers), all the depressions (unavailability of goods like tea and coffee), all of the church reform (the bishop-*cum*-gardener thinks he's a "worker-priest"!), all of the individual acts of personal homicide caused by the class structure (a peasant has killed his mean bourgeoisie employers, to no ultimate avail), all of the "sexual revolutions" (the scenes of mad love-making), and—not least—all of the philosophies like Freudianism (the first soldier's story) and existentialism (the second soldier's story). Yes, the bourgeoisie has survived all of these, and, indeed, learned to treat them as nothing but petty annoyances, to maintain its cool, its grace, its . . . well, its discreet charm.

But toward the middle of the movie the interruptions become *so* ruinous that they can't be survived but only "resolved"—by turning out to be dreams by one of the three businessmen. *These* events may—just may—represent *real* threats; they may harbinger the *next* revolution. A dinner party turns out to have occurred on a stage, when the window curtain becomes a stage curtain and rises to a jeering audience ("exposure" of the bourgeoisie by theoreticians, journalists, and artists like Buñuel?)—and the group flees in panic. Cassel wakes up; it was a dream. At another party someone has never heard of Rey's country and a duel ensues—a ridiculous war over nothing but national honor (Vietnam?—the kind of meaningless conflict which could *cue* the revolution?). Frankeur wakes up; it was a dream. Finally the six, at the film's last dinner party, are interrupted by a bunch of gunmen who kill them all. And Rey wakes up, and it was a dream.

Buñuel is, of course, far more ambiguous and less linear than I've made him sound; indeed, during the second half, the entire group gets arrested for its drug-trafficking and then goes free after political strings are pulled—hardly an event harbingering a revolution. What is more, the identity of the gunmen at the end is deliberately left open. Are they friends of the Mirandan terrorist seen earlier in the film? Aligned with the Maoist student we have seen tortured by the police (the detective who has arrested the six wakes up; it was a dream)? Are they revolutionaries at all? Or just "the Marseilles gang"—the rival group of heroin-traffickers about whom Rey and his friends are so worried? Will there *ever* be a revolution? Or just another capitalist realignment designed to keep the bourgeoisie in power—like the formation of the Common Market or the resurgence of Japan?

But Buñuel is ambiguous not only in his plotting and structure but in his *attitude* toward his people as well. *Discreet Charm* is one of the most brutally *honest* films ever made; maybe only a seventy-two-year-old man could be so honest. Buñuel's people in *Discreet Charm* are dope-dealers and vapid and blind and silly but, damn it, they *are* charming.

From the very beginning, when Seyrig *smiles* as she notices evidence that her hosts have not prepared for her arrival at a dinner party, you admire her discreet charm. As you do Audran's delicate fingering of her collar as she inspects her garden, or Rey's "with pleasure" whenever he's asked if he wants a second helping of food. And the style permits Buñuel a balletic use of camera movement and staging: A maid passes a door with a tray exactly when the doorbell rings. Such a thing would look foolish done by any other director; Buñuel makes it the most natural coincidence in the world. And the resultant freedom permits him to present an equality of people and objects which expresses a materialist vision of the universe: a diplomatic pouch, a vase, a doorknob gets as much attention, as much placement as a person. *The Discreet Charm of the Bourgeoisie* will influence movies for years to come. I should add one thing: It's one of the funniest pictures ever made.

[1972]

# THE PHANTOM OF LIBERTÉ
## Joy Gould Boyum

It's surrealism's golden anniversary, fifty years to the month since French poet and one-time medical student André Breton published the First Surrealist Manifesto. And what better way to celebrate this semicentennial than with Luis Buñuel's *The Phantom of Liberté?*

This superb and marvelously witty movie by the brilliant seventy-four-year-old director whose very first film back in 1928, *Un Chien Andalou,* was a collaboration with Salvador Dali, almost incarnates the principles laid down in Breton's document. The "liberty" with which it is concerned and which is referred to in its title is not, as one might assume, our traditional political liberty: freedom of speech, assembly, the press, etc. It is instead the very untraditional *liberté totale* of the surrealists: freedom from order, logic, consistency, or, in Breton's own words, from "any control exercised by reason . . . from any aesthetic or moral concern."

The surrealist aim was to assert the absolute autonomy of the creative mind, to release the spontaneity and imaginative capacity which rationalism had imprisoned in the depths of that mind and which could assert themselves only through dream, hallucination, magic. Where artists had traditionally imitated the order and forms of nature, the surrealists would disarrange and reshape them, just as they would the inherited conventions of their poetry, their paintings, their films.

In *The Phantom of Liberté,* there is, for instance, no consistent narrative, no logical continuity, no sequential progression in time such as we are accustomed to find in films. We move from the past to the present, from one locale to another, from one set of characters to another via a word said in one context and repeated in another or as one character quite unconsciously crosses the path of another. A man whose story we have been following enters a doctor's office, at which point we pick up the adventures of the doctor's nurse; the nurse, driving along in her car, gives a lift to another man, a professor at a police school, and we leave her to follow him; one of the student-policemen stops a man in a car, and we shortly drive away with the driver. Where we are at any given moment is, then, a matter of chance, especially since we enter each story in the middle and leave it before its end.

Clearly, the construction of the film counters any conventional expectations we might bring with us. But these expectations are perhaps even more challenged by the events and images that are presented within the film's separate segments. Throughout, Buñuel surprises us with impossible, often mystical phenomena: statues which suddenly come to life; clocks which leap ahead at incredibly rapid speed; events which we first accept as dream but which later assert themselves as reality, as when a man seems to imagine a postman on a bicycle riding into his bedroom to deliver a letter only to discover in the morning that he has the letter in hand, or when a dead woman telephones her brother and the brother, on investigation, finds a pastel-colored Princess phone lying in the dead woman's crypt. Contradictions also abound: a sniper tried for the murder of eighteen people, on having the court pronounce the death sentence, is immediately set free to become a sought-after celebrity; a little girl who is unquestionably present to us and to everyone on screen is declared missing by her school and is brought by her parents to the police station where she provides her own description for the search party being formed.

Aside from these outright impossibilities, there are also in the film all kinds of more plausible—if equally absurd—incongruities: a poker game in which all the players are monks and who are, moreover, using religious medals as chips ("I raise you two Saint Christophers"); a set of apparently obscene postcards given by a strange man in a playground to a couple of young girls and which turn out, as we look at them over the shoulders of one of the girl's aghast parents, to be pictures of familiar Parisian monuments.

The immediate effect of these outrageous images is, of course, to make us laugh, since the incongruity which qualifies surrealist art is at the same time the basis for comedy. But there are other effects as well. For what Buñuel is asking us to do here is to break up our conventional modes of perception, our ready-made habits of thought and to see and think about the world in new terms. Watching a professor and his wife pay a visit to friends we are compelled to consider the relativity, the arbitrary nature even, of our social customs. Similarly, to see a picture of the Arch of Triumph and hear it called at that moment "obscene" is to force us both to reconsider our received judgments of the monument and to raise questions about just what ultimately constitutes "obscenity." The point is that in the surrealist world the conventional values of things are destroyed and the usual connotations of words and images are demolished. Nothing whatsoever, not even our sanity, can be taken for granted and so we must perceive with a new and heightened awareness the relationships between words and images and between images and their emotional meanings.

And in *The Phantom of Liberté,* this awareness is made all the more intense by the extraordinary imaginativeness of the screenplay (for which Buñuel must share credit with his long-time coscenarist, Jean-Claude Carrière) and the astounding technical mastery that marks that screenplay's realization. Buñuel has used all the resources of his medium to saturate us with sensuous richness, and his film is from beginning to end exquisite to look at. He has also assembled an incredibly capable cast—among others, Monica Vitti, Jean-Claude Brialy, Michel Piccoli—and elicited from each an impeccable performance.

Just as Buñuel in his direction never stresses the fantasy but in poker-faced style presents it in absolute continuity with the everyday appearances that surround it, so his actors never play out the madness but matter-of-factly express it as sanity. When Jean-Claude Brialy looks at a spider and announces, "I'm fed up with symmetry," he does so without any indication that he has made either an unusual or crucial observation. When Michel Lonsdale invites some acquaintances "to celebrate chance" and tells them that he "loves the unexpected," he shows no self-consciousness in articulating a major theme.

But perhaps the film's most memorable performance and the one that is at the same time richest in metaphorical suggestiveness and most consistent with Buñuel's wit, is that of a terrified ostrich we see at the film's conclusion. Shown to us in close-up while on the sound-track we hear gunfire and revolutionary cries recalling the film's opening sequence—which has been set in Toledo during the Napoleonic invasion of Spain—the ostrich can't help but become for us the "phantom" of a "liberty" essentially and yet other than surrealist.

[1974]

# INGMAR BERGMAN

## SMILES OF A SUMMER NIGHT
### Pauline Kael

Late in 1955 Ingmar Bergman made a nearly perfect work—the exquisite carnal comedy, *Smiles of a Summer Night.* It was the distillation of elements he had worked with for several years in the 1952 *Secrets of Women* (originally called *The Waiting Women*), the 1953 *A Lesson in Love,* and the early 1955 *Dreams;* these episodic comedies of infidelity are like early attempts or drafts. They were all set in the present, and the themes were plainly exposed; the dialogue, full of arch epigrams, was often clumsy, and the ideas, like the settings, were frequently depressingly middle-class and novelettish. Structurally, they were sketchy and full of flashbacks. There were scattered lovely moments, as if Bergman's eye were looking ahead to the visual elegance of *Smiles of a Summer Night,* but the plot threads were still woolly. *Smiles of a Summer Night* was made after Bergman directed a stage production of *The Merry Widow,* and he gave the film a turn-of-the-century setting. Perhaps it was this distance that made it possible for him to create a work of art out of what had previously been mere clever ideas. He not only tied up the themes in the intricate plot structure of a love roundelay, but in using the lush period setting, he created an atmosphere that saturated the themes. The film is bathed in beauty, removed from the banalities of short skirts and modern-day streets and shops, and, removed in time, it draws us *closer.*

Bergman found a high style within a set of boudoir farce conventions: in *Smiles of a Summer Night* boudoir farce becomes lyric poetry. The sexual chases and the round dance are romantic, nostalgic: the coy bits of feminine plotting are gossamer threads of intrigue. The film becomes an elegy to transient love: a gust of wind and the whole vision may drift away.

There are four of the most beautiful and talented women ever to appear in one film: as the actress, the great Eva Dahlbeck, appearing on stage, giving a house party and, in one inspired suspended moment, singing "Freut Euch des Lebens"; the impudent love-loving maid, Harriet Andersson—as a blonde, but as opulent and sensuous as in her other great roles; Margit Carlquist as the proud, unhappy countess; Ulla Jacobsson as the eager virgin.

Even Bergman's epigrams are much improved when set in the quotation marks of a stylized period piece. (Though I must admit I can't find justification for such bright exchanges as the man's question, "What can a woman ever see in a man?" and her response, "Women are seldom interested in aesthetics. Besides, we can always turn out the light." I would have thought you couldn't get a laugh on that one unless you tried it in an old folks' home, but Bergman is a man of the theater—audiences break up on it.) Bergman's sensual scenes are much more charming, more unexpected in the period setting: when they are deliberately unreal they have grace and wit. How different it is to watch the same actor and actress making love in the stuck elevator of *Secrets of Women* and in the golden pavilion of *Smiles of a Summer Night.* Everything is subtly improved in the soft light and delicate, perfumed atmosphere.

In Bergman's modern comedies, marriages are contracts that bind the sexes in banal boredom forever. The female strength lies in convincing the man that he's big enough to act like a man in the world, although secretly he must acknowledge his dependence on her. (J. M. Barrie used to say the same thing in the cozy, complacent Victorian terms of plays like *What Every Woman Knows;* it's the same concept that Virginia Woolf raged against—rightly, I think—in *Three Guineas.*) The straying male is just a bad child—but it is the essence of maleness to stray. Bergman's typical comedy heroine, Eva Dahlbeck, is the woman as earth-mother who finds fulfillment in accepting the infantilism of the male. In the modern comedies she is a strapping goddess with teeth big enough to eat you up and a jaw and neck to swallow you down; Bergman himself is said to refer to her as "The Woman Battleship."

But in *Smiles of a Summer Night,* though the roles of the sexes are basically the same, the perspective is different. In this vanished setting, nothing lasts, there are no winners in the game of love; all victories are ultimately defeats —only the game goes on. When Eva Dahlbeck, as the actress, wins back her old lover (Gunnar Björnstrand), her plot has worked—but she hasn't really won much. She caught him because he gave up; they both know he's defeated. *Smiles* is a tragicomedy; the man who thought he "was great in guilt and in glory" falls—he's "only a bumpkin." This is a defeat we can all share—for have we not all been forced to face ourselves as less than we hoped to be? There is no lesson, no moral—the women's faces do not tighten with virtuous endurance (the setting is too unreal for endurance to be plausible). The glorious old Mrs. Armfeldt (Naima Wifstrand) tells us that she can teach her daughter nothing—or, as she puts it, "We can never save a single person from a single suffering—and that's what makes us despair."

*Smiles of a Summer Night* was the culmination of Bergman's "rose" style and he has not returned to it. (*The Seventh Seal,* perhaps his greatest "black" film, was also set in a remote period.) The Swedish critic Rune Waldekranz has written that *Smiles of a Summer Night* "wears the costume of the *fin-de-siècle* period for visual emphasis of the erotic comedy's fundamental premise

—that the step between the sublime and the ridiculous in love is a short one, but nevertheless one that a lot of people stub their toe on. Although benefiting from several ingenious slapstick situations, *Smiles of a Summer Night* is a comedy in the most important meaning of the word. It is an arabesque on an essentially tragic theme, that of man's insufficiency, at the same time as it wittily illustrates the belief expressed fifty years ago by Hjalmar Söderberg that the only absolutes in life are 'the desire of the flesh and the incurable loneliness of the soul.' "

[1961]

# AFTERWORD:
# SOME THEORETICAL OBSERVATIONS

A theory of comedy is no laughing matter. Much of the world's least humorous writing has been devoted to analyses of merriment, its roots and its rationales. There are few topics as predictably solemn, or as hopelessly subjective, which is to say that the conjugation of the verb "to laugh" is highly irregular. Also, people seem to become very pompous when they talk about humor. Hence, humor is always considered a healthy thing until someone steps on our own toes or prejudices, or kicks our own crutches out from under our armpits, or throws up all over our new Persian rug. Then the humor is in bad taste. It all depends upon the point of view.

—Andrew Sarris

Satire is subversive; camp isn't.

—Molly Haskell

Built into all urban humor are the derisive acceptance of oneself as part of a mass and techniques for bringing down those who would deny their membership in that mass.

—Pauline Kael

Perhaps funniness often occurs when everything is in good order except for one small thing that has slipped.

—Penelope Gilliatt

Comedians have never been the happiest of men. No small part of their appeal is the wry or jaundiced eye with which they view the world and its ways, pointing up with savage or what passes for affectionate humor the follies of their fellow men. Theirs is no lovers' quarrel: Jokes are their armor in a never-ending war against stupidity, convention, prejudice, or merely the opposite sex; gags are their scarcely camouflaged weapons of counterattack.

—Arthur Knight

A laugh is an exhalation. Which is funny, if you think about it. It comes from inside us. Somebody slips on a banana peel. And we involuntarily exhale air. The laugh was poised awaiting its release.

Laughter is conspiracy, an acknowledgment of your recognition. You can't laugh at a joke that has to be explained to you. And only humans laugh. Because that shock of recognition presupposes consciousness. And, therefore, comedy is almost a sacramental celebration of our humanity. And tragedy, of course, is the celebration of that other uniquely human function, crying.

We historically reward those who can invoke awe and pity and cathartic tears. And, as well, those who deflate authority and custom, make fun of bodily functions or basic animal drives, and give us the tension-release of joyful laughter.

Not surprisingly, it is the mixture of these two human emotions that is most prized. The synthesis produces a dual release, a simultaneous surrender to two ecstatic sensations. Few have the breadth to embrace what is funny and sad. Shakespeare could, because his deaths were as powerful as his clown scenes. And though Chaplin's Victorian sentimentality often blunted his compassion, he could nonetheless make us laugh and cry for a blind flower girl and a tramp.

—Joseph Gelmis

Screwball comedy is probably not so much a genre as, like comedy of humors, a comic idiom.

—William S. Pechter

During the past three or four years, many directors have tried to put revue humor on film, and, except for some of the early comedy sequences in *The Graduate*, it has failed, painfully—as in *Luv, The Tiger Makes Out*, the Eleanor Bron–William Daniels bits of *Two for the Road*, parts of *Bedazzled*, the Elaine May role in *Enter Laughing, The President's Analyst*, and so on. Revue theater is a form of actors' theater; even when the material isn't worked up by the actors—even when it is written by a Murray Schisgal (or, in England, transformed into more serious drama by Harold Pinter)—the meaning comes from the rhythm of clichés, defenses, and little verbal aggressions, and this depends on the pulse and the intuition of the performers. It would be as difficult to write down as dance notation. Typically, as in the Nichols-and-May routines, the satire is thin and the thinness is the essence of the joke. We laugh at the tiny, almost imperceptible hostilities that suddenly explode, because we recognize that we're tied up in knots about small issues more than about big ones, and that we don't lose our pretensions even when (or especially when) we are concerned about the big ones.

This style developed here (and in England) in the fifties, when college actors went on working together in cabarets, continuing and developing sophomoric humor. That word isn't used pejoratively; I *like* sophomoric college-revue humor, and one has only to contrast its topicality and freshness with the Joe Miller Jokebook world to understand why it swept the country. In revue, the very latest in interpersonal relations—the newest clichés and courtship rites and seduction techniques—could be polished to the point of satire almost overnight. Mort Sahl and the stand-up comics might satirize the political *them*, but cabaret, with its interacting couples, satirized *us*. We laugh at being nailed by these actors who are cartoons of us, all too easy to understand, and though there's a comic discomfort in listening to what our personal and social rituals might sound like if they were overheard, it's a comfortable form of theater—the disheveled American's form of light domestic comedy.

But it didn't work in the movies. A skit builds by the smallest of inflections, and each inflection becomes important because we construct the whole ambience from the performers—mainly from their voices. And that's what, in the past, killed this kind of acting on the screen: the performers did too much with voices and pauses, and when the director interrupted them with camera shifts and cuts, the performers lost their own rhythm and rapport. In relation to how it was being used, their acting was overdeveloped in a specialized way, and the result was, oddly, that they seemed ugly and rather grotesque and terribly stagy. And the milieu always felt wrong, because we didn't need it; instead of getting our bearings from the performers we looked at the sets and lost our bearings.

—Pauline Kael

The difference between satire and comedy, like the difference between a telegram and a letter, is one of kind, not degree. It is the difference between institutions and individuals, between characters who are succinct and representative and characters who are complex and resonant. It is the difference, in *Divorce American Style,* between Debbie Reynolds and Dick Van Dyke on the one hand and Jean Simmons and Jason Robards on the other. It is the difference between Bob and Carol and Ted on the one hand and Alice on the other. It is the difference between the husband and the wife in *Diary of a Mad Housewife,* or between the old and the young in the "youth" films. It is not that one mode is better than the other. More feeling is attached to comedy, but satire can be just as original—e.g., all of Feiffer's creations, including those in *Little Murders.* But they represent two different conventions, two different styles, and demand two different responses, and are mixed at great peril to a film's equilibrium. When the two types coexist within the same film or—as in *I Love My . . . Wife*—within the same characters, there are usually disconcerting differences in tone, degree of stylization, and point of view. American directors and screenwriters, like Americans in general, want to be loved and can't bear to leave a savage situation without extracting a little sentimental juice from it. On the other hand, the derisive impulse is strong nowadays. Film, after all, is a reflection of life and life has become instant satire of the institutional variety. Just try to make a phone call. Or go to a movie. Or breathe.

—Molly Haskell

In the movies, the sex queen, the Theda Bara, the Mae West, the Harlow, the Marilyn Monroe—even the Garbo—always ends up playing a parody of herself. It is as if the audience cannot stand for long this physical manifestation of its dream life. It must at a certain point relieve the inner tension engendered by such stars through laughter. With considerable relief, the critics burst into print with the information that the Symbol has become an extremely talented comedienne.

—Richard Schickel

I suppose there's a touch of maliciousness in most comedy. We are nearly always amused at someone or other's expense. But a certain attitude toward that person and his situation are essential, if we are to find mirth in his misery. First of all, we must believe he deserves his discomfort: that his vanity or pretentiousness or selfishness has at last received its comeuppance. Second, and perhaps even more crucial a condition for laughter, the punishment for even the most deserving must not be too severe. Disney, for example, making a comedy of a pretty grim tale with *The Three Little Pigs,* didn't boil his wolf alive at the end but merely burned his bottom a bit. In this case, we'd all probably agree that the wolf didn't suffer too much, but it is precisely in the thrust of "just deserts" that we have our greatest disagreements about the comic or comic effects. Our thresholds for pain are all different and what one man perceives as agony, another perceives as mere ache.

Consequently, there are certain films which will leave some of us squirming in our seats while our neighbors sit laughing convulsively.

—Joy Gould Boyum

Movie comedies nowadays are like large airplanes with every conceivable flying feature except aerodynamics. They roar around the runways making the right noises, the jet engines go like a dream, the seat belts and ashtrays are flawless. And none of it lifts as much as an inch from the ground.

—Richard Eder

The dominant mode in movies today is derision. No target is too low or too broad or too decrepit for today's cinematic satirists. Indeed, there are times when the target has become so vague and indistinct that the derisory smile of the filmmaker becomes as disembodied as the grin of the Cheshire Cat.

—Andrew Sarris

The distinction between Horatian and Juvenalian satire, between the specific optimism of one approach and the general pessimism of the other, was appropriately invoked in the eighteenth century to define two modes of satire of which Pope and Swift were the leading exemplars. But it is a distinction which runs through all art, at least in its critical and indignant moods. It is the difference between the cast of mind which sees human ills in terms of institutions and is to some degree corrective, and the bleaker vision which sees, beneath it all, only the depravity of the human animal, a fundamentally nihilistic vision which at its most "beneficial" is merely salutary.

The prevailing impulse today is in the former vein—activist, political, corrective. From Brecht and Artaud to the new forms of theater, from Dadaism to the antimuseum movement in art; it includes the creative offspring of Marx, Freud, and their contemporary modifiers; most black writers. In the second category, social criticism may be expressed, but it is overshadowed, even undermined, by a deep pessimism regarding human possibility. Godard, with *Weekend,* crossed over into this group, which includes such desperate artists as Céline, Beckett, Orton, and Francis Bacon.

—Molly Haskell

# AFTERWORD: SOME THEORETICAL OBSERVATIONS

Let any reliable movie historian chart the decline and fall of the belly laugh and the awful truth emerges: The god of mirth is moribund in Hollywood. It's too bad, because Hollywood's claim to greatness rests most securely on comedy—witness the golden age of the silents, dominated by such geniuses as Chaplin, Keaton, Langdon, and Lloyd. Though excellent in their way, almost all of the best of recent comedies inspire the kind of laughter that dies in the throat. These satires, built on a bedrock of bitter social commentary—M*A*S*H, Joe, The Boys in the Band, and Catch-22—tend to be coldly black rather than sidesplittingly funny. Much less admirable but nonetheless making it are Andy Warhol movies, Robert Downey's Pound, and mean-spirited creations such as Myra Breckinridge and Where's Poppa?, which invite audiences to leer and snigger at the creeps on display. We go to see them because today—with lamentably few exceptions—that's what passes for comedy. We pay our money, but do we have much of a choice?

Some moviemakers themselves have become nostalgic for the pure visual comedy of yesteryear. And such men as Richard Lester, Blake Edwards, and Mel Brooks, in their different ways and with varying degrees of success, have been trying to revive the old spirit. Today, a broad romp such as Start the Revolution Without Me, done in vintage style, can easily be mistaken for a milestone if it delivers a hearty laugh once every ten minutes.

Why has so much of the fun gone out of comedy? There are pundits who insist that the reasons are psychological. Maybe they have something. The past jittery decade has produced perhaps one not-so-light classic—Dr. Strangelove, a black comedy to end all comedies in the age of the bomb. Can anyone be really amused, or amusing, after all, with doomsday at hand? Whatever the reasons, today's stylish young taste makers—though hip to drugs, love, and revolution—are sorely lacking in humor. Perhaps the discussion is academic, since the decline of comedy is inextricably connected with harsh economic realities. The great silent comedies cost more and took longer to make than the average dramatic films of the time, because the men who made them were not hacks but young, relatively independent artists who, if they had to, would spend days or weeks perfecting a single unforgettable gag. When the big-studio organization men took charge, they demanded finished scripts and shooting schedules. The party was nearly over and filmdom's fruitful age of innocence began to evolve into the big business we know now. Which means that comedy has become, by and large, a package of big-box-office names cavorting on an easily exploitable topic. Everything goes into it but the key ingredients of ample time and incomparable talent.

—Bruce Williamson

# ABOUT THE CONTRIBUTORS

Gary Arnold is film critic of *The Washington Post.*

Joy Gould Boyum writes on film for *The Wall Street Journal.* She also teaches literature and film at New York University, where she is professor of English.

Stuart Byron is a film critic for Boston's *Nightfall* and has written for *The New York Times,* the *Village Voice, Rolling Stone, Creem, Movie, Film Quarterly,* and *Gay.* He was for two years on the staff of *Variety* and for another two the film editor of the *Real Paper.* He is a contributing editor of *Film Comment.*

Vincent Canby is film critic of *The New York Times;* he was a critic and reporter for *Variety* from 1960 until 1965, and is an associate fellow of Pierson College, Yale. He is the author of a novel, *Living Quarters,* published in 1975.

Charles Champlin is film critic of the *Los Angeles Times;* he was host of the "Film Odyssey" series for NET.

Jay Cocks reviews for *Time* magazine.

Richard Corliss is the film critic of *New Times* magazine and the editor of *Film Comment.* He has written for *The New York Times,* the *Village Voice, Commonweal,* the *Real Paper,* and most of the major specialized film magazines. He is the editor of *The Hollywood Screenwriter* and the author of *Talking Pictures* and *Greta Garbo.*

Judith Crist is film critic of *The Saturday Review* and *TV Guide.* She has been film critic of *The New York Herald Tribune, The World Journal Tribune, New York* magazine, and NBC-TV's "Today" show. Her reviews were collected in *The Private Eye, the Cowboy and the Very Naked Girl* and in *Judith Crist's TV Guide to the Movies.* She is an adjunct professor at the Columbia University Graduate School of Journalism.

Bernard Drew is film critic and feature writer for the Gannett News Service. He has written original material for movies and television.

Roger Ebert, film critic of the *Chicago Sun-Times,* won the 1975 Pulitzer Prize for criticism. His pieces have appeared in *Esquire, The New York Times, Film Comment,* and *The Critic.* He is lecturer in film at the University of Chicago and he wrote the original screenplay for *Beyond the Valley of the Dolls.*

Richard Eder was formerly foreign correspondent for and is now film critic for *The New York Times.*

Joseph Gelmis is film critic of *Newsday,* film writer for the *Los Angeles Times / Washington Post* News Wire, and the author of a collection of interviews, *The Film Director as Superstar.* He is an adjunct assistant professor at State University of New York at Stony Brook.

Penelope Gilliatt is a film critic for *The New Yorker* and was formerly film critic of the London *Observer*. She is a Fellow of the Royal Society of Literature. Her latest books are *Nobody's Business*, a collection of short fiction and a short play; *Unholy Fools*, a collection of writing on film and theater; *Jean Renoir*; and *Jacques Tati*. She has also written two novels, *One by One* and *A State of Change*, and two collections of stories, *Come Back If It Doesn't Get Better* and *Penguin Modern Stories No. 5*. Her original screenplay for *Sunday, Bloody Sunday* is available in hardcover and paperback.

Roger Greenspun is film critic and contributing editor for *Penthouse*, and associate professor of English at Rutgers, where he teaches film criticism. He has been a film critic on the staffs of the New York *Free Press*, *Rolling Stone*, *The New York Times*, and the *Soho Weekly News*. His articles on film have appeared in *Moviegoer, Sight and Sound, Second Coming, On Film*, the *Village Voice, Cahiers du Cinéma in English*, and *Film Comment*, for which he is a contributing writer. He is a member of the Selection Committee of the New York Film Festival and a panelist on film and video for the New York State Council for the Arts.

Molly Haskell is a film critic for the *Village Voice* and a free-lance writer on film. Her pieces have appeared in *Vogue, Saturday Review, Intellectual Digest, Show, USA, Film Comment, Film Heritage, Inter/VIEW, Cahiers du Cinéma in English*, and *MS*. She is the author of *From Reverence to Rape: The Treatment of Women in the Movies*.

Pauline Kael is a movie critic for *The New Yorker*. She has written for *Partisan Review, Sight and Sound, Film Quarterly*, the *Atlantic, McCall's*, the *New Republic*, and *Harper's*. Her criticism has been collected in *I Lost it at the Movies, Kiss Kiss Bang Bang, Going Steady, Deeper Into Movies*, and *Reeling*. Her long essay "Raising Kane" appears in *The Citizen Kane Book*. Her collection *Deeper Into Movies* won the National Book Award for Arts and Letters in 1973.

Arthur Knight, author of the *The Liveliest Art*, is a professor in the University of Southern California's Cinema Division and director of its History and Criticism program. Formerly assistant curator of the Museum of Modern Art Film Library, he was also a film critic and contributing editor of *The Saturday Review* for twenty-four years and now writes for the *Hollywood Reporter, Westways*, and the *Soho Weekly News*. With Hollis Alpert, he is coauthor of *Playboy*'s long-running "The History of Sex in the Cinema" series.

Janet Maslin is a critic of film, theater, and music for *Newsweek*. She was formerly film editor of the *Boston Phoenix* and music columnist for *New Times*. Her pieces have also appeared in the *Village Voice, Rolling Stone*, and *Film Comment*.

William S. Pechter is film critic of *Commentary*. His pieces have also appeared in *Commonweal*, the *Kenyon Review, Moviegoer, Sight and Sound*, the *London Magazine, Contact, Tulane Drama Review, Kulchur, Film Quarterly*, and *Film Comment*, and have been collected in *Twenty-four Times a Second*.

Rex Reed is the film critic for the New York *Daily News* and *Vogue.* He has been the film critic for *Women's Wear Daily, Holiday,* and *Cosmopolitan* in past years, and his reviews and articles on film have appeared in most major publications. He is the author of four books: *Do You Sleep in the Nude?, Conversations in the Raw, Big Screen, Little Screen,* and *People are Crazy Here.*

Frank Rich is film critic of the *New York Post.* Previously, he was film critic and senior editor of *New Times.* His journalism has also appeared in *Esquire,* the *Village Voice, TV Guide,* the *Washington Monthly,* and, in England, the *Guardian* and *Harper's Bazaar & Queen.*

Andrew Sarris is film critic of the *Village Voice* and associate professor of cinema at Columbia University. His books are: *The Films of Josef von Sternberg, Interviews with Film Directors, The Film, The American Cinema: Directors and Directions 1929–1968, Film 68/69,* coedited with Hollis Alpert, *Confessions of a Cultist: On the Cinema 1955–1969, The Primal Screen,* and *The John Ford Movie Mystery.*

Richard Schickel was film critic of *Life* from 1965 until its demise in 1972. He now reviews films for *Time* magazine. He was producer-writer-director of the Public Broadcasting Service series, "The Men Who Made the Movies." His books include *The Disney Version, The Stars, The World of Goya, His Picture in the Papers, The Platinum Age, Harold Lloyd: The Shape of Laughter, The World of Tennis, The Fairbanks Album,* and a collection of film criticism, *Second Sight.* He coedited *Film 67/68* with John Simon.

Elisabeth Weis serves the Society in the nonvoting position of secretary. She teaches film at Brooklyn College of the City University of New York and has written for the *Village Voice, Film International,* and *American Film.*

Colin L. Westerbeck, Jr., is film critic for *Commonweal* and has written for *Sight and Sound* and *Artforum.*

Bruce Williamson is film critic and contributing editor of *Playboy* magazine and has taught at St. John's University, Long Island; he was a film critic at *Time* magazine from 1963 to 1967 and has written satirical songs and sketches for revues in New York and London.

# INDEX

# INDEX

# INDEX

# INDEX

# INDEX

## ACKNOWLEDGMENTS

*(Continued from copyright page.)*

Commentary magazine: reviews of *M\*A\*S\*H, Love and Anarchy,* and *What's Up, Doc?* by William S. Pechter, Copyright © 1970, 1972, 1976 by the American Jewish Committee; reprinted by permission of the publisher.

Commonweal magazine: reviews of *Day for Night, The Heartbreak Kid, Young Frankenstein,* and *Nashville* by Colin L. Westerbeck, Jr.; reprinted by permission of the publisher.

Connecticut magazine: "The Ache of a Belly Laugh" (here titled "An Allen Overview") by Joseph Gelmis; reprinted by permission of the publisher.

Darien House, Inc.: from Judith Crist's Introduction to *A Flask of Fields* edited by Richard J. Anobile, Copyright © 1972 by Darien House, Inc., distributed by Avon Books; reprinted by permission of the publisher.

Dial Press: from *The Stars* by Richard Schickel, Copyright © 1962 by Richard Schickel and Allen Hurlburt; reprinted by permission of the publisher.

E.P. Dutton & Company, Inc.: from *The American Cinema: Directors and Directions 1929–1968* by Andrew Sarris. Copyright © 1968 by Andrew Sarris; reprinted by permission of the publisher.

Film Comment: "Paul Mazursky: The Horace with a Heart of Gold" by Richard Corliss, Copyright © 1975, The Film Society of Lincoln Center, *Film Comment,* Vol. XI, Number 2, March/April 1975 issue; reprinted by permission of the publisher; all rights reserved.

Harper & Row, Publishers: from *Twenty-Four Times a Second* by William S. Pechter, Copyright © 1962, 1970 by William S. Pechter; reprinted by permission of the publisher.

Holt, Rinehart and Winston, Publishers: from *The Private Eye, The Cowboy and the Very Naked Girl* by Judith Crist, Copyright © 1967, 1968 by Judith Crist; reprinted by permission of the publisher. From *From Reverence to Rape* by Molly Haskell, Copyright © 1973, 1974 by Molly Haskell; reprinted by permission of the publisher.

Little, Brown and Company in association with The Atlantic Monthly Press: review of *Bob & Carol & Ted & Alice* from *Deeper into Movies* by Pauline Kael, Copyright © 1969 by Pauline Kael (originally in *The New Yorker*); reprinted by permission of the publisher. Review of *Weekend* by Pauline Kael, Copyright © 1968 by Pauline Kael (originally in *The New Yorker*) and "Trash, Art and the Movies" by Pauline Kael, Copyright © 1969 by Pauline Kael (originally in *Harper's Magazine*), from *Going Steady* by Pauline Kael; reprinted by permission of the publisher. Reviews of *The Golden Coach* and *Smiles of a Summer Night,* Copyright © 1964 by Pauline Kael (originally in *Kulchur*), and of *Shoot the Piano Player,* Copyright © 1965 by Pauline Kael, from *I Lost It at the Movies* by Pauline Kael; reprinted by permission of the publisher. "So Off-Beat We Lose the Beat," Copyright © 1966 by Pauline Kael, and "A Shaggy Man Story: *Boudu Saved from Drowning,*" Copyright © 1967 by Pauline Kael (originally in *The New Republic*), from "Spoofing: *Cat Ballou,*" Copyright © 1965 by Pauline Kael (originally in *The Atlantic Monthly*), from "It's a Great Technique, but What Can You Do With It?" (review of *The Knack* and *Help!*) and "Notes on 280 Movies" *(Kind Hearts and Coronets, The Lavender Hill Mob, The Man in the White Suit, Miracle in Milan, Zazie),* Copyright © 1965, 1966, 1967, 1968 by Pauline Kael, from *Kiss Kiss Bang Bang* by Pauline Kael; reprinted by permission of the publisher.

Little, Brown and Company in association with the New York Graphic Society: From *Harold Lloyd: The Shape of Laughter* by Richard Schickel, Copyright © 1974 by Time-Life Films; reprinted by permission of the publisher.

Los Angeles Times: "The Odd Couple Is a Laughing Matter" by Charles Champlin; reprinted by permission of the publisher.

Macmillan Publishing Company, Inc.: From *The Liveliest Art* by Arthur Knight, Copyright © 1957 by Arthur Knight; reprinted by permission of the publisher. From *Big Screen, Little Screen* by Rex Reed, Copyright © 1968, 1969, 1970, 1971 by Rex Reed; reprinted by permission of the publisher.

Millimeter: review of *Beat the Devil* by Cha⬛ ⬛plin; reprinted by permission of the publisher.

New Times magazine: review of *Phantom of the Paradise* by Frank Rich; reprinted by permission of the publisher.

New York Daily News: review of *Harold and Maude* by Rex Reed, Copyright © 1971 by the New York News, Inc.; reprinted by permission of the publisher.

New York Times: reviews of *King of Hearts, Putney Swope, Trash, Playtime, Amarcord,* and *One Flew Over the Cuckoo's Nest,* and "Laurel and Hardy" by Vincent Canby; review of *La Ronde* by Roger Geenspun; and "Hail Chaplin—The Early Chaplin" by Richard Schickel, Copyright © 1967, 1969, 1970, 1972, 1973, 1974, 1975 by The New York Times Company; reprinted by permission of the publisher.

The New Yorker: from "God Save the Language, at Least" (here titled "Marriage Comedies") by Penelope Gilliatt, Copyright © 1970 by The New Yorker Magazine, Inc.; reprinted by permission of the publisher.

Newsday: reviews of *Two for the Road, Monty Python and the Holy Grail,* and *Seven Beauties,* and "Interview with Gene Wilder" by Joseph Gelmis; reprinted by permission of the publisher.

On Film: review of *Stolen Kisses* by Roger Greenspun; reprinted by permission of the publisher.

Overlook Press, Inc.: From *Talking Pictures* by Richard Corliss, Copyright © 1974 by Richard Corliss; reprinted by permission of the publisher.

Playboy magazine: "Buster Keaton" and "On Late Chaplin Films" by Bruce Williamson, Copyright © 1971, 1973 by Playboy; reprinted by permission of the publisher.

Real Paper: "Blake Edwards" and review of *The Girl Can't Help It* by Stuart Byron; reprinted by permission of the publisher.

Rolling Stone: reviews of *Bananas* and *Carnal Knowledge* by Roger Greenspun and review of *The Discreet Charm of the Bourgeoisie* by Stuart Byron, Copyright © 1971, 1972 by Rolling Stone; reprinted by permission of the publisher.

Andrew Sarris: "The World of Howard Hawks" (here titled "Hawksian Comedy") by Andrew Sarris; reprinted by permission of Mr. Sarris.

Saturday Review: reviews of *Gold of Naples* and *Tom Jones* by Arthur Knight, Copyright © 1957, 1963 by Saturday Review; reprinted by permission of the publisher.

Simon & Schuster, Inc.: from *Confessions of a Cultist* by Andrew Sarris, Copyright © 1970 by Andrew Sarris; reprinted by permission of the publisher. From *Second Sight* by Richard Schickel, Copyright © 1971 by Richard Schickel; reprinted by permission of the publisher.

Time magazine: reviews of *Traffic* and *The Three Musketeers* by Jay Cocks, *Blazing Saddles* by Richard Schickel, and *The Loves of a Blonde* by Bruce Williamson, Copyright by Time, Inc.; reprinted by permission of the publisher.

Time, Inc.: review of *What's New Pussycat* by Richard Schickel for *Life,* Copyright © 1965 by Time, Inc.; reprinted by permission of the publisher.

The Viking Press: from *Unholy Fools* by Penelope Gilliatt, Copyright © 1960–1973 by Penelope Gilliatt; reprinted by permission of the publisher.

Village Voice: from reviews of *The Producers, Blazing Saddles,* and *Royal Flash,* and "A Theory of Comedy" and "Preston Sturges" by Andrew Sarris; reprinted by permission of the publisher. Reviews of *Futz, Taking Off, The Heartbreak Kid,* and *Sleeper* by Molly Haskell; reprinted by permission of

Wall Street Journal: reviews of *The Heartb⬛* ⬛ *Love, The Phantom of Liberté,* and *Love and L⬛* © 1973, 1974, 1975 by Dow Jones and Compa⬛ publisher.

Washington Post: reviews of *The Miracle o⬛* ⬛ *dles,* and *Young Frankenstein,* by Gary Arnol⬛ ⬛lisher.

Whitney Communications Corporation: revi⬛ and *Seduced and Abandoned,* by Judith Cris⬛ reprinted by permission of the publisher.

7407

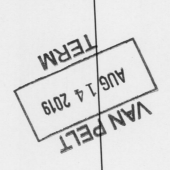